THE MODERN CITY

An Introduction to Urban Sociology

PRENTICE-HALL SOCIOLOGY SERIES

Herbert Blumer, Editor

THE MODERN CITY

An Introduction to Urban Sociology

SVEND RIEMER

Professor of Sociology
The University of California
at Los Angeles

1952

PRENTICE-HALL, INC.

NEW YORK

For Carol

Preface

Urban sociology recently has had to cope with an abundant growth of factual information. It has become increasingly difficult, particularly for the beginner, to reach the core of the subject. Many empirical sciences contribute to the knowledge of the city. The city planner, the architect, the highway and the sanitary engineer, the political scientist, and the social psychologist assist in the collection and interpretation of information about the city. Books have been written about urban sanitation, about recreational planning, about city planning, and about housing alone. Available information overflows traditional lines of classroom instruction. To Municipal Government are added courses on Urban Finances and Public Utilities. City Planning has been divided into a number of specialties. Both Urban Sociology and the related field of Urban Land Economics have been embarassed by an excess of incoming information.

Under the circumstances, the author's objective in this volume has been to concentrate argument and to eliminate stray information that might bewilder rather than educate the beginner. This study emphasizes sociological orientation. It satisfies a specific interest in urban problems of those who are mainly concerned with liberal education and, simultaneously, lays a sound groundwork for those who intend to devote themselves professionally to some aspect of urban administration or urban planning. It should furnish the urban engineer, the land economist, and the architect with an approach to the social aspects of the city.

Carefully selected reading lists — with a limited number of major sources — are provided at the end of each chapter. Some fifty problems have been carefully worked out for individual chapters.

SVEND RIEMER

Contents

ix

Introduction

CHAPTER 1

The City in Western Civilization

THE DAWN OF URBANIZATION

Village Growth. The beginning of urbanization was not sudden. During a period of no less than 1,500 years (5000 to 3500 B.C.) something stirred in the scattered stone-age villages of southwestern Asia and northeastern Africa. They tended to overshoot the customary village size, which so far had encompassed from 8 to 35 individual houses. The modest wealth gained from both food production and craftsmanship provided the sustenance for larger permanent settlements. To begin with, urbanization was not more than this: the growth in size of permanent human settlement.

This change of size in itself, however, caused social change sufficiently profound to lead from barbarism to civilization, i.e., an urban society and continued social progress.

A variety of circumstances can be mentioned as prerequisites of early urban development: (1) a food supply sufficient to free some members of the social group from the burden of agricultural labor, (2) a water supply sufficient to satisfy the needs of increasing human settlements and their livestock, and (3) means of transportation to increase the range from which food supplies could be gathered in support of incipient urban populations.[1]

---

[1] For the "Environmental Factors in the Rise of Urban Cultures," see Ralph Turner, *The Great Cultural Traditions,* Vol. I. New York: McGraw-Hill Book Company, Inc., 1941, pp. 123-125.

3

The crafts of the Bronze Age (from about 2500 B.C.) had considerably improved available means of transportation. From the use of exclusively human carriers, transportation advanced to the utilization of the pack ass. The invention of the wheel led to the construction of the oxcart. The sailing vessel made its appearance simultaneously along the shorelines of the open sea.[2]

Systematic food production in the peasant-village cultures of the early Bronze Age had already permitted the development of specialized craftsmen operating for the benefit of local needs. Yet the bronze-age villages and some of the towns of that period, never exceeded very narrow boundaries in space. They may have covered a few acres.

It remained for the marshy delta and valley regions of the Nile in Egypt and the Euphrates and Tigris in Mesopotamia to provide an economic base for sizable urban developments.[3] Here we find cities — like Sumar, Ur, and later Babylon — which measured their geographical area in square miles. This change in size had far-reaching effects upon social organization. The quality of urban culture and civilization can be distinguished clearly from that of the bronze-age village.

Location close to the waterways of Mesopotamia provided for another basic need. There are those who suggest that early cities might have originated from nomadic populations and their livestock, which thronged toward the sources of abundant water supplies. Such notions overemphasize the importance of one of several relevant factors; but it is undoubtedly true that the location at river valleys not only eliminated one of the basic supply problems, but also provided for easy means of water transportation to accumulate the food products from an extended hinterland. Water transportation also facilitated the importation of building materials, such as timber,[4] and raw materials for urban crafts, such as bronze, and later, iron.

The dawn of urbanization thus leads us to a natural environment where various circumstances combined to supply a peasant-village culture with the means of doing on a more extended scale what they had been doing previously on a small scale.

---

[2] *Ibid.*, "The New Means of Transport," pp. 259-260.
[3] *Ibid.*, p. 124.
[4] *Ibid.*, p. 62.

Social Change. Early urbanization brought revolutionary changes to mankind. The pre-urban village was small enough to retain the clan, the large consanguinal family group, as the basic frame work of

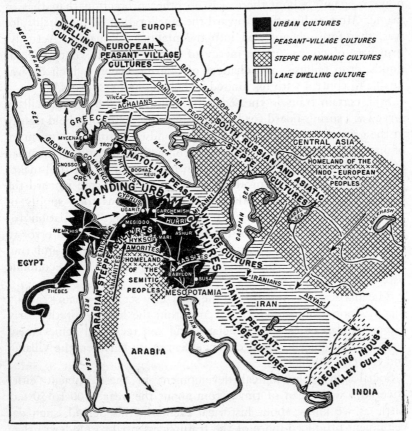

FIGURE 1. Expanding Urban Cultures in the Near East. About 2000 B.C. From Ralph Turner, *The Great Cultural Traditions.* New York: The McGraw-Hill Book Company, Inc., 1941, p. 223.

social organization. Man's actions were dictated by prevailing folk-ways sanctioned to the point of discouraging social or technical innovation. Pre-urban societies stagnated in firmly established routines. Superstition thwarted man's initiative in attempts to improve his well-being in this world.[5]

---

[5] *Ibid.,* pp. 89-90.

The universe was assumed to be reigned by demonic powers, which, teasing or favoring, maliciously or benevolently, interfered with the destiny of man. Man felt at the mercy of supernatural powers, against whom there was no other protection than that of magic. Most of his effort toward the amelioration of his earthly lot was, therefore, channelized into the practice of magic. Actually, man was, of course, at the mercy of purely natural events, such as floods, crop failures, and changes of climate, events which he was unable to control with his limited techniques and resources.[6]

Still, certain traits in the sedentary culture of the peasant-village served as a spring-board for later urbanization. Although held tightly in the grip of custom, man laid the groundwork for the "invention of inventions," the full development of which demanded an urban setting.[7] In the sedentary village man had turned into a tool-maker and made tools for the production of tools, a first step toward the development of modern industry. The continuous food supply of the village economy released parts of the village population for specialized tasks. The performance of these led in trial and error to inventions which, once they were sanctioned by magic and thus made acceptable to prevailing folkways, improved the economic base of the village culture.

The increase of population in the early city set off a chain-reaction that has not terminated yet. Even within the history of the early Mesopotamian cities, man's social world and technical achievement were revolutionized. Deep estrangement arose between the villager and the city dweller.

Social and technological development in these ancient cities covered a wide span of time, from about the year 4500 to 50 B.C. Little as we know about historical events in this period, such development produced more of the features essential to modern urban life than any later development. Early urban history provided mankind with: (1) an elaborate system of division of labor, i.e., occupational specialization; (2) a principle of social organization to facilitate the co-ordination of individual efforts, i.e., a class system; (3) a form of government that exercised authority on a territorial rather than a family basis; (4) a system of trade and commerce; (5) effective

---

[6] Gordon Childe, *What Happened in History*. New York: Penguin Books, Inc., 1946. p. 33.

[7] Ralph Turner, *op. cit.*, p. 28.

means of communication to integrate a cosmopolitan crowd; and finally (6) science and its application to technology.

The controls of social organization in the early cities were concentrated within the temple. It took religious sanction to guide the city dweller from the confines of custom to a new way of life apart from the village in-group. Organized religion dispelled the powers of magic. To work for the "greater magic" of the city deity, the villager made himself part of a highly intricate occupational organization of bakers, brewers, metalworkers, spinners, and sailors.

The production of surplus foods in the fertile river valleys provided nutrition for a growing urban population able to devote itself to non-agricultural pursuits. The delivery of these surplus foods was enforced by exploitative relationships between the city and the surrounding hinterland, i.e., by either slavery or serfdom.

Urban production was centered around the temple. Permanence of religious worship was guaranteed by the formation of a priest class, which monopolized magic powers and later sacred learning, replenished its ranks from new disciples, and administered the vested interests of the city in a relatively stable system of social organization.

As the "divine household" of the temple gave way to inter-urban trade and commerce, the institutions of government and production underwent a process of secularization. The dominant position of the priest class yielded to the powers of royalty.

In city architecture, the palace was added to the temple. Royalty, to be sure, had to claim divinity or divine origin to make possible the transference of authority from the temple to the palace. The people still obeyed what they thought to be the command of supernatural powers.

These early cities could not have survived without new instrumentalities to co-ordinate a cosmopolitan crowd that carried with it the traditions of innumerable local cultures. The supreme power of a territorial deity satisfied the early city dweller's need for supernatural sanction. To establish orderliness in everyday life routines, new means of communication had to be devised.

Contributions in labor and in kind on the part of the motley urban crowd and its rural satellites had to be checked by way of reliable records communicable to all. A simple system of imprints upon clay tablets provided for such needs. To facilitate the recording of larger numbers, specific symbols were used for units of counting. The decimal system came into use, later in this era to be replaced by a system of sexagesimal reckoning.[8]

To the need for numerical notation was added that for written language. Hieroglyphic scripts predominated. Graphic symbols were used to represent specific meanings as well as objects; these were gradually correllated to the spoken language. In some of these cities, phonetic denotations replaced the use of hieroglyphic script and led to the systematic use of the first crude alphabets.

Standard weights and measures were introduced to facilitate the exchange of goods. Unspoilable, easily subdivisible, and frequently traded goods assumed the function of monetary exchange. Increasingly wider territories were culturally unified by trade and the use of standard means of communication. Man raised his eyes to widening ranges of social intercourse.

Urbanization also promoted first developments of science. Empirical observation, to be sure, was obscured by traditional folklore. Yet, invention met fewer obstacles where organized religion, rather than magic and superstition, stood guard over social traditions.

GREECE

Diffusion, Conquest, and Commerce. The European city cultures of antiquity in Greece and Italy are the result of a diffusion of urban culture traits that had evolved in the Near East. They do not represent a spontaneous development, another beginning similar to that of early urbanization in the river valleys of the Niles, Euphrates and Tigris. In the history of the ancient oriental cities a successful pattern of economic and social organization had worked itself out. The instruments of diffusion were conquest and commerce.[9]

The wealth of the early oriental cities attracted nomadic tribes that ventured forth from the plains of central Asia in search of conquest and booty. As conquerors, they imposed their yoke upon existing urban communities. As a parasitic group, they exploited the urban workers, as well as the peasants of the hinterland who provided the necessary food supplies.

In this process, the knowledge of writing passed from a priestly

---

8 Gordon Childe, *op. cit.*, p. 95.
9 Ralph Turner, *op. cit.*, p. 446.

monopoly into the hands of the military upper classes, and, later on, into the hands of a growing merchant class that made practical use of it.

The sacred traditions, which, already in the hands of the priest class, had represented a source of power, were enriched by heroic epics like the Greek Iliad and Odyssey depicting barbaric conquests, inter-urban strife, and the calamities of social change and readjustment to new power structures.

While the barbaric conquerors intruded from the north, the lore of urban crafts and skills spread from the south, promoting the growth of relatively permanent village cultures in central and southeastern Europe. The use of copper and, later, bronze and iron spread in a sedentary village environment that forged the weapons which in turn were used in conquests aimed at the wealth accumulated in the cities of Greece and the Near East.

Minoa. Between the 15th and the 8th centuries B.C. Greek city culture evolved where Indonesian invaders from the north came upon outposts of the Minoan culture. This urban culture had its center on Crete. Its influence reached to Troy and to other cities at the Asiatic shores of the Mediterranean Sea. Historically, the urban culture of Greece is linked to earliest city developments in Mesopotamia and Egypt. Removed from the invading nomadic tribes, Egyptian city culture experienced the longest history of uninterrupted development.[10]

The superior bronze armor of Indonesian war bands checked the spreading influence of Minoan culture at the shores of the Agaean Sea. The earliest cities of the invaders were not much more than fortresses from which to raid the countryside and to which to withdraw from the onslaught of counter-attacks. Among these costal fortresses, Mycenae gained prominence between 1400 and 1200 B.C.

These cities grew by conquest and commerce. The existence, at the opening of the 8th century, of a large number of such urban settlements testifies to the economic and political superiority of city culture. The labor of the villagers in the region was exploited by conquering hordes which established themselves as a permanent upper class located at fortified strong points of military power.

Greek Cities. At this time we hear of Sparta and Corinth, of Argos

---

[10] *Ibid.,* "The Egyptian Cultural Tradition," pp. 174-214; see also "The Minoan Cultural Tradition," pp. 214-221.

and Megara, of Athens, Thebes, Ephesus, and Miletus. To agricultural production were added the output of urban industry, such as the crafts of metalworking, pottery, and mining. Trade and commerce were protected by the military activity of Greek citizenry, which kept pirates from the Agaean shores. Merchants from the Near East established relations of economic exchange with the trade routes of the orient.

Greek aristocracy did not participate directly in either trade or industry. Work was beneath the dignity of the warrior. The pursuits of the free Greek citizens were limited to the administration of their land holdings, to warfare, to concern with city politics, and to the extraction of tolls and taxes from commerce and the craft's industry.

In physical appearance these cities were not unlike those of the early Middle Ages. They were similarly based upon military protection and the payments of tributes to a warrior class. The urban dwelling units were clustered around the fortified strong point located on a hill — the acropolis. In case of attack, the citizenry withdrew to the shelter of the fortress.

The dwelling units carried gabled roofs which protruded beyond the walls of the structure and thus had to be supported by those wooden posts, which in later public construction — the well-known temples of the classic period — became marble columns serving the purpose of ornamentation. Even at the time of Athenian supremacy in the 5th century B.C., however, the dwelling units of the city presented a rather shabby appearance. The street layout in the residential sections was irregular, and only narrow alleys were left between individual structures.

The interest in architecture was concentrated upon monumental public buildings such as the Parthenon (447 B.C.), the gate of the Acropolis (437 B.C.), and the Erechtheum. There were theaters and office buildings. It was a man's city, and the life of men did not have its center in the home, but rather in the market place, the public square, and the theater.

There is only one example, in the culture of Greek cities, of purposeful city planning. When, in the second half of the 5th century B.C., the commercial and seafaring population of Athens overflowed to the peninsula of the Piraeus, construction was held to the design of a gridiron plan by the architect Hippodamus. This was the first attempt at city planning in Western civilization. Wholesale construction of square public and private buildings suggested a simple rectangular layout.

Class Structure. Throughout the history of Greek cities, class conflict was limited to a struggle between the nobility and the free peasants. Both groups had been part of the original conquering war bands; all were members of the citizenry. In addition, the city population contained craftsmen, hired men, and slaves. These latter groups had no political rights whatsoever. Craftsmen and merchants were exploited to the benefit of the city treasury, the property of all full-fledged citizens. Economic exploitation went just far enough not to discourage these occupations in the city confines.[11]

The foundation of status was primarily landed property, managed by absentee owners living in the city, and operated by hired men and slaves. The need for capital in the operation of olive groves gave a considerable advantage to the owners of the large estates. The small land owners, free peasants, were ever in danger of falling into debt and bankruptcy. The monopolization of landed property in the hands of the nobility was a continuous source of political strife. The tyrants of the Classic Period of Greek culture were political demagogues who rose to power on the complaints of small land holders and other underprivileged groups of the urban population.

Colonization. Economic pressures led to colonization. Well-known are the Greek colonial cities at the eastern shore of the Mediterranean sea such as Chios, Miletus, Cos, Chidos, Halicarnassus, Mytilene, Phocaea, Smyrna, Teos, and Ephesus. The poor peasants and the less prominent members of the nobility left their home towns to establish lucrative land holdings elsewhere.

Colonization was linked to ancient traditions of warfare, conquest, and economic exploitation. The colonizing Greeks worked as little as did the upper classes at home, at either agriculture, trade, or industry. They organized an administrative and political machine that lent itself to the systematic exploitation of the indigenous population. They intermarried with the native population, but held their women in low esteem.

Such colonial outposts spread eastward to the shores of the Black Sea and westward to the coasts of Gaul and Spain. Marseille, on the

---

[11] *Ibid.,* "The Social and Political Development of Greek Culture," pp. 454-473.

Mediterranean coast of France, was thus founded as a Greek colonial city at about 600 B.C.

On the North African shores, Greek colonization followed in the wake of earlier colonizing enterprises by the Phoenicians. These early conquering traders had emphasized the extension of commerce rather than the exploitation of indigenous labor. Carthage, founded at about the middle of the 9th century B.C., never lost its reputation as an urban center with a population set on commercial gain rather than exploitative colonial administration; yet Greek influence promoted the opening up of the vast hinterland for agricultural and industrial production.

Greek colonial cities also flourished in Sicily and in southern Italy (Magna Graecia) where, at the beginning of the first millennium B.C., they ran into conflict with the expanding urban culture of Italy. The founding of Rome is dated at 753 B.C.

Culture.[12] Greek culture reflects the tensions between the close in-group ties of the nomadic clan, on the one hand, and a cosmopolitan way of life on the other. Different folkways intermingled in the environment of urban crowds. Questions of right and wrong began to occupy the mind of the philosopher, who replaced the priestly diviner and searched for rules of correct behavior in a world exposed to the counter-claims of tribal deities.

Problems of ethics dominated Greek philosophy. Such philosophy developed side by side with remnants of a pre-urban type of religion, which by oracle, divination, and mystic communion with the diety tried to provide guidance in the conduct of worldly affairs. The Cynic, the Stoic, and the Epicurean furnished systematically elaborated attitudes toward a cosmopolitan way of life in which the individual found himself at the mercy of powers greater than himself. The task was to develop an attitude of passive acceptance.[13]

Greek science never overcame the handicap inherent in the separation of work and learning. Members of the upper classes did not work with their hands, and thus had to forego the advantage of pertinent empirical observation. The lower classes lacked the leisure required for detached scientific observation and speculation.

The contribution of Greek science rests in the systematization of

---

12 *Ibid.*, Chapter X, "The Greek Definition of Western High Intellectual Tradition," pp. 530-601.

13 *Ibid.*, "The Development of Greek Philosophy and Science," pp. 554-595.

random information, gained fortuitously by trial and error, or handed down within a web of priestly superstition and derived from the lore of ancient urban civilization. In rounding out stray bits of information into internally consistent theory, Greek science stumbled into and clearly formulated many basic problems of epistemology, of method and subject matter in medicine, astronomy, mathematics, mechanics, and so forth.

Exhaustion. Greek urban culture never died. It lost importance as it exhausted the possibilities inherent in its principle of social organization. It never overcame the limitation set by its focus upon the individual city and the exploitation of regional resources by a privileged minority. Intercity strife prevailed and weakened Greece for imperialistic enterprise.

The commerce of tolerated foreigners, rather than missionary zeal on the part of the free citizens in Greek territory, led to the extension of its sphere of influence. The vision of democracy (limited to the nobility and the free peasants of individual cities) inhibited the formation of a supreme central power that might have built an empire. This task was left to Rome under different social conditions.

ROME

Village Background. The Italian cities grew out of villages that combined to make larger urban settlements. In gradual moves, these village populations pressed southward from the Alps. The early Romans combined the virtues of the farmer and the soldier.

Early cities were defensive strongholds in an area of constant population pressure. In the Etruscan tradition of northern Italy, the citizens were divided into patricians and plebeians. Forced labor and slavery were known throughout Roman history.

The basic political and social institutions survived the strife of social classes more or less inviolate. They allowed for some social mobility, for the displacement and the regrouping of entire social strata, and for the assimilation of ambitious and wealthy citizens into the ruling class. Among the groups assimilated were ignoble Romans; second-class citizens of other Italian cities; and, at the time of the Empire and its decline, even colonials prominent merely through wealth.

Classes. At the time of the Roman Republic, wealth and political influence were tied to landed property. Political strife centered around the interests of the small landholder liable to become indebted to the large estate owner in the cultivation of vineyards and olive groves, which required capital until the original investment yielded results. Carrying the financial burden for the conduct of political affairs, the large estate owners claimed privileges of power and compensation from military conquests. Their political power in the Roman senate, however, was contested by the plebeians who were able to make their demands felt by withdrawing from military service.

In the long run, the political tug-of-war favored the lower classes, who gained access to important political offices, and finally even to the Senate. The laws of indebtedness were changed to ease the burden of the debtor. Intermarriage between patricians and members of the lower classes was legalized. The distribution of conquered wealth was changed to benefit the entire citizenry. Commitment to a written and codified law eliminated arbitrary rulings in favor of patricians in the law courts.

The Empire. In the Roman Empire,[14] original class divisions were further obviated in favor of a conglomerate upper stratum of society which continuously renewed itself from the ranks of second-rate citizens and colonials. Political and military success, landed and commercial wealth, and favoritism made entrance into the ruling class possible. The restricted democracy of the Greek city widened to a regimen which, in principle, excluded nobody from wealth or power.

The source of prestige, to be sure, remained in landed property. The newly rich had to buy themselves in, if their source of wealth stemmed from commerce, conquest, or colonial exploitation. A large-estate economy was the foundation of the Roman Empire. Latifundia were worked by tenants, serfs, and slaves, while the owners consumed their wealth as residents of the city.

Colonial government employed similar extractive policies within the dominions of the Roman Empire. At home as well as abroad mines were worked by slaves. They were administered as public enterprises for the benefit of the state treasury. The urban crafts served, aside from the production of weapons, to fill the demands of the wealthy urban residents for luxuries. A mass market for

---

[14] *Ibid.,* Chapter XV, pp. 856-948.

consumer goods did not exist. The urban mob of poor Roman
citizens was supported by state-organized food shipments and gifts
distributed by politically ambitious citizens eager to buy their voting
power.

Culture. The rule of Rome imposed a unified cultural pattern
upon all parts of the civilized world with which communication was
possible. It allowed a cosmopolitan culture to flourish. Within the
large city, different religions and philosophies found a way of existing side by side.

On the village level, this would never have been possible. Different
deities and value systems would have had to fight each other to the
point of extermination. There was no room for divided loyalties
among the villagers and their close-knit in-group.

In Rome, different cults of local origin were sustained by different
groups of immigrants who came (or had been brought as slaves) to
the central seat of the Empire. As temporary fads, oriental mystery
cults caught the imagination of the urban populace and led, inter-
mittently, to the worship of such deities as Cybele, the Great Mother;
Isis and Serapis (who extended their influence from Egypt); and
Mithra, the god of the dead in the Zoroastrian religion. Religious
tolerance, however, was not practiced consistently. In occasional
spurts, the state religion asserted itself by the persecution of foreign
sects.

The deification of the emperor bears witness to the fact that the
state religion had its purpose in binding the loyalties of immigrating
villagers from foreign lands. It took a supremely powerful deity to
loosen the immigrant's ties from home traditions, to enforce conformity where a conflict of loyalties might have arisen. Still, inasmuch as the state religion was concerned primarily with political
loyalties rather than religious sentiment, with the observance of
symbolic rituals rather than communion with supernatural powers,
it could afford tolerance with regard to the inner life of man.[15]

Intellectually, the culture of Rome was eclectic, providing the
background for the assimilation and dissemination of Greek and
oriental traditions without adding original contributions in any field
but that of jurisprudence (history, philosophy, and interpretation of
the law).

Roman law provided an institutional setting for the administrative

---

15 *Ibid.*, Vol. II, Chapter XVI, pp. 949-1025.

integration of the Empire. In defining clearly the concept of private property, developing flexible economic institutions, and providing a codified law to replace an arbitrary class justice based on avowed legal traditions, it set the scene for a growth of urban industry and commerce on an "international" basis and encouraged individual initiative.[16]

Christianity. The most important cultural and social contribution of the Roman Empire to Western urban civilization was the foundation and organization of the Christian Church. It developed as a distinctly urban phenomenon. The "pagans" were the unconverted villagers who were not able to tear themselves away from a supernatural world that was filled with deities and demons who arbitrarily interfered with the well-being of man on this earth. These demons had to be controlled by magic, and their favors had to be gained by sacrifice and flattery. Man, in the pre-urban world, was definitely not the master of his own destiny.[17]

Christianity combined a variety of religious and intellectual traditions to give adequate expression to emotional needs growing out of urban existence. It replaced tribal deities, which were concerned only with the well-being of their own people. It replaced them by the idea, foreshadowed in Greek philosophy, of the one and only supreme and all-pervasive God guarding the destiny of humanity in its entirety, a truly cosmopolitan notion.

As a religion of salvation, Christianity gave spiritual shelter to the footloose urban masses in their endurance of social change and exploitation. It anchored them to the solid rock of hope for a better life in the hereafter. It gave dignity to the isolated individual removed from in-group protection, a dignity that rested in his personal relation to the forgiving and saving deity. It proposed the notion of spiritual, if not economic, equality. Missionary activities penetrated class lines and national boundaries. The entire civilized world was visualized, under Christianity, as one cohesive unit. In Christianity, the cosmopolitan tendencies of urban existence found full expression.

Construction. In architecture and physical construction, Rome and the cities dominated by Rome did not surpass the achievements of the Greek polis in anything but size and grandeur. The public

---

[16] *Ibid.,* pp. 1004-1019.
[17] *Ibid.,* Chapters XVII-XIX, pp. 1026-1233.

buildings of the forum were the center of attention. They were devoted to commerce, administration, and amusements, as well as to the worship of different deities. New building methods permitted the erection of larger structures than before. The Etruscan arch supported great weight, and local volcanic materials furnished the basis for strong cement.

Peculiar to the Roman scene under the Empire was the construction of triumphal arches. They gave symbolic expression to military power and glamorized the achievements of individual emperors. The street pattern of the city was shaped to focus attention upon the architectural symbols of military, dictatorial, and commercial greatness and religious dedication.

Peculiar to Rome, also, was the technical improvement of utilitarian structures such as aqueducts, sewers, and port facilities. The road system planned and constructed by Roman highway engineers established means of rapid communication between different parts of the empire, and aided in the movements of troops and administrative colonial personnel.[18]

The style of Roman architecture was eclectic and profusely ornamental. It elaborated on the Greek column as a decorative feature. With improved building methods, the column increasingly lost its function of support and faded into the facade of public structures such as temples, office buildings, courts of justice, baths, and circuses.

Slums and mansions. The private lives of the citizens were hidden away in crowded beehives of multistory apartment buildings dissected, as in some modern slums, into the greatest possible number of "kitchenettes," that is, dwelling units of not more than two rooms, one of them to serve for kitchen purposes.

The palaces of senators and knights in the city were more elaborately equipped for the semi-public services they rendered in fostering the relations between political leaders and their individual followers. Also, they were more centrally located.

The country house of the landed gentry deserves mention for the ease and the luxury of living which it suggested. The art of landscaping was in high esteem, and domestic comforts with luxurious baths and, in some cases, even central heating exceeded the standards of living for many centuries to come. To be sure, only a small section of the nobility enjoyed these spectacular advantages.

---

[18] *Ibid.*, p. 966.

Function of Urbanization. In the Roman Empire, the urban culture of Western civilization realized for the first time the cosmopolitan intentions inherent in the urban way of life. The colonial administration of the Empire foreshadowed the need for wide territorial domination, without which large urban settlements cannot subsist.

Roman law and the concept of individual property provided an institutional setting for unimpeded commercial activities. As Greece had eliminated priestly rule and divine sanction from the core of urban life, Rome eliminated the hereditary rule of a conquering oligarchy and opened the ranks of its upper classes to individual achievement in military, political, and commercial pursuits.

Christianity offered a cultural framework for the spiritual unification of the entire urban population and, in the long run, its rural subsidiaries. All these achievements were retained throughout the period of stagnation into which urban culture lapsed at the end of the Roman Empire.

THE CITY OF THE MIDDLE AGES

Collapse of Rome. The city of the Middle Ages arose from the debris of the dead Roman Empire. Somewhere between the 4th and 8th centuries, A.D., the economic basis of Roman city culture had begun to exhaust itself.[19]

Production, in the Roman empire, had been primarily agricultural production. Manufactured consumer goods found only a narrow market among the absentee owners of landed estates, who lived within the orbit of the city. Land holdings were worked by slaves and serfs within the womanless household of the so-called latifundia. These slaves did not replace themselves through procreation. Thus, the agricultural production which made large urban settlements possible by supplying the food necessary for survival of the city was predicated upon a continuous importation of slaves. As Roman conquests abated, agricultural surplus production slowed down. Consequently, taxes diminished, the resources for further military operations were depleted, and — in a vicious circle — the importation of slaves was furthermore reduced.

Left without cash income, the absentee land owners withdrew

---

[19] *Ibid.*, pp. 1086-1092.

from the city and went to their estates to live and to supply themselves in kind with goods required for their everyday needs. Urban culture, based on specialization and division of labor, was replaced by a self-sufficient agriculture, a feudal system in which a military upper class was supported by the toils of serfs bound to the land.

Great importance for the decline of Rome has also been attributed to the Islamic invasions of the 7th century which — by the conquest of the southern, eastern and western shores of the Mediterranean sea — reduced the trading area of the cities of the Empire.[20]

Piracy added to the insecurity of commercial relations. Gold went out of circulation to be horded and stored in the treasuries of churches and monasteries. It was replaced by silver coinage. The large merchant population that had supported the growth of teeming trading centers, such as that of Marseilles, dwindled away. City finances were undermined by the decrease of revenues from tolls and taxes.

Urban Stagnation. When the city culture of the Middle Ages started to arise from the preceding stagnation,[21] there remained only city-like fortifications sustained for two purposes: (1) as strong points in defense against invaders, and (2) as administrative seats for the international organization of the Christian clergy.

The defensive burghs consisted of little more than fortifications into which the rural population of the surrounding countryside withdrew in case of raids and invasions. Within the confines of the burgh, the feudal lord reigned supreme. At most times, the arsenal was protected by a small resident guard. There was little commerce. Industry was confined to the manufacture of weapons by feudal serfs.

The seats of the clergy, the cathedral towns, the bishoprics, and monasterial settlements attracted some local trade to supply the consumer needs of the resident population. Few articles were shipped from outside the immediate region. The region remained a relatively self-sufficient unit of production and consumption. Trade, as a matter of fact, was discouraged by religious ethics which frowned upon commercial gain not wrought from the toil of the hands. The

---

[20] Henri Pirenne, *Economic and Social History of Medieval Europe.* London: Kegan Paul, Trench, Trubner & Co., Ltd., 1936, p. 3.

[21] For European urban stagnation preceding the year 1000 A.D., see *Ibid.,* Introduction, pp. 1-15.

church limited the opportunities for free enterprise by condemning the receipt of interest as usury.[22]

Urban Revival. After the year 1000, both commerce and industry gradually revived. This year had not brought judgment day and the second coming of Christ; hence, the minds of men turned back to worldly pursuits. The feudal system had reached sufficient stability to permit a daring minority of adventurers to try their luck in the shipment of goods from places where they were abundant to places where they were in great demand.[23]

Traditions of commerce had not completely faded out of the picture. Some exchange of goods had continued even through periods of extreme feudal stagnation, between Constantinople, the center of the Byzantine Empire with its luxury trade, and Venice, the city on an island which did not command the services of a natural hinterland and, therefore, was dependent upon commerce for its survival.

Trade. Timber, iron, and slaves went east on this remaining trade route, while spices, silks, perfumes, and manufactured luxury goods arrived at Venice, to be distributed from here to other Italian cities and territories beyond the Alps. Trade stimulates trade; thus, from Venice commercial relations extended to the cities of the Lombardian plain, to Genoa, Pisa, and the Sicilian cities. These cities aided in freeing the Mediterranean Sea from piracy.

At the North Sea and the Baltic Sea, conquest and commerce combined to create a new orbit for trade relations beyond the boundaries of local markets. The pirate raids of the Vikings had established outposts from as far as the British Isles to the city of Kiev in the Ukraine. Their maritime and commercial activities embraced, in a wide arc, the stagnant agrarian culture of the central European feudal system. They traded with the Orient and were in communication with the Byzantine Empire by contacts established over the Russian river routes. Along navigable rivers, they penetrated deeply into the territories now held by France and Germany. As the Vikings retreated, they left behind a system of trading centers in close communication with each other.[24]

Outside the range of the Italian cities, a new nucleus of inter-urban

22 *Ibid.,* p. 14.
23 *Ibid.,* p. 46.
24 *Ibid.,* p. 22

trade centered around the cities of the Flemish coast. Fortified raiding camps grew into mercantile settlements. Honey, furs, and slaves were exchanged for spices, wines, silk, and metal products. A belt line of trade relations spanned the continent connecting, via the valleys of the Rhine and the Rhone, the Italian cities with those of the Flemish coast.

Commerce. Mercantile tradition was not entirely disrupted in the period of stagnation prior to the year 1000. Apart from the art of writing and the development of the concept of private property, antiquity had fashioned the rudiments of commercial techniques and a law of commerce. It protected both debtor and creditor in financial transactions, and knew the institute of entrepreneurial partnership.

In the Middle Ages, the development of commercial techniques radiated from Venice and the Italian cities. In the later phases of medieval commerce and industry, the art of double bookkeeping and the participation in private enterprise through shares (the stock company) originated. This development aided in the rationalization of commerce and tapped hitherto unused financial resources of small property owners.

The commercial activities of the cities were alien to the primarily agrarian base of the feudal system. The economic base of urban culture in the Middle Ages was thrust like a wedge into a civilization functioning by a different principle of social organization.

City development, however, was welcomed as a source of revenue by the feudal aristocracy, particularly the princes with vast territorial interests. The cities payed well for their privileges; and many impoverished knights exploited urban wealth by highway robbery as well as by the collection of tolls.

The emancipation from serfdom was granted the city dweller after an urban residence of a year and a day. The arbitrary justice of the feudal world was replaced, in the city, by municipal courts and a codified, or prescribed, commercial legislation.[25]

Industry. Commerce, in turn, stimulated industry. The cities of Flanders owed their importance not only to favorable location, but also to local production of high quality woolen products. These were shipped far into the Orient and functioned at times as generally-accepted currency. City fairs and city markets begged for merchandise. The urban crafts flourished under the stimulus of com-

---

[25] *Ibid.*, p. 72.

mercial outlets. Attracted by urban opportunities, city populations swelled with the runaways from serfdom, particularly the second and third sons of peasants and tenant farmers who found themselves without a livelihood due to the rights of primogeniture.

Later on, guild restrictions limited the access to urban occupational opportunities. In the wake of political freedom, class struggle raged throughout the Middle Ages. It gradually reduced the influence of the feudal nobility and that of the wealthy merchants, in favor of the craftsmen who successfully defended their privileged position against the competition of surplus populations.[26]

The Middle Ages are often looked upon as a time of relative social stability. This conception is misleading. In social structure and physical construction, the city of the Middle Ages underwent fundamental changes from its revival in the 12th and 13th centuries to the exhaustion of its economic potentialities in the 16th century. In the discussion of medieval urban culture, we frequently pay attention only to medieval city ruins that have survived to the present day.

Early Construction. The cities of the Middle Ages were planned cities. Present air views make the ruins of medieval cities appear as random agglomerations of dwellings crowded like the chicks of a hen into the protective shelter of walls and moat, with a minimum of rational internal organization. The original structure of the city is no longer apparent. In the later phases of the Middle Ages, the city outgrew its original design. In the course of centuries, it filled up and, unable to sprawl beyond the limits of its fortifications, developed differently from the metropolis of the industrialization period.

The main streets and thoroughfares of the medieval cities were deliberately and rationally planned. They led directly — and frequently in a straight line — from the central market place to the city gates.

At times, an element foreign to our conception of purposeful planning entered into the picture. The street system was occasionally determined by symbolic references, dividing the city area, for example, into 12 sections representing the 12 apostles of Christ. A straight north-south and east-west direction was frequently preferred to arrangements more convenient to inter-urban traffic. But plans there were; although subservient to values different from ours.

___
[26] *Ibid.*, pp. 67-68, and p. 173.

Originally, the medieval cities were planned with a generous lay-out, leaving room for additional expansion. The belt of fortifications was wide enough to encompass tillable land for food supplies in case of prolonged siege. The gardenland of the urban residents was also enclosed within the city walls.

City location, of course, was determined by defense purposes. A variety of strong defense positions were exploited. Cities were located on the tops of cliffs and mountains; we also find them on islands, and at river deltas and peninsulas. The winding course of a river offered many opportunities for well protected urban locations.

Yet what was an advantageous position in the beginning later often turned into an embarassing restriction to further growth. Neither the hill-top nor the island could be extended to allow for un-limited population increase. Many urban settlements thus fell by the wayside due to geographical obstructions. They fell into a state of stagnation from which they never recovered. Others ex-tended in suburban settlements beyond their natural borders. They continued to grow at the foot of the hillside or overflowed the river line behind which the early settlement had sought protection.

Expansion. From the 12th to the 16th century, not only were these cities filled up, but most of them were repeatedly extended beyond earlier ranges of fortification. As the medieval city filled up, additional populations settled in clusters outside the city walls in the faubourg. By the concerted efforts of these peripheral settlers, something like a stockade was thrown around their dwelling units to hold the site against the enemy at least long enough to permit the suburbanites to withdraw to the inner ring of fortifica-tions.

Sooner or later, the city walls proper were extended to embrace all the outlying settlements in a widened ring of defensive construc-tion. Successive rings of abandoned protective belts are still clearly visible in the street system of cities that have survived from the Middle Ages. The famous boulevard ring of "Hausmannized" Paris represents only the last phase of such a conversion.[27]

Medieval Ecology. Inside, the medieval city pattern expressed the class structure of a feudal society and that of the urban community itself. Not all, but many of the earlier cities nestled at the feet of

---

[27] See Harold MacLean Lewis, *Planning the Modern City,* Vol. I. New York: John Wiley & Sons, Inc., 1949, pp. 24-26.

burghs. As the city spread in a circle or semicircle, it retained a hierarchical arrangement of residential construction according to status. Advanced status groups pre-empted the grounds in the center of town. Members of the nobility had their city residences close to the central market place. As the nobility declined in power and numerical importance, their place was taken by the family residences of wealthy merchants or craftsmen with seats in the city council.

Unlike our modern cities, these cities had no slums close to their centers; instead there were pretentious stone structures, palaces, and stately mansions. Here was the place also for the numerous public buildings. Many of these have since been converted to residential use, thus obscuring their original function. Cathedrals and city halls, to be sure, still stand out as such. In addition the innermost ring of urban construction contained the guildhalls and the ballhouses, the public baths, and the wholesale markets with indoor as well as outdoor space for commercial activities.

At the periphery of the medieval city, we find the residences of the poorer members of the community, squeezed close to the wall and crowded together in a frantic scramble for space. The modest dwellings of the early Middle Ages, as a matter of fact, have not endured to the present times. These one-story and often one-room structures were later replaced by more elaborate three-floor structures protruding over the street front to increase the amount of dwelling space.

If the main streets of the medieval city were laid out according to a uniform plan, the same cannot be said for the side streets and alleys. The winding network of sidestreets often leaves us with an esthetically pleasing impression.

These side streets of the Middle Ages were never laid out with a view to purposes of communication. They were spaces left over in the built-up area of the city, as farm and garden land, vineyards, barns, and stables were gradually cut up into lots for residential construction. There were no premeditated plans for as much as a single city block. As a matter of fact, there were no city blocks.

Sanitary conditions in the medieval city were such as to endanger by either plague or fire its very survival. There was progress, but the growing population pressure continuously made obsolete the water system and the sewerage system, as well as the protective measures designed to forestall the devastating fires that annihilated entire cities.[28]

City ordinances determined the distance between individual structures in order to limit the spread of possible fires. Streets were paved, restrictions were imposed upon the elimination of waste products, public toilets were installed. The pigsties had to disappear from the street system and, in the late Middle Ages, many cities installed plumbing systems that piped running water into the individual dwelling units.

To permit a minimum of sunlight to penetrate into the side alleys, building ordinances restricted the custom of letting the upper floors of residential construction protrude to the point where the houses almost touched at the top-level. Street-lighting helped to improve the citizen's safety from robbery by night, and the organization of the fire brigade was improved as these cities grew and filled up into dense clusters of humanity within the confines of the city wall.

Gunpowder. With the invention of gunpowder, this entire social scene crumbled into oblivion. City walls ceased to be obstacles to military conquest. The urban residents sought relief from central congestion and spread their dwellings far and wide beyond the belt line of fortifications. The basic conditions for residential location changed so radically that now the wealthy citizens moved to the periphery, leaving the urban slums behind.[29]

Inventions rarely stand by themselves as causal factors in the determination of social change. At the time of the first use of gunpowder for military purposes — an urban invention in itself — the social structure of the medieval city was ready to fall. The mercenary armies which laid siege to the cities formed part of that population surplus, which, in the late Middle Ages, failed to find access to either the feudal system of agriculture or the guild system of urban commerce and industry.[30]

---

[28] See Svend Riemer, *Functional Housing in the Middle Ages.* Proceedings, Wisconsin Academy of Sciences and Letters, 1949 (Published 1951), pp. 77-91.

[29] "It was gunpowder — the ability to strike at a distance — that brought about the first major changes in city planning since the days of Jericho." Henry S. Churchill, *The City is the People.* New York: Reynal & Hitchcock, 1945, p. 14.

[30] See Georg Rusche and Otto Kirchheimer, *Punishment and Social Structure.* New York: Columbia University Press, 1939, "Social Developments in the Middle Ages," pp. 11-14.

In the service of territorial princes, these mercenary armies forcibly broke down the isolation of the city from its hinterland. Within the larger unit of the national state, the production of both city and countryside in co-operation could absorb a larger total population.

THE MODERN CITY

Metropolitanization. When the defensive walls of the medieval city fell, the main effect was not the ensuing military weakness of the urban community. The city now merged with its own hinterland and that of other urban communities into a larger society. Industrial society was to appease the clash between the agrarian (feudal) and urban (guild) principles of social organization that had endured through the Middle Ages.

Modern economic enterprise emerged from innovations in urban commercial techniques. Industry grew contagiously from the urban centers into the regional environment of the city. Manufacturing plants were located in the country. Agriculture itself was, in the long run, to drop the fetters of feudalism, and to follow the urban trend that promoted freedom of labor as well as individualized and flexible property relations. The social and economic structure of the medieval city, driven as an alien wedge into the essentially rural world of feudalism, expanded its influence beyond the city walls that had now been razed. Modern capitalism knew no division between rural and urban enterprise. The modern farmer is an entrepreneur just as are the urban craftsman and the industrial "tycoon."

As the centers of commerce and industry, and as large aggregations of consumers, the cities now tend to dominate the rural environment.[31] This is domination, not in terms of force, but in terms of relations of interdependence which have their focus in the ctiy.[32]

Without the existence of modern cities, modern agriculture would not be what it is. It depends upon the city for markets to absorb the products of efficient one-crop farming. It depends upon the city

---

[31] For urban dominance in the contemporary scene, see Don J. Bogue, *The Structure of the Metropolitan Community. A Study of Dominance and Subdominance.* Ann Arbor: Horace H. Rackham School of Graduate Studies, University of Michigan, 1949.

[32] See Roderick D. McKenzie, "The Ecological Approach to the Study of the Human Community," *American Journal of Sociology,* Vol. XXX, No. 3 (November, 1924), pp. 287-361; "The Scope of Human Ecology," *American Journal of Sociology,* Vol. XXXII, No. 1 (July, 1926), pp. 141-154; "Human Ecology," *Encyclopedia of the Social Sciences,* Vol. 5 (1931), pp. 314-315.

for the purchase of agricultural machines without which the farmer could not produce his crops at a reasonable price. The agricultural section of modern society depends upon the city for the purchase of food, clothing, housing, and all those durable consumer items, like interior plumbing, stoves, radios, and refrigerators, which have changed the rural mode of living in a revolutionary manner and moved it closer to the urban way of life.

The modern city, of course, is equally dependent upon an agricultural economy that makes it possible for large urban populations to survive without active participation in the production of food.[33] The modern city is dependent upon an agricultural surplus production of tremendous proportions.

If, nevertheless, we talk about metropolitan dominance of modern society, we do so in recognition of the following circumstances:

1. Modern society has its center of organization in the city, for both government and industry.

2. All communications, so vitally important for the maintenance of an intricate system of economic, social, and political relations, are gathered in and disseminated from urban centers.

3. The city holds the centers of science and technology, and thus determines the direction of progress.

4. If studied by itself, the modern city reveals most of the social relationships that constitute modern society; the rural hinterland does not.

5. Urban attitudes, those attitudes which obviously (with their emphasis upon impersonal social relations and their easy acceptance of social change) stem from the urban way of life, have spread and are still spreading to the rural environment, while the tradition-bound folkways of the self-sufficient peasant village fail to influence city ways and city manners.

The modern city has not remained without critics. The artificialities of urban life have so impressed some writers that they felt justified in raising the question whether or not urbanism had to be considered "abnormal." To many the modern city presents an uncontrollable power structure that bends human purposes to its own end.[34] There are those who sincerely wish to reduce the modern

---

[33] In 1787, it took 9 farm families to feed 1 city family. In 1945, 1 farm family provided food for 8 city families. See William F. Ogburn and Meyer F. Nimkoff, *Sociology*. New York: Houghton Mifflin Company, 1950, p. 315.

[34] See Jose L. Sert, *Can Our Cities Survive?* Cambridge: Harvard University Press, 1942.

city to what they call a "human scale." The assumption is that city size in our days has exceeded its optimum, that our largest metropolitan centers operate at lower efficiency than smaller urban communities.[35]

Nobody, to be sure, dares recommend a way of life from which urban communities would be entirely absent. The reduction of our material standards of living that would be necessitated by the absence of urban concentrations is too obvious. Quite often, however, the opinion has been expressed that the extremes of modern metropolitanization might well be checked to the advantage of the modern way of life. Small town life is favored by many writers as compared to life in the large modern city. These writers are very much concerned with the appeasement of culture conflict that might be gained from life in close contact with friendly neighbors.

Unfortunately, the disadvantages of the metropolitan way of life are closely linked to its advantages. Advancement in the production of material goods is dependent upon the further extension of typically urban principles of social organization. We have to continue in the direction of further specialization of human labor and further segmentalization of human experience, lest we interrupt that dynamic push in the direction of ever higher standards of living that is at the very base of modern industrial society. In the process, to be sure, certain values are trampled underfoot. Perhaps we are sacrificing in vain for material progress. Those many millions, however, who still stand to benefit from further improvements in their standard of living, do not falter in their choice. If further specialization and psychological segmentalization is necessary to raise nutritional standards of the entire population of this country, of the Western world, and of the entire world, that is what we are going to have. If it takes even larger cities, even larger human aggregations of specialized workers to achieve this end, our cities are going to grow still more.

All that we can hope for is that improved means of communication will make it possible to loosen the urban fabric. Air travel may extend commuting distances into sparsely settled suburban parklands. Increased industrial efficiencies may reduce our working hours so that the boredom of a monotonous job may be compensated for in diversified leisure-time activities. Such developments, however, will lead to metropolitanization of a yet unimaginable scope.

---

[35] See Otis Dudley Duncan, *Optimum Size of Cities*. Ph.D thesis, Department of Sociology, University of Chicago, 1948, unpublished.

Nor dare we hope that suburban life will regain the stability of tradition-bound life in the contemporary small town. In spite of the recreational amenities of suburban life in a setting close to nature, suburbanites share the social attributes of those who live closer to the center of the city. They are not friendlier neighbors, nor do they feel more restricted in their personal conduct than the inhabitants of the downtown areas.

The modern city is, irrevocably, the fate of modern civilization as we know it. Human existence today is collective, not individual. We share in the blessings and the blemishes of modern civilization by giving ourselves to a group life that is more powerful than our individual lives can possibly hope to be. In the aggregate of the modern city, the horizon of possible human achievement is without limit. Through co-operation in the urban way of life, we can participate in the mastery of our own destiny, in the control of those awe-inspiring natural resources which our modern science and technology have unleashed.

The Atomic Age. The Atomic Age has made the physical structure of the modern city most vulnerable; and it has therefore been proposed that our large urban communities be decentralized by either:

(1) dispersal and reconstruction in the form of smaller cities, or by

(2) reconstruction of our metropolitan centers in the form of ribbon developments running far and wide over the countryside.

Either solution would entail a cost approximating that of World War II to this nation.[36] Only the stress of extreme emergency, it seems, will lead to the implementation of such plans.

Thinking ahead, we realize that a revolution in means of communication will be necessary to permit our society to function in the face of such revolutionary resettlement. Business is negotiated and ideas disseminated through methods which depend upon face-to-face relationships. The contractual structure of modern urban commerce, industry, and government demands the keeping of reliable records. We have become accustomed, in the modern city, to associate even our leisure time with those who share our interests. To retain these values in the face of defensive decentralization of our large cities, we would need means of transportation and communica-

---

[36] See William F. Ogburn, "Sociology and the Atom," *American Journal of Sociology*, Vol. LI, No. 4 (January, 1946), pp. 270-75.

tion which would surpass by far in range and efficiency the present system.

Suffice it to say that the modern city is probably here to stay, if we view it as a principle of social organization. Its powers of recuperation and adaptation are tremendous. The modern city is not merely a creation in brick and stone; it is a creation of the human mind. The shape of the future city will be the outcome of constant new adaptations to changing technological, social, and political conditions.

SELECTED READINGS

1. Gorden Childe, *What Happened in History*. New York: Penguin Books, Inc., 1946, pp. 82-105.

2. Henry S. Churchill, *The City is the People*. New York: Reynal & Hitchcock, 1945, pp. 1-64.

3. Lewis Mumford, *The Culture of Cities*. New York: Harcourt, Brace and Company, 1938, pp. 13-72.

4. Henri Pirenne, *Economic and Social History of Medieval Europe*. London: Kegan Paul, Trench, Trubner & Co., Ltd., 1936, pp. 1-223.

5. Ralph Turner, *The Great Cultural Traditions*. New York: McGraw-Hill Book Company, Inc., 1941, pp. 3-1333.

PROBLEMS

1. *The Dawn of Urbanization.* Present in a systematic essay different theories about the causes of city formation, particularly at the dawn of Western civilization. References in this chapter will be helpful to you in locating important contributions. In addition, you will have to devote some library work to the location of further sources. Remember that careful reading of one publication will lead to further materials. Publications related to the following authors should be helpful: Toynbee, Spengler, Turner, Childe, Sorokin.

If causation cannot be fixed, as some authors want it, what are the conditions productive of city formation?

Can you arrive, by comparisons of developments of Western civilization with those of other civilizations, at a general theory of city development?

2. *Philosophical Reactions to Urbanization.* This problem will be based primarily upon a general review of philosophical developments and ideological currents in antiquity. For an instructive survey, you may refer to Ralph Turner, *The Great Cultural Traditions*. New York:

McGraw-Hill Book Company, Inc., 1941. Make your own selections from this two-volume work.

It is your task, specifically, to analyze philosophical and ideological currents of antiquity as reactions to the new urban way of life. Consider (1) philosophical schools, (2) social movements, and (3) Christianity.

If previous training and study permits, you are encouraged to consider also contemporary philosophical trends (from the Renaissance to the present day) in their relationship to the experience of industrialization and urbanization.

3. *Capitalism in the Middle Ages.* For this problem, you will have to read and study closely:

Max Weber, *The Protestant Ethic and the Spirit of Capitalism.* Translated by Talcott Parsons. London: George Allen & Unwin, Ltd., 1930.

———, *General Economic History.* Translated by Frank H. Knight. London: George Allen & Unwin, undated.

Henri Pirenne, *Medieval Cities.* Princeton: Princeton University Press, 1925.

———, *Economic and Social History of Medieval Europe.* London: Kegan Paul, Trench, Trubner & Co., Ltd., 1936.

The first of the above books poses the well-known thesis that capitalism is the outcome of religious developments intitiated in the era of reformation. The other three contain information that shows the presence of features of capitalism in the economic and social life of the Middle Ages.

Draw carefully quotations from these last three publications to demonstrate that the transition from a pre-capitalistic to a capitalistic economy has not been as abrupt as assumed by Max Weber in the first mentioned publication.

Discuss the origin of capitalistic features in the urban economy of the Middle Ages.

How do you explain the apparent contradiction in the two above mentioned contributions by Max Weber.

Give your best judgment, on the basis of what you have learned, about the causes of capitalism and urbanization, and their relation to each other and to precipitating conditions.

PART I

Urban Growth

CHAPTER 2

The Growth of Cities

CITY LOCATION

The Sea Coast. Cities, that is, large and dense population settlements, tend to be located at breaks of transportation lines.[1] The crowding of urban developments at the Atlantic seaboard of this continent is undoubtedly due to the need for unloading facilities for ocean-going freighters. In addition to docks and piers, and to warehouses for temporary storage, there must be facilities for inland transportation. Thus, cities are located where the inland waterways connect with the open sea, or where highways and, later, railroad lines terminate at the edge of the continent, providing coast-to-coast distribution of all incoming goods.

It takes both personnel and equipment to transfer goods from one means of transportation to another. This need provides the germ for urban settlement. There are opportunities for work as well as commercial gain where the boats come in. Harbor facilities must be provided, and the final distribution of incoming goods must be decided upon. Manpower is needed for the operation of physical as well as commercial processes in demand at such locations. Thus a

---

[1] "Population and wealth tend to collect wherever there is a break in transportation." Charles H. Cooley, "The Theory of Transportation," Publications of the American Economic Association, Vol. IX, No. 3 (May, 1894), p. 91. See especially Chapter X, "The Location of Towns and Cities."

sufficient population is attracted and retained to provide for the first foundation and further growth of an urban settlement.

Breaks of Transportation Lines. The seacoast shipping centers furnish only the most obvious example of a principle of city location that has much wider application. There are urban settlements at river crossings which in earlier days necessitated reloading activities. There are urban settlements along the inland waterways where goods were transferred from barges to wagon trains, railroads, or trucks. There are urban settlements at the edges of mountain ranges that formerly made necessary the shifting from one means of transportation to another.

In the history of the United States, the transcontinental railroad system was only gradually expanded. Wherever railroad construction came temporarily to an end, urban settlements developed to accommodate the transfer of goods from the freight train to the horse-drawn wagon. Today, the break of transportation which caused original city location has in many instances been obliterated by further extensions of the rail system. Railroad construction was continued with devastating effects upon inland trading centers. Bridges were thrown over rivers to eliminate the need for reloading to and from ferries. In this process, many urban communities came to outlive their usefulness. The location of new communities and their development changed continuously with the improvement of our means of transportation. Ghost towns were left in the wake of the transcontinental advance of our railroads.

The Problem of City Growth. In addition to the reason for city location, we are interested in the reasons for city growth. We want to understand fully the present spread and size of urban settlement in the United States. The function of the city as a trading center is overemphasized by the theory that points exclusively to location at breaks of transportation lines.

In the early Middle Ages, city location was determined primarily by the needs of defense. We find remnants of these ancient cities on almost inaccessible hillsides, on the estuaries of rivers, or perched on peninsulas. With the development of trade and commerce, many of these cities lost importance, ceased to grow, and drifted into stagnation. They became obsolete with a change in urban function. Nor is urban growth entirely explainable anymore by location in relation to transportation facilities. Most modern cities have developed from centers of commerce and trade to centers of industry. Under the circumstances, new economic considerations have to be added to the explanation of urban growth and development.

Modern industry needs bulky raw materials. The mileage these raw materials have to travel from their place of origin (for example, from the mines) to the place of industrial transformation enters heavily into industrial cost calculations. Quite often several raw materials are required in the process of production. Every one of these raw materials exerts a pull upon the location of the manufacturing plant.

The Pull of Raw Materials. Location of industry and location of urban settlement are attracted to the places where raw materials are extracted. On top of the mines, obviously, the cost of cross-country transportation is reduced to nothing. In the see-saw between different raw materials, that one wins which loses a maximum of bulk and weight in the finished product. Thus, total costs of transportation are reduced to a minimum.[2]

Coal proves to be more effective in attracting the steel industry than iron. More coal than iron ore — in weight and bulk — is used and lost in the production of any given amount of steel. For this reason, the steel industries of western Europe are located in the Ruhr valley where coal is found, rather than in France where the iron ore is mined. In this country, there are steel mills on top of the coal mines of Pittsburgh and in Gary, Indiana, where the coal is shipped from the nearby coal mines of Illinois. Iron ore, on the other hand, is shipped a considerable distance from northern Minnesota to either of the above mentioned locations. In Sweden, where iron ore is found in abundance but coal is entirely lacking, only an industry for high-quality steel products has developed. Most of its iron ores are shipped to various parts of Europe where coal is found.

The relationship of industrial and urban location to coal and iron ore is, of course, only a striking example of a more general principle. Location is determined by the attempt to reduce the total cost for

---

2 See Alfred Weber, *Theory of the Location of Industry.* English Edition, with Introduction and note by Carl Joachim Friedrich. Chicago: The University of Chicago Press, 1929. This book contains a concise statement about the different factors that influence the location of industry. Of particular interest are the chapters on "Transport Orientation," "Labor Orientation," "Agglomeration," and "The Total Orientation," pp. 41-211.

transportation to the lowest possible level. The pottery industry moves to deposits of suitable clay; oil refineries hover over the most productive wells; and paper mills cluster around our diminishing resources of timber. Urban settlements provide the necessary manpower for industrial and commercial activities in such locations.

The Pull of the Market. The transportation costs of raw materials are not the only factor in industrial location. Shipment of the final product to the market also influences the location of industry. For our heavy industries, to be sure, the pull exerted upon plant location by the market is of less importance than that exerted by the location of raw materials. In the heavy industries, a considerable amount of bulk and weight of the raw material disappears in the process of production. The costs of shipping the final product are so much less than those required for the movement of the raw materials that the location of the heavy industries is rarely attracted far toward the market site.

The less weight and bulk of the raw materials is lost in the process of production, the greater becomes the inducement to take advantage of industrial location close to the buyer and the final consumer. For many products, the costs of shipping the goods from the end of the production line are not calculated in terms of weight, bulk, and mileage alone. The problem of spoilage enters into the picture.

There is an advantage, also, in close contact between the commercial and industrial areas of modern enterprise. Costs for crating and other shipping materials as well as the costs for labor have to be taken into consideration. Under the circumstances, we find that many of our consumer industries move closer to the site of sales on either the retail or wholesale market.[3]

The most extreme example for this condition is that of the production and the delivery of fresh and easily spoiled foods. The truck-farming belt around the large urban settlement bears testimony to the need for market proximity. One-crop farming, on the other hand, is sufficiently dependent upon suitable climatic and soil conditions to resist the attraction of the market site. This type of farm-

---

[3] An elementary but thorough discussion of the entire problem of industrial and city location will be found in Edgard M. Hoover, *The Location of Economic Activity.* New York: McGraw-Hill Book Company, Inc., 1948. See particularly Part I, "Locational Preferences and Patterns," pp. 15-145.

ing, in turn, will attract urban trading centers and urban storage facilities.[4] The reduction of spoilage is also achieved by improvement in the means of transportation.[5]

Cumulative Growth. The markets to which many of our industries are attracted consist of consumers, that is, they are dependent upon already existing urban settlement. A city, once established, holds certain advantages for the growth of trade and commerce in the service of effective consumer demands.

Such secondary growth is likely to occur in urban settlements of small as well as gigantic size. The metropolis particularly attracts vast industries subsidiary to the needs of the city dweller.

Cumulative urban growth is also enhanced by the availability of a labor supply easily diverted into other industrial channels than those which determined the early growth of the city. Industry is attracted to locations where it is able to compete on the labor market with less profitable production.

Overlapping Causes. Urban growth is a highly complex phenomenon not easily reduced to conditions of natural environment alone.

Breaks in lines of transportation may explain why small urban settlements developed here and there all over the countryside. But, although it may be possible to refer to an early Indian trail as a cause for first foundation of an urban settlement, the Indian trail does not explain why this settlement grew to tremendous proportions while others have remained villages or hamlets.

The changing importance of different raw materials and changing techniques of exploitation and transportation have to be taken into account for the explanation of modern urban growth. In addition, the process of cumulative urban growth due to the concentration of

---

[4] Consider the huge silos in Omaha, Nebraska; Minneapolis, Minnesota; Kansas City, Kansas; and other cities of the midwestern wheat belt.

[5] The impact of various transportation improvements has been timed in the following manner:

Canals	1830
Railroads	1843, 1862, 1878
Electric railways	1895
Automobiles	1918

See Walter Isard, "Transportation Development and Building Cycles," *Quarterly Journal of Economics*, Vol. LVII, No. 1 (November, 1942), pp. 90-112; also, Walter Isard, "The Transportation-Building Cycle," *Review of Economic Statistics*, Vol. XXIV, No. 4 (November, 1942).

labor and the consuming masses calls for analysis. The full explanation of city growth is tied to the entire history of industrial and technological advancement, which does not submit to treatment by formula.[6]

Spread of Trading Centers. Modern agriculture is dependent upon an interchange of goods and services with the modern city. Its tools and machinery are not homemade but factory-produced. Farm machinery is mass-fabricated where the process of specialization has gone so far as to lead to the production of machinery to make machinery. It is produced in the city. Modern methods of farming are unthinkable in the absence of the metropolis.

In addition to large urban concentrations for the production of farm machinery and other goods that raise the farmer's standard of living, agriculture requires smaller trading centers, urban settlements of limited size which gather the crops of the region for shipment toward the metropolis and its food industries, and which carry city-produced machinery and equipment to the trading orbit of the villager and the isolated farmer.

Modern farming guarantees the survival of the American small town. Because farming is more or less ubiquitous, a network of small towns is spread over the American countryside. These towns are of varying size, but there is regularity in the manner in which smaller and larger urban settlements are found side by side.

The smaller towns are more abundantly distributed than the larger urban settlements. The farmer is willing to travel increasingly farther for specialty trading required at increasingly rarer occasions. The more specialized trades and the more specialized institutions are dependent for economic survival upon an ever increasing number of potential consumers.

Time of Foundation. The contemporary urban panorama was not laid out in one sweep. The sequence of city foundation has influenced the extent of growth of the individual cities. Existing cities pre-empt the economic opportunities which otherwise might have caused the formation and growth of another city in close proximity.

Without the existence of Chicago, Milwaukee might have assumed the role of providing a midwestern railroad and transportation center.

---

[6] A good case study of historical change in urban function is provided by Blake McKelvey, *Rochester. The Flower City. 1855-1890.* Cambridge: Harvard University Press, 1949.

A small village may be thwarted in its growth, because the farming population in its environs has learned to depend for specialty shopping upon the business district of a nearby town. The country town may owe its prominence to its previous function as a railroad terminal where goods were transferred to other means of transportation.

Cities and towns have a certain amount of staying power. Once established, they survive due to habit on the part of potential consumers and due to the difficulty of duplicating in a nearby settlement the investment in trade and service institutions that have already been formed in answer to effective demands.

In urban settlement, the first-comer holds a certain advantage. Priority has a good chance to succeed in competition within the established service area. Thus, social history carries over into the location and growth of our contemporary cities. Different stages of adjustment to physical and social environment are overlaid in the contemporary scene.

TYPES OF CITIES

The Problem of Classification. Any classification of cities is somewhat arbitrary. The criteria of classification are a matter of choice. We classify cities according to function, but we recognize that most modern cities are dedicated to a plurality of overlapping functions. The "type" is derived from the predominating function. Some cities, of course, are distinct types, such as college towns, one-industry towns, or agricultural trading centers. But such clear distinction is the exception rather than the rule.

To establish a tentative system of classification, we arrange function according to the manner in which it occurred in urban history. There are cities that function as (1) seats of institutions, (2) trading centers, (3) industrial centers, (4) metropolitan centers, and (5) resort towns.

The historical progress of city types according to predominant function may be represented in the following manner:

Seats of Institutions
— Mesopotamian Cities
— Cities of Antiquity
— Urban Stagnation at the Fall of Rome

Trading Centers——————Early Middle Ages

Industrial Centers ⟨ Late Middle Ages
Early Industrialization Process

Metropolitan Centers
Resort Towns ⟩ Late Industrialization Process

Seats of Institutions. The first mentioned city type, characterized as the seat of one or several institutions, reaches back into the dawn of urban history when city life was centered around the temple or the palace of divine royalty. There were economic reasons, of course, that made the foundation and growth of such cities possible. They were dependent upon an agricultural surplus in the immediate hinterland. Yet the economic function of these early cities was subsidiary to religious worship or secular homage.

The cathedral town of the Middle Ages furnishes a similar example with diversified construction for the use of the clergy. In the contemporary environment, the college town, the county seat, the seat of the state government, the agricultural experiment station and towns devoted to a variety of such purposes, containing schools, governmental institutions, churches, and libraries, fall into this same category.

Trading Centers. The city as a center exclusively for trade and commerce was prominent at another phase of urban development. Such singleness of purpose is unusual for the large city in the contemporary scene. The cities at the shores of the Mediterranean Sea in antiquity, however, could be considered primarily centers of trade and commerce.[7] Upon these cities the products of a vast rural hinterland converged. Between these cities, products of the hinterland were exchanged. From the urban centers, these products were distributed to the country population in the region.

In the Middle Ages, urban commerce developed before urban in-

---

[7] "The Roman Empire, at the end of the third century, had one outstanding general characteristic: it was an essentially Mediterranean commonwealth. Virtually all of its territory lay within the watershed of that great land-locked sea." Opening sentence of Henri Pirenne, *Medieval Cities*. Princeton: Princeton University Press, 1925. The primarily commercial function of early medieval cities is treated in the subsequent chapter. See also Henri Pirenne, *Economic and Social History of Medieval Europe*. London:Kegan Paul, Trench, Trubner & Co., Ltd., 1936.

dustry. Trade gave a livelihood to merchants and to those engaged in transportation before it stimulated the development of crafts and industries which were later to replace the commercial activities in importance.[8] In the contemporary scene, we have to look to our agricultural trading centers for a similar type of town.

Industrial Centers. The industrial city reaches its full development during the industrialization process itself. It is dependent, in both location and growth, upon the availability of raw materials within a favorable range of transportation. It is also dependent upon a supply of labor, and not unconcerned with the distance at which the final product can be marketed.

Metropolitan Centers. In the metropolitan center, the process of urbanization reaches its climax. The metropolitan center is characterized by a multiplicity of functions. It contains industry as well as commerce, educational as well as governmental institutions. The metropolitan center feeds on the cumulative processes of urban growth.[9]

The metropolis may start its development from any of the above mentioned types. Let us assume a trading center favorably located near existing means of transportation. Large masses of consumers will be attracted by commercial activities and provide a sufficient market for the development of consumer goods industries. Nearby sources of raw materials may give further impulse to industrial development. The labor supply so collected induces an ever widening range of diversified industrial enterprise to locate within the metropolitan area. Educational and governmental institutions are prone to move into the already established large urban settlement where they will be close to the people they intend to serve.

The process may proceed along different lines. The metropolis may start as a center of industry which — at a certain point of development — begins to attract banks, warehouses and other establishments to promote commerce in either raw materials or finished products. The metropolis may have its origin in a seat of government or an educational center, although we have to go far back in urban history to find examples for such developments.[10] The begin-

---

[8] "On that wonderful plain (Lombardy) cities bloomed with the same vigor as the harvests. . . . There, commerce gave rise to industry," Henri Pirenne, *Medieval Cities. op. cit.,* p. 95.

[9] *Ibid.,* p. 15.

[10] See Henri Pirenne, *Economic and Social History of Medieval Europe. op. cit.,* "The Revival of Urban Life," pp. 40-45.

ning, however, is not very important once the metropolis has come into its own.

In its full bloom, the metropolitan center becomes an end in itself, gaining increasing advantage as an agglomeration of a large resident population. It fulfills regional as well as national and world-wide services in the pursuit of governmental, educational, commercial, and industrial activities.

Resort Towns. We place the resort town at the very end of our historical continuum. The resort town appears as the outgrowth of a metropolitan way of life that requires specialized services for purposes of human recuperation. We need not elaborate upon its function. Suffice it to say that the resort town is economically dependent upon the existence of large urban settlements at a reasonable distance.

The resort town is most frequently tied to small urban settlements which function simultaneously as agricultural trading centers. Accessibility to metropolitan travelers and a site which appeals through natural features such as lakes and meadows and mountains are important prerequisites. Such conditions establish for the indigenous population the opportunity of gaining additional income through boarding houses, hotels, cabins, and artificial recreational facilities.

URBANIZATION IN THE 19TH CENTURY: INTERNATIONAL COMPARISON

Population Increase. In the social history of Western civilization, industrialization, general population increase, and urbanization travel hand in hand. Many social scientists have claimed that the population increase was the sole cause.[11]

The theory has been proposed that modern industrialization has been the manner in which social institutions in the Western world adjusted themselves to an ever-growing population. This seemingly spontaneous population increase, which — practically all over the world — started in the 17th century and reached its climax

---

[11] Max Weber referred to the "widespread error that the increase of population is to be included as a really crucial agent in the evolution of western capitalism" in *General Economic History*. London: George Allan & Unwin, Ltd., undated, p. 352.

To prove that capitalism is not the necessary result of population increase, Max Weber pointed to China, where a startling population growth had occurred — just as in Europe — from the beginning of the 18th century to the end of the 19th century without causing capitalism or urbanization, but instead making "China the seat of a swarming mass of peasants." *Ibid.*, p. 352.

in the 19th century has been looked upon by some as the cause of modern capitalism. Others have refuted this idea by pointing to China where a similar population increase generated a system of intensive agriculture.

Population increase cannot be looked upon as a primary cause of urbanization. In Western history, it may have been the outcome of good harvests. It may have been the outcome of more successful prevention of epidemics. It may have resulted from the spread of new starch products yielding a higher output per acre (like the potato), or it may have been the outcome of the thrift and frugality cultivated by the early pioneers of a capitalistic mode of life.[12] Thus, population increase may be in itself an outcome of the capitalistic enterprise which it is said to have brought about. Whatever we may want to consider the primary cause, it cannot be doubted that a close connection exists between population increase and industrialization. A similar two-way path of influence exists between population increase and urbanization. Urbanization enables a country to support a larger population than that surviving on a merely agrarian basis.

Agriculture and Urbanization. Agriculture gains in productivity by increased urbanization. Larger food supplies become available where city-produced implements are used to till the soil and to reap the harvest, where urban commerce assists in the distribution of diversified food products and permits the farmer to devote himself to specialized one-crop farming.

City growth means more efficient agriculture. More efficient agriculture provides for the survival of a larger number of people in the city as well as in the country. Finally, a larger number of people provides for that continuous population surplus within the rural section of society that will tend to flow city-ward.

We shall leave aside the problem of *first* causes. We are unable to answer the question whether it is the city that causes population increase or whether it is population increase that causes the city. We remain satisfied with the understanding that population increase and city growth are somehow closely interrelated. At the threshold of the modern industrialization process, both population increase and city growth unfolded in a cumulative development which exceeded any population increase or city growth known previously.

---

[12] See Max Weber, *The Protestant Ethic and the Spirit of Capitalism.* Translated by Talcott Parsons, with a foreword by R. H. Tawney. London: George Allen & Unwin Ltd., 1930.

TABLE I

URBANIZATION IN THE 19TH CENTURY

Country	Per cent Population in communities roughly 100,000 or more *			Per cent Population in communities roughly 20,000 or more			Per cent Population in communities roughly 10,000 or more		
	1800†*	1850	1890	1800	1850	1890	1800	1850	1890
England and Wales	9.73	22.58	31.82	16.94	35.0	53.58	21.30	39.45	61.73
Scotland	0.	16.9	29.8	13.9	27.7	42.4	17.0	32.2	49.9
Belgium	0.	6.8	17.4	8.7	16.6	26.1	13.5	20.8	34.8
Saxony	0.	0.	22.6	7.7	9.9	30.0	8.9	13.6	34.7
Netherlands	11.5	7.3	16.6	24.5	21.7	29.3	29.5	29.0	33.5
Prussia	1.8	3.1	12.9	6.0	7.8	23.0	7.25	10.63	30.0
United States	0.	6.0	15.5	3.8	9.8	23.8	3.8	12.0	27.6
France	2.8	4.6	12.0	6.7	10.6	21.1	9.5	14.4	25.9
Denmark	10.9	9.6	17.3	10.9	9.6	20.2	10.9	9.6	23.6
Sweden	0.	0.	7.34	3.0	3.4	10.84	3.9	4.7	13.74

* Rough estimates only.
† Somewhat earlier or later years have been used as available.
Source: Adna Weber, *The Growth of Cities*. New York: 1899, pp. 144-145.

The process of urbanization was timed differently in different countries. Whether city growth started early or late, whether it reached a relatively high degree of urbanization, or whether it leveled off at a relatively modest degree of urbanization was dependent upon industrial developments in these countries.

Countries like England and France, where industrialization had an early beginning, have achieved today a relatively high degree of urbanization. The relative number of people in these countries who devote themselves to agricultural pursuits has dwindled. The farming population has become a minority within the nation.[13]

---

[13] For international statistical comparisons of the history of urbanization, see Adna F. Weber, *The Growth of Cities in the 19th Century*. New York: The MacMillan Company, 1899. This source book of information copes with the tremendous task of making the statistics of many countries comparable to each other. For a quick comparison of urbanization in different countries consult Table CXII, p. 144, and the diagram on p. 151. Comparable data are here computed for the years 1800, 1850, and 1890. Later information, up to 1930, is compiled in *Our Cities. Report of the Urbanism Committee to the National Resources Committee*. Washington, D.C.: U.S. Government Printing Office, June 1937, pp. 25-27.

The city dwellers have become a preponderant majority in these countries. Once under way, the process of urbanization seems to press relentlessly onward. Thus, an early start seems to guarantee a lead position in the race toward ever increasing urbanization, a race in which no nation seems as yet to have reached a saturation point beyond which urbanization will not proceed.

Urbanization has a background in both urban and rural developments. In modern times, events occurring in the country and in the city cannot be considered separately. This might have been possible in the Middle Ages when both country and city were dominated by entirely different social systems. At the dawn of the industrialization period, both industry and agriculture submit to a process of relentless rationalization. Both have in common a tendency toward rationalization in the service of increased efficiencies and in exploitation of the discoveries of natural science.

For the advance of urbanization the social reorganization of agriculture through the redistribution of land, the abandonment of strip-farming, and the application of the concept of individual property to rural landholdings was just as important as the development of commercial and industrial institutions in the city.

When the Napoleonic code of law was applied to agriculture, demanding an equal distribution of inherited property to all siblings, family holdings were cut into minute parcels of arable land insufficient to provide a living even for the small conjugal family of modern times. Due to indebtedness or outright poverty, rural families sold their stakes in the land and turned their steps city-ward. Agricultural machinery and the trend toward one-crop farming lowered the demand for female labor in agriculture. Unmarried girls tended to drift into the nearby city.

Both rural and urban industrial developments combined in a reorganization of the productive processes that favored city growth. The timing of the process of urbanization in different countries in Western civilization was affected by propensities for, as well as resistances to, rural and urban rationalization.

National Differences. Leadership in the process of urbanization did not always fall to England, Wales, and Scotland. In 1800 urbanization in the Netherlands surpassed that of England by a considerable margin. In the Netherlands, intense urbanization had its roots far back in the Middle Ages. There, urban growth was the outcome of large scale commercial activities. Industrial developments in the 19th century left the country relatively untouched. In 1850 the Netherlands was surpassed in urbanization by England, Wales, and Scotland, and England has remained the most urbanized country ever since.

In Denmark, as well as in the Netherlands, the degree of urbanization did in fact recede during the first half of the 19th century. This does not indicate that urbanization in these countries had reached something like a saturation point. Later on, the urban sections of these countries continued to grow at the cost of the rural population. The importance of the city shrank only temporarily while commercial urban functions all over the Western world were outdistanced by industrial urban functions.

Second only to the Netherlands in 1800, England took the lead when the combination of commercial and industrial urban activities in that country caused a population displacement from the rural areas to the coastal cities unmatched anywhere else.[14]

In other countries, such as France, Saxony, and Prussia, urbanization started from a relatively low level at the beginning of the 19th century, but forged ahead toward the middle and the end of the 1800's. These are the countries distinguished by primarily industrial urbanization. Commerce, in these countries, never played an overwhelming role.

The United States is in a somewhat unique position. The commerce which at the threshold of the 19th century was concentrated at the Atlantic coast was heavily outbalanced by non-urban pursuits of the pioneers pushing inland. Later industrial developments never outdistanced rural expansion enough to match the degree of urbanization reached in England, France, and Germany.

There is still another group of countries, such as Sweden and Norway, where urbanization remained practically stagnant during the first half of the 19th century, only to occur with a sudden onrush during the last half of that century. These countries were affected late but vigorously by the industrialization process.

Urbanization and Population Density. City growth seems to be stimulated by population density, or vice versa. There are, however, exceptions to this rule. In the 19th century, some countries

[14] For different statistical distinctions between urban and rural settlement see Adna F. Weber, *The Growth of Cities in the 19th Century, op. cit.*, pp. 9-19.

TABLE II

PROPORTION OF RURAL AND URBAN POPULATION

Country	Latest census urban	rural	1880 urban	rural
United States (1950)	64.0	36.0	29.5	70.5
England and Wales (1931)	80.0	20.0	67.9	32.1
Germany (1933)	56.5	43.5	29.1	70.9
France (1946)	53.2	46.8	34.8	65.2

with relatively high population density, such as Italy, the Bengal in India, and Japan, did not show a correspondingly high degree of urbanization. Conditions in these countries were characterized by intensive agriculture or a relatively low standard of living, or both. If a certain standard of living is to be maintained, population increase must be met by increasing urbanization.

A comparison based on degree of urbanization in the different large countries of Western civilization shows England and Wales in the lead throughout the 19th century. This lead has been retained up to the immediate present, although both Germany and the United States have managed in the 20th century to catch up somewhat with the British Isles. With only about 20 per cent of the total population retained in rural residence, England may well have surpassed that degree of urbanization beyond which the dependence upon food imports from abroad leaves the country in a precarious economic situation.

Metropolitan Growth. Urbanization differs from metropolitan growth. As cities surpass the million mark, they function on more than a regional or even a national basis. They become world cities, centers of international trade and travel. There have been such cities since antiquity. Carthage, on the North African coast has been given credit for a population of more than a half million people. Rome, at the height of its importance, was estimated to contain a population of a million. In the late Middle Ages, other cities loomed high in numerical importance.

The trade that passed in the Middle Ages between the orient and the occident converged upon Constantinople and permitted this city to grow larger than any other urban community of its time. Trade also stimulated the growth of Naples and Venice. These two cities represented the commercial link between Asia and the urban civilization of northern Europe. Paris held the center of the stage in medieval Europe proper. Even the population of this latter city, however, did not rival that of ancient Rome until the early beginnings of the industralization process.

At the beginning of the 19th century, London gained supreme numerical importance. In 1950 the largest city of the world was New York, its metropolitan area containing a population of almost 13 million. Throughout the world, there were about 54 cities with populations of more than a million people. Of these, the United States claims 14, New York, Chicago, Los Angeles, Philadelphia, Detroit, Boston, San Francisco, Pittsburgh, St. Louis, Washington

TABLE III

MILLION CLASS CITIES IN THE UNITED STATES,
INCLUDING STANDARD METROPOLITAN AREAS — 1950

Standard Metropolitan Area	Total Population	Increase since 1940 (in per cent)	Population in Central City
New York-Northeastern New Jersey	12,831,914	10.	8,573,403
Chicago, Ill.	5,475,535	13.5	3,606,436
Los Angeles, Calif.	4,339,225	48.8	1,957,692
Philadelphia, Pa.	3,660,676	14.4	2,064,794
Detroit, Mich.	2,973,019	25.1	1,838,517
Boston, Mass.	2,354,507	8.1	790,863
San Francisco-Oakland, Calif.	2,214,249	51.5	1,141,329
Pittsburgh, Pa.	2,205,544	5.9	673,763
St. Louis, Mo.	1,673,467	16.9	852,623
Washington, D.C.	1,457,601	50.6	797,670
Cleveland, Ohio	1,453,556	14.6	905,636
Baltimore, Md.	1,320,754	21.9	940,205
Minneapolis-St. Paul, Minn.	1,107,366	17.7	826,751
Buffalo, N.Y.	1,085,606	13.3	577,393

1950 Census of Population. Preliminary. Series PC-3, No. 3. Table 2.

D.C., Cleveland, Baltimore, Minneapolis and St. Paul, and Buffalo, all arranged here according to size of metropolitan area.

URBANIZATION IN THE UNITED STATES

The time sequence. In the United States urbanization advanced most rapidly during the first half of the 19th century.[15] It is remarkable that cities should have grown at all at a time when the arable land of a continent stood ready to absorb any surplus population that might have grown from within or arrived from abroad by immigration. The city population of the United States reached its highest rate of growth in the decade between 1840 and 1850. In these ten years, the urban population of this country almost doubled, increasing by 92.1 per cent. During that same decade, the rural population of the United States did not increase by more than 29.1 per cent. Consequently, a heavy displacement must have occurred from the rural to the urban sections of American society.

In 1840 not more than 10.8 per cent of the entire population of the United States lived in cities. In 1850 this percentage had increased to 15.3. Ever since, urban population increase has slowed down until the rate of increase sank to a low of 7.9 per cent between 1930 and 1940. During the 1940's, the rate of urban population increase in the United States bounced back from the low ebb of the depression decade.

---

[15] All figures quoted on urbanization in the United States are related to the statistical definition of urban residence as applied by the Census Bureau. Such definition, of course, is somewhat arbitrary:

"Urban-Rural Residence.— According to the definition adopted for the 1950 Census, the urban population comprises all persons living in:

1. Places of 2,500 inhabitants or more incorporated as cities, boroughs, towns, and villages (except towns in New England, New York, and Wisconsin, where 'towns' are minor civil divisions of counties and are not necessarily densely settled centers like the towns in the other States);

2. The densely settled urban fringe, including both incorporated and unincorporated areas, around cities of 50,000 or more; and

3. Unincorporated places of 2,500 inhabitants or more outside of any urban fringe.

The remaining population is classified as rural.

According to the urban definition used in previous censuses, the urban population comprised all persons living in incorporated places of 2,500 inhabitants or more and in areas (usually minor civil divisions) classified as urban under special rules relating to population size and density."

Key to Published and Tabulated Data for Small Areas. United States Census of Population and Housing. 1950. United States Department of Commerce. Bureau of the Census. U.S. Government Printing Office. Washington D.C.: 1951. pp. i/2.

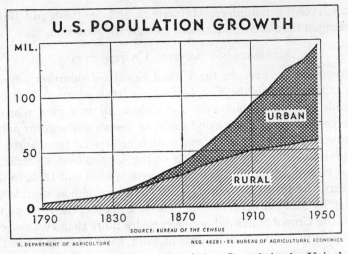

S. DEPARTMENT OF AGRICULTURE   NEG. 46281-XX BUREAU OF AGRICULTURAL ECONOMICS

FIGURE 2. Urban and Rural Population Growth in the United States, 1790-1940. (Strictly comparable figures for 1950 are not available.)

Rural Versus Urban Increase. All through the 19th century and ever since, urban population increase was above that for the rural section of the United States. The only exception is the decade between 1810 and 1820 when, due to the War of 1812 and its interference with commerce, the rate of growth in the urban population of this country fell to a relative low of 33.1 per cent, while the rural section of the population continued to grow by 33.2 per cent.

Thus an ever growing sector of the American population found residence in the urban environment. By 1850 the cities harbored about 15 per cent of the United States population. In 1900 they contained about 40 per cent of all inhabitants. In the census year of 1920 the size of the urban population in this country for the first time surpassed that of the rural population. Since then the urban share of the population of the United States has climbed to more than 60 per cent.

Historical Backgrounds. Behind these figures there is a colorful story of industrial developments, of wars, of improvements in the transportation system, and of waves of immigration which reached this country from various parts of the European continent all through the 19th century.[16]

---

16 See p. 77 below.

In 1821 the Erie Canal was opened, with its consequent effects upon urban development in the State of New York. During the following decade, New York City forged to the front as the largest metropolis of this country, outdistancing Philadelphia. In upstate New York a row of urban settlements grew up along the transportation system provided by the canal, including Buffalo, Rochester, and Syracuse. Simultaneously, railroad construction through the New England states had given impetus to the development of urban manufactures in this area.

The Influence of Transportation. Urban growth in the United States was dependent upon the development of its means of transportation. Until 1840 direct access to the ocean was almost a prerequisite to urban growth. New York, Baltimore, Boston, and New Orleans rose to prominence during this period. The interior was opened up for urban development while transportation flowed inland through rivers, canals, and the Great Lakes.

Two separate urban empires established themselves in the United States with relatively little connection between them: the urban development along the shores of the Great Lakes, and that of the Mississippi basin. These two territories were closely fused commercially only after the Civil War, when transportation became predominantly dependent upon the railroads' push westward, favoring the development of such cities as Chicago, Minneapolis, Kansas City, Omaha, Denver, and the west coast cities.[17]

As the railroad had emancipated urban development from its close dependence upon the waterways of the country, motor transportation permitted urban growth on a widening regional basis. It welded more closely the individual city and its immediate hinterland. Local exchange of agricultural and industrial services became sufficiently intensive to make urban growth somewhat independent of the inter-urban and international division of labor and exchange of goods.[18]

---

[17] For the development of our national transportation system from the Indian trial to modern air travel, see *Highways in Our National Life. A Symposium.* Edited by Jean Labatut and Wheaton J. Lane. Princeton: Princeton University Press, 1950.

The relationship of the prevailing road system to the growth of cities is discussed in Homer Hoyt, *The influence of highways and transportation on the structure and growth of cities and urban land values. op. cit.*, pp. 201 ff.

[18] "Thus the new automotive transportation tended to spread out the great metropolitan conglomerations over a wider area, because a mile or so further means little to a man in an automobile." *Highways in Our National Life*, p. 205.

The Influence of Boom and Bust. More important for city growth than improvements of the transportation system were the cycles of economic prosperity and depression. Economic prosperity causes accelerated urban growth, but urban growth is retarded in times of economic depression. Thus, paralleling the boom and bust cycle, the decades of 1840-50, 1860-70, and 1880-90 were characterized by substantial urban growth; and the decades following the years 1850, 1870, and 1890 contain periods of relatively retarded urban growth.

The decade 1910-20 was a time of relatively active urban growth. The rate of urban growth, which had been declining ever since the middle of the 19th century, experienced, during this decade, a decided increase. The same was to happen later during the 1940's.

Although the Napoleonic wars, with their stifling effects upon international trade and commerce, had retarded urban concentration in the United States, the Civil War and World Wars I and II affected the process of urbanization in a positive manner. This was due to the stimulating effect of these wars on urban industry in the process of mobilization and armament. The tremendous slackening of urbanization in the 1930's is just another reflection of economic stagnation during these years.

Growth by City Size. Urbanization does not affect cities of different size in exactly the same manner. We want to know how the urban population was distributed throughout the 19th century over different size groups of communities. It makes a difference

TABLE IV

NUMBER OF CITIES IN THE UNITED STATES,
BY COMMUNITY SIZE GROUPS *

	1790	1840	1880	1930	1940
2,500 to 10,000	28	123	872	2183	2387
10,000 to 25,000	3	27	150	606	665
25,000 to 100,000	2	9	57	283	320
100,000 to 250,000		2	12	56	55
250,000 to 500,000		1	4	24	23
500,000 to 1,000,000			3	8	9
1,000,000 & over			1	5	5

* 16th Census of the United States: 1940, Vol. I, Population, p. 25. Washington, D.C.: U.S. Government Printing Office, 1942.

whether people live in the shadow of sky-scrapers in metropolitan communities of more than a million people, or whether they are residing predominantly in small towns of less than 100,000.

In 1790 there was no city in the United States that held more than 100,000 inhabitants. In 1810 only Philadelphia had grown beyond the 100,000 mark. In 1790 less than 10 per cent of the population of the United States lived in urban communities, and of these city dwellers more than half were located in communities of less than 10,000 people. In 1950 about 15 per cent of the entire population of the United States, and about 25 per cent of the entire urban population in this country live in metropolitan cities of more than a million.

The number of individual communities has increased much more rapidly in the smaller groups. Since 1790 there have always been fewer communities in the larger and more communities in the smaller groups. That there should be fewer cities of large size, that there should be a relatively limited number of metropolitan settlements as compared to thousands of small urban centers with less than 10,000 population is not surprising.

Population in Community Size Groups. Yet, if we consider popu-

TABLE V

PER CENT OF POPULATION IN URBAN COMMUNITY
SIZE GROUPS *

	1790	1840	1880	1930	1940
2,500 to 5,000	1.1	1.0	3.2	3.8	3.8
5,000 to 10,000	1.2	1.9	3.4	4.8	5.1
10,000 to 25,000	1.2	2.4	4.4	7.4	7.6
25,000 to 50,000	1.6	1.4	2.9	5.2	5.6
50,000 to 100,000		1.1	1.9	5.3	5.6
100,000 to 250,000		1.2	3.6	6.1	5.9
250,000 to 500,000		1.8	2.6	6.5	5.9
500,000 to 1,000,000			3.8	4.7	4.9
1,000,000 & over			2.4	12.3	12.1
Total Urban Population	5.1	10.8	28.2	56.2	56.5

* 16th Census of the United States: 1940, Vol. I, Population, pp. 26-27. Washington, D.C.: U.S. Government Printing Office, 1942.

lation rather than number of communities in different size groups, we are not confronted with a similar hierarchical structure. We do not consistently find more people in the smaller as compared to the larger community groups. There is no broad base of small town development in terms of population, upon which rises the glory of the modern metropolis. About 30 per cent of our urban population is located in communities with less than 25,000 people each; urban centers with a population of more than 100,000 persons contain another 30 per cent of the entire urban population.

The distribution of the total urban population over community size groups in the United States is not weighted at the base. There is some emphasis, indeed, upon the population concentrated in our large metropolitan areas. In these cities with more than a million people, we find a larger number of city dwellers than in any other census category. Between the other size groups, however, the total urban population is fairly evenly distributed.

Recent Trends of Urban Growth

The Economic Base. In recent decades, the process of urbanization has proceeded in a very erratic manner. The relative growth of urban and rural populations is, of course, dependent upon business conditions.

The boom of the 1920's permitted our urban population to grow at a rate of 27.3 per cent, while the rural population was held back to a growth of only 4.4 per cent. During the long and severe depression of the 1930's, urban growth was much lower than during any decade since 1790, with a rate of 7.9 per cent. In the 1930's rural population increase was accelerated. During these years the rural population of the United States gained by a rate of 6.4 per cent. Since the Napoleonic wars, rural population increase had never come as close to that of the rate of urban population growth. The decade of World War II again reversed conditions.

Future Trends. Undoubtedly the long-term decrease in the rate of urban population growth will continue as time goes on. Yet urban growth will not come to as abrupt a standstill as was apparently indicated by the unusual conditions of the depression decade.

In 1924 immigration to this country came practically to an end. Natural population increase is rapidly and irreversibly falling off.

TABLE VI

GROWTH OF THE URBAN POPULATION OF THE
UNITED STATES, 1790 TO 2000

Year	Total Population	Urban Population			
		Number	Per Cent of Total	Number	Per Cent of Total
1790	3,929,214	201,655	5.1		
1800	5,308,483	322,371	6.1		
1810	7,239,881	525,459	7.3		
1820	9,638,453	693,255	7.2		
1830	12,866,020	1,127,247	8.8		
1840	17,069,453	1,845,055	10.8		
1850	23,191,876	3,543,716	15.3		
1860	31,443,321	6,216,518	19.8		
1870	38,558,371	9,902,361	25.7		
1880	50,155,783	14,129,735	28.2		
1890	62,947,714	22,106,265	35.1		
1900	75,994,575	30,159,921	39.7		
1910	91,972,266	41,998,932	45.7		
1920	105,710,620	54,157,973	51.2		
1930	122,775,046	68,954,823	56.2		
1940	131,669,275	74,423,702	56.5		
1950	149,855,592	88,369,716	60.0		
Projection		*Medium*		*High*	
1960	153,375,000	98,620,000	64.3	104,448,000	68.1
1970	159,847,000	107,897,000	67.5	119,246,000	74.6
1980	163,877,000	116,189,000	70.9	133,724,000	81.6
1990	164,585,000	122,616,000	74.5	147,139,000	89.4
2000	163,312,000	127,710,000	78.2	159,719,000	97.8

From: Philip M. Houser and Hope T. Eldridge, "Projection of Urban Growth and Migration to Cities in the United States"; in *Postwar Problems of Migration.* New York: Milbank Memorial Fund, 1947, pp. 160-163, 165, 170-173.

The two alternate projections are related to assumptions of either medium or high economic prosperity.

Technological advances in our agriculture are not of a sufficiently revolutionary nature anymore to release a substantial surplus population for internal city-ward migration.

It is safe to base estimates of future urban growth in the United

States on the assumption that the declining trends of the past will continue through the coming decades. Allowance must be made for alternate economic conditions. The trend toward further urbanization should be assisted by economic prosperity, or slowed down by adverse economic conditions.

Two alternate series of estimates for the continuation of the process of urbanization up to the year 2000[19] have been offered. The assumption of medium economic prosperity is probably closest to realistic expectations. It would leave the United States, in the year 2000, with an urban population encompassing almost 80 per cent of the entire population, a condition which resembles that currently existing in the British Isles.

DECENTRALIZATION OR CONCENTRATION?

Metropolitanization. In recent years, urbanization has taken a turn toward "metropolitanization." Since the beginning of World War II, the growth of cities in the million class has proceeded at a higher rate than that of cities with less than a million population.

It has been claimed that the modern metropolis has reached ungainly size, that city size needs to be held down to a "human scale." Lost in the anonymous crowd of the metropolitan area, the individual city dweller is said to lose out in the experience of a full social life. He fails to establish friendly relations with his neighbors. His specialized work routines give him little opportunity to understand all angles of the production process of which he is a part. From suburb to place of work, he has to commute over ever increasing distances. He becomes hardened to the misery of millions of slum dwellers whose fate he is unable to avert. The city — at this size — is looked upon as too powerful to be controlled by humans.

Nobody has ever shown at what community size exactly these nefarious influences of city growth start making themselves felt. Yet, any tendency toward the relative growth of other than our largest urban settlements has been hailed as a movement toward the "human scale" of city living. The splitting-up of urban agglomera-

[19] See Kingsley Davis, Harry C. Bredemeier, and Marion J. Levy, Jr., *Modern American Society*, Vol. I. New York: Rinehart & Company, Inc., 1948, p. 50.
See also Philip M. Hauser and Hope T. Eldridge, *Projection of Urban Growth and Migration to Cities in the United States. The Milbank Memorial Fund Quarterly*, Vol. XXV, No. 3 (July, 1947), pp. 293-307.

tions into a larger number of smaller units and the dispersion of metropolitan populations to smaller cities of the rural hinterland are somewhat uncritically looked upon as improvements of existing social conditions.

Ironically enough, the more rapid growth of relatively small-sized

TABLE VII

METROPOLITAN GROWTH, 1940 - 1950

Area	Population Increase	
	absolute	per cent
United States	18,186,317	14.3
Standard metropolitan areas*	14,653,382	21.2
Central cities	5,652,053	13.0
Outlying parts	9,001,329	34.7
Outside standard metropolitan areas	3,532,935	5.7

1950 Census of Population. Series PC-3, No. 3. Preliminary Report.
* About the definition of 'standard metropolitan area,' see note p. 60.

urban communities in past decades is now being reinterpreted as a statistical expression of highly concentrated metropolitan growth. The growing smaller communities have been found, at closer inspection, to be largely located in the outlying districts of our large metropolitan population centers.[20]

Decentralization, Dispersion, and Peripheral Growth. Let us distinguish between *decentralization* and *dispersion.* Both terms are

[20] "Population growth in the United States during the last ten years was very largely growth within the standard metropolitan areas. More than four-fifths of the national population increase (1940 to 1950) took place within the 168 standard metropolitan areas. . . . On the whole, the communities on the outskirts of the large cities of the United States grew much more rapidly than did the central cities themselves or the remainder of the country. . . . It appears that nearly half of the population increase of the entire country took place in the outlying parts of the 168 standard metropolitan areas. Since standard metropolitan areas are very largely urban, the population changes of the last decade point to an increasing urbanization of the country, with the more spectacular development occurring in the smaller urban and suburban communities adjoining our metropolitan centers." 1950 Census of Population. Preliminary Counts. Washington 25, D.C.: Nov. 5th 1950, Series PC-3, No. 3, p. 1.

often used indiscriminately to represent the opposite of concentration. Population concentrations can be loosened either by having population drift off to other communities of smaller size or by having the urban fabric thinned through lowered density of settlement. The latter occurs when new land is claimed for construction at the periphery of the built-up city, and the city grows in land as well as in population.

We conform fairly well with common usage, if we apply the term decentralization both to the spread of metropolitan populations to communities of smaller size and to the settlement of these populations at the fringe of the metropolitan territory itself. To distinguish between these two alternate conditions, we assign the term *dispersion* to the former and the term *peripheral growth* to the latter. Dispersion thus means the loss of metropolitan populations to distant communities of smaller size. Peripheral growth, on the other hand, does not interfere with the expansion of the metropolitan community as such. On the contrary, it refers to the extension of the metropolitan territory — although the outlying territory may not as yet have been annexed.[21]

The question arises whether modern decentralization is taking the form of dispersion or of peripheral growth. If only the latter is the case, the trend toward metropolitanization has not necessarily reversed itself. Peripheral growth does not indicate that our modern cities have overshot their optimum size, or that urban concentration is automatically dissolving itself.

---

[21] "A standard metropolitan area contained at least one city of 50,000 or more in 1950, and each city of this size is included in one standard metropolitan area. In general, each standard metropolitan area comprises the county containing the city and any other contiguous counties which are deemed to be closely economically integrated with that city. In a broad sense the country's standard metropolitan areas include all the leading urban centers together with all adjoining territory that has been demonstrated to be closely linked with the central cities." *Ibid.*, p. 1.

With the conception of the standard metropolitan area, the Census of 1950 has made an exceedingly valuable contribution to social science research; it has made it possible to clarify the facts regarding urban decentralization. Peripheral growth rather than dispersion has been found to be the most striking phenomenon of the 1940's.

This procedure abandons the collection of data in relation primarily to a *legal* definition of the city (incorporated places) in favor of a more functional definition (criterion of economic integration). The influence of the lag of annexation procedures upon city statistics is thus practically eliminated.

Because present tendencies toward decentralization express themselves primarily in terms of peripheral growth, nothing very unusual is involved. Cities always grew at the only place where they could grow, namely at the periphery. There is a tendency toward standards of lower density of settlement in our large cities. They are growing more in land than in population.

REGIONAL DIFFERENCES IN URBAN GROWTH

The Northeast. The most highly urbanized section of the United States is located north of the Ohio River and east of the Mississippi River. In 1950, the following states had more than 80 per cent of their populations residing in cities: Rhode Island, Massachusetts, New York, and New Jersey.

A hundred years ago, the predominance of urban concentration in the northeastern section of the United States was even more pronounced than today. At that time, urbanization was practically absent from the rest of the country. After the Civil War, however, railroad transportation pushed westward across the continent. Urban centers such as Minneapolis, Milwaukee, Kansas City, and Denver grew in its wake.

The Southeast. At the Gulf of Mexico, New Orleans remained in isolated splendor. It never did spearhead (as did the cities of the Atlantic coast) a development of city foundation and city growth inland along the waterways accessible by cheap and easy transportation. The settlement of the lower Mississippi Valley after the Civil War remained predominently a rural movement. At the northern end of the region, St. Louis established contact with the more highly urbanized and industrialized part of the northeastern United States.

The Far West. At the Pacific coast, we observe a relatively independent development of urban growth in and around the three centers of far-western urbanization: Los Angeles, San Francisco, and Seattle. To reach sizable proportions, these cities were dependent upon railroad communication with the East as established after the Civil War.

The gold rush of 1849 gave San Francisco an early start at a time when the West Coast could be reached only by ocean travel or a cross-country trek. Today, the Los Angeles metropolitan area surpasses those of San Francisco and Seattle in size of population.

Large subsidiary urban centers have developed at Portland and San Diego.[22]

Regional Trends. During the years of World War II and immediately thereafter, the rate of urban growth recuperated from a state of relative stagnation in the depression years. Urbanization in this period was characterized by three distinct features: (1) a cumulative emphasis upon cities that were already relatively large in size, (2) an emphasis upon the growth of cities in the southwestern part of the country, and (3) an emphasis upon the growth of cities located close to our ocean shorelines or connected with them by inland waterways deep enough to accommodate ocean-going vessels.

The cumulative emphasis upon the growth of cities already large in size is often ignored. Some old urban centers, indeed, did lose in population during the early war years. Such displacements were dictated by the demands of a war emergency that required a rapid flow of manpower to develop new war industries in the Southwest.

In 1950 the temporary deficit had been more than made up for; not, however, without leaving the cities of Texas and other southwestern states with a lasting advantage. In the urban panorama of the United States the cities of the Southwest will loom more important in the future than might have been guessed from their relative size before World War II. The industrial use of oil as a source of energy has given emphasis to southwestern industrial location in this country.

The competitive pull of relatively cheap transportation at the deep sea waterways of this country, on the other hand, reinforces the strong economic position of the oldest and most urbanized section of this country, its northeast corner. The wave of urbanization has swept over this country from coast to coast in search of economic advantages in terms of transportation and available raw materials. The natural resources and inland transportation facilities have been exploited to a point of inner equilibrium. Now urban growth withdraws again to the fringes of this continent to develop world-wide trade and industrial relations.

At this stage, our coastal cities have an internally well-urbanized continent behind them. They do not have to support themselves

---

[22] For a visual impression of the regional distribution of urban growth in the United States, see *Our Cities, op. cit.* Maps based on official census enumerations are presented opposite pp. 2, 8, 30, and 66.

primarily on foreign trade. The cities of the United States stand as the climax of the industrialization process in Western civilization, powerful centers of our industrialized and urbanized world.

SELECTED READINGS

1. Cooley, Charles H., "The Theory of Transporation," *Publications of the American Economic Association*, Vol. IX, No. 3 (May, 1894), pp. 13-148. This work is reprinted in Charles H. Cooley, *Sociological Theory and Social Research*. New York: Henry Holt and Company, 1930, pp. 17-120.

2. Hoover, Edgar M., *The Location of Economic Activity*. New York: McGraw-Hill Book Company, Inc., 1948, pp. 15-145.

3. *Our Cities. Report of the Urbanism Committee to the National Resources Committee*. Washington, D.C.: United States Government Printing Office, June, 1937, pp. 1-87.

4. Pirenne, Henri, *Medieval Cities*. Princeton: Princeton University Press, 1925, pp. 1-243.

5. Weber, Adna F., *The Growth of Cities in the 19th Century*. New York: The Macmillan Company, 1899, pp. 1-142, 230-284, 446-475.

PROBLEMS

1. *Land Use Profile*. Drive toward and into a city of 50,000 population or more. On your way from the outmost periphery to the central business district record —mile by mile or block by block — the prevailing land uses. Repeat this performance on another highway approaching the same city. Compare the sequence of land uses so obtained. Explain the difference in terms of the total geographical layout of the city, about which you will have to inform yourself with the help of a land use map available for that community.

In your recordings of land uses, don't limit yourself to the very general categories applied in standard land use maps, such as "commercial," "residential," and so forth. Give a detailed account of the type of establishments and the type of housing observed.

2. *Analysis of Urban Location and Growth*. For the largest city of your state or one of your neighboring states, give reasons for location as well as growth. For such an analysis you will need the help of Edgar M. Hoover's book as quoted in the selected readings for this chapter. This book will provide you with a systematic framework of possible factors in location and growth, to be considered one by one.

Historical incidents as well as economic trends, success in the competition with other cities, raw material location as well as potential labor markets, and similar conditions will have to be ascertained to explain why the community under observation has reached its present size, and why it hasn't grown more.

3. *Concentration or Decentralization?* With the help of the appropriate census reports, ascertain for your own state or one of your neighboring states the growth of different community size groups since the turn of the century. Sketch a simple diagram showing the development of population distribution on different community size groups.

CHAPTER 3

Population Resources for City Growth

THE IMPORTANT DEMOGRAPHIC RELATIONS

Migration. The modern city is a consumer of manpower. Our cities are not demographically self-supporting; no cities ever have been. In the city the death rate tends to surpass the birth rate. In order not to dwindle away and disappear, cities have to be fed demographically by a constant stream of city-ward migration. Thus there can be neither city growth nor urban survival without support from a recruitment area.

The dependence of the city upon its hinterland [1] is demographic as well as economic in nature. City-ward migration, however, is frequently gathered from a much wider territory than that from which food products are shipped to the city. City-ward migration has reached a world-wide scope. Occupational opportunities in the city attract both the farmer from the immediate hinterland of the urban community and the peasant dissatisfied with his lot in a foreign country. They lure the American small-town boy as well as the savage in the jungle. A world-wide recruitment area for city-ward

---

[1] "Hinterland. . . . The region lying behind the coast district; hence, a region remote from cities and towns" *Webster's New Collegiate Dictionary.* Springfield, Mass: G. & C. Merriam Co., 1949. In most modern discussions, this term is applied more generally to the area surrounding the city, standing economically in close relationship to the city, without being characterized by an urban type of settlement in itself.

65

migration is exposed to the competitive pull exerted by a large number of widely-scattered urban centers.

Natural Increase. Before the industrialization period and during its earliest phases, the natural population increase of the city was insufficient for survival, due to excessive mortality rates. Births did not make up for natural population losses. Diseases flourished in the urban environment and reached, at times, epidemic proportions. Tuberculosis and other contagious diseases took a high toll among congested urban populations not yet protected by preventive sanitation and medical care.

With the improvement of urban standards of living, mortality in the city was reduced considerably. Today, urban mortality compares favorably with that in the non-urban environment, due to a greater abundance and a higher quality of medical facilities. The reduction of deaths in the city, however, coincided historically with a numerically even more impressive decline in births.

Thus the natural population budget of the city has only seldom shown an absolute gain. In our times, the American city is further from reproducing itself demographically than it has ever been since the first collection of pertinent statistical records in 1790.

The Population Budget. City populations grow or shrink under the impact of the following demographic factors: [2]

1. Births
2. Deaths
3. Immigrations
4. Emigrations
5. In-migrations
6. Out-migrations.[3]

The balance of the population budget is established by subtracting the negative from the positive factors (by subtracting the sum of items 2, 4, and 6 from the sum of items, 1, 3, and 5). We distinguish

---

[2] For a thorough discussion of related demographic problems, see T. Lynn Smith, *Population Analysis*. New York: McGraw-Hill Book Company, Inc., 1948. Data on urbanization will be found in Chapter 2, "Residence," pp. 27-44.

[3] A concise analysis of the co-ordination of these factors in the process of urbanization has been offered in Dorothy Swaine Thomas, *Social and Economic Aspects of Swedish Population Movements, 1750-1933.* New York: The Macmillan Company, 1941, pp. 19-31.

between immigrations and in-migrations as well as between emigrations and out-migrations. The former concepts (immigration and emigration) refer to migrations across national borderlines, the latter concepts (in-migration and out-migration) refer to migrations originating and terminating within the same country.

In subtracting deaths from births, we arrive at the *natural population increase*. If the natural population increase is negative, urban growth and survival are dependent upon a migration surplus that makes up for the deficit. Under the circumstances, here are the conditions for urban growth:

$$\text{(immigration} - \text{emigration)} + \text{(in-migration} - \text{out-migration)} > \text{(births} - \text{deaths)}.$$

We can formulate the conditions for urban growth more generally in the following manner:

$$\text{(births} + \text{immigration} + \text{in-migration)} - \text{(deaths} + \text{emigration} + \text{out-migration)} > 0, \text{ or}$$
$$\text{(births} + \text{immigration} + \text{in-migration)} > \text{(deaths} + \text{emigration} + \text{out-migration)}.$$

Comparable to the concept of natural population increase is that of *net migration* [(immigration + in-migration) − (emigration + out-migration)]. Net migration gives us the result of all migratory movements either to or from the city, originating either in foreign countries or within the United States.

Of secondary importance for our interests is the concept of *mobility*, applied to the sum total of all migratory movements (immigration + emigration + in-migration + out-migration). Mobility refers to the bulk of all movements, regardless of whether they displace population toward or away from the city. In principle, high mobility may well coincide with either low net migration or no net migration at all.

Important Demographic Rates. We must have these simple relationships clearly in mind before we consider demographic rates. Rates are computed to eliminate from consideration certain secondary factors contributing to urban growth and survival. We have a special interest in demographic rates, which — like reproduction rates — eliminate from consideration secondary factors of growth which influence the situation for a short time only.

Most important is the computation of demographic rates in relation to population size. In handling absolute figures of births and deaths and migrations, our judgment is easily thrown off by sheer size of the basic population that produces these phenomena. A certain number of births or deaths may mean very much or very little according to the size of the total population in which these phenomena occur. In order to be able to compare population growth in communities of different size, we compute demographic rates per 100, per 1,000, and per 10,000 of total population. The choice of reference is entirely arbitrary. Conventionally, demographic rates are recorded per 1,000 of total population.

More refined rates are computed to let reproductive capacity as such stand out more clearly without the interference of factors other than the willingness to reproduce.

Fertility rates are computed to eliminate the influence of sex and age composition upon the birth rate. A community with relatively few women of marriageable age is likely to have relatively few children. This is certainly an interesting fact in itself; we get such information from ordinary birth rates. There is further interest, however, in the willingness and the ability of the relatively few women present in that community to reproduce. We want to know whether these women are doing better or worse than women in communities with different sex and age compositions.

For this purpose, fertility rates are computed which give us the number of births, not per 1,000 of general population, but per 1,000 women in the reproductive age ranges. In official census analyses the reproductive age ranges usually are made to encompass the ages from 15 to 45. This is somewhat crude and arbitrary. Still, it gives us a close approximation to the information we need.

The general age composition also may affect the number of births produced in a certain community. Women in their forties are not likely to have as many children as those in the twenties. Birth rates differ for each separate age, that is, each section of the population being, at any given time, of a certain specified age. To eliminate from the analysis of reproductive capacity the influences of the distribution of the population among individual age cohorts, reproduction rates have been computed by somewhat intricate procedures.

The *gross-reproduction rate* answers the question whether 1,000

females in a given community will, in the course of their reproductive years, have given life to another 1,000 female children. The
gross-reproduction rate is computed on the basis of information
about present birth rates in each age group. These rates are added
up for the entire span of life, at the end of which each 1,000 females
may or may not have reproduced themselves and may have contributed either to a population increase or a population loss.

The *net-reproduction rate* adds a further refinement by taking
into consideration mortality rates prevailing in the community.
Some of the young mothers today will die in the course of their
reproductive years, and some of the children they bear will also
have died by the time these mothers disappear from the reproductive
age ranges. The net-reproduction rate answers the question whether
the women at present entering their reproductive years will, at the
end of their reproductive period, actually have reproduced themselves; that is, whether in spite of losses in their ranks and in spite
of the deaths of some of their children they will have left to posterity
1,000 young females. With regard both to gross and to net reproduction rates, full replacement is indicated by an index of either 1 or
100. Excesses or losses are indicated by the addition or subtrac-
tion of proportionate fractions. The net-reproduction rate offers
a fairly refined index of the capability of a population to reproduce
itself. In this index, the influences of age and sex distribution and
the influences of differential birth and mortality rates are eliminated
by meticulous statistical procedures.

NATURAL POPULATION INCREASE IN THE MODERN CITY

Births and Deaths in the Modern City. By and large, modern city
growth has occurred in spite of natural population losses or very
small natural population gains due to a one-sided age distribution.

At the present time, the number of deaths in all cities of the United
States is somewhat below the number of urban births. The natural
population increase is due to an urban age distribution that favors
the reproductive age ranges. With relatively few children and old
people living in the cities of the United States, natural increase of
population results. Assuming a normal age distribution, there would
be no natural population increase in the modern American city.
Without positive net migration, our cities in all size groups would be
shrinking in population at the present time.

TABLE VIII

U.S. BIRTH RATES BY COMMUNITY SIZE GROUPS IN 1940

Number born per thousand of population.

Cities of 100,000 or more	42.8
Cities of 25,000 to 100,000	47.5
Cities of 10,000 to 25,000	49.5
Cities of 2,500 to 10,000	56.9
Rural	59.8
Total United States	52.0

U.S. DEATH RATES BY COMMUNITY SIZE GROUPS IN 1940

Number of deaths per thousand of population.

Cities of 100,000 or more	11.3
Cities of 10,000 to 100,000	11.4
Cities of 2,500 to 10,000	12.4
Rural	9.8
Total United States	10.8

From: Vital Statistics Rates in the United States. 1900-1940. U.S. Department of Commerce. Washington, D. C., 1943, pp. 198 and 685.

Social Backgrounds of Urban Mortality. Urban death rates have been on the decline since the beginning of reliable records. This is due to the advance of medical science and the improvement of urban medical facilities.

No reliable records are available for the very early days of the industrialization period. Certain diseases, to be sure, have been increased by urban living conditions; congestion promotes the spread of contagious diseases. We are not able to retrace changes in the death rate experienced at early times of city formation and urban growth on either the European or American scene. It is not unlikely that right up to and into the industrialization period changes in the death rate were a more important factor to consider in the fluctuation of urban population losses than comparable changes in the birth rate.

Throughout the 19th century, however, the urban death rate has been on the decline due to improved standards of living. Improved standards of living influence the death rate both indirectly, through improved nutrition and concomitant resistance to disease, and directly, by making available to ever-widening sections of the urban population better hospital facilities and better and more abundant medical care.

Urban mortality rates have recently shown a tendency to level off. They have been reduced remarkably due to the combat of contagious diseases, infant mortality, and childbed fever. Urban longevity, under the circumstances, has reached unprecedented heights. An increasingly larger number of deaths, in recent decades, have been caused by degenerative diseases, such as heart diseases, the failing of other organic functions, and cancer (which is not a degenerative disease but is mentioned here because it takes its toll predominantly in the older age ranges).

Urban death rates have been reduced to a level at which no further startling improvements can be expected. Therefore, our interest in the natural population increase of the city population shifts to the other factor upon which it is dependent, the birth rate.

TABLE IX

LIFE EXPECTANCY

	Males		Females	
	Urban	Rural	Urban	Rural
1901	43.97	54.03	47.90	55.41
1910	47.32	55.06	51.39	57.35
1930	56.73	62.09	61.05	65.09

From: T. Lynn Smith: Population Analysis. McGraw-Hill Book Company, Inc. New York, 1948, p. 274.

Social Backgrounds of Urban Nativity. In recent Western civilization, the decline of the birth rate has been pre-eminently an urban phenomenon. During the 19th century, birth-rates declined earlier and more precipitously for urban than for non-urban populations. In 1950, fertility rates were lowest for the largest urban communities in the United States. Fertility rates decreased with city size. This low urban fertility rate is so marked that many arguments have been presented to explain it. Low urban fertility is also one of the main objections raised against city growth. Low urban birth rates have been blamed on the invention, manufacture, and spread of means of contraception. Of the urban origin of technical means of contraception in recent history, there can be no doubt. In the early parts of the 19th century, contraceptives were used by the urban upper classes of France. From there, the knowledge and the use of contraceptives spread to other urban centers in the Western world.

TABLE X

URBAN AND RURAL GROSS AND NET
REPRODUCTION RATES

Area	1905-10		1930-35		1935-40		1942-47	
	Net	Gross	Net	Gross	Net	Gross	Net	Gross
Total U.S.A.	1,336	1,793	984	1,108	978	1,101	1,292	1,402
Urban	937	1,298	747	839	726	815	1,085	1,177
Rural-nonfarm	1,499	1,956	1,150	1,296	1,150	1,294	1,465	1,586
Rural-farm	2,022	2,663	1,632	1,844	1,661	1,878	1,859	2,029

From: Statistical Abstract of the United States, 1948. U.S. Department of Commerce, p. 55.

Still, urban birth control cannot be attributed entirely to an invention which, although it made birth control more convenient, was not the only possible means of achieving it. The invention and manufacture of contraceptives has probably accentuated and accelerated a trend dictated by consumer demands. We are inclined to assume that the invention and spread of contraceptives was encouraged by urban social needs.

In the city children have changed from an asset to a liability. Children are not looked upon as potential farm hands but as a burden to the family budget. This becomes increasingly true with the increasing demands for prolonged education.

In the 19th century children started earlier in gainful employment. They were raised by their parents to late adolescence. Then they gained occupational experience on the job. According to merit, they advanced flexibly to a more or less elevated position in life. The parental family was earlier released from the burden of providing room and board and from educational expenses.

Today, diplomas are far more important in determining the income bracket within which the child will make a living and from which the child will gradually advance by seniority to higher salary scales. The urban family concerned with the improvement of its social status, thus prefers to have a smaller number of children. Funds available to advance children to a higher social position will go much further if they are not split into too many parts.

TABLE XI

UNITED STATES INFANT MORTALITY AND COMMUNITY SIZE, 1948

Deaths per thousand live births.

Area	Under 1 year	Under 1 month	1-11 months
Urban	31.2	23.0	8.3
Rural	33.1	21.0	12.1
Places of 100,000 or more	28.9	21.9	7.0
Places of 25,000 to 100,000	31.4	22.9	8.5
Places of 10,000 to 25,000	32.6	23.7	8.9
Places of 2,500 to 10,000	36.0	25.4	10.6

Source: Vital Statistics. Special Reports. National Summaries. Volume 35, No. 17. October 16, 1950, p. 305.

These changes in our economic and social institutions are probably of influence upon the birth rates in the urban environment.[4] In addition, we have to remind ourselves that the prestige attached to large families has diminished.

Middle class resentment is directed against the idle pursuit of personal pleasures. It was directed against the so-called two-child system as practiced by the upper classes in France. With the spread of birth control, the urban upper and middle classes all over the Western world have become the target of similar criticism.[5] But these barriers to birth control are fast disappearing. Concern with the family unit is being replaced by concern with the individual

[4] For related discussions, see Chap. 10.

[5] For middle class resentment against the luxurious way of life, see Svend Ranulf, *Moral Indignation and Middle Class Psychology.* Copenhagen: Levin & Munksgaard, 1938, especially the section, "Upper Middle Class," pp. 27-35.

family members and their well-being. Companionship is more nearly the purpose of modern urban family living than procreation.[6]

MIGRATION TO THE MODERN CITY

The Background of General Mobility. The modern city gains population through migration. With the exception of periods of outright urban stagnation, this has probably always been the case. Due to high mortality rates and low birth rates, and to the presence of relatively large numbers of unmarried people, urban populations were seldom in a position to reproduce themselves. They have been dependent upon population gains by migration.

Migratory population gains occur as the end result of population mobility. In the modern city, urban net migration appears as a relatively slim margin resulting only from the circumstance that migrations from the city are surpassed, numerically, by migrations toward the city.[7]

Many people leave the city for a less urbanized environment. There are people who return to the country, and there are people who retire to the country. The city is left by people who have learned to shun the urban way of life, and it is left by large numbers of those who give up trying to make a living or to get ahead in the city. It is left by families whose children need the country air and by women who marry into a rural environment. It is left by old people who find that their pensions at retirement last longer and buy more if used outside the range of urban competition.

Still, there are more people attracted toward than away from the city. Occupational opportunities are the main incentive; urban migratory gains result from the availability of gainful employment, from the lure of higher wage levels, from opportunities not only for a job but for progressive careers that point to gradually increasing wage levels and positions of advanced social status.

---

[6] "Historically the family has discharged several characteristic functions which have been of service to its members and to the community. These include the bearing and rearing of children."

"The loss of historic functions by the family permitted it to perform efficiently its essential function, that of developing the personalties of its members through intimate association, affectional interdependance and emotional security."

Ernest W. Burgess and Harvey J. Locke, *The Family, From Institution to Companionship.* New York: American Book Company, 1945, pp. 501, 718.

[7] See Dorothy Swaine Thomas, *op. cit.,* Tables 76-79, on pp. 299-303.

The Influence of Industrial Fluctuations. Urban net migration and general mobility fluctuate with the business cycle. They reach a climax immediately preceding the economic crisis. They fall off to a relative minimum at times of economic depression.[8]

In these fluctuations, the development of urban migration gains and general mobility (as the sum total of migratory movements away from and toward the city) travel hand in hand. Migration in all directions is stimulated in periods of economic prosperity. But movement toward the city is even more encouraged than movement away from the city.

City-ward migration, in short, is primarily a function of economic opportunities offered in the urban environment. For this reason, we do well not to pay too much attention to discussions of the "lure of the city" which emphasize the bright-lights, the interest in urban recreational facilities, and the zest for independence from social restrictions imposed by a small town or farm environment.[9] People who move to the city do so in order to find work. Mainly the occasional visitor is attracted to the city as a fascinating playground.

Migration in Stages. City-ward migration occurs typically in stages. Urban migration gains are not entirely the outcome of direct movements from areas that lose population because of insufficient employment opportunities to the city as an area in need of labor. Migration gains appear as relatively narrow margins resulting from ample migrations back and forth between the different types of community under consideration. Migration gains are accompanied by high mobility.   They are the outcome of relatively large migratory exchanges between the larger urban communities, and urban communities of smaller size, and rural areas. Migrations from the farm are likely to terminate in the small town. But the small towns, in turn, are apt to lose population by migration to urban communities of larger size. Our large industrial centers are probably the population reservoirs, which (replenished from small towns) contribute most to migrations to the metropolis.

---

[8] *Ibid.*, Chapters 8 and 9, entitled "Internal Migration and Business Cycles" and "Emigration and Business Cycles," pp. 304-322; see also Dorothy Swaine Thomas, *Social Aspects of the Business Cycle.* London: George Routledge and Sons, Ltd., 1925.

[9] For a historical study on motivation in favor of city-ward migration, see Arthur Meier Schlesinger, *The Rise of the City. 1878-1898.* New York: The Macmillan Company, particularly Chapter III, "The Lure of the City," pp. 53-77.

Individual migrations are apt to cover relatively short geographical distances. Arrivals in the large city are more often small-town people than farmers. Adjustment to life in the metropolis does not necessarily have to cover the entire span between a rural way of life and metropolitan emancipation. Direct migrations from the farm to the metropolis form an exception rather than the rule. As the outcome of all population exchanges, however, our metropoles record the largest population gains, while population losses through migration are largest in non-urban communities. Cities of intermediate size are more apt to hold their own, receiving population from the smaller, and yielding population to the larger communities.[10]

In the earlier phases of the industrialization process, immigration to this country occurred in a large part as the migration of rural populations in the Old World, joining the mass of unskilled urban labor in this country. Unfortunately, we are unable to reconstruct the manner in which, at the period of most impressive urban migration gains, the rural-urban displacement of population resulted from individual migratory movements.[11]

Internal and International Migrations. City growth in the United States has been affected by both international and internal migrations. Both, as they occurred in the 19th century, may be looked upon as somewhat different aspects of the same social process.

Rural populations were set free by processes of rationalization such as the redistribution of land on the European continent, improved methods of farming, and the shift to one-crop farming both in

---

[10] "People tend to migrate between communities resembling one another in degree of industrial development." Jane Moore, *Cityward Migration.* Swedish Data. Chicago: The University of Chicago Press, 1938, p. 124.

[11] Due to the lack of a registration system in the United States that requires the official recording of every individual change of residence within the country and every individual move across the borderlines of the country, all of our information about internal migration in the United States is based upon place-of-birth statistics. See *The Problems of a Changing Population.* National Resources Committee. Washington, D.C.: U.S. Government Printing Office, May, 1938. See particularly III, "Trends in Population Redistribution," pp. 83-118. For the "Continuous Register System of Population Accounting," see pp. 276-297.

"The complete absence of information about internal migration tends to make the numerators and denominators of vital statistics rates approximations to the actual measurements desired." See Philip M. Hauser, "Present Status and Prospects of Research in Population," *American Sociological Review.* Vol. 13, No. 4 (August, 1948), p. 375.

Europe and the United States. These populations were absorbed wherever economic opportunities offered themselves. They went city-ward, either in their own country or across the borderlines of national states, to fill the need for unskilled industrial labor in the growing urban communities of Western civilization.[12] The exploitation of natural resources[13] and a process of urbanization in the United

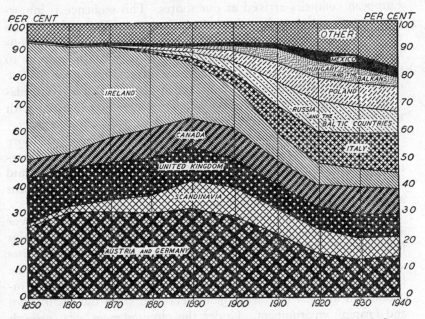

FIGURE 3. Nationality Background of Immigration to the United States, 1850-1940. From: T. Lynn Smith, *Population Analysis*. New York: McGraw-Hill Book Company, Inc., 1948, p. 319.

States gave emigration to this country a particularly prominent part in the city-ward population displacements within the Western world.

Immigration. Immigration gains from the European continent proceeded throughout the 19th century with shifting national em-

---

[12] For Sweden, the coincidence of emigration losses with urban migration gains is shown in Dorothy Swaine Thomas, *op. cit.*, table on p. 27.

[13] That the immigration terminal in the United States has shifted from country districts to cities, has been shown for the period from 1890 to 1930 by Walter F. Willcox, *Studies in American Demography*. Ithaca: Cornell University Press, 1940, p. 159.

phasis. English, Scotch-Irish, Dutch, and Irish immigration gains
were gradually replaced in numerical importance by German and
Scandinavian immigrations, to be followed later by immigrations
from Italy, the Balkans, Greece, and Near Eastern countries. European
political events, famines, and the impoverishment of entire social
groups influenced the sequence in which emigrants from different
European countries arrived at our shores. This sequence is important for present considerations of ethnic status. The early arrivals
found better opportunities to participate in the appropriation of potential wealth. Also, the families of early arrivals had more time to
make a place for themselves within the status and income hierarchy
of our urban communities. The nationality groups that arrived relatively early in this country have become generally associated with
higher economic and social status than those that came later.

The nationality groups of relatively early arrival have had more
opportunities, also, to move away from the central slum neighborhood of the city. They have moved to a less central position, and
individual members of the group have shifted to a greater extent
away from areas of ethnic segregation.[14]

Internal Migration. Internal migration gains in our cities never
attained numerical proportions similar to those of migration gains
from abroad. Since 1924, of course, immigration to this country has
come practically to a standstill. Since that time, urban growth in the
United States has been dependent upon the two factors of natural increase and internal migration gains recruited from the small town
and farming environment. Under the circumstances, city growth
in this country has been slowing up.[15]

Migration gains resulting from the population exchanges between
the country and the city have always been less sizeable than population gains from immigration. Moreover, urban population gains
from internal migration are shrinking and will probably continue
to do so. The reason is twofold. First, the rationalization of agri-

---

[14] For a study of segregation as a function of social rank, see Eshref Shevsky
and Marilyn Williams, *The Social Areas of Los Angeles*. Berkeley and Los
Angeles: University of California Press, 1949, pp. 37-40, 47-57.

The study shows that the ethnic groups with lowest social status find themselves most isolated in the urban environment. The different European immigrant groups appear in the following order from low to high status: Italians,
Russians, Scandinavians, Germans.

[15] See Chap. 2.

culture and the tightening of the urban labor market leave increasingly less of an economic discrepancy between these two environments. Increased mobility and improved means of communication minimize the margin between the rural and urban wage levels.[16]

A second reason for the slowing up of city-ward population displacements is the reduction of rural population reserves. They are reduced, in absolute figures, due to the slowing down of the rural birth rate in the wake of comparable urban conditions. Moreover, rural population reserves available for movement in a city-ward direction are relatively reduced, due to the continuous shift of the proportion of the rural and urban populations in favor of the latter. As our urban population grows in proportion to the non-urban population, further urban growth proceeds on a continuously shrinking population basis.

Major Streams of Internal Migration. Internal city-ward migration has always had a strong regional character. At present two major streams of city-ward migration are very clearly defined with regard to the region from which they originate, the types of population they involve, and the urban regions to which they are attracted. The first example that might be cited is the migration of economically unfavored Negro farm laborers and small tenants from the southern states to the large expanding urban centers of the Northeast and the Middlewest, where they are likely to settle down in positions of unskilled industrial labor or as service personnel. The second is the migration of impoverished white farm laborers and tenants from the so-called "dust bowl" in the South to the Far West of this country, where they settle down in a variety of urban or rural, unskilled or semiskilled positions.

Similar population shifts inside the United States have been known in the past. At the depletion of forest reserves in the northern parts of Michigan, Wisconsin, and Minnesota, a large population of workers in the lumber industries of these territories found themselves out of work and migrated to the Northwest. These were the "second-jumpers" of the present Northwest. A substantial number of these midwestern lumbermen were attracted to the urban communities of the Northwest where they found work in unskilled and,

---

16 For the effect of "Wages and Hours in Agriculture" upon migratory movements, see Dorothy Swaine Thomas, *op. cit.*, pp. 66-68.

later, semi-skilled and skilled employment.[17]

The above-mentioned stream of migration formed part of the prevailing westward migration in this country during the 19th century. This migration is divided according to its termination in either a rural or an urban environment. Wherever urban development promised better employment opportunities on this westward route, a relatively large part of this stream of unskilled labor was diverted city-ward. The cities of the Far West have grown in this manner up to the immediate present. They still show strong population gains from internal migration.

In recent decades the character of migratory populations has undergone considerable change. Urban population gains are no longer necessarily related to rural population losses in other regions. Urban populations are growing also through populations withdrawn from other urban communities. City-ward migration has to some extent been replaced by inter-urban migration.

Inter-urban Migration. Inter-urban mobility is the result of a flexible urban labor market. Skilled laborers and professional people drift in the direction of employment opportunities and higher wage scales. They go wherever their services are economically most highly rewarded.

The urban labor market, particularly at the higher income levels, is a very sensitive market. Information about supply and demand is readily exchanged between different urban centers. We know of the business executive who moves from town to town in the fullfillment of ever-growing responsibilities, possibly in the service of one and the same company.

There has been some change, also, in the type of unskilled labor that moves from one city to another. In addition to skilled labor and trained personnel, another labor category moves between the cities. It is somewhat different from the unskilled industrial labor that formerly arrived from the rural environment and still does, to considerable extent.

Our urban occupational structure has opened a wide range of

---

[17] In Seattle, the number of foreign born Norwegians and Swedes surpassed that of any other nationality group since 1890. The time of most rapid increase was between 1900 and 1910. See Calvin F. Schmid, *Social Trends in Seattle*. Seattle: The University of Washington Press, 1944, p. 98.

positions of gainful employment in the service industries.[18] There is room in the expanding service industries for relatively unskilled labor, attracted to urban centers that are prospering economically.

Thus, urban migration gains are today partly derived from other cities. They indicate interregional population displacements rather than a further trek from a rural to an urban environment. Some cities still gain, but many have come close to losing by internal migration. Long distance migration gains in the modern city especially tend to come, to an ever increasing extent, from other urban centers.[19] Exceptions to this pattern are mass movements from economically-deteriorating rural areas like the southern farming areas and the dust bowl.

The Urban Age and Sex Distribution

Effects of Differential Fertility and Selective Migration. The population development of the city is dependent upon its age distribution. A high birth rate may be due to the fact that many people in the child-bearing age ranges are present in the population. It may be due, also, to the willingness of individual members of the group to have a relatively large number of children. The prospects for reproduction on the part of a given population can be assessed only if its age distribution is taken into consideration. Age distribution determines crudely what fraction of the population is biologically able to reproduce. Age distribution also determines future age distribution. Apart from trends in differential fertility, the birth rates of the future are dependent upon the number of people who, from year to year, will move into the potentially reproductive age ranges. This, in turn, depends upon the manner in which the younger age

---

[18] "The Changing Occupational Structure" of our cities is discussed in Eshref Shevsky and Marilyn Williams, *op. cit.*, pp. 2-7.

For the United States as a whole, the working population in the service industries (including trade, transportation, communication, and personal and professional services) has advanced between 1820 and 1940 from 15.3 per cent to 50 per cent of the entire working population.

[19] "Movement to Los Angeles was predominantly an urban movement (in the 1930's). The largest group of migrants to Los Angeles came from New York and Illinois. San Francisco attracted migrants from Washington and Oregon as well as from Illinois and New York." See Eshref Shevsky and Marilyn Williams, *op. cit.*, p. 27. Read their concise historical statement about migration to the Far West on pages 28 and 29.

groups are represented in the population and, thus, upon selective migrations that may enforce either the reproductive or the non-reproductive age ranges.

For the demographic future of the modern city, its age distribution and the age distribution of its area of recruitment are strategic items. The urban age distribution garners the effects of differential fertility and selective migrations in the past and projects them into the future demographic history of the city.

Overpresentation of Child-bearing Age Ranges. City-ward migration has been selective in the past. It has consisted mainly of migrations of young adults.[20] Radical change of environment is most easily accepted when young men and women sever their ties from their parental families and start on their own careers. The change in environment occurs at a time in the life history when it does not interfere with already established occupational routines, when there is no chance that acquired skills will be wasted, and when advancement is not blocked by lack of previous occupational experiences.

Children, in the past, were best raised in the country. Old people had little reason to leave the farm or small town environment to spend their years after retirement in the large modern city, where they would be strangers, and where the purchasing power of their savings provided a lower standard of living. The retirement of farmers to small towns and hamlets is not an unusual move, but population gains in the age ranges beyond reproductive capacity do not occur in the large city to any sizable extent.

Thus, city-ward migration gains have been highly age selective in the past, favoring people of marriageable age. Due to this fact, most of our urban communities have retained, in spite of rapidly declining fertility rates, a positive natural population budget. Migration gains have benefited the population resources of the modern city in two ways: directly, through a surplus of immigrations and in-migrations over emigrations and out-migrations; and indirectly, through results of differential migration gains which influence the urban age distribution in such a manner as to stimulate natural population increase.

Where migration gains abate due to shrinking economic opportunities selective migrations cease to distort the prevailing age dis-

---

[20] See *The Problems of a Changing Population, op cit.,* "The Cityward Movement of Young Adults," pp. 109 and 110.

tribution. The age distribution becomes more "normal," that is, shaped more or less exclusively by prevailing birth and mortality rates in the city. At this point, the natural population increase of the modern city ceases and is replaced by a natural population decrease.

The cessation of migration gains, again, will affect the population growth of the modern city in two ways simultaneously: directly, by the decrease in the number of new arrivals who become city residents, and indirectly, by changes in the age distribution of the city population which decrease the opportunities for procreation.

Sex-Selective Migration. Urban population growth is also influenced by sex-selective migrations. Where city-ward migration results in relatively high or relatively low urban sex ratios (a large surplus of men or of women), there is relatively less chance for marriage and child-raising. In the history of American cities, relatively unequal sex ratios have been the rule rather than the exception.

In the early statges of city formation and urban growth, high sex ratios (surpluses ot men) were preponderant. Our urban communities were developed under conditions of hardship which attracted the venturesome part of the single male population. This is as true of early pioneer settlements at the Atlantic coast of this continent, as it is of later urban developments in the interior and the Far West. We know of historical instances in which women were imported for the purposes of housekeeping and procreation.[21] The migration of entire families followed the pioneering crowd of single men.

Since the late 19th century, selective migrations toward the American city have produced low urban sex ratios. Particularly since the opening of employment opportunities for female workers in urban manufacture, in domestic service, and in urban white collar positions,[22] urban migration gains were drawn from

---

[21] "In 1619 Sir Ewin Sandys sent out (to Jamestown in the southern Colonies) ninety young women, carefully selected, to be wives of the turbulent colonists." See Willystine Goodsell, *Backgrounds of the American Family*. Quoted in *Marriage and the Family*. Howard Becker and Reuben Hill, editors. Boston: D. C. Heath and Company, 1942, p. 75. Similar importations of women for purposes of marriage occurred later in the colonization of the Far West.

[22] "Between 1900 and 1940, the number of women in the United States increased by 102 per cent, the number of women in the labor force increased by 151.2 per cent, the number of married women in the labor force increased by approximately 500 per cent." See Frieda S. Miller, "Women in the Labor Force," in "Women's Opportunities and Responsibilities," *The Annals* of the American Academy of Political and Social Science, Vol. 251 (May, 1947), p. 39. For the shift toward clerical work during World War I, see Alice Rogers

the female as well as the male part of the population. To the pull of urban opportunities for gainful employment was added the push of rationalized one-crop farming that set female labor free, by eliminating much of the demand for female labor that existed in the days of relatively self-sufficient farming units.

At present, most American cities are characterized by a low sex ratio. This condition is less pronounced in some cities of the Far West where a relatively large population of old single men still presents an after-effect of pioneering days in this part of the country. In other cities of the Far West with a preponderance of old people, the greater size of the aged female population counteracts the above-mentioned condition.

Age and Sex Composition in the Urban Environment. The urban age and sex distribution differs, of course, in different parts of the city. There is the single men's district close to the center of town, clearly segregated from other residential or commercial areas and overpopulated by aged men. There are the downtown apartments and hotels where the stenographers and other female white collar workers establish living quarters for themselves in rooms or separate households, and there are the suburbs with a relatively large number of unmarried females, employed or unemployed.[23]

For the city as a whole, this one-sided distribution of age as well as sex is not without importance. To have a fairly even sex distribution in the city as a whole does not do much good for the procreation of the city population if the men are living in a different part of the city from the women. The unbalanced sex ratio of different urban environments must be considered a factor contributing to the low urban birth rate.

Social contacts between the two sexes are impaired, in the city, by the anonymity of prevailing relationships. The "Lonely Hearts' Club," a typical urban institution attempting to overcome the lack of social contacts between marriageable adults, has the function of reducing — for the purpose of mate selection — both geographical

---

Hager, "Occupations and Earnings of Women in Industry," in "Women in the Modern World," *The Annals* of the American Academy of Political and Social Science, Vol. 143 (May, 1929), p. 68. Between 1910 and 1920, the proportion of women among clerical workers in the United States increased from 34.2 per cent to 45.6 percent.

[23] The uneven spread of the sex ratio in different parts of the large American city is well demonstrated in Calvin F. Schmid, *op. cit.,* p. 87.

and social distance in the city. The domestics from the fashionable suburbs are given an opportunity to meet young factory workers or white collar laborers through either correspondence or social get-togethers. Lonely widowers are brought into contact with equally lonely widows, and shy members of both sexes avail themselves hesitatingly of the services of the professional matchmaker.[24]

SOME SOCIAL CONSEQUENCES OF URBAN DEMOGRAPHIC CONDITIONS

Distrust. Urban social relations are affected by sheer number and size of populations living together in a relatively limited territory. They are continuously replenished by new arrivals who, at least temporarily, consider the city a place to make their fortune in fierce competition with the rest of the population. Their loyalties will often remain with their home towns, while their urban neighbors are considered as competitors and as suspect because of different backgrounds.

Indifference toward neighbors and business acquaintances is not only a matter of numbers that exhaust the individual capacity for commiseration and identification. It is also a matter of estrangement to the city environment which the migrant enters with exploitative purposes in mind. This attitude spreads contagiously to old city residents always ready to defend themselves against intruders they feel do not belong. In the anonymous city environment, the worst experiences with all sorts of social contacts set the tone. An attitude of mutual distrust prevails.

Family Formation as Social Achievement. Migration to the city, we have seen, is concentrated in the years of young adulthood. It occurs in the initial stages of the occupational career and during those phases of the life cycle when young people get ready to settle down to married life. Under the circumstances, family formation in this environment often coincides in time and is therefore associated with social achievement.

Status has always been associated with the ability to support a wife and children. Also, the city environment emphasizes the prestige involved in family formation, particularly for the newcomer from a non-urban environment. To be settled in the big city with

---

24 For "The Role of Intermediaries" in modern marriage, see Ernest W. Burgess and Harvey J. Locke, *op. cit.*, pp. 404-415.

a wife, a house of his own, and a car is no small financial achievement for the man who arrived in the city as a migrant. Family formation becomes the symbol of a firm foothold in the city, and thereby a symbol of success.

For these reasons, conspicuous consumption is [25] more and more frequently expressed in durable household equipment and other instruments of family living. Conspicuous consumption is a privilege freely granted to the housewife,[26] who carries the symbols of status and success within the confines of a family home that has come to mean not merely a residence, but the final foothold in an initially hazardous urban environment.

Separation of Private and Occupational Life. The constant occurrence of arrival and settling-down divides the urban population into two distinguishable sections: the world of the roaming and striving new arrivals, finding a foothold in the industrial and commercial sections of the city with temporary shelter in hotels, apartment dwellings, and cheap rooming houses; and the world of settled residents in outlying districts which are carefully guarded against the intrusion of commercial competition.

The modern American city has gone further than any other in the conscious separation of commercial activities and the environment in which the private family life unfolds. There is a tendency to withdraw from the jungle of cosmopolitan intermingling in the central parts of the city, and to settle down to family living in an environment that promises the shelter of a small town or village, that is characterized by limited social contacts in the everyday routines of family living and excludes the disturbing influences of social change.

In the conduct of business affairs, the family breadwinners have to plunge back daily into the turmoil of the central city. At the cost of long commuting distances, however, and at the cost of cumbersome shopping trips, urban residents try to retain the semblance of a stable village existence at their place of residence, at the place where they house their families and raise their children.

---

[25] See pp. 275 ff.

[26] "In this lower middle class there is no pretence of leisure on the part of the head of the househould . . . but the middle class wife still carries on the business of vicarious leisure, for the good name of the household and its master." Thorstein Veblen, *The Theory of the Leisure Class.* New York: The Modern Library, 1934, p. 81.

Generations Conflict. The continuous flow of new arrivals to the city environment has profound influence upon the relation between the different family members. The superior status of the father in the family group has given way to more democratic arrangements. There are two reasons for this development: (1) the father, separated daily by long commuting distances from the family home, loses contact with everyday family routines; and (2) the father and mother experience — as new arrivals to the city — the city environment in a different manner than do their children.[27]

The older generation finds itself in a position analogous to that of immigrant parents from the Old World who struggle — through the remaining years of their life — with a cumbersome process of assimilation that is greatly facilitated for their children by institutional devices such as city schools. The children learn to take for granted the city which to their parents has been something to conquer.

SELECTED READINGS

1. Gunnar Myrdal, *Population, A Problem for Democracy.* Cambridge: Harvard University Press, 1940, pp. 1-237.

2. *The Problem of a Changing Population.* National Resources Committee. Washington, D.C.: U.S. Government Printing Office, May, 1938, pp. 6-148.

3. Arthur Meier Schlesinger, *The Rise of the City, 1878-1898.* New York: The Macmillan Company, 1933, pp. 1-436.

4. Calvin F. Schmid, *Social Trends in Seattle.* Seattle: The University of Washington Press, 1944, pp. 1-150.

5. Dorothy Swaine Thomas, *Social and Economic Aspects of Swedish Population Movements, 1750-1933.* New York: The Macmillan Company, 1941, pp. 3-360.

PROBLEMS

1. *Comparison of City-ward Migration in Sweden and the United States.* Acquaint yourself with the information available on city-ward migration in Dorothy Swaine Thomas, *Social and Economic*

---

[27] Margaret Mead explains American personality traits in a similar manner through the experience of large scale immigration to this country. See Margaret Mead, *And Keep Your Powder Dry.* New York: William Morrow and Company, 1942.

Aspects of Swedish Population Movements, 1750-1933. New York: The Macmillan Company, 1941; and in *The Problem of a Changing Population.* National Resources Committee. Washington, D.C.: U.S. Government Printing Office, May, 1938.

Compile comparable information from these two sources with regard to city-ward migration in Sweden and the United States. Discuss differences and similarities. Don't forget to compare the timing of peak and recession in these migratory movements, and to discuss the influence of selective migrations upon the urban population composition in either country.

Try to sharpen your argument by the use of simple comparative graphs.

2. *Statistical Description of Natural Areas in Seattle.* Read the following Chapters 3, 4, 5, 6 of this book and pay particular attention to everything said about "natural areas." Then, turn to Calvin F. Schmid's book about Social Trends in Seattle and study the statistical attributes of the different census tracts. Continue until the clustering of these attributes furnishes evidence for some crude or hypothetical delineation of at least three "natural areas" in that city. Discuss homogeneities and interdependence relations which might explain the statistical characteristics of these areas.

3. *The Urbanite and the American as Social Types.* Read Margaret Mead, *And Keep Your Powder Dry.* New York: William Morrow and Company, 1942. and Chapters 10-13 of this text. Acquaint yourself with sources quoted on urban personality in these chapters. Then write an essay comparing the characteristics attributed to the American by Margaret Mead and those attributed to the typical urban resident. To what extent do they coincide, to what extent do they differ? What causes these characteristics? Make a hypothetical statement about causes that might explain either the coincidence or the difference of urban and American characteristics.

CHAPTER 4

Geographical Patterns of City Growth

ORDER OUT OF CHAOS

Random Growth. The modern city is not shaped by either plan or tradition. It has grown at random. The center of the modern city has no symbolic meaning. Neither the temple, nor the factory, nor the office building are moved purposely into prominent position. At its fringes, the modern city is not confined by fortifications. The modern city sprawls haplessly into its own hinterland.

There are those who claim that the modern city has grown "naturally" because it has grown without plan.[1] That the city has grown according to something like a "natural law" is suggested by the fact that it follows a more or less regular pattern. We are not confronted with a jumble of public and private construction, differently arranged in every city. As a matter of fact, the experienced traveler will easily find his way around from the business district to the slums, from the slums to the bright light district, and from the bright light district to the parkland of fashionable urban residences in any city that he comes to.

---

[1] "The city is discovered to be an organization displaying certain typical processes of growth. Knowledge of these processes makes possible prediction of the direction, rate, and nature of its growth. That is, the city is found to be not an artifact, but a natural phenomenon." Harvey W. Zorbaugh, "The Natural Areas of the City," in *The Urban Community*. Ernest W. Burgess, editor. Chicago: The University of Chicago Press, 1926, pp. 220-21.

89

The sociologist is interested in the regularities of city patterns that have grown without premeditated purpose and yet repeat themselves from one urban community to another. As a scientist, he is interested in generalization. It may look to him as though some guidance had been provided to place a more or less similar stamp upon all our modern urban communities.

Competition for Land. The cities of the industrialization process grew without plan, but under fairly similar conditions of economic competition. An attitude of laissez-faire prevailed. In principle, all builders had an equal chance to build on whatever land they were able to claim. They all had to make their claims, however, on the real estate market in terms of purchasing power; and the most desirable land went to the highest bidder.

Desirability of location and effective demands for land use were very much the same wherever modern cities grew. Desirability of location raised the land values in certain parts of the city. Here, only those land uses could survive economically which were backed by purchasing power sufficiently large to win out in competition on the real estate market. Similar clients came to cluster on similar tracts of land. Through competition some order established itself without either plan or tradition.

Change of Preference. Desirability of location did not remain the same throughout the course of urban growth. In the early American city topographical conditions were of greater importance for differential construction than they have been since. Spectacular and more sanitary sites were pre-empted for the residences of the more affluent members of the community. They sought pleasant views on highlands not endangered by recurrent floods. The poor clustered on the less desirable lowlands.

As urban settlement grew, the importance of topographical features diminished as compared to various aspects of the man-made environment itself. Proximity to or distance from the central nucleus of commercial, governmental, and industrial construction became a matter of primary consideration. Advantages and disadvantages of either central or peripheral location shifted constantly during the history of American city growth. In the beginning, there was an obvious advantage for the wealthy in settling close to the center of town, within easy walking distance from their places of work, close to the docks and wharves, the storehouses, and the office buildings.

The poor had to come in daily from the fringes of town where they lived in relatively primitive shelter.[2]

As means of transportation improved, as wealthy citizens traveled to town by carriage, as the street car, the cable car, the train, the subway, the bus, and the private automobile made their entrance to ease the commuting problem, the wealthier citizens turned their eye to the outskirts of the city where they found an opportunity to settle in relatively spacious mansions on well landscaped grounds. They leap-frogged beyond the ranges of less desirable housing and left their city homes to be taken over by other land uses.

There are exceptions to this rule. The stately city homes of Beacon Hill in the center of Boston testify to the survival of earlier forms of city development.[3] At the fringes of many of our large metropolitan areas, we still find poor housing, simple shacks, and deteriorating farm housing converted to residential use.[4]

ABOUT CONCENTRIC URBAN GROWTH

European Cities. The American [5] city expresses more clearly than the European city the competitive forces inherent in the industralization process. This is true for two reasons: (1) American cities are not superimposed upon urban settlement that survived from previous historical conditions; and (2) American cities have grown more rapidly than those of the European continent.[6]

---

[2] "*The Mirror's* articles included comments . . . on the immigrants and ragged beggars who came into the city from the suburbs each morning." James Ford, *Slums and Housing,* Cambridge: Harvard University Press, 1936, pp. 94-95.

[3] See Walter Firey, *Land Use in Central Boston.* Cambridge: Harvard University Press, 1947, Chapter III, "The Influence of Spatially Referred Values Upon Land Use: Beacon Hill," pp. 87-135.

[4] For the "tendency for residences to gravitate to the lowest use in terms of class status" in the urban fringe, see Walter Firey, "Ecological Considerations in Planning for Rurban Fringes," *American Sociological Review,* Vol. 11, No. 4 (August, 1946), pp. 418-419.

[5] Where we talk about the "American" city, we have in mind specifically the city of the United States. Cities in South America differ markedly from cities in this country with regard to most social conditions.

[6] "The European cities have assumed their urban character and proportions more gradually than have those of the United States." *Our Cities, Their Role in the National Economy.* Report to the National Resources Committee. Washington, D.C.: U.S. Government Printing Office, 1937, p. 26. Consider the entire section on "Comparison between American and European Urbanism," pp. 25-27.

Most European cities were already fairly well structured by the time the industrialization process got under way. There were public buildings in the center of the city, castles and cathedrals, theaters and museums, public squares and stately boulevards. The business centers of these cities developed close to, but remained clearly segregated from, the centers of public construction.[7] Public functions, parades, speeches, and performances took place in convenient proximity to, but did not quite intermingle with, the functions of the business districts where the department stores attracted their customers, where the newspapers went to press, and where the bankers dealt with their clients. At their inner cores, these cities reflected the presence of royalty and aristocracy alongside new shopping districts that displayed glamorously the wares turned out by the advancing industrialization process.

Beyond the central part of the European city, the urban area tended to fall apart into a limited number of more or less distinct sections. The workingmen's section was easily distinguished from the area where the well-to-do lived in relatively pretentious apartment housing. Far toward the outskirts, large sections were built up entirely of single-family housing.

The European city tends to be partitioned into segments that serve distinctly different purposes. Close to the docks and the early manufacturing plants, there had always been the homes of the workers and the poor. On hills and near lakes, there had always been the homes of the wealthy. These tendencies were reinforced by the push and pull of "natural" segregation, by the desire of like to live with like, and by the resistance of different groups of city dwellers against association in their private lives with those either above or below their social station. Never did these cities grow fast enough to obliterate the sectional pattern into which they had chanced to fall before the onset of the process of industrialization.

American Cities. The concentric pattern of city growth has found its most blatant development in the American scene. Even here, the simple geometrical design rarely achieves full perfection. It is warped by natural man-made obstacles. These obstacles arise in the form of

---

[7] "We find many of the European cities divided into two major parts: the ancient city at the center and the new or modern city outside the line of former walls which enclosed the inner core." *Our Cities, op. cit.*, p. 26. Consider that the "line of former walls" enclosed only a minute section of the modern metropolis.

lakes, rivers, or other waterways, hills, freight yards, warehouses, or early industrial plants. They either bring urban construction to a standstill or are by-passed by urban growth.

Chicago, the city pattern of which has been more thoroughly investigated than that of any other urban community in the world,[8] grew very rapidly in the second half of the 19th century and has obtained a fairly regular outlay of construction and land use. Geometrical regularity exists there, but Chicago's lake shore location has sent out waves or rings of successive expansion that bulge in the form of semicircles of increasing radius.

Minneapolis has grown in a southwesterly direction. At the northeast end, this city was cut off from further growth by spacious freight yards and railroad tracks. Toward the east, it was hemmed in by the Mississippi river.

Seattle extended inland on terraces that rose from Puget Sound. In New York City, urban growth has been restricted and forced into a vertical direction (by means of tall buildings) due to its position on Manhattan Island. At present, this largest city of the world is overflowing into the four other boroughs of its metropolitan area, and also into Long Island, Westchester and New Jersey. This development is dependent upon means of transportation, such as ferries, bridges, and tunnels. Thus any semblance to a strictly concentric pattern of construction is obscured by the unique configuration of natural hindrances and man-made facilities.

Concentric Growth. That our fast growing cities have expanded in approximately circular form is not hard to understand. In the circle, a maximum surface is contained within the shortest distance from the center. A circular form of city development eases the burden of the intra-urban communication.

Without the desire to keep commuting distances to a minimum, our cities might well have sprawled indiscriminately. As it is, urban construction is influenced by centripetal tendencies. Economy of transportation does not permit building activities anywhere but at the shortest possible distance from the central nucleus of the city. Usually, until everything is built up within six miles of the city center in all directions, few will venture into construction activities as far removed from the city center as 7 miles.

---

[8] For the development of urban sociology at the University of Chicago, see Edward Shils, *The Present State of American Sociology.* Glencoe, Ill.: The Free Press, 1948, "Urban Sociology," pp. 7-14.

Concentric Rings. At varying distances from the city center, belt lines of similar construction run through the entire urban area. Workingmen's homes did not always cluster in either the north or the south, the east or the west, of the city. They once ran like a belt line relatively close to the center of the city, encircling the downtown business district. Today, the situation is somewhat different.

In the American city of the 19th century, a relatively homogeneous type of construction was found at the same distance from the central business district in all directions that permitted construction. This statement holds completely true only where equally good transportation facilities run in all directions from the center. Otherwise, the circles are extended in immediate proximity to transportation lines. We have to express distance from the central business district in terms of commuting time to find similar types of construction at all locations equally close to the city center.

The ring theory of urban development confronts us with a simplified theoretical structure realized to perfection only under highly-simplified conditions.[9] If we take cities as they have actually grown, we shall see the theoretical structure "shine through," being approximated by observable land use and construction. There are innumerable deviations, however, which necessitate the consideration of local conditions.

Burgess' Five Zones. With these limitations in mind, a useful orientation is provided in Burgess' well known theory of concentric city development.[10] Not only does he emphasize concentric growth as such; he tells us specifically what sequence of land uses to expect as we move away from the center of the city.

The Business District. Burgess distinguishes five zones of urban construction and land use. Zone I contains the "loop," or central business district. Here we find the department stores and office buildings, frequently in the form of skyscrapers. Here are the specialty stores which cater to the entire urban population. Here we

---

[9] For equally simplified assumptions with regard to human motivation in the foundation of economic theory, see Talcott Parsons, *Essays in Sociological Theory, Pure and Applied*. Glencoe, Ill.: The Free Press, 1949, "The Motivation of Economic Activities," pp. 200-217; also Adolf Loewe, *Economics and Sociology*. London: George Allen & Unwin, Ltd., 1935.

[10] See Ernest W. Burgess, "The Growth of the City," in Robert E. Park, Ernest W. Burgess, and Roderick D. McKenzie, *The City*. Chicago: The University of Chicago Press, 1925, pp. 47-62.

find the courthouse, the library, the museum, and other public buildings.

The Zone of Transition. Zone II girds the central business district. It is often called the "Zone of Transition." This designation is well-deserved. It harks back to times when one wave of immigration after another reached this country and settled in the large cities, finding a first temporary residence in the centrally-located city slums.

As they improved their economic status, as they learned to speak the language of this country, as they acquired skills in industry and were able to move to outlying districts with more expensive, better constructed, better equipped, and better maintained homes, these immigrants left their quarters in the Zone of Transition, only to be followed by a group of new arrivals. The Zone of Transition changed from an Irish to a Swedish, to a German, to an Italian or Negro neighborhood.

While different nationality groups moved through, leaving traces of their former dominance in the German club, the Irish Catholic church, the Swedish Salvation Army station, and the Italian restaurant, the area retained a more or less similar character. This area continued to harbor the slum (housing considered dangerous to the health of its inhabitants according to modern American standards).[11]

The Zone of Transition harbors a mixture of changing land uses. Within this first ring of urban construction surrounding the central area, we also find "skid row," or the single men's district; we find hangouts, headquarters, and residences, of the criminal underworld. In glaring contrast to this sordid environment, yet located in immediate proximity and at the same distance from the central area, we find some of the fanciest apartment buildings, and the bright light district with luxurious eating places, night clubs, and theaters. In the modern metropolis, the Gold Coast hugs the slum. Both of them are located in the Zone of Transition.

Workingmen's Homes. The Zone of Transition is followed, in Burgess' scheme, by zone III, the Zone of Workingmen's Homes. This zone is given a somewhat unified character by housing conditions which, although not quite as bad as in the Zone of Transition, are bad enough to be used for living quarters only by the relatively poor. Though there may be no slums (outright insanitary housing)

---

[11] For further discussion of the slum environment, see Chapter 6.

in this environment, it is quite customary to talk about this part of the city as being "blighted." The term blight does not relate as much to health hazards as to economically unsound housing conditions.[12] Conditions tend to be economically unsound not because of physical, but because of functional deterioration. Construction may be strong, fireproof, and well equipped with elementary sanitary facilities. Yet, being unplanned and converted from construction previously intended for different use, the desirability of homes in this environment is decreasing. These parts of town are unattractive at best, and sordid where they are at their worst. They were built at a time when little consideration was given to park planning and the provision of attractive green spaces to improve the livability of residential districts. This zone contains former stately mansions now cut into kitchenette apartments. Residential construction expresses the change from former glory to present humiliation.

Residential Zone. Most middle class residences are packed into the wide zone IV, designated as the "Residential Zone." Home construction, in this environment, runs the entire gamut from multiple dwellings to one-family homes, from modest quarters to expensive mansions, from rental housing to conditions of stable home ownership.

By and large, the better homes are found located more closely to the outer than the inner belt-line of this area. Home ownership, lower construction, and less densely built-up lots increase as we proceed from the inner to the outer rings of this zone. Such ring-formed regularities, however, are interrupted by neighborhood business districts, so-called "satellite loops," or by fashionable apartment hotels that might spring up anywhere close to a city park or a train station.

At the outer edge of zone IV, we find a mixture of land uses which can be compared only to the Zone of Transition close to the city center.[13] In large metropolitan communities, the outer fringe of zone IV appears as a secondary bright light district. Space consuming entertainment facilities, such as eating places (road houses), night clubs, golf courses, drive-in theaters, racetracks, and baseball

---

[12] Causes for blight formation are discussed on p. 100.

[13] Burgess did not give much attention to a breakdown of these developments at the urban fringe. These developments did not become apparent until the 1930's and 1940's. His theory was published in 1925.

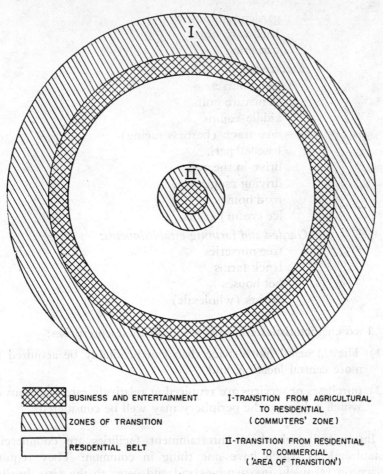

BUSINESS AND ENTERTAINMENT

ZONES OF TRANSITION

RESIDENTIAL BELT

I-TRANSITION FROM AGRICULTURAL
TO RESIDENTIAL
(COMMUTERS' ZONE)

II-TRANSITION FROM RESIDENTIAL
TO COMMERCIAL
('AREA OF TRANSITION')

FIGURE 4. Peripheral and Central Transition.

parks are located in this vicinity. In the modern city, the residential area turns outward as well as inward for entertainment.

The commercial and entertainment belt at the outer edge of the residential belt shows this list of land uses at Harlem and North in Chicago:

> *Business related to residential development:*
> realtors
> contractors
> furniture stores

garden equipment
hardware stores
carpeting

Entertainment enterprises:
golf courses
miniature golf
kiddie camps
race track (harness racing)
baseball park
drive-in theaters
driving ranges
road houses
ice cream parlors

Garden and farming establishments:
tree nurseries
truck farms
hot houses
florists (wholesale)

Two characteristics are inherent in all these enterprises:

(1) They demand more space than can profitably be acquired in more central location, and

(2) purchases or services are required at relatively rare occasions at which a drive to the periphery may well be considered.

Intermixed with these entertainment facilities are commercial establishments which have one thing in common: They require space on relatively inexpensive land and cater to the city dweller at special occasions only. Located upon relatively large tracts of land and engaged in business less lucrative than downtown commerce, these facilities have lost out in competition for downtown real estate and moved to areas of second choice which offer relatively low land values and relatively easy access to the residential areas of the city.

Commuters' Zone. The outermost zone (V) is designated by Burgess as the Commuters' Zone. This zone may stretch far into the urban hinterland and is not necessarily part of the built-up section of the urban community. It may extend to semi-rural communities outside the incorporated city. Along rapid transit lines, this area will reach right into the midst of primarily agricultural land uses.[14]

REASONS FOR CONCENTRIC GROWTH

The Real Estate Market. The reasons for concentric urban growth are found in the dynamics of the real estate market.[15]

Our cities have grown rapidly. At any given time, building activities did not reach further beyond the built-up area than was absolutely necessary. Land at a certain distance from the central business district had to be exhausted before the realtor ventured into the development of further outlying areas. Thus, a relatively even growth extended in all directions.

The question remains why the wealthier residents of the urban community seem to have preferred peripheral sites for their building activities, being followed in more or less regular succession by lower status groups and economically less-powerful citizens. It has been argued that the more well-to-do city dwellers in the 19th century sought refuge from urban grime and congestion by placing their residential housing close to the urban fringe.[16] They escaped the central city to enjoy an easy access to nature, fresh air, and sunlight.

---

[14] For an empirical study of recent fringe developments in the outer rings of Burgess' concentric pattern, see Walter Firey, *Social Aspects of Land Use Planning in the Country-City Fringe. The Case of Flint, Michigan.* East Lansing, Mich.: Michigan Agr. Exp. Sta. Special Bulletin 339, June, 1946; also Solon T. Kimball, *The New Social Frontier: The Fringe.* East Lansing, Mich.: Michigan Agr. Exp. Sta. Special Bulletin 360, 1949. For a French statement of the problem, see Pierre George, M. Agulhon, L. A. Lavandeyra, H. D. Elhai, and R. Schaeffer, *Études sur la Banlieue de Paris.* Paris: Librairie Armand Colin, 1950.

[15] The economist is concerned with the direction of effective demands as the foundation of his analytic reasoning; the sociologist probes deeper into the causes for such direction, and thus finds himself very much concerned with the background of preferences and values. What is a fact for the economist becomes a problem for the sociologist. Walter Firey seems to have misunderstood, somewhat, this relation when he pleaded for the consideration of values in human ecology. See Walter Firey, *op. cit.,* "Introduction to the Problem," pp. 3-40.

[16] "Among the factors that push the people out of the city are: (1) the expansion of commerce and industry in the central zones; (2) expansion of racial and ethnic belts; (3) hazards and discomforts associated with heavy traffic; and (4) presence of vice and crime in certain parts of the city." Noel

These new-arrivals to the urban fringe vacated residential facilities in the inner city. These, in turn, were occupied by city dwellers next in line with regard to social status and purchasing power. These followers moved into the abandoned mansions of the well-to-do and made themselves at home in a type of construction which often did not fit their needs of everyday living. Thus, urban home construction in the residential belt changed hands not only once but many times.[17]

With each sale and purchase, original design and construction lost in functional relationship to the housing needs of its occupants.[18] The discrepancy between original design and present usage of real estate property grew to such proportions that the landlord considered the possibility of conversions. The usefulness of the available structure was improved by makeshift remodeling. One-family mansions were transformed into apartment housing. Additional sets of kitchen and bathroom facilities were installed. Once begun, this process continued to the point where the entire building, whatever its original shape or form, was cut into a maximum number of minimum-sized kitchenette apartments with bathroom facilities shared by several families and kitchen facilities offered in the form of hot plates.

Succession. During rapid city growth, the entire urban fabric was continuously in a state of transformation.[19] The highest status and

---

P. Gist and L. A. Halbert, *Urban Society.* New York: Thomas Y. Crowell Company, 1948, p. 127.

"The peripheral expansion in Milwaukee county is a movement of people from the better sections of the city who seek to avoid certain disadvantages of the city without depriving themselves of the urban services to which they have become accustomed." Richard Dewey, "Peripheral Expansion in Milwaukee County," *The American Journal of Sociology,* Vol. LIV, No. 2 (September, 1948), p. 118.

[17] "The great mass of the housing supply consists of used housing . . . the average ratio between the annual production of non-farm dwellings and total supply was 2.3 percent from 1900 to 1940, ranging from 1.3 to 3.2 percent." *American Housing. Problems and Prospects.* New York: The Twentieth Century Fund, 1947, pp. 182-183.

[18] "Many of these depreciated (filtered-down) houses are not particularly well suited to the low income groups. They may have too many or too few rooms; the rooms may be too large and inconveniently arranged to suit simpler modes of living; or they may require too much maintenance and service. In the filtering down process, therefore, a large number of houses are bound to lose their utility." *American Housing, op. cit.,* p. 185.

[19] See also p. 95.

income groups pushed toward the periphery of the city to escape congestion and other urban nuisances. They were followed by their immediate "inferiors" trying to penetrate the home environment of their "betters." This race continued all down the line through the various strata of the middle classes and through the lower income brackets. Even the slum-dwellers stood ready to push in an outward direction.

This centrifugal pattern of urban growth and succession stratified the urban fabric in layers of increasing social status toward the outskirts. Most urban sociologists have explained this phenomenon with the desire for residential location at the urban fringe.[20]

At close scrutiny, this explanation is not satisfactory. Peripheral residential location may be desirable, but it should not matter much whether — once encased in the urban fabric — the family residence is removed one, two, or three miles from the semi-rural playgrounds.

Second Hand Housing. Thus, it remains unexplained why inside the outmost peripheral belt-line of urban residential construction housing conditions arrange themselves in a regular status sequence. To understand this pattern better, we have to recall that only a few of the urban residents in the 19th century were able to have their houses built for themselves and designed for their unique needs. To build at all, the well-to-do families had to go where building was possible, namely to the edge of the built-up city. New building activities in any other part of the already built-up city were economically encumbered by the necessity of demolishing existing construction, still in use and still yielding an income.

The status arrangement of subsequent residential belt-lines, thus, explains itself more easily. Competition does not struggle only for decreasing distances to the city fringe, but struggles also for a functionally less obsolete type of residential housing. It may not make a difference whether the city dweller lives one or two miles removed from the open country, but it does make a difference what vintage housing his family occupies. The poorer families lose out in this competition. They have to live in far outdated housing. Age of construction decreases in approaching the urban fringe. We

20 "Factors which attract or pull city people toward the outer zones include: (1) improved transportation facilities; (2) a rising standard of living expressed in terms of exclusiveness, spaciousness, and freedom from traffic noises; (3) advertising and propaganda, particularly the influence exerted by merchants and realtors; and (4) the tendency to conform to prevailing fashions and customs." Noel P. Gist and L. A. Halbert, *op. cit.*, p. 126-127.

need not be surprised to find ourselves confronted here with occupants of increasingly higher income brackets.

Central Rehabilitation? Few of our cities have reached the age
where thorough rebuilding and rehabilitation programs can profitably be undertaken in the inner city. In the future, we shall have
better opportunities for central rehabilitation. At that time, the
wealthier members of our urban communities will consider the
advantages of open developments at the city outskirts as well as the
advantages of residential location in close proximity to the central
business district.

As complete physical deterioration makes inner city areas available for new construction, the now existing status arrangement in
our city pattern may reverse itself. Land values rise also as we move
close toward the central business section of the urban settlement.
One day, perhaps, there may be a sequence of residential housing
that improves as we advance toward the city center rather than
the other way around.

The Riddle of the Slums. The utter deterioration of the slum
environment in the immediate vicinity of the downtown business
district needs explanation. Here is desirable land in closest proximity
to the heart of the city, yet standing construction deteriortes visibly,
maintenance is neglected, and only the least successful members of
the urban community are willing to put up with living conditions
in this environment. The combination of high land values in this
Zone of Transition with low incomes derived from real estate available at this location presents a paradox.

The answer to the riddle is conventionally given as follows: Land
values in the slum environment are high not because of the income
derived from the slum property, but because of the high income
expected sometime in the future, when the central business district
will extend into this area. Thus, the high land values in the slum
environment have a speculative basis.[21]

---

[21] "One fruitful source of error in studying land values is to regard the
problem as involving only a point of time instead of a period of time." Richard
M. Hurd, *Principles of City Land Values.* New York: The Record and Guide,
1903, p. 18.

"Inquiry will disclose that much of the land in the area (area of transition)
is in the hands of absentee owners who hold it for speculative reasons, hoping
that as the city grows, the business district will expand and skyscrapers will be
erected on these lots. Consequently, land values are inflated, but rents in comparison are low." *Our Cities, op. cit.,* p. 7.

There is some doubt today whether the expectations of property holders in the slum environment will ever be borne out. The growth of the core of the modern city has practically come to a standstill. This is not entirely due to the slowing down of city growth. It is also due to the business district's tendency of growing vertically rather than horizontally. Additional office space and other building needs are provided for in skyscrapers.[22]

The owners of slum property, thus, find themselves "holding the bag." One might ask whether it wouldn't be justified to leave them in that unenviable situation. They speculated on profitable sales; their speculations misfired; why not leave the real estate business to the free play of the market?

The community, however, has somehow committed itself to the support of high land values in this environment through tax assessments based on similar expectations.[23] It will seem unfair to have demanded a payment of dues on fictitious basis.

There also remains the concern for future taxable income. With annexation procedures lagging behind the growth of urban construction at the periphery of the urban community, the municipality becomes increasingly dependent upon its source of income in the central city.[24] Under the circumstances, there is little enthusiasm for

---

[22] "The central business district of a city can expand in two ways, vertically and laterally. . . . The invention of the steelframe skyscraper and the electric elevator has facilitated vertical as against lateral expansion in many cities." Arthur M. Weimer and Homer Hoyt, *Principles of Urban Real Estate*, New York: The Ronald Press Company. 1948, p. 99.

"Vertical expansion of business and industry and decentralization made many early zoning ordinances look ridiculous and defeated the speculative hopes of owners of property close-in to central business districts. Erroneous anticipations tended to frustrate appropriate development and rebuilding." S. E. Sanders and A. J. Rabuck, *New City Patterns. The Analysis of and a Technique for Urban Reintegration.* New York: Reinhold Publishing Corporation, 1946, p. 6.

[23] One of the causes of central slum development is said to be "High taxes and the unwillingness of both public officials and property owners to adjust inflated assessments and values to realities."

"It is a well known fact that present assessments in urban blighted areas are much higher than legitimate land use values." S. E. Sanders and A. J. Rabuck, *op. cit.*, p. 16.

[24] "During the last 20 years numerous industries have moved from central to outlying urban areas and the employees of these industries are gradually moving out in order to live near the factories where they work. Moreover, it is a well known fact that local business tends to follow population movements. As these movements take place, what is happening to the tax structure of the central city? The obvious answer is that sources of municipal revenue are drying up and disappearing." S. E. Sanders and A. J. Rabuck, *op. cit.*, p. 15.

letting the bottom drop out of the real estate market of slum properties. Nor is the economic situation in the slum necessarily as grim as our reasoning would have it.

Recent investigations have not definitely proven, but have indicated the likelihood that residential slum properties are yielding a fair return on capital investment. Rentals in this environment may be extremely low but total income seems to have been raised at many places by crowding a very large number of occupants into available dwelling units. Expenses for maintenance are reduced to a negligible portion of the total income and, thus, a fairly acceptable economic situation is temporarily established — at least until neglected construction deteriorates further and physically falls apart, or is condemned as a hazard to the life and health of its occupants.

Scattered Slums. The dynamics of slum formation are not confined to the Zone of Transition. Slums blossom forth wherever inferior and less renumerative land uses are replaced by relatively superior and more renumerative land uses.

Any student knows the slums or blighted areas that flourish in the immediate environment of the university campus. Here, land is expected to change over from residential to institutional use. The university is expected to buy up sooner or later most of the residential properties that border its campus. Under the circumstances, it is smart to wait for the university to branch out, not to waste any money for new construction on lots that are going to be sold profitably in the near future anyway, to reduce expenses for maintenance to a minimum, and yet to try to use available construction for rooming and boarding houses.

Although slums are not limited to the central Zone of Transition, they are more prevalent here than in any other part of the city. Nor are slums found in every changing residential environment; if so, they would have to be found all over the city, because the entire urban fabric is continuously in a state of gradual transformation, superior land uses being gradually replaced by inferior ones. To make a slum, the changeover from one type of land use to another has to take more than a gradual step. The gain in income from property has to be so substantial as to make present usage irrelevant in view of expected sale prices.

This condition prevails on a large scale in two parts of the modern city: in the Zone of Transition skirting the central business district, and at the very edge of the solidly built-up city. At the former location, residential land uses are held in readiness for replacement by commercial land uses that are economically more powerful. At the latter location, rural land uses are being replaced by urban residential land uses which are also economically more powerful.[25]

There results in either location a period of confusion during which we find deteriorating construction of the disappearing type side by side with new construction that anticipates future developments. During this period of temporarily mixed land uses, the central Zone of Transition as well as the "rurban fringe" are temporarily entered by short-term ventures in the entertainment industry, such as restaurants, night clubs, road houses, carnivals, and theaters. Such business establishments find little access to consolidated residential areas. They are forced to find a place for themselves in the central and the peripheral Zones of Transition. Short-term profits are large enough to warrant substantial investment in construction that may not, in either location, serve its purpose for more than a very limited number of years.

RECENT CHANGES IN THE PATTERN OF URBAN GROWTH

New Patterns of Urban Settlement. The ring theory of urban development will be used in the future to explain a historically limited phase of spectacular urbanization in the United States. It cannot be accepted as a theory of city growth with general validity and universal application.

In the 1930's, American modern city growth had changed in pattern and direction. With the help of the W.P.A., real estate inventories were undertaken in a large number of American cities.[26]

---

[25] "This fundamental identity between seemingly unrelated land uses suggests the possibility of a single inclusive theory of slums, in which the rurban fringe, the ghetto, the rooming house area, and the rural creek-bottom or forest-farm slum all appear as varieties of a single land use phenomenon." Walter Firey, "Ecological Considerations in Planning For Rurban Fringes." *American Sociological Review*, Vol. II, No. 4 (August, 1946), p. 411.

[26] "As the techniques for making real property surveys were refined through the cooperative efforts of the Works Progress Administration, the Central Statistical Board, the Federal Home Loan Bank Board, the Housing Division of the Public Works Administration, and Division of Economics and Statistics of the Federal Housing Administration, the possibilities of utilizing the voluminous data (available for over 200 American cities) in developing principles of city structure were recognized. Thus, the present study was conceived." Homer Hoyt, *The Structure and Growth of Residential Neighborhoods in American Cities.* Federal Housing Administration Form No. 2088. Washington, D.C.: U.S. Government Printing Office, 1939.

These revealed interesting empirical evidence of recent changes in the pattern of urban growth. Homer Hoyt, a well known land economist, stands out as the most prominent interpreter of these data.[27] He made them the basis not only for a thorough criticism of the ring theory of urban growth, but also for tentative predictions regarding the future structure of American cities.[28]

The Sector Theory. These observations about modern city development refute the simple regularity claimed earlier by Burgess' ring theory. The claim of the ring theory that belt-lines of homogeneous land uses will be found at similar distances from the city center, collapses completely.[29]

At the very periphery, there are fashionable mansions as well as factories and workingmen's homes. These different land uses hold themselves to different sectors of the city outskirts. They are segregated from each other, but they are found at the same distance from the central business district.

In the center of the city, we find the Gold Coast in immediate proximity to the slum environment.[30] High class apartment housing along New York's East River is located directly adjacent to the tenement slums of Manhattan Island. For quite some time, we have looked at this phenomenon as the exception that proves the rule. Recent developments have made the fashionable apartment hotel in the downtown district such a regular phenomenon that we shall either have to explain it by some central theory, or give up such theory altogether.

Many Factors in Residential Location. It has become more difficult, also, to make generalizations about the residential areas between

---

[27] Homer Hoyt is known as the originator of the "Sector Theory" of urban development, to be discussed below. "This theory was worked out by Homer Hoyt and first presented in a series of articles in the FHA's *Insured Mortgage Portfolio*, Vol. I, Nos. 6-10." Footnote in Arthur M. Weimer and Homer Hoyt, *op. cit.*, p. 96.

[28] Homer Hoyt, "The Structure of American Cities in the Post-war Era," *The American Journal of Sociology*, Vol. XLVIII, No. 4 (January, 1943), pp. 475-481. See also "The Future Growth and Structure of Cities," in A. M. Weimer and Homer Hoyt, *op. cit.*, pp. 104-119.

[29] See p. 94 ff. above.

[30] The social problems arising from this condition have found artistic elaboration in Sidney Kingsley's play "Dead End," popular in the 1930's. The classic sociological study of these conditions is Harvey W. Zorbaugh's *The Gold Coast and the Slum. A Sociological Study of Chicago's Near North Side.* Chicago: The University of Chicago Press, 1929.

A CITY OF THE FUTURE

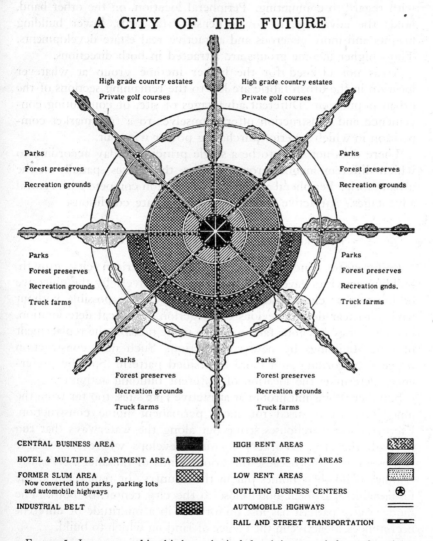

High grade country estates
Private golf courses

High grade country estates
Private golf courses

Parks
Forest preserves
Recreation grounds

Parks
Forest preserves
Recreation grounds

Parks
Forest preserves
Recreation grounds
Truck farms

Parks
Forest preserves
Recreation gnds.
Truck farms

Parks
Forest preserves
Recreation grounds
Truck farms

Parks
Forest preserves
Recreation grounds
Truck farms

CENTRAL BUSINESS AREA

HOTEL & MULTIPLE APARTMENT AREA

FORMER SLUM AREA
Now converted into parks, parking lots
and automobile highways

INDUSTRIAL BELT

HIGH RENT AREAS

INTERMEDIATE RENT AREAS

LOW RENT AREAS

OUTLYING BUSINESS CENTERS

AUTOMOBILE HIGHWAYS

RAIL AND STREET TRANSPORTATION

FIGURE 5. Incorporated in this hypothetical sketch is recent information about actual changes in the pattern of urban growth in this country. From: Arthur M. Weimer and Homer Hoyt, *Principles of Urban Real Estate.* New York: The Ronald Press Company, 1948, p. 117.

the fringe of the city and its central core. Central location may be pre-empted by the higher income groups because of its convenience with regard to commuting. Peripheral location, on the other hand, holds the advantage of lower density standards, lower building heights and more generous and attractive real estate developments. Thus, higher income groups are attracted in both directions.

Areas not claimed for the higher income group at whatever location in the urban fabric are left to the remaining sections of the urban population. Different advantages of site, of commuting convenience and construction offer themselves to a free market competition in which superior purchasing power wins out.

There does not seem to be a single principle today according to which different income groups arrange themselves spatially in the urban fabric. Peripheral advantages of location compete with central advantages. Attractive sites further complicate conditions.

DIFFERENTIAL PREFERENCE AND SEGREGATION

Preferences. Since the slowdown of American city growth, building activities have not been guided exclusively by the objective of locating as close to the center of the city as possible without having to tear down previous construction. Physical deterioration, in many cities, has gone far enough to make possible the replacement of older buildings by new construction. Such new construction proceeds according to a more diversified pattern. Specific preferences determine the location of different building activities.

Summer cabins mushroom at attractive lake sites, too far from the inner city to be used for more permanent home construction. Factories and warehouses string out along the waterways that run through the city. Workers' housing develops wherever available real estate is cheap because of various kinds of nuisances. Wealthy families build their homes out in the country, or rent them in the fashionable apartment hotel close to the city center, or both. The modern city pattern has lost uniformity in a multitude of different preferences, all active in the choice of land on which to build.

"Octopus with Tentacles" The city does not grow slowly and systematically today in a spiral of ever widening concentric rings. The appearance of the city is no longer that of a circle. Homer Hoyt described the shape of the modern city as that of an octopus with its

tentacles stretched far out into the rurban hinterland. The tentacles stretch out wherever rapid transit lines reduce commuting time to the inner city area. They consist of apartment housing and a narrow belt of one-family homes following the railroad lines far out into the countryside.[31]

Developments during the 1930's have somewhat obscured the protruding tentacles. Two modern technological devices, the automobile and the septic tank,[32] enabled the city dweller to move into the space left open between the rapid transit lines. The automobile made the city dweller independent of public means of transportation. He found his way into territory previously inaccessible to those gainfully employed in the downtown business district. The septic tank made it possible for the city dweller to build his home with all modern conveniences in an environment not yet reached by the urban network of underground facilities.

Segregation. Within the built-up city, we observe a tendency toward segregation, which is gaining influence upon the structure or urban land uses. This tendency asserts itself as the tempo of city growth slows down and as the problem of distance loses importance due to improved means of transportation.

In Europe, where city growth never was as hectic as in the United States of the 19th century, segregation has always been noticed as one of the most prominent features in the arrangement of land uses. If the workingmen's housing in one city was to be found in a generally northern direction from the city center, the villas and the apartments of the upper classes were most likely in the opposite direction.

In the United States, the tendency toward segregation was temporarily obscured by the circular growth which alligned homogeneous land uses in the shape of rings rather than in the shape of clusters. The tendency toward the clustering of similar land uses was overshadowed by a pattern of growth that added one belt-line of construction to another. Homogeneous land uses assembled in

---

[31] See Fig. 18, "A City of the Future," in A. M. Weimer and Homer Hoyt, *op. cit.,* p. 117.

[32] "These unincorporated suburbs (of the 1930's) were located almost at random because the automobile, the septic tank, and the power-driven pump made a vast number of sites available and freed the new developments from dependency on fixed transportation routes and established sewer and water systems." Homer Hoyt, *op. cit.,* p. 477.

the form of citywide belt-lines rather than relatively compact clusters.

Segregation has been universal in urban construction and the urban way of life. Similar needs are better satisfied in unison. There is need for cheap grocery stores, cheap taverns, and low rentals in the workingmen's district. Special services are attracted where a settlement of definite character establishes a need for them. Once these services are being provided for a cumulative process accentuates the peculiarities of any given urban environment.

Nuisances. Nuisances also contribute to the establishment of homogeneous city areas. City nuisances, such as odors and noises, congestion, and unattractive appearance, are to some extent inescapable for those who cause them. Under the circumstances, land uses that create nuisances are usually found in close proximity to each other. In the inner city, industrial establishments, warehouses, and centers of commercial activity will seldom stray far from each other. Whatever nuisances they are here exposed to, they could not escape, anyway, because they produce such nuisances themselves. In sticking close to each other, they are not exposing themselves to any nuisances they could escape by going elsewhere. In the single men's district, the burlesque show does not provoke any feeling of moral indignation because it is closely related to fairly universal needs.

Yearning for Homogenity. The trend toward segregation is all-pervading in the modern city. It is supported by the similarity of needs and nuisances. Another motivating force is the reaction against occupational life in the cosmopolitan atmosphere of the central business district.

In his work, the city dweller mingles with a heterogenous crowd of coworkers. He learns to get along with them. He learns to get along with Swedes and Scots, with Negroes, Poles, or whatever people may come his way in the pursuit of his business. He meets rich and poor, Catholics and Protestants, family men and bachelors. To relax from his working day, the city dweller seeks a residential environment where he will be free from the constant alertness that is forced upon him by mingling with the motley crowd of a heterogeneous urban population. To relax in his private life, the city dweller wants to be with "his own kind."

Status Considerations. Residential location in the city carries status connotations. The city dweller's "address" tells not only where he lives, but where he belongs in the social scale.

The realtor who takes his client around to arrange the purchase or the rental of a home carefully inquires about his background, his job, his "race," and his social contacts. On that basis, he will select the most suitable location for a family residence. An environment of people with similar social backgrounds is considered the most suitable location.

The total effect is a clustering of relatively homogeneous housing conditions and occupancy standards all over the city. From street to street and from block to block, there is a consciousness of social status as conveyed by residence in that very location.[33]

Preferential location develops into the formation of relatively homogeneous city areas. The orderliness of the ring-pattern of urban development may have been abandoned in recent decades. In a more haphazard manner, the orderliness of relatively homogeneous settlement in distinct clusters has remained.

Suburbia. Beyond the outer Zone of Transition, suburban developments and new functions of the metropolitan area find manifestation in types of construction not foreseen by the classical ring theory. Our suburbs are not all of one type.[34]

Not only the spaciously laid-out homes of the well-to-do are to be found in this Commuters' Zone. There are settlements of workers' homes, summer cabins, apartments, and prefabricated housing placed on vacant land for middle class families who need housing urgently. There are factories, and there are whole industrial towns, there are resort areas, and large tracts of land pre-empted by the truck farmer.[35]

---

[33] An intricate system of status designations will be found in W. Lloyd Warner, Marchia Meeker and Kenneth Eells, *Social Class in America*. Chicago: Science Research Associates, Inc., 1949; see chart on p. 19.

For the measurement of segregation, consult Eshreff Shevsky and Marilyn Williams, *The Social Areas of Los Angeles. Analysis and Typology*. Berkeley and Los Angeles: University of California Press, 1949. See particularly the Chapter on "Segregation," pp. 47-60.

[34] For the suburban trend in the United States and a classification of types of suburbs, see Chauncy D. Harris, "Suburbs," *The American Journal of Sociology*, Vol. XLIX, No. 1 (July, 1943), pp. 1-13.

[35] "Nearly half of the population increase (1940-1950) of the entire country took place in the outlying parts of the 168 metropolitan areas . . . the population changes of the last decade point to an increasing urbanization of the

In a manner of speaking, these mixed land uses in the suburbs are protruding offshoots from the outer Zone of Transition. The Commuters' Zone of 50 years ago has changed into an area teeming with highly variegated productive, residential, and recreational land uses. So far, there are no distinct regularities in this environment. The metropolitan area is truly fuzzy at the edges.

SELECTED READINGS

1. Richard M. Hurd, *Principles of City Land Values*. New York: The Record and Guide, 1903, pp. 1-159.

2. Ernest W. Burgess, "The Growth of the City," Robert E. Park, Ernest W. Burgess, and Roderick D. McKenzie, *The City*. Chicago: The University of Chicago Press, 1925, pp. 47-62.

3. Homer Hoyt, *The Structure and Growth of Residential Neighborhoods in American Cities*. Federal Housing Administration Form No. 2088. Washington, D.C.: U.S. Government Printing Office, 1939, pp. 3-169.

4. Walter Firey, *Land Use in Central Boston*. Cambridge: Harvard University Press, 1947, pp. 3-340.

5. S. E. Sanders and A. J. Rabuck, *New City Patterns. The Analysis of and a Technique for Urban Reintegration*. New York: Reinhold Publishing Corporation, 1946, pp. 1-197.

PROBLEMS

1. *From the Ring Theory to the Sector Theory of Urban Development.* Consult *The Growth of the City* by Ernest W. Burgess and *Principles of Urban Real Estate* by Weimer and Hoyt. State clearly the tenets of both the ring theory and the sector theory of urban development. Write an essay on whether and how they can be combined in the analysis of contemporary city structure. Do the two theories contradict or do they supplement each other? In what respect do they contradict each other to the point of making integration impossible? In what respects can they be reconciled with each other?

country, with the more spectacular development occurring in the smaller urban and suburban communities adjoining our metropolitan centers." *1950 Census of Population.* Preliminary Counts. Series PC-3, No. 3. November 5. 1950.

2. *Application of the Ring Theory and the Sector Theory to Seattle.*
Consult the readings as recommended in problem 1, and also Calvin
F. Schmid's *Social Trends in Seattle.* First, study the materials offered in Calvin F. Schmid's publication in the light of the ring
theory. Second, study the same materials in the light of the sector
theory. Write your conclusions as to the usefulness of either theory
for your purpose.

Informal Survey of an Urban Fringe. This problem calls for repeated visits to the fringe of one of the larger cities in your state
or in one of your neighboring states.

Consider carefully what has been said in Chapter 4 about the
fringe of the modern city, about recent developments in that environment, about assertions pertaining to that environment, and
about speculations regarding future fringe development. Read the
books by Walter Firey and Solon T. Kimball, as quoted in footnotes
to Chapter 4. Look up further references offered in Chapter 4 which,
in part, may bear on the problem of the modern fringe. Then visit
the fringe of an actual city, and note as systematically as possible
your observations about prevailing land use patterns. Decide whether
your observations bear out or contradict any statements or speculations you have come across in your readings.

PART II

Urban Environment

CHAPTER 5

Ecological Units and Processes

THE ECOLOGICAL APPROACH

The Study of Urban Environment. We have seen how different urban land uses are geographically distributed in the modern city. We got a total view of the modern city, with its breakdown into areas serving industrial, commercial, residential, recreational, and other purposes. None of the discussed city areas, however, are as uniform as might be expected from our discussion.

Residential areas are not entirely residential, but interspersed with shopping districts and recreational areas. Industrial areas are not entirely industrial, but interspersed with workingmen's homes, taverns, occupational schools, gasoline stations, and eating places. We shall now explain the manner in which different types of urban construction, different land uses, and different types of people find their way to each other or separate themselves from each other.

The detailed study of urban environment avails itself of the "ecological approach." [1] This is a term borrowed from the natural sciences. The ecological approach to urban problems carries a valu-

---

[1] "Ecology has been defined as 'that phase of biology that considers plants and animals as they exist in nature, and studies their interdependence, and the relationship of each kind and individual to its environment.'" Robert E. Park, Ernest W. Burgess, and Roderick D. McKenzie, *The City*, Chapter III, "The Ecological Approach to the Study of the Human Community," Chicago: The University of Chicago Press, 1925. p. 63.

"In the absence of any precedent let us tentatively define human ecology as a study of the spatial and temporary relations of human beings as affected by the the selective, distributive, and accomodative forces of the environment. Human ecology is fundamentally interested in the effect of POSITION, in both time and space, upon human institutions and human behavior." *Op. cit.,* pp. 63-64.

117

able emphasis. It is committed to detached observation and registration of time and space relationships.

Urban ecology has been narrowed further by scientific convention. Ecological studies tend to limit themselves to the recording of phenomena or events that are easily demonstrated by means of graphical presentation. The field of urban ecology is conventionally delimited as much by a unique set of problems as by the use of unique techniques of investigation.

Administrative Spot Maps. The spot map, as an instrument for the presentation of the spatial distribution of social phenomena, can be used for administrative or analytic purposes.

In the administrative use of spot maps, the interest is generally limited to the presentation of one set of data. The spot map furnishes the means of making the spatial distribution of these data clearly visible. It shows their distribution, and thus facilitates administrative action and sound allocation of institutional services.

A few examples will make this clear. Any large city hospital staff is interested in knowing what area it serves. A spot map of past patients will give the answer and may assist in suggesting best possible location in case of either relocation or the construction of extension buildings. The parole and probation service of any large city cannot operate successfully without a residence spot map of parolees. The "beat" of the individual parole officer will have to be based upon the distribution of parolees.

A further development of this technique is the use of moving spot maps. These are spot maps continuously brought up to date to permit a close scrutiny of operations at any given time. A case in point is the large map at police headquarters equipped with movable gadgets to designate the location of traveling police cars. During World War II we saw movies of Air Force Headquarters, where a sizable staff was continuously engaged in spotting all incoming information on a colossal map that indicated the location of enemy bombers and fighter planes as well as the location of home forces.

Analytical Spot Maps. In scientific investigation, the spot map has a more complicated function. It is used with interest in the coincidence of different sets of data. Coincidence in space, for example of bad housing, poverty, delinquency, and suicide may be taken as a tentative indication for the existence of cause and effect relationships.

There is no analytical interest in isolated spot maps giving the distribution of a single datum. Nor is the spot map always the best means of establishing significant correlations. It should be used only where we are interested in spatial relationships, or where information about spatial coincidence is more easily available than information with different points of reference.[2]

The Ecological Slant. For the detailed study of urban environment, the spot map technique is invaluable. It shows how different social conditions overlap in one and the same area, thus inviting the consideration of more than one facet of any given environment, making it possible to think in terms of social configurations rather than single factors.

Ecological studies are said to be unconcerned with social "meaning."[3] They state what is, and leave the interpretation of accumulated data to other social scientists. Such a program is, of course, hard to live up to. The mere fact that certain data are selected for recording while others are ignored involves a value judgment. It directs the reader's focus of interest into desired channels. There is more to the ecological approach than its proclaimed minimum creed.

Plant Communities. In the study of plants, interesting information is lost if they are considered as individuals only. They exist together in patterns which do not occur by accident. The plant community, rather than the individual plant, is the object of study for the plant ecologist. He assures us that the interrelationships prominent in these plant communities are just as complex, and in their complexity just as worthwhile for study, as the communities of humans.[4]

---

[2] A discussion of the possibility of correlating mental disorder with categories of either space or time or with individual attributes will be found in H. Warren Dunham, "Social Psychiatry," *American Sociological Review*, Vol. 13, No. 2 (April, 1948). Note especially the section on "Ecological and Statistical Studies," pp. 18-190.

[3] "It was characteristic of these (early ecological) studies that they were not motivated by a central scientific problem or by any clearly-defined hypothesis. They represented simply an attempt 'to see the life of the community as a whole' in all its concreteness." Edward Shils, *The Present State of American Sociology.* Glencoe, Ill.: The Free Press, 1948, p. 8.

[4] "Plants do not ordinarily live alone like hermits but are growing along with other plants in communities that usually consist of many individuals. When an ecologist goes into a forest he does not see merely a number of trees, shrubs and herbaceous plants with no relations one to another except that they happen to be growing in close proximity. What he sees is a plant community

Plants, we learn, live together, and have to be studied, "in a state of social disjunctive symbiosis."[5] They are so closely interdependent that their community as a whole "may be considered as an organic entity" of its own. Plant life exists in layers of vegetation. The tallest plants have immediate access to the sunlight. In their shadow, other plants exist with less sun. They form the underbrush in our forests; and below the underbrush the grasses, the mosses, and the flowers lead an even more economical existence.[6]

Competitive adjustment occurs between the life requirements of different species. Some species do not fit into the arrangement and are eliminated from existence.

Animal Communities. Animal communities exist in similar relationships of interdependence. Carnivorous (meat-eating) animals are organized in food chains; each species may serve as the nutritional base for another. If one species dies out, others are bound to follow it into annihilation. Some animals destroy the insects that bother another species. If the decimation of certain animal populations ceases, they may outgrow their food supply and either emigrate or perish in starvation. The animal ecologist is concerned with the equilibrium that will permit the perpetuation of the community through mutual instinctive adaptation.

Ecological Equilibrium. This concern with the conditions of survival on the part of mutually interdependent individuals and species has been carried over into the study of urban environment. In the community of humans, to be sure, instinctive adaptation is replaced by folkways and culture. The urban ecologist starts with

---

which is just as simple and understandable but with its multitude of activities just as complex, just as inevitable in its structural make-up but with its succession of life problems just as intensely interesting as any city or other community dominated by the genus of bipeds to which we belong." W. B. McDougall, *Plant Ecology.* Philadelphia: Lea and Febiger, 1927, p. 206.

[5] "The individual plants that make up a plant community are living together in a state of social disjunctive symbiosis but they are so intimately associated that the community as a whole may be considered as an organic entity; that is, an individual organism." W. B. McDougall, *op. cit.,* p. 206. "Symbiosis" means "The living together in intimate association or even close union of two dissimilar organisms." *Webster's New Collegiate Dictionary.* Springfield, Mass.: G. & C. Merriam Co., 1949.

[6] For an elaborate comparison between plant, animal, and human societies, see H. G. Wells, Julian S. Huxley, and G. P. Wells, *The Science of Life.* New York: Doubleday, Doran & Company, Inc., 1931, Vol. II, Chapter V, "The Science of Ecology," pp. 961-1011.

the assumption that equilibrium is achieved in the urban environment by processes of automatic adjustment.[7]

A relatively stable equilibrium is considered to result from the struggle for survival on the part of individuals. Unless disturbed in its delicate internal balance, the equilibrium is expected to perpetuate itself. Like the plant or the animal ecologist, the human ecologist focuses attention upon conditions existing in the community as a whole rather than upon its component parts, the individual city dwellers.[8]

THE NATURAL AREA

Determining Conditions. Natural selection in the urban environment leads to the establishment of natural areas. The natural area is the product of ecological processes at work in the city environment.[9]

The "natural area" is, of course, "natural" only in a limited sense. Natural areas are configurations of construction, of people and activities which are drawn toward each other because they depend upon each other. The "natural area" is neither planned nor manipulated.

The single men's district in the American city forms such a natural area. In this environment we find cheap eating places to serve the needs of single men with limited means. There are flophouses and inexpensive hotels. Pawn shops lend assistance in case of sudden need for cash. Burlesque shows cater to the yearnings of an unmarried adult population, and in the barbershops we may find female attendants to satisfy the desire for fleeting female companion-

---

[7] "In contrast with the view of society which regards social institutions and the community itself as the mere instruments and tools of the individuals who compose it, is that which conceives society as resting upon biological adaptations." Robert E. Park and Ernest W. Burgess, *Introduction to the Science of Sociology.* Chicago: The University of Chicago Press, 1921, p. 162.

[8] For the ideological implications inherent in the concept of "equilibrium" in the social sciences, see Gunnar Myrdal, *An American Dilemma.* New York: Harper & Brothers, 1944, Vol. II, p. 1045-1057. A do-nothing policy suggests itself where a delicate "natural" equilibrium has established itself. The notion of an ecological equilibrium parallels the assumption of an economic equilibrium in classical economic theory where it furnishes the rationale for laissez-faire policies.

[9] For a first systematic and elaborate formulation of the concept, see Harvey W. Zorbaugh, "The Natural Areas of the City" in *The Urban Community.* Ernest W. Burgess, editor, Chicago: The University of Chicago Press, 1926, pp. 219-229.

ship. In this environment, we also find missions and innumerable taverns. This type of a natural area is duplicated in the same stereotyped manner in all major cities of the United States, from Seattle to New York.

This is equally true of communities of recent immigrants, the Little Sicilies, the Ghettos, the Chinatowns, and other ethnic neighborhoods. Still, present social expediency rather than human nature in general accounts for the repetitiveness of these patterns.

Other natural areas are related to specialized occupational activities, such as the department store section, providing facilities for customers as well as employees in a characteristic fashion. Others are related to facilities, grouped together in the downtown entertainment district, in the "satellite loop," or in the resort areas of the urban fringe.

Human nature cannot explain the tremendous differences observed in the urban environment. Human nature by itself is far too flexible.[10] It certainly makes possible the multitude of different environments in the modern city. It cannot, however, account for the specific differences.

Absence of Plan. Natural areas are "natural" only in that they are unplanned. The connotation is negative rather than affirmative. It refers to the absence of restrictions, regulations, and joint commitments in the clustering of urban real estate. The natural area is the outcome of individual action based on free choice.

This does not exclude the consideration of other propensities than those for money-making.[11] Free choice is based upon all values and desires which may induce man to build, to live, and to do business in one part of the city rather than another. It includes all motivations that make it desirable for residences as well as business establishments to either congregate or segregate.

Changeability. The natural area cannot be considered a constant,

---

[10] For early but still fundamentally correct statements about the "nature of human nature," see George H. Mead, *Mind, Self and Society.* Chicago: The University of Chicago Press, 1934, and Charles H. Cooley, *Human Nature and the Social Order.* New York: Charles Scribner's Sons, 1922.

[11] This position is not shared by Walter Firey. He discriminates between rational calculation as based upon the profit motive, and "values" as the foundation of preferences not based upon the profit motive. His viewpoint does not coincide with that of modern economic theory. See Walter Firey, *Land Use in Central Boston.* Cambridge: Harvard University Press, 1947. Consult Chapter I, "Introduction to the Problem," pp. 3-40.

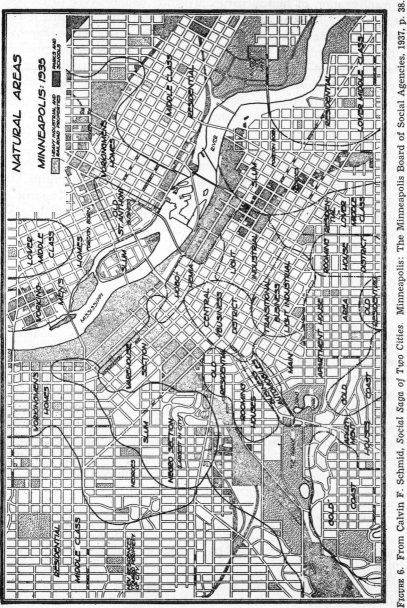

FIGURE 6. From Calvin F. Schmid, *Social Saga of Two Cities*. Minneapolis: The Minneapolis Board of Social Agencies, 1937. p. 38.

a manifestation of human nature which is bound never to change. It should not be considered an outrage against human nature, if and where these natural areas are tampered with in order to improve urban environment. The concept invites ideological judgment.[12] Such judgment enters into the discussion of urban problems when existing conditions are considered as based upon "human nature," and therefore beyond the range of improvement.

This is the point at which the analogy to plant and animal communities presents a danger. If natural areas are thought of as based upon eternal characteristics of human nature, if they are considered to be super-historical, if any attempt to change them is looked upon as a deviation from human nature and therefore detrimental to human well-being, then we are confronted with ideological assertions rather than empirical conclusions. "Natural" areas should be discussed with due regard to their historical setting.

Delineation. A difficult scientific problem is connected with the discovery, the objective definition, and the delineation of natural areas in the city environment. Criteria for the existence of natural areas have been sought in two different conditions.

Many authors have laid stress upon the criterion of internal homogeneity.[13] They have emphasized the circumstances that city dwellers tend to congregate with like-minded and similar people and institutions. Also, certain people and certain types of construction may be repelled by certain other people and other urban land uses. They will cluster by default, by not being admitted freely to other city areas than those already settled by their own kind.

Therefore, many investigators interested in the systematic description of natural areas have been on the lookout, primarily, for homogeneities. They have tried to establish the preponderance of similar land uses in any given city area. They have found statistical measures of the clustering ethnic groups.[14]

---

[12] For a critical analysis of the ecological approach to sociological problems, see M. A. Alihan, *Social Ecology*. New York: Columbia University Press, 1938.

[13] Statistical methods of area delineation are most easily applied to criteria of "homogeneity." See Margaret J. Hagood, "Statistical Methods for Delineation of Regions Applied to Data on Agriculture and Population." *Social Forces*, Vol. 21, No. 3 (March, 1943), pp. 287-297.

[14] See Eshref Shevsky and Marilyn Williams, *The Social Areas of Los Angeles*. Berkeley and Los Angeles: University of California Press, 1949, Chapter V, "Segregation," pp. 47-60. Other approaches to the measurement of degree of segregation are quoted in the above-mentioned source.

Thus the preponderance of commercial land uses defined the commercial areas, the central business district, and the so-called satellite-loops. The preponderance of workingmen's homes determined the spread of the workingmen's residential zone. Somewhere along the line of lowered frequencies, the borderline of the natural area was more or less arbitrarily established on a definite numerical basis.

Early in the discussion of natural areas, however, attention was also called to the co-existence in many city areas of highly divergent land uses and occupancy patterns. The very concept of "ecology," as a matter of fact, had called attention to interdependance relations between different types of people and different commercial as well as institutional establishments.[15]

The students' residential area was also found to be an area of concentration for middle aged landladies. Domestic servants were found to be concentrated in the upper class residential districts of the suburbs. One sociologist delineated the single men's district of a western city by designing a spot map that indicated the location of barber shops with female attendants. Another sociologist was able to indicate the limits of the crime district in Chicago by pointing, at the edges of the crime district, to the appearance of the first chain store. He explained the absence of chain stores in the crime district by referring to all-too-frequent hold-ups, which did not affect the local stores, the latter being considered part of the community and, therefore, inviolate.

These delineations of natural areas are based on intricate reasoning. They are not based on frequencies of the main characteristic of the area. They are based upon the presence of secondary attributes. Sometimes these secondary attributes are more easily observed and recorded.

Meaningful Relations. At this point, ecology becomes more than a matter of recording sociologically relevant data without reference to their sociological "meaning." Through informal empirical observation, the sociologist encounters a number of obvious interdependence relationships that are easily understood in their "meaning." He is then, of course, committed to checking statistically upon the

---

[15] "These areas of selection and function may comprise many subformations or associations which become part of the organic structure of the district or of the community as a whole." Roderick D. McKenzie, "The Ecological Approach to the Study of the Human Community," in Robert E. Park, Ernest W. Burgess, and Roderick D. McKenzie, *op. cit.,* p. 77.

regularity of the interrelationship. He must make sure that he is not misled in his hypothetical understanding of the situation.

Unfortunately, it is much more difficult to handle statistically a configuration of attributes than a single attribute by itself. Under the circumstances, rigorous statistical research has been limited to the study of natural areas on the basis of internal homogeneties. The definition of natural areas that points to interdependence relationships, and which attempts to account for the co-existence in the same natural area of highly divergent attributes, has had to confine its usefulness to informal and exploratory research.[16]

THE NEIGHBORHOOD

Neighboring. Unlike the natural area, the city neighborhood can be either planned or unplanned. A neighborhood exists where neighboring occurs. Neighboring is a matter of repeated face-to-face contacts and close personal relations within a contiguous city area. Such neighborhood contacts are generally related to more than one single purpose and they tend to recur at more or less regular intervals in the course of daily living.

Some urban neighborhoods have been planned.[17] Other urban areas have been laid out to function as neighborhoods, but in actual fact have failed to do so. The latter are not true neighborhoods.

We need more information about social conditions that either favor or impede active neighboring processes. As yet, no definitive knowledge has been accumulated on this subject. Neighboring is apt to coincide with a process of internal socialization of a given city area. From an anonymous crowd of city dwellers who happen to make their residence in the area more or less accidentally, the residents mold themselves into a structured social group with a focus of interest on shared activities, with the formation of informal leader-and-follower relationships in the pursuit of common interests,

---

[16] Theoretical problems related to the definition of the natural area and methodological problems related to its delineation are discussed in Paul Hatt, "The Concept of Natural Area, *The American Sociological Review*, Vol. 11, No. 4 (August, 1946), pp. 423-427, and Svend Riemer, "Theoretical Aspects of Regionalism," *Social Forces*, Vol. 21, No. 3, pp. 275-280.

[17] See Chapter 17.

and with the development of some proud "we" feeling, an identification with other residents.[18]

Some groups of city dwellers are more likely than others to participate in the neighboring process. Young people are more likely to become good neighbors than old people. New arrivals to the city are more likely to establish informal social contacts within their residential environment than are families that have lived for years in another part of the city and have established friendships there and in other residential areas. Young and recently married couples may be eager to establish a new circle of friends and acquaintances, to sever relations established during their previous lives as isolated individuals and to step into new social contacts as a family unit.[19]

Community of Interests. Community of interests furnishes a more permanent basis for neighboring activities, and holds the ethnic groups in our large cities closely tied together. Immigrants from the same country are held together by adherence to the same folk festivals, celebrations, and religious services. All members of the ethnic group meet the problems of adjustment to the ways of the modern American city in more or less the same manner.[20] The sharing of problems invites close communication; it invites gossip and the exchange of gripes; it invites mutual help and the exchange of advice on how to meet typical emergency situations.

Community of interest exists also among young married couples who are raising infants or young children of about the same age. In the suburban fringe of low- or medium-cost homes, we frequently find neighborhoods with an unusual degree of internal cohesion

---

[18] "There is evidence . . . that the face-to-face condition is a normal feature of the environment of society and that man tends to degenerate when it is missing." Clarence Arthur Perry, *Housing for the Machine Age.* New York: Russell Sage Foundation, 1939, p. 215. The author's bold assertion is not based upon empirical fact.

[19] The positive experiences with veterans' neighborhoods may be due to both new arrival and community of interest. See Svend Riemer, "Trailer Communities on a University Campus, *The Journal of Land and Public Utility Economics,* Vol. XXIII, No. 1 (February, 1947), pp. 81-83.

[20] For the similarity of adjustment problems faced in most immigrant communities, see William Foote Whyte, *Street Corner Society.* Chicago: The University of Chicago Press, 1943; Walter Firey, *op. cit.,* Chapter V, "The Influence of Localized Social Solidarity Upon Land Use. The North End," pp. 170-225. Both publications deal, from slightly different viewpoints, with the Italian immigrant community.

due to the fact that the resident families meet the same vital problem of child care and child raising.

Uncertainty about ways to meet a new problem pulls people together. In crises and emergency situations, they find reassurance in close neighborly contact. As the problem resolves itself, as the children grow into school and high school age, neighborhood contacts are apt to lose intensity. Neighboring is related to the lives of the people rather than to any features of construction, layout, and location. The urban neighborhood is of the social rather than the physical dimension.[21]

Modern urban neighborhoods tend to be centered around leisure-time activities. Such bonds are not nearly as strong as those of vital problems shared.[22] Still, most contemporary planning efforts pertain to the private and recreational life of the neighborhood. In the large audience hall of the community center, on playgrounds, in workshops and clubrooms, the occupants of a residential neighborhood congregate in the pursuit of leisure-time activities that are designed to hold an interest for all.

THE SERVICE AREA

Economic Foundation. The natural area, we have seen, is based upon social homogeneities and interdependence relations which establish themselves in a more or less clearly delineated city area. The existence of an urban neighborhood is predicated upon active neighboring activities, in a more or less clearly delineated city area. Another unit of urban environment is the service area dependent upon the service radius of either economic enterprise or public service institutions such as libraries, hospitals, fire stations, schools,

---

[21] In the small urban community, neighboring is more likely to be related to shared problems and economic relations, while it is most often limited, in the large city, to leisure time activities. See Svend Riemer, "Hidden Dimensions of Neighborhood Planning," *Journal of Land Economics,* Vol. XXVI, No. 2 (May, 1950), pp. 197-201.

[22] Interesting information about the history of urban neighboring is contained in the following publication, albeit influenced by Nazi ideology: Ernst Lehmann, *Volksgemeinschaft aus Nachbarschaften.* Berlin: Noebe & Co. K.-G. Verlagsbuchhandlung, 1944. See particularly Chapter III, "Geschichtliches." On pages 46-49, the author deals with "Brunnenschaften," organizations for the upkeep and administration of local water supplies which led to the development of friendly social relations.

and seats of municipal government. The service area does not pre-empt completely a given territory.[23]

Service areas are easily ascertained on the basis of enrollments, memberships, purchases, records of treatments, accidents, and so forth. Therefore, the service area has more frequently been delineated than other ecological units in the city environment. Another reason is the importance of such information for the operation of these same services.[24]

The individual store and the business district are concerned with the residential location of their customers. Sales campaigns will depend upon the distribution of customers and the means of communication by which they can best be reached. There is particular interest in the marginal area contested by nearby competition.[25]

Public institutions are duty-bound to provide equitable service on a community-wide basis. Where do the children go to school who do not reside within a radius of one mile or two from the nearest elementary school? From what area are the patients of a hospital recruited? Should the local library establish another annex somewhere at a five-mile distance, where residents are not reached by convenient services? Are there outdoor playgrounds for all children in the city, available within easy walking distance? The answer to such questions will have to be given on the basis of city-wide surveys. The spot map designed for administrative purposes will be an easy means of discovering loopholes in the services rendered.

INVASION AND SUCCESSION

Environmental Change. Neither natural areas nor neighborhoods nor service areas are stable units in the urban environment. They are based on social relationships rather than permanent construction.

---

[23] We are dealing here with "ideal types." As far as the service areas are concerned, however, the thinning out of customers and clients toward the periphery of the area is so much an expected phenomenon that even the conception of the ideal type has to concede that no contiguous area is fully pre-empted by it.

[24] See the discussion of "Administrative Spot Maps," p. 118.

[25] The economic problems related to the establishment and extension of a commercial shopping area are discussed in Robert M. Lillibridge, "Shopping Centers in Urban Redevelopment," *Journal of Land Economics*, Vol. XXIV, No. 2 (May, 1948), pp. 137-160. The attached bibliography will be useful for further exploration of the problem.

Consequently, they are subject to change in close connection with social needs arising in the environment.

Ethnic groups might lose internal cohesion as their members advance in their adjustment to the modern American city. Competition might interfere with the service area of the local business district. Better medical services elsewhere may reduce the number of patients seeking admittance to the local hospital. The delicate equilibrium of social interdependence in any natural area may be disturbed by social change.

The hobo culture flourishing in the single men's district of the 1930's perished with the replacement of migratory agricultural labor by agricultural machinery and the employment of foreign seasonal labor. Thus, the single men's district in our Midwestern and Western cities changed function and appearance. Dormitory construction on our university campuses leads to a reduction and dilapidation of the area of rented rooms within easy walking distance of the halls of learning.

Ecological units are in a continuous state of flux. They may disappear, change their function, and adjust to new circumstances. New social needs in the urban environment may lead to the formation of new ecological units.

Real estate developments, providing so many separate dwelling units, might turn into neighborhoods teeming with activity and held together by bonds of mutual loyalty. Commercial services will continuously be extended into unexploited residential areas. New schools are built in the suburbs to take care of new generations of elementary school children. Whether the modern city expands or shrinks; whether the urban fabric settles with a relatively stable population that grows only in age, exposed to either economic failure or success; the urban environment cannot remain static.

Centrifugal Trends. In the course of the 19th century our cities were growing at a rapid pace. Ecological change was dominated by a continuous push of central land uses to the periphery. Two aspects of this process of change caught the eye of the social scientist:

1. Land uses that commanded superior purchasing power tended to replace economically less powerful land uses.[26]

---

26 "In general the basis of the distribution of all business utilities is purely economic, land going to the highest bidder and the highest bidder being the one who can make the land earn the largest amount."

2. Less desirable land uses tended to replace more desirable land uses.[27]

Where different land uses are attracted to the same site, the economically more powerful ones will win out. The pull toward advantages of site favors the highest bidder.

The push away from city nuisances, on the other hand, leaves these nuisances in shunned isolation. This is particularly true with regard to residential housing. The more desirable living quarters move away in all directions.

Residential land uses are sensitive both to the traction from desirable sites and to the repulsion from nuisances connected with urban congestion and undesirable associations with the housing of lower status groups. Commercial and industrial land uses are more exclusively subject to pull toward locations desirable for their purposes. They are more or less immune to status associations with the environment.

Superior purchasing power always has the last word in competition for desirable real estate. Under special circumstances, however, the desirability for residential land uses is lowered through the presence of undesirable patterns of occupancy.

Push from the Center. Thus, inducements to change of residential occupancy were generally received from the direction of the city center. Such change was by no means confined to the slums surrounding the business district in a belt-like formation. Status groups of ever increasing rank were exposed to pressures which originated in the slum environment but which extended secondary

---

"The basis, of residence values is social and not economic — even though the land goes to the highest bidder — the rich selecting the locations which please them, those of moderate means living as near by as possible, and so on down the scale of wealth, the poorest workmen taking the final leavings, either adjacent to such nuisances as factories, railroads, docks, etc., or far out of the city." Richard M. Hurd, *Principles of City Land Values.* New York: The Record and Guide, 1903, pp. 77-78.

[27] About the repellent and pre-empting effect of nuisances, see Arthur W. Weimer and Homer Hoyt, *Principles of Urban Real Estate.* New York: The Ronald Press Company, 1948, pp. 132-33.

Consider also Walter Firey's discussion of the rurban fringe, where he discovered the "tendencies for residences to gravitate to the lowest use in terms of class status."

Walter Firey, "Ecological Considerations in Planning for Rurban Fringes. *American Sociological Review,* Vol. 11, No. 4 (August, 1946), p. 413.

effects over the entire orbit of the city environment. These pressures extending from the city center called forth the formation of city gradients, that is, an arrangement of land uses in a concentric pattern with ever improving residential conditions at increasing distances from the center and in approach to the periphery of the urban settlement.

Only the highest status groups were able to build for their own residential needs. When they moved, they left secondary homes for purchase or rental to be taken over by lower status groups, who in turn left their own homes to those next in line, and so forth.

The pull toward the periphery was accompanied by a push from the city center. The pressure from the city center impressed itself on all city dwellers as a painful experience. In all residential areas, lower status groups tended to infiltrate and initiate the exodus of those financially best able to leave and to compete for more valuable housing further removed from the city center.

To escape identification with lower prestige groups, city dwellers found themselves continuously on the move. Any area in the residential sections of the modern city was subject to dynamic change. Even if the upper strata of urban society might have wanted to remain longer in any given environment before turning to greener pastures, they were not allowed to do so because of pressures exerted from the inner city. What happened within the individual residential area of the city has been described in terms of "invasion" and "succession."[28]

Reaction to Invasion. Intensive studies are available describing the manner in which a residential area reacts when first invaded by occupants previously excluded from making their homes in it.[29]

To begin with, the invaders are held back by financial means. Rentals are kept sufficiently high to discourage the invasion of status groups considered inferior by public opinion. Pressures originating in the center of the city, however, threaten the existing

[28] Burgess first called attention to the need for investigations of what he called "Expansion As a Process." Robert E. Park, Ernest W. Burgess, and Roderick D. McKenzie, *op. cit.*, pp. 50-53.

Since then it has become customary to talk about "invasion" and "succession" rather than "expansion."

[29] See Ernest W. Burgess, "Residential Segregation in American Cities, *The Annals* of the American Academy of Political and Social Sciences, Vol. 140, No. 229 (November, 1928), pp. 105-115.

equilibrium. As the area is invaded by residents spilling over from residential sections further downtown, some of its most well-to-do residents will try to rent or buy property in a more outlying area to which — for economical reasons — they did not seek access earlier.

After invasion has taken place in a few isolated instances the invaded residential area will be alerted to the fact that its homogeneity is endangered. If lower status groups are permitted to move in, the entire residential area may soon lose in status. If economic self-defense of the area — in terms of high rentals and land values — proves inefficient as a means of keeping the intruders out, other than economic means have been resorted to in attempts to stem the tide of invasion and area change.

These noneconomic means may range all the way from giving the newcomers the cold shoulder, from embarrassing them and letting them understand that they are not welcome, to outright violence. Bombs may be thrown to discourage the newcomers, or they may find themselves the target of pot-shots smashing their windows under cover of darkness. The children of these newcomers will not easily be accepted by established playgroups in the new residential environment.

Restrictive covenants may bind owners not to rent or sell to groups of city dwellers who through income, ethnic, or "racial" affiliation are considered of lower social status than the group presently in possession or residence. Although these restrictive covenants will no longer stand up in court, their binding force is sufficiently based on custom to serve as a real obstacle in the process of invasion and succession.

Violence is apt to occur at the height of conflict. It occurs when some owners have yielded to pressure and started to sell. It will not always occur; but such violence, stimulated by racial and other prejudices, occurred frequently during the course of rapid city expansion.

In recent years, social scientists have begun to notice that the change of occupancy from higher to lower status groups does not necessarily cause a decline of income. By skillful remodeling and adaptation, available residential real estate can be broken up into a larger number of smaller dwelling units yielding just as high or even higher total rental income than before. The decrease of yield

appears as a temporary phenomenon lasting only for the duration
of the processes of invasion and succession.

CLUSTERING, SEGREGATION AND CONCENTRATION

Refuge in Homogeneity. The ecological processes of clustering
and segregation are closely related to those of invasion and succession. Were it not for a tendency of the same types of people
to cluster their residences close to each other and to withdraw from
identification with other types of people, the entire process of urban
expansion and residential change might flow more smoothly.

The tendency toward segregation was encouraged by the large-
scale immigration to our urban centers. Immigrant groups, in their
early stages of adjustment to the American way of life, sought
shelter in a residential environment which surrounded them with
people of similar background.

The primary purpose of clustering was the desire for close neighborly relations between like-minded people. It had secondary effects
of considerable consequence. Residential location became closely
associated with ethnic affiliation and gained symbolic significance.
Ethnic affiliation carried very definite status associations in the
modern American city. By and large, recent immigrants were considered to be of lower status than earlier arrivals.[30]

In second, third, and following generations of immigrants, the
pattern of residential location becomes more diffused. This process
coincides with the achievement of economic success. The successful
members of the ethnic group tend to leave the shelter of a Little
Sicily, a Ghetto, or a Greek neighborhood. They become able
to get along by themselves. At this point, their social status may
begin to suffer from close residential association with an immigrant
group which, by and large, is characterized by more limited
economic means.

. *Segregation by Income.* The symbolic significance of residential
location has extended to environments that differ in economic rather
than ethnic status. Status-consciousness on the part of the city
dweller supports this tendency. Home ownership is, after all, one
of the most conspicuous forms of conspicuous consumption.[31]

The anonymity of urban existence — where family history re-

---

[30] See p. 143, footnote 11.
[31] For conspicuous consumption, see 275 ff.

mains a secret and where bank accounts are neither open to inspection nor made public by way of gossip — encourages patterns of conspicuous consumption. For family status, residential location must be considered the most revealing index. The "address" of the city dweller tells the initiated a great deal about his financial achievement. Residential location has become a means of placing a family on the ladder of social advancement.

Thus the trend toward segregation is continuously re-enforced in the competitive urban environment. It is used defensively as well as affirmatively as a means of displaying achievement. Lower status groups will remain confined to their own quarters; in a way, they may even enjoy their concentrated clusterings of homogeneous housing and occupancy patterns as a defense against being snobbed in their private lives. Other members of the lower income groups will try to push forward into residential sections occupied by higher status groups, thereby recognizing and re-enforcing existing status differentials.

SELECTED READINGS

1. Robert E. Park, Ernest W. Burgess, and Roderick D. McKenzie, *The City*. Chicago: University of Chicago Press, 1925, pp. 1-160.

2. Edward Shils, *The Present State of American Sociology*. Glencoe, Ill.: The Free Press, 1948, "Urban Sociology," pp. 7-14.

3. Harvey W. Zorbaugh, "The Natural Areas of the City" in Ernest W. Burgess, editor, *The Urban Community*. Chicago: The University of Chicago Press, 1926, pp. 219-229.

4. Arthur M. Weimer and Homer Hoyt, *Principles of Urban Real Estate*. New York: Ronald Press Company, 1948, pp.3-221.

5. Walter Firey, *Land Use in Central Boston*. Cambridge: Harvard University Press, 1947, pp. 3-340.

PROBLEMS

1. *Shopping Areas and Neighborhood Formation.* Your problem is to find out whether a shopping district in your community has an integrating or distintegrating influence upon the establishment of social contacts. You want to know whether a business street serves to get the people living on both sides of it more closely together, or whether it serves as a demarcation line beyond which social contacts are likely to be disrupted.

Part of your task is to translate this general problem into specific behavior or attitudes to be ascertained from the people concerned. You may well proceed on the basis of informal interviewing. Conclusive research is beyond the scope of your class contribution. But, as the result of informal interviewing, you may be able to work out and to present for criticism by your instructor a questionnaire or a schedule to cope with the above-mentioned problem in a more conclusive manner.

Store managers may reveal information about the distribution of their customers. Residents may reveal their attitudes, their contacts, and specific institutional relationships with residents beyond the commercial development.

2. *Conservative Conclusions from the "Organism" Analogy.* The ecological approach to problems of urban environment makes ample use of analogies or organic matter, as evidenced by such terms as "natural area," "equilibrium of interdependance," and so forth. Frequently, the conclusion suggests itself that an intricate natural balance ought not to be disturbed by rational improvements desirable for specific reasons but undesirable because of the havoc raised with neglected aspects of the problem situation.

Read Chapter 5 carefully with this problem in mind. Consult the literature quoted as it bears upon your problem. You will find M. A. Alihan's *Social Ecology*, a critical study, particularly valuable.

Then, indicate passages in our urban ecological literature which reveal a bias against change of existing conditions. Write an essay about the extent to which ideological assertions have or have not sneaked into our literature on the basis of the "organism" analogy.

3. *Stages of Invasion and Succession.* The process of invasion and succession has been broken down by different authors into three, four, or five phases. Consult Noel P. Gist and L. A. Halbert, *Urban Society*. New York: Thomas Y. Crowell, 1948, pp. 152-159, and the literature quoted there for documentation. Draw a conceptual sketch synchronizing the various phases. Develop a scheme of your own that incorporates in chronological order all phenomena of "invasion and succession" about which you have gained information. Break up — if it is warranted — major phases into minor subcategories. Write an essay comparing the relative analytical value of different classifications.

CHAPTER 6

The Slum and Its People

THE SLUM AS AN OBJECT OF REFORM

Early Attitudes. At the beginning of urban reform was the slum.[1] In the American city of the 19th century, slum conditions were experienced as a blot of shame by the otherwise prospering urban community. During the earlier phases of the industrialization process and accompanying city growth, the tide of misery in the urban slum environment was stemmed exclusively by means of charity. As described by Charles Dickens, the wealthier members of urban society carried soup, food, clothes, and Christmas presents to their unfortunate neighbors.

Gradually, some understanding developed of the economic mechanism that placed the curse of unemployment recurrently upon large segments of the urban population. The Poor Laws of the earlier 19th century represent legislative attempts to cope with the problem of economic insecurity. The community accepted responsibility for large-scale and epidemic poverty among the urban masses.[2]

With better understanding of the causes of poverty, the well-to-do city dweller could not assuage his conscience any longer by reference to divine predestination. Temporarily, economic theory and social philosophy tried to place the blame for poverty, starvation,

---

[1] See J. L. Hammond and Barbara Hammond, *The Bleak Age*. New York: Penguin Books, 1947, Chapter V, "The State of the Towns," pp. 52-74.

[2] *Ibid.*, Chapter VII, "The New Poor Law," pp. 91-115.

disease, and unhygienic living conditions upon the shoulders of the individuals so afflicted.[3] Assuming equal opportunities for economic and social advancement, the suspicion of idleness and laziness was carried to the threshold of the miserable homes of indigent city dwellers.

Contemporary Attitudes. Our thinking about the causes of urban slum formation has not developed very rapidly. Ministers, students of society, reformers, and philanthropists are found among the pioneers of new thought. Those holding vested interests in the status quo, on the other hand, remain unwilling to take concerted action to alleviate the misery of the slum dweller. Different interpretations of the urban slum are found side by side in the contemporary scene. There are those who consider the urban slum as (1) a punishment of God, (2) the result of neglected individual responsibilities, and (3) a community responsibility, to be met by the concerted efforts of all city dwellers, not by the slum dwellers alone.

In controversies about the rehabilitation of urban slums, these different viewpoints find themselves engaged in a fierce ideological and political struggle. Conservative opinion objects to spending the taxpayer's money on slum rehabilitation projects. From this viewpoint, the slum dwellers are challenged to extricate themselves by their own means from their predicament. More liberal opinion emphasizes the unequal opportunities for economic advancement in our society and seeks community assistance in giving the slum dweller a fair deal.

The urban slum is one of the effects of industrialization and mass unemployment. For this reason, the urban community as such is not alone responsible for slum-grown misery and famine, for death on the sick-bed, and moral depravity. These conditions are part of our industrialized society, although their most extreme repercussions are felt in the modern city environment. The modern city functions as a climax area for the damages of modern industrialization.

IMMIGRANTS TO THE SLUM

An Area of Social Transition. As a "natural area" even the slum serves important purposes in our urban communities. Lest we re-

---

[3] For the ideological implications of economic theory, see Adolf Loewe, *Economics and Sociology.* London: George Allen & Unwin, Ltd., 1935, Chapter V, "The Sociological Factor in Modern Economic Theory," pp. 74-101.

main satisfied with the elimination of the slums as a blatant symptom of more deep-seated social disorder, we have to form a clear conception of the tasks which in the past, have been fulfilled by the slum environment.[4]

The urban slum has always been a two-way station of social transition. It has harbored both those on the way up and those on the way down. The slum has furnished temporary shelter for new arrivals to the city. It also has received those members of the urban community who have lost their economic and social foothold in more elevated strata of urban society. The two-fold character of the slum's social function has not always been recognized.

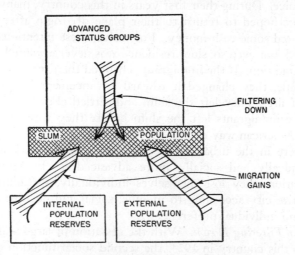

FIGURE 7. The Slum's Population Resources.

New Arrivals to the City. In the early days of modern city growth, the slum environment was dominated by the task of providing a domicile for newcomers to the city. The slum provided cheap housing for single men and impecunious families. Such housing was often considered mere temporary shelter, to be abandoned for better

---

[4] Compare Merton's interest in "social structures (which) exert a definite pressure upon certain persons in the society to engage in nonconformist rather than conformist conduct." Robert K. Merton, *Social Theory and Social Structure.* Glencoe, Ill.: The Free Press, 1949, pp. 125-126. Study the functional approach applied to immigrant subcultures in this country in the same source, "Social Structure and Anomie," pp. 125-149.

quarters in the course of time and with the achievement of moderate financial success.

This function of the modern city slum was retained throughout the 19th century, through the recurrent arrival of immigrants in the urban settlements of this country. Temporarily, the slum became the seat of entire immigrant communities, as described by Upton Sinclair in "The Jungle," and analyzed by W. I. Thomas and Florian Znaniecki in their study of *The Polish Peasant in Europe and America.*[5]

The slum quarters of these immigrants were intended for temporary occupancy only. Slum residence was a matter of emergency, not choice. During their first years in this country, many of the immigrants hoped to return to their place of origin after having accumulated some cash money. For many, these intentions were later changed, but even so, slum residence was never accepted as a permanent condition. If the immigrants changed their intention of returning home, they changed it toward advancement in the American way of life. They left the slum and settled elsewhere in the city.[6]

If the immigrants left the slum before they were quite adjusted to the American way of life, they moved out in clusters, establishing elsewhere in the urban fabric secondary ethnic settlements on an economically and socially more advanced level. After complete assimilation, they lost themselves individually, spreading out over the entire city according to income, social and occupational affiliation, and individual preferences.

Social Filtering Down. With the cessation of large scale immigration to this country in 1924, the second social function of the slum environment gained in relative importance. The German Club, the Polish Mission House, and the Swedish Station of the Salvation Army may still stand as reminders of a different past. Yet, with few

---

5 Upton Sinclair, *The Jungle*. New York: Moffat, Ward & Co., 1905.

William I. Thomas and Florian Znaniecki, *The Polish Peasant in Europe and America*. New York: Alfred A. Knopf, Inc., 1918, Part III, "Organization and Disorganization in America," pp. 1467-1827.

6 "The slum is a residual area whose occupants live there because they have to rather than because they have voluntarily chosen to. . . . Inferentially such families, once they acquire sufficient means, will move to more desirable districts." Walter Firey, *Land Use in Central Boston*. Cambridge: Harvard University Press, 1947, p. 174. The author, by the way, goes on to show that slum residence is often retained on a voluntary basis, due to "Localized Social Solidarity."

exceptions such as those of the Puerto Rican immigration to New York City, the modern city slum has changed both face and function. It is not primarily a way station to success anymore. It has more and more become a receptacle for the driftwood of urban failure.

Types of Immigrants. Of immigrants from abroad, the present slum harbors two categories: (1) the arrivals from relatively recent waves of immigration from southeastern Europe, Asia Minor, and East Asia; and (2) the remnants of preceding waves of immigration that have not attained successful adjustment to the American way of life, either financially or culturally.

More remnants are left, needless to say, from immigrations of more recent date. The Greeks, Syrians, and Assyrians are still clustered in close-knit neighborhoods in the slum environment. So are the Chinese. More Italians will be found to linger within the confines of the slum area than Swedes or Germans. There are enough Italians left to establish the Little Sicilies in most of our large cities. The Ghetto also remains as a relatively self-sufficient community in the slum.[7]

The earlier waves of immigration, however, have not remained intact in the slum environment. They have suffered a process of drainage and lost valuable members of their communities. They may have established satellite ethnic communities outside the slums by a process of leap-frogging into more peripheral residential location. Some of these immigrants and their offspring may have remained in the area of first settlement through cultural ties rather than financial inability to rent better quarters.

As the wealth of the immigrant community increases to a level of moderate comfort, some of its members may attempt to purchase and improve residential real estate in the slum environment. Older members of the immigrant community may decide to stay where they first found shelter in the American city. Instead of moving out to a middle class residential neighborhood, they may use their

---

[7] Immigrant communities in the slum environment have been given elaborate descriptive treatment in the following sources:

Walter Firey, *op. cit.*, Chapter V, "The Influence of Localized Social Solidarity Upon Land Use: The North End," pp. 170-225.

William Foote Whyte, *Street Corner Socity*. Chicago: The University of Chicago Press, 1943.

Louis Wirth, *The Ghetto*. Chicago: The University of Chicago Press, 1929.

financial means to acquire property within the confines of a neigh-
borhoood they are familiar with.[8]

They invest in remodeling residential construction. As landlords
or store owners, they form a dwindling upper social stratum in the
slum environment. Through conversion, they provide housing for
the impecunious members of their own ethnic group. As his own
ethnic group loses itself increasingly in the wider urban community,
the immigrant landlord or store owner may cater to the needs of
other populations in the slum environment. The Italian landord
may start renting to negroes; the Jewish grocer may cultivate an
Italian clientele.

Toward the end of this process, early immigrants will stay in the
slum only on an individualized basis. Some may remain in the slum
only during working hours, with their private homes pushed further
out into the urban periphery. Others remain because of childhood
memories, actual cultural ties within the immigrant community
having become increasingly meaningless due to the dispersal of the
immigrant group. Others return to the immigrant slum during their
hours of leisure.

Sooner or later, the social ties between isolated remnants of a
previously well-established ethnic group and its straying members
are cut off. Only the memorials of once important public buildings — churches, community centers, missions, schools, and so forth
— testify to earlier occupancy patterns.

In-migrants to the Slum

Arrivals from Rural U.S.A. When immigration slowed down
it was replaced by migrations to the city from rural sections of the
United States. Such in-migrations were particularly attracted at
times of heavy demands for manpower, at periods of industrial
expansion due to either economic prosperity or war.

Farming in the 20th century may not provide living conditions
comparable to those connected with urban occupations, but neither
does it encourage mass migrations toward the industrial city from all
rural sections of this country. At the present time, the lure of the
city forms a persistent challenge mainly to highly underprivileged

---

[8] "Italians, more than most immigrant nationalities, attach a great deal of
significance to the ownership of real estate." Walter Firey, *op. cit.*, p. 214.

groups of farm labor, such as Negro farm laborers and tenant farmers in the South.

To get a first foothold in the city environment, many of these in-migrants have to remain satisfied temporarily with the lowest possible standards of living. They drift in masses toward the slum and settle in living quarters of minimum rentals. Their gainful employment is predominantly in the heavy industries where they are more or less limited to the performance of unskilled labor.

All over the country, farm and small town populations are drained of talented and ambitious youth. They come to the city to rise educationally and in social status. These people do not tend to drift into the slum environment. Their in-migration is based upon individualized decision, and it spreads more or less evenly over the entire orbit of the modern city.[9]

Prejudice and Slum Residence. Due to race prejudice, most of the recent in-migrants to the urban slum are — if they belong to a racial minority group — retained within the slum environment even after having made an economic adjustment through which they could afford better housing conditions located closer to the urban periphery. The problem of recent urban in-migration and the problem of race prejudice are closely intertwined.[10]

The lower the status of an urban minority group, the more closely do its members tend to keep their residential housing concentrated within contiguous areas.[11] Many in-migrants cursed with the disadvantage of minority status are unable to disperse over the rest of the city area. They do not cluster here voluntarily because they have a great deal in common with each other. Many have nothing in common but the stigma placed upon them all by prejudice.

---

[9] See Noel P. Gist and Carroll D. Clark, "Intelligence as a Selective Factor in Rural-Urban Migrations," *The American Journal of Sociology*, Vol. XLIV, No. 1 (July, 1938), pp. 36-58; also W. Parker Mauldin, "Selective Migration from Small Towns," *American Sociological Review*, Vol. 5, No. 5, pp. 748-758.

[10] For the location of the Black Belt in Chicago and housing conditions in that area, see St. Clair Drake and Horace Cayton, *Black Metropolis. A Study of Negro Life in a Northern City.* New York: Harcourt, Brace and Company, 1945, Chapter 8, "The Black Ghetto," pp. 174-213.

[11] "(It was pointed out earlier that) isolation of groups is differentially related to social rank, and (that) the five most isolated groups are largely concentrated in in the lowest level." Eshref Shevsky and Marilyn Williams, *The Social Areas of Los Angeles.* Berkeley and Los Angeles: University of California Press, 1949, p. 57.

Under such circumstances, the entire ethnic group tends to cluster wherever the average income of the members of the group makes residential location most suitable. Predominantly limited to unskilled labor positions, recent Negro in-migration has terminated in and around the urban slum.

Earlier immigrants stayed together because they wanted to, because they appreciated the shelter of the ethnic group while undergoing a process of acculturation to the American scene. Recent in-migrants are more likely to stay together because there is no other place for them to go.

Race prejudice keeps most of these in-migrants together even after they have become differentiated with regard to occupation, income, and status. Social stratification may become quite pronounced within the confines of such minority groups.[12] At times, there are attempts at leap-frogging on the part of minority groups.[13] They are vigorously opposed, however, in such attempts to establish secondary settlements closer to the periphery of the city.

The well-to-do members of the Negro community or the Mexican settlement try to forge ahead and to establish themselves wherever they may find a loophole in the otherwise restricted residential areas of the urban middle classes. Such opportunities are limited due to the defensive attitude of the rest of the urban community. Consequently, we observe a tendency of the minority group as a whole to strain against its borderlines. Retaining contact with the major settlement of the minority group, individual members slowly and gradually send out spearheads of residential occupancy penetrating the urban fabric outward into borderline districts designating higher social status. The population center, however, remains in or close to the slum.

Overcrowding. Due to prejudicial restrictions, population densities reach their highest degree in that urban environment occupied by recent in-migrants of low racial status. The Negro communities in our large metropolitan centers are cracking at the seams. The

---

[12] For class differentiations within the Negro community, see St. Clair Drake and Horace R. Cayton, *op. cit.*, Chapters 19-22, pp. 526-715; also Allison Davis, Burleigh B. Gardner, and Mary R. Gardner, *Deep South*. Chicago: The University of Chicago Press, 1941, Chapter X, "The Class System of the Colored Caste," pp. 228-251.

[13] See William K. Brussat, "Incidental Findings on Urban Invasion," *American Sociological Review*, Vol. 16, No. 1 (February, 1951), pp. 94-96.

housing shortage after World War II impinged upon them severely.[14]

For the extension of living quarters these immigrants are dependent upon homebuilding activities of such generous scope that the residents surrounding the contiguous ethnic settlement find it possible to withdraw. Indirect effects of new building activities have to be awaited before the population pressure in these areas can be relieved. Adjacent slum dwellers are not likely to withdraw directly to new real estate developments at the urban periphery. Most of them can only hope to occupy vacated housing of remote vintage located nearby. Thus, a succession of movements to the outer rings of urban settlement has to occur before the Negro settlement has a chance to expand without danger of serious conflict.

In the meantime, additional housing is provided in the "Black Belt" by progressive conversions of available shelter. This process is accompanied by ever intensified crowding inacceptable in any other area of the city. In the course of this process the individual dwelling unit is cut down to the proverbial "kitchenette." [15]

SOCIAL FILTERING-DOWN TO THE SLUM

Contrasts. The slum is an environment of contrast. In addition to the new arrivals in the city, it harbors many citizens of long standing. In addition to those who seek a temporary stopover in the slum while gaining a foothold in the city economically, there are those who find in the urban slum the termination of a faltering and failing career. In addition to those who have remained poor, the slum harbors those who have become impoverished.

Poverty is not the only thing the two groups whose roads cross in the urban slum have in common. They are not only both poor but suffer similarly from the indignity of not being accepted elsewhere on a basis of equal status. The newcomers, the immigrants, and in-migrants are ostracized as "greenhorns" as long as they cling together, as long as they have not adjusted sufficiently to the American way of life to disperse over the entire city environment. The human wreckage that filters down into the slum is ostracized on a more individual basis. For them many roads lead into the slum.

---

[14] For in-migration and the housing shortage in the Black Belt, see St. Clair Drake and Horace R. Cayton, *op. cit.*, pp. 61-64.

[15] "The bulk of the lower class . . . was getting used to 'kitchenette' living." St. Clair Drake and Horace R. Cayton, *op. cit.*, p. 576.

The slum existence of immigrants and in-migrants is apt to be a group experience. Individualization to them means success, the abandonment of the ethnic group and the ability to stand on their own feet without the support of the sheltering in-group. The process is reversed for those who filter down into the slum. They have lost foothold within the highly individualized existence that is the lot of the average city dweller. They have lost the ability of standing on their own feet and drift helplessly into an environment where the individual is lost in a motley crowd that congregates for the purpose they all have in common — the purpose of elementary survival.

About the background of slum dwellers who come from other parts of the same city, little information has been collected systematically. Descriptive case study and life history materials are the only sources that tell us about this part of the slum population.[16] These people are best subdivided according to the type of misfortune to which they owe their residence in the slum environment:

1. Economic failure (bankruptcy, and so forth)

2. Illness and consequent unemployability

3. Emotional instability and consequent unemployability

4. Divorce and consequent loss of support

5. Alcoholism

6. Drug addiction

7. Gambling

8. Crime, delinquency, and prostitution

9. Ostracization from a specific occupational group to which the individual's earning capacity is limited

10. Irregular sex life, perversions, and consequent ostracization

Social Disorganization. These conditions are well recognized as symptoms of social disorganization. Such deviant behavior does not always originate where it is found in the city environment. It may originate in the fashionable suburb, in the middle class neighborhood, or in the apartment hotel frequented by the "artist colony."

---

[16] For good descriptive materials see Harvey W. Zorbaugh, *The Gold Coast and the Slum.* Chicago: The University of Chicago Press, 1929, Chapter VIII, "The Slum," pp. 127-158.

After defeat in the individual life history, however, the wreckage withdraws into a group of those similarly afflicted. Personality disorganization turns here into social disorganization.

It would be an injustice to blame the slum environment entirely for the concentration of social disorganization in its confines. What we observe in the slum is the cumulative effect of individual failure to retain conformity or to survive economically in different environments all over the entire city. The modern slum functions in relation to the entire urban community. Conformity and advanced standards of living are retained in the rest of the city due to the service provided by the slum, the service of accepting those who are deemed inacceptable elsewhere.

Individual Failure. Economic misfortune, of course, rarely comes alone. The ten items in the above classification are by no means mutually exclusive. Economic failure, as a matter of fact, is typically related to one or more of these symptoms of personality disorganization. The interrelationship between economic failure and various types of deviant behavior can take any of the following directions: (1) Despair over economic failure may lead to indulgence in vice either as a substitute satisfaction or on the basis of inclinations that were repressed as long as repression was economically rewarded; or (2) indulgence in vice or other deviant behavior may lead to economic failure due to dismissal from employment or withdrawal of patronage.

Downward mobility that terminates in slum residence must be considered the end product of a cumulative process in which psychological and economic factors interact. The process might originate in any part of the modern city. We do not know whether downward mobility of this nature tends to be gradual or sudden. Such mobility may occur in successive steps, or the connection between the background environment and the slum residence may be a direct one. We do not know whether the loss of foothold in a neighborhood with high social and economic status leads immediately to slum residence or to attempts at surviving in urban neighborhoods of intermediate status.

Suicide. The alternative to "filtering-down" may well be found in suicide.[17] Suicide frequently occurs at a location removed from

---

[17] "Another index of man's difficulty in adjusting to city life is the high suicide rate to be found there." William F. Ogburn and Meyer F. Nimkoff,

the original residence. Slum dwellers commit a large percentage of suicide at their own places of residence. Suicide in the downtown hotel and suicide at a slum residence, however, do not differ greatly in their intentions. In both cases, the shelter of an anonymous environment is sought to spare friends and relatives embarrassment. Slum residences will frequently not represent more than a temporary and unsuccessful struggle for survival before the final step of self-annihilation is taken.

Anonymity in the Slum. Economic failure and noncomformity are not the only factors making the anonymity of slum living desirable. Slum conditions may be sought not only after defeat elsewhere, but on the basis of actual preference.

The slum is an environment of contrast. It shelters populations in the process of either upward or downward mobility with regard to economic success and social advancement. The slum shelters the very cohesive ethnic group as well as highly individualized populations. Side by side, we encounter immigrants bound together by deep-seated loyalties, dedicated to the preservation of shared values and closely connected by friendship ties and mutual help, and also the human flotsam that wants to be left alone for various reasons.

In this urban slum, the deviants of our culture congregate. Deviant behavior is not necessarily inferior behavior. The anonymity of the slum environment is sought by the artist as well as the criminal, by the young writer as well as the sex pervert. In one respect, these different types of people find themselves in the same situation. They all try to escape from convention and from the control of environments where the individual is the concern of any neighbor who might want to pass judgment.

The refuge of urban anonymity in the slum is offered to all comers. They do come from the farm and the small town as well as from other parts of the metropolitan community. We stand without knowledge with regard to the background composition of these

Sociology. New York: Houghton Mifflin Company, 1950, p. 290.

For an intensive statistical case study, see Calvin F. Schmid, *Social Trends in Seattle.* Seattle: The University of Washington Press, 1944, Chapter IX, "Suicide," pp. 203-215. For further materials consult the references in this source.

For the year 1929, a graphical presentation of urban and rural suicide rates will be found in *Our Cities. Their Role in National Economy.* National Resources Committee. Washington, D.C.: U.S. Government Printing Office. 1937, p. 12.

groups. There might be more young people from small towns in the artist colonies of our large cities than people with a metropolitan background. Many talented young people from the small towns are channelled through Greenwich Village in New York City before they are able to establish themselves professionally in the big city. Many of these artists and professionals remain in this location, once established. The "Village," partly because of its tourist appeal, has become the site of luxurious apartment buildings and expensive renovations, and deteriorated slum sections remain only at the edges. This bohemian part of the urban slum fills a nationwide function.[18]

Crime and Vice. Anonymity is not always sought for constructive purposes. More conspicuous are the shady activities that cause one to seek cover in an environment where nobody cares what the next fellow does, where the entire neighborhood can be relied upon not to "squeal" to the police. Apart from the so-called "bohemian" group, the criminal and the vice addicts are slum dwellers intent upon profiting from the shelter of anonymity.

The criminal may be either one who stayed in the slum, or one who found his way to the protective slum environment. There can be no doubt that the slum environment is crimogenic.[19] On the other hand, it would be wrong to blame the slum alone for all the criminals who congregate within its confines.

Traditions of criminal behavior are certainly carried in the slum environment and handed down from generation to generation.[20] The first American-born generation of immigrant stock is particularly tempted by the glamor and the rewards of crime.[21] Their

[18] "The story of Greenwich Village during the post-War decade (World War I) is a chapter in the history of American culture — the chapter which shows the inherited pattern of American social life repudiated by many to whom it was traditional, and without sufficient vitality or relevance to mould the lives of immigrant newcomers." Caroline F. Ware, *Greenwich Village 1920-1930.* Boston: Houghton Mifflin Company, 1935, p. 3.

[19] Edwin H. Sutherland, *Principles of Criminology.* New York: J. B. Lippincott Company, 1939, Chapter IX, "Culture Areas and Crime;" see especially pp. 138-144.

Marshall B. Clinard, "Secondary Community Influences and Juvenile Delinquency," *The Annals* of the American Academy of Political and Social Science, Vol. 261 (January, 1949), pp. 42-53.

[20] Crime is even handed along within the family in the sibling sequence. See Clifford R. Shaw, Henry D. McKay, and Harold B. Hanson, *Brothers in Crime.* Chicago: The University of Chicago Press, 1938.

[21] "The second generation of immigrants has been generally believed to be more criminalistic than their foreign-born parents and also more criminalistic

loyalties are divided and, obviously, confused. Temptation is bound to be challenging where prestige — otherwise missing — is easily gained within a value system that makes the most daring delinquent or criminal the idol of his associates.[22]

In all American cities, criminals find their way easily to each other. Somewhere close to the central business district, somewhere in the slum there will be found that part of the city where the professional criminal is likely to hang out.[23] Inasmuch as the police are not always on the lookout for every person who ever committed a crime, the individual criminal is fairly safe in the crime community, where anonymity prevails.

Grossly deviant behavior is just as much in need of protection against discovery as aggressive criminal behavior. Homosexual activities are punishable by law just as is safe cracking. Thus all sorts of illegal activities seek refuge in a group, the members of which have in common with each other their fear of and their opposition to law enforcement.

There are hotels notorious as hang-outs for perverts. There are stores where stimulating drugs are sold over the counter. There are houses of prostitution and the apartments where call girls reside when not at work.

The clustering of deviant behavior is a truly metropolitan phenomenon. It is to some extent a question of numbers. There are enough deviants in the large city to make it possible for groups of them to congregate, to provide each other with sympathy in the isolation of illicit activities and to help each other and to instruct each other in the skillful pursuit of their vice.

---

than the native whites of native parents. Recent statistics indicate that this belief is not generally true at the present time."

Edwin H. Sutherland, *op. cit.*, p. 126. Consult the entire section on "Immigration," pp. 123-129.

[22] See Robert K. Merton, *op. cit.*, "Functions of the Political Machine for Diverse Sub-groups," pp. 73-81.

[23] A good descriptive account will be found in Edwin H. Sutherland, *The Professional Thief*. Chicago: The University of Chicago Press, 1937, Chapter VII, "The Social and Personal Life of the Thief," pp. 154-171.

Due to the mobility of the criminal population, the crime community is best charted according to frequences of juvenile delinquency. See Clifford R. Shaw and Henry D. McKay, *Juvenile Delinquency and Urban Areas*. Chicago: The University of Chicago Press, 1942, Chapter III, "Distribution of Male Juvenile Delinquents in Chicago," pp. 43-85; also Calvin F. Schmid, *Social Saga of Two Cities*. Minneapolis: The Minneapolis Council of Social Agencies. 1937, Chapter XIII, "Juvenile Delinquency in Hennepin County," pp. 349-360.

THE SHATTERED LIFE PLAN IN THE SLUM

Hand to Mouth. Most slum dwellers are living on a hand-to-mouth basis. Whether immigrants or members of the Negro community, drug peddlers or prostitutes, their life plan lacks perspective. They are unable to plan much more than a day ahead. The extreme type is the drunk on skid row, happily clutching his bottle and willingly giving all his money away, unable to foresee that tomorrow his bottle will be gone.

The shattering of the life plan is, of course, not a matter of deficient intelligence. The case lies somewhat differently with different categories of slum dwellers.

The alcoholic has injured his nervous system through prolonged indulgence to the point of personality disintegration. He lives like a child for the satisfaction of immediate needs, prominent among which is combating the "shakes." Immediate needs are preponderant also in the life situations of recent immigrants, and of criminals and other deviants. They claim also the attention of the artist and other members of the "bohemian" group.

Immigrants. Recent immigrants are involved in a fierce struggle for survival. From day to day, they have to earn the bread with which to feed themselves and their families. Simultaneously, they are beset by elementary problems of adjustment. From the day of their arrival, they have to be alert against attempts to exploit their ignorance economically. They have to learn what wages they can demand. They have to guard against the signing of exploitative contracts that will claim their earning power for many years ahead. Immigrant housewives have to learn how to shop profitably and without being "taken for a ride."

All this they have to do in a language foreign to them, acquired at a relatively low level of literacy and relatively late in life. They have to acquaint themselves with the legal institutions and with the institutions of government, of relief, of welfare, of child care, and education, the services of which are offered to them in the country of their choice.

Occupied in unskilled labor, they live a life of continuous insecurity with regard to the provision of elementary needs. Economically, they have little opportunity to plan far ahead. Meager savings are quickly exhausted at times of economic depression, during tem-

porary layoffs, and as they look around for better jobs. They are so
deeply immersed in the problem of keeping things going from week
to week and from day to day that they don't have a chance to look
ahead. For years, or perhaps for a lifetime, the bank account, home
ownership, or the attainment of an American education for the
children must remain a vague day dream projected into an indefinite
future.[24]

Under the circumstances, there is no place for an integrated life
plan. The span of time for which conditions can be foreseen is in-
finitesimally short. This influences behavior and general orientation.
Money will be spent generously at times; it will be hoarded miserly
at others, in exaggerated yearning for economic security and social
advancement. Hopes rise and fall with the turns of the business
cycle and with individual good or bad fortune. No deep-seated
loyalties develop in the attitude toward a community of which the
immigrant does not feel himself to be a stable part.

Within the immigrant family, close co-operation is demanded by
the older generation. The younger generation rejects such demands
as the imposition of an un-American way of life which it does not
accept.[25] Co-operation is withdrawn from the family unit, and the
struggle for survival and advancement proceeds on a highly individualized basis. Without the security provided by close family
co-operation, the hazard of income fluctuations is intensified. The
immigrant and his offspring are, under the circumstances, just as
dependent upon the pawnbroker and indebtedness for temporary
financial relief as the drug addict, the "bohemian," and other types
of slum dwellers.

Criminals. The insecurities connected with a career in crime need
little elaboration. After a big haul, the safe cracker spends money
profusely. Such spending undermines his economic security. Years
of want and years in the penitentiary have to be compensated for
in brief spells of riotous living.

A rich man one day, the criminal has to go borrowing and begging
the next, the safe cracker may even have to go shoplifting to be able

---

[24] The function of the bank account as a symbol of economic security in
the immigrant family was the subject of a recently popular play: John Van
Druten, *I Remember Mama* (Adapted from Kathryn Forbe's *Mama's Bank
Account*) *The Best Plays of 1944-45*. New York: Dodd, Mead and Company,
1945, pp. 67-102.

[25] For "culture conflict" in the city, see pp. 211 ff.

to eat, sleep, and drink (shoplifters have very low status in the prestige hierarchy of the criminal underworld).[26]

Vice Addicts. Those given to the indulgence of vice find themselves in a similar situation. All activities are concentrated upon the procurement of the next dose of the stimulant. Little time is left, therefore, to plan far ahead.[27]

The drug addict steals and begs without consideration of his future earning power or his social prestige. The enjoyment of life is encapsuled in those few beatific moments after the stimulant has been taken. The neglect of all other pursuits sooner or later even interferes with the continuous purchase of the drug. Fortunes, if if there are any, are wasted. Belongings are sold; necessary equipment and clothing sent to the pawnbroker, redeemed, and sent back again. Money is gained by begging and borrowing at ever increasing costs of humiliation, and finally stealing remains as the only door left open for the continuance of a futile existence — if the afflicted person has enough energy and mental power left for the pursuit of a criminal career.[28]

Failures. In some life histories, to be sure, vice is not a primary factor of personality disorganization but serves as an escape only from other failures. The professional misfit and the bankrupt merchant are liable to drift into the slum environment, because their existence in a more stable urban environment has become meaningless or economically unrewarding.

They may indulge in vice to lift themselves temporarily out of their mood of defeat. But vice is habit-forming, and sooner or later they find themselves immersed in a life sometimes dedicated entirely to the procurement of a stimulant.

"Bohemians." For somewhat different reasons, the "bohemian" group also loses time-perspective. It is a somewhat heterogeneous group, and the individual life histories take somewhat different courses.

---

[26] This information was gained in informal interviews with a former safecracker in the Institute for Juvenile Research in Chicago.

[27] See excerpts from the diary of a drug addict in Harvey W. Zorbaugh, *The Gold Coast and the Slum.* Chicago: The University of Chicago Press, 1929, pp. 136-137.

[28] "It is popularly believed today that most addicts are criminals or derelicts prior to addiction. As we have seen, this impression requires considerable qualification as it applies to contemporary drug users." Alfred R. Lindesmith, *Opiate Addiction.* Bloomington, Ind.: Principia Press, Inc., 1947, p. 181.

Not all members of the "bohemian" group are artists. Some are students with many different interests. Others may be gainfully employed in steady white-collar jobs, but intensely occupied with the enjoyment of art and literature, as well as the association with artists and writers. Show people of different talents, on their way up or down the ladder of success also seek living quarters in the slum where rentals are cheap. In addition, there are the hangers-on, the critics, agents, and managers. All of them are engaged in the guidance or promotion of talent and in its economic exploitation.

They may be writing books, or painting pictures, or developing a stage talent. Work at the product they are trying to perfect calls its own measure. Work and leisure are not clearly separated where work is not performed for wages and where perfection rather than quantity of performance is the goal. Work may continue to the point of exhaustion. Or it may never start, if the creative individua! persuades himself to wait for the right mood. Family ties are abandoned, and friendship provides only fleeting loyalties. Students join in this pattern of existence. Temporarily, at least their studies also demand exclusive attention to a subject in which they are trying to accomplish something.[29]

The financial basis of bohemian existence is apt to be either derivative or erratic, there is not much the individual can do about it by way of sustained effort. Income may flow from an inheritance or a monthly check from parents, relatives, or some "angel"; or from occasional remunerations through early sales of a talent that is being developed. The erratic flow of self-earned income sets the pattern for expenditures. They are bound to be erratic also. When a painting is sold, the lump sum is spent lavishly. It would be unreasonable to economize and to plan for a step-by-step higher standard of living.

The way to the pawnbroker is, thus, traveled as frequently by members of the bohemian group as by other slum dwellers. In their pursuit of the arts and the sciences, these individuals are just as isolated from the rest of the urban community and its standards of financial success as the immigrant or the dope peddler.

In two respects only does the attitude of the bohemian group

---

[29] About family patterns prevailing in Greenwich Village, see Caroline F. Ware, *Greenwich Village 1920-1930*. Boston: Houghton Mifflin Company, 1935, Chapter XIV, "The Family," pp. 404-421. Since publication of this book, however, many conditions in Greenwich Village have changed.

differ from that of its neighbors in the slum environment. Their lot is self-chosen, and it is assumed to be temporary. These people have come to the slum environment for the sake of the opportunities it offers for concentrated dedication to a self-imposed task. They hope to leave their bohemian quarters once they have attained success.

PHYSICAL DETERIORATION IN THE SLUM

Housing. Physical construction of the residential slum environment leaves an impression of extreme deterioration. Buildings in the last years of their usefulness are made available as residences for those willing to occupy them at low cost. It matters little whether we look at the tenement or the duplex occupied by recent immigrants, at the housing facilities provided in the metropolitan "Black Belt," or some of the back alleys and side-streets of Greenwich Village. Demands for sanitary facilities are limited. Inadequate heating facilities are readily endured.

Expenses for maintenance and remodeling in accordance with modern demands for hot water, electric lights, and adequate sewerage facilities are held back. But the most striking phenomenon is a complete disregard for exterior appearance. Apart from some immigrant neighborhoods with a growing home ownership percentage and meek efforts to make buildings look neat and slightly respectable with a fresh coat of paint, it seems that appearance is the last item on which the landlord is willing to lavish his financial resources. With this attitude, of course, he follows the trend of prevailing demands. Nobody cares about appearances. The more ambitious inhabitants of the slum environment consider their stay there as temporary. They don't have status associations with present quarters. Most others are beyond pride, and mainly concerned with the provision of a roof over their heads at minimum expense.

The Gold Coast. There is one important exception to this rule. The fashionable and well-equipped apartment house has, in recent decades, made its appearance in close proximity to the central slum.[30] Such construction has never been free of considerable financial risk. Yet large scale developments at spectacularly attractive sites have been successful. Such residential development had to be of sizable

---

[30] Coleman Woodbury, *Apartment House Increases and Attitude toward Home Ownership. Studies in Land Economics.* Research Monograph No. 4. Chicago: The Institute for Economic Research, 1931.

scale. Only in this manner was it possible to overcome difficulties involved in the possible transfer of low prestige from the slum.

Pertinent examples are the Gold Coast in Chicago and some of the apartment houses overlooking the East River from Manhattan Island. In both cases, the sites have been unusually attractive, with sweeping views over adjacent waters. Such location could overcome whatever initial resistance there might have been to residence on previous slum properties.[31]

In some ways even these recent intruders into the urban slum share the characteristics of other slum dwellers. They consist of a relatively mobile group in the higher income strata. The modern apartment hotel here provides services demanded by people relatively well-to-do but without a permanent family home. There are young executives with their families, bachelors and widows and divorcees. There are other people who have permanent family homes far out in the country, to whom the downtown residence does not mean more than temporary quarters within a convenient distance from the downtown business and shopping area.

There are relatively few children and many broken families. These people, too, are intent upon remaining anonymous. They do not identify on a permanent basis with this environment as a status determining factor.

MIXED LAND USES IN THE SLUM

Contrasts. The slum is characterized by physical deterioration. It also stands out as the area of mixed land uses. We are struck by the seemingly incompatible mixture of land uses contained in this district.

The art school is located close to the crime district, the first-rate restaurant close to the flophouse, and Little Sicily a short walking distance from the winter residences of the most wealthy members of the urban community. The slum even extends into the glamorous sections of the bright light district, of downtown apartment houses and fashionable eating places.

Ecological Integration. Some ecological relationships (relationships of social interdependence) exist between the bleak and the glamorous sides of this Zone of Transition. The chorus girls and the "available" hostesses of the downtown night club are not in-

---

[31] See Harvey W. Zorbaugh, *op. cit.*

frequently recruited from the impoverished sections of the slum environment. There they meet with the financially affluent members of the community.

Criminal behavior is stimulated by the close proximity of poverty and wealth on a spree of spending and indulgence. The poor kids steal bicycles from the nearby fashionable high school. The jack-roller starts his career under a dark bridge close to the entertainment district.[32] Many a swanky party ends with a "slumming" trip. The artists live modestly, a stone's throw away from their wealthy clients.

Land Values. For the causes of this quaint mixture of land uses, we have to look — as we have done before — to the dynamics of land values.[33]

Slums are gradually being rehabilitated, not, as previously expected, by the extension of the central business zone, but by a growing interest of the well-to-do in the convenience of central residential location. To this are added the economic interests of a consumer-oriented entertainment industry which, close to the downtown area, caters to the temporary visitor to the modern city.

Once connected in space, however, these divergent land uses foster interrelations that mold the slum into something of a social unit, including the anonymous environment of the fashionable downtown residence, the apartment hotel, and even the light industries remaining here and furnishing with their occasional empty lots, storehouses, and unguarded cash registers the night-time playground of adventurous slum youth.

Rehabilitation. Slum rehabilitation, therefore, requires more than the condemnation of dilapidated residential construction and the provision of low-cost housing elsewhere in the city. It requires the re-channelling of firmly established social relations. It requires the provision of substitutes for a highly variegated system of needs covered by the present slum environment.

If we are to do away with the slum as it is today, we must plunge into a program of municipal policies which will have to consider the needs of the poor who live in the slum because they cannot afford to live anywhere else. This will always be an important aspect of the rehabilitation program.

---

[32] Clifford R. Shaw, *The Jack-roller.* Chicago: The University of Chicago Press, 1930.

[33] See pp. 99 ff.

It will also have to be decided where the entertainment industry is to be moved, where the nonconforming members of the community, the perverts, and other deviants are to be taken care of. More adequate housing facilities and a congenial environment will also have to be provided for the bohemian group, our students and young artists, who want to associate with each other while dedicating themselves to their training in a temporary situation of poverty and economic insecurity. We have to provide homes for our unattached urban workers,[34] for transients at all economic levels, and for the rising executive who is likely to be transferred to another city in the near future.

SELECTED READINGS

1. J. L. Hammond and Barbara Hammond, *The Bleak Age.* New York: Penguin Books, 1947, pp. 13-246.

2. W. I. Thomas and Florian Znaniecki, *The Polish Peasant in Europe and America.* New York: Alfred A. Knopf, 1918, Part III, "Organization and Disorganization in America," pp. 1467-1827.

3. Harvey Warren Zorbaugh, *The Gold Coast and the Slum.* Chicago: The University of Chicago Press, 1929, pp. 1-279.

4. St. Clair Drake and Horace R. Cayton, *Black Metropolis. A Study of Negro Life in a Northern City.* New York: Harcourt, Brace and Company, 1945, pp. 31-97, 379-754.

5. Caroline F. Ware, *Greenwich Village 1920-1930.* Boston: Houghton Mifflin Company, 1935, pp. 3-424.

PROBLEMS

1. *Interdependence of Mixed Land Uses.* Select for your investigation an area in the downtown business district, the Zone of Transition, or the residential fringe (see pp. 96-98). Visit that area and record painstakingly the land uses observed, and the manner in which they are located in relation to each other.

   If office buildings of several floors are included, the land uses at different floor levels will have to be reported.

   It is your task to give as complete an interpretation as possible of the reasons why these different land uses are found in such close proximity to each other.

2. *Location of the "Black Belt."* What generalizations can we make about the location of the "Black Belt," the residential areas pre-

---

[34] See Arnold M. Rose "Living Arrangements for Unattached Persons," *American Sociological Review,* Vol. II, No. 4 (August, 1947), pp. 429-435.

empted by Negroes in our American cities? Consult *Black Metropolis* by St. Clair Drake and Horace R. Cayton; and Calvin F. Schmid's *Social Saga of Two Cities*, pp. 172-188, and *Social Trends in Seattle*, pp. 137-141. Try to amplify your information from other sources, particularly, if possible, about your own community.

Make the best general statement about the location of the urban Black Belt borne out by the above-mentioned materials. Then discuss the reasons for deviations from the general patterns that may be found in individual cities.

3. *The Life Plan in Different Urban Environments.* Read the discussion of the "shattered life plan" in the slum, pp. 151-155. If the span of time taken into account in the individual life plan is significant for social attitudes in the slum environment, the same must be true for different urban environments. As a matter of fact, unless differences are found, our discussion would remain pointless.

Make a comparative study of planning perspectives as found in the slum and in contrasting environments.

For documentation, consult Walter Firey's *Land Use in Central Boston*. The author discusses different urban environments. It is your task to scrutinize his description and analysis in search for relevant materials about individual planning perspectives. You will probably find the discussion of "Beacon Hill" (pp. 87-135) particularly valuable by way of contrast to the life plan of slum dwellers. Consider also Caroline F. Ware's *Greenwich Village*, pp. 404-421. The more materials you can interpret with this viewpoint in mind, the better.

CHAPTER 7

The Urban Fabric

Construction, Social Relations, and Transportation. The city consists of *urban construction* and *urban social relations.* Without the
former, we would find ourselves without the urban problems of how
to build and where to build. Without the latter, urban construction
would not hold any interest to the social scientist. The city is a
construct of steel, stone, brick, and wood, and also a maze of interpersonal relationships. These interpersonal relationships must be projected upon the geographical dimension of the urban territory.[1]

Urban construction is welded into a functioning whole through
the urban transportation system. Different people, residing in
different parts of the built-up city, have to be brought together for
a number of purposes. They have to be brought together for trade
and commerce and for industrial co-operation. They have to be
brought together for purposes of self-government. City dwellers also
need opportunities to get together in stimulating and relaxing leisure
time activities. They want to be able to meet their friends and to
associate with all members of the large consanguinal family [2] which

---

[1] "Neighborhood planning is an attempt to make spatial arrangement subservient to social function." Svend Riemer, "Hidden Dimension of Neighborhood Planning," *Journal of Land Economics*, Vol. XXVI, No. 2 (May, 1950),
p. 197.

[2] "Organized on a blood relationship basis, the consanguinal family is made
up of a nucleus of blood relatives, surrounded by spouses who are only inci-
dentally important to the family unit." H. Scudder Mekeel, "Preliterate Family
Patterns," in Howard Becker and Reuben Hill, editors, *Marriage and the
Family.* Boston: D. C. Heath and Company, 1942, p. 50.

is scattered more or less haphazardly over the entire urban fabric. The modern city depends for survival upon its means of transportation. Whenever the intra-urban transportation system breaks down, urban social relations are paralyzed. In such an emergency situation, city functions are interfered with more threateningly from hour to hour up to the moment of complete disorganization, starvation, and death. Health services and food distribution are interrupted. The maintenance of law and order by the police force is incapacitated. Without its system of internal communications, the city dies.[3]

These consequences are largely due to urban size. In the village and small town, no artificial means of transportation and communication are required to keep necessary social relations going. Different people and different institutions and services are here contained within easy walking distance. The territory of the large modern city, on the other hand, requires an effective system of transportation to "normal" social relations.

We sometimes talk about the urban transportation system as the "arteries of the city." Like the arteries of the human body, the urban transportation system keeps the various sections of the city supplied with foods necessary for survival. It takes products out of the city to their destination; it eliminates the waste products of industry and those of private living; it connects labor with its place of work. In the city, both goods and people pass in a continuous stream through the internal transportation system. Without these "arteries," urban life comes to a standstill.

The System of Transportation. Urban transportation is provided in a highly diversified system. Different means of transportation supplement each other. They are carefully attuned to each other. Within the system of railroad transportation, express services and local distribution co-operate in providing speed as well as approximation of door-to-door transportation.[4]

Long distance movements within the urban fabric set the need for

---

[3] Consider the paralyzing effects upon the transportation system and the functioning of the city as a whole, of Chicago's railroad strike in 1948 and New York's snowstorm in 1949. Contemporary editions of news magazines carried interesting documentary photography.

[4] For express highway design, see Gilmore D. Clarke, "The Design of Motorways," in Jean Labatut and Wheaton J. Lane, editors, *Highways in Our National Life. A Symposium.* Princeton: Princeton University Press, 1950, pp. 299-308.

speedy and uninterrupted displacements of population. To increase speed, it is necessary to minimize local stops for the unloading and loading of commuters. This, in turn, increases the need for subsidiary means of transportation, feeding into the rapid transit lines. Within the highly differentiated urban transportation system, the rapid transit lines are the most vulnerable part. They are the most vulnerable because more difficult to replace by transportation on foot in case of emergencies.

Motor Transportation. The very existence of the combustion engine and its use for purposes of transporation has increased the importance of the intra-urban highway system.[5] Both public transportation, in the form of bus lines, and private transportation, in the form of automobiles owned by the individual city dwellers, have caused a revolution in the circulation of both goods and people in the city.

The combustion engine has made the intra-urban transportation system much more flexible. Motor vehicles are not dependent upon an inflexible rail system. They also satisfy demands for door-to-door transportation, for direct transportation between place of work and place of residence. We are therefore faced today with problems of highway congestion that were less acute in the days when rail transportation dominated the urban scene.

When the present street system of most cities was laid out, nobody was able to foresee the future needs for transportation. Present urban construction pre-empts space badly needed for a flexible widening of our street system. To adjust our urban street system to present needs of motor transportation often entails the abandonment of valuable investment in standing urban construction. Thus, the more important arteries of modern city transportation are clogged. This is particularly true in the inner parts of the city where high land values make street-widening a very expensive enterprise.[6]

---

[5] Homer Hoyt, The Influence of Highways and Transportation on the Structure and Growth of Cities and Urban Land Values. *op. cit.*, pp. 201-206.

[6] In our cities the paradoxial situation prevails that our streets are the most narrow where they ought to be widest to accommodate the differential traffic needs. A system of widening streets toward the periphery would be functional only where communication with the rural hinterland exceeds the inner traffic in numerical importance. For a unique economic and social situation where such conditions prevailed, see an ecological study of the cattle raising communities of the Hungarian plains, A. N. J. Den Hollander, *Nederzettings-vormen en -problemen in de Groote Hongaarsche Laagvlakte*. Amsterdam: J. M. Meulenhoff, 1947.

Commuting. With all its shortcomings, the intra-urban transportation system provides valuable service for the city. Its most important function is the shuttle service, by which thousands of commuters are daily concentrated at their places of work in the city center, to be dispersed after the working day to widely scattered residential habitations.

Still, "commuting" refers to more than the journey to work.[7] It refers to any long distance travel between a predominantly residential area and the central business district that is apt to occur repeatedly and with a certain amount of regularity. So considered, commuting needs arise in connection with specialty shopping trips to the central business district.

Commuting also connects the city residence with the downtown bright light district. Specialized entertainment facilities, such as drama, opera, nightclubs, large movie theaters, and good eating places draw large sections of the population daily from their living quarters to the central parts of the city. Nor dare we forget the associational life of the urban community, which takes place to a large extent in the downtown area. Commuters with special interests are able to gather here from all over the city through the use of transportation facilities to which they have become accustomed through their daily journeys to work.

Local Transportation. In addition to commuting services, the urban fabric requires local means of public and private transportation. This involves different orbits of transportation within the relatively self-contained residential areas, within the downtown business district and within the residential areas serviced by the so-called satellite loop.

Within the relatively self-contained residential area, communications can be assumed to be primarily pedestrian in nature. If some member of the family dashes to the local drug store to pick up a pint of ice cream in the family car, he does so more for fun than out of necessity. Children, by and large, walk to the elementary school,

---

[7] "The American term 'commuter' refers to the individual who alternates between his residence and place of work every week-day." For a treatment of the problem according to this more limited definition, see the excellent study in Kate K. Liepmann, *The Journey to Work.* New York: Oxford University Press, 1944.

See also Gerald Breese, *The Daytime Population of the Central Business District of Chicago.* Chicago: The University of Chicago Press, 1949.

and the daily shopping trip in the well developed neighborhood is usually carried out on foot.

Due to the precipitous development of new residential areas, commercial facilities follow along with some lag in time. In the sparsely settled outskirts years may pass before daily shopping facilities are provided within easy walking distance of the individual family home. Protective zoning restrictions often make it impossible for local grocery stores and drug stores to move within close range of newly developed residential housing. Under such conditions, bus services are in strong demand, unless the family income permits the purchase of a second car, or proximity to lines of rapid commuting services free the family car for use in local transportation.

Within the downtown business district, local transportation is required to forward the commuter from the terminal of rapid transit lines to his final destination at his place of work, the department store, or the desired place of entertainment. Most modern cities provide for some such service. Such downtown transportation, however, suffers from congestion due to the overlapping of incoming commuter transportation in buses or privately owned automobiles with the services needed for the circulation of populations within the downtown area itself.[8]

Many urban commercial and recreational facilities cater to a larger population than that residing within walking distance. With regard to shopping needs, the satellite loop has to be reached by some means of artificial transportation. For more or less regular contacts we must also consider such vital needs as those of the high school student, the church member, the sports fan, or the child who wants to go swimming during the summer months. In between rapid transit lines and local transportation, these needs are not always well taken care of in the urban fabric.

Most modern cities are not well supplied with circular transportation that interconnects the outlying residential districts of the city with each other.[9] In the American city, the typical route from one outlying suburb to another leads to the terminal of rapid transit lines

[8] For planning problems concerned with downtown transportation, see pp. 446.

[9] Some European cities achieved a ring-formed central street system by utilizing space previously occupied by fortifications that had become obsolete. See Harold MacLean Lewis, *Planning the Modern City*. New York: John Wiley & Sons, Inc., 1949, pp. 24-26.

in the central city, and then out again by way of a different rapid transit line, thus prolonging tremendously the distance to be covered by means of artificial transportation.

DAILY POPULATION MOVEMENTS

Rythmical Movement. The analysis of the urban fabric must consider the time element. The city is the people, and these people are found at different places during the different hours of the day.

Our conception of the city must not remain static. Unfortunately, we have no hour-to-hour census of the location of the entire urban

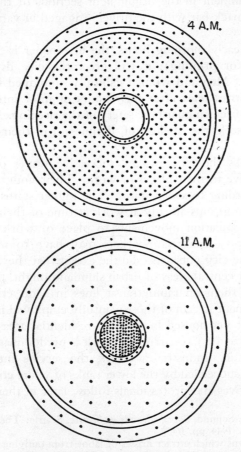

FIGURE 8.   Urban Population Distribution.
Different Hours of the Day. (Schematic)

population within the confines of the city. Population spot maps are generally related to place of residence.[10]

Morning Hours. In the early morning hours, the city lies dormant. Preparatory to the awakening of the city, certain consumer services reach greatest intensity in their operation. Life at the commission houses, the wholesale grocery markets, and the meat and fish markets stirs more vigorously than at any other time of the day. From here, and from the local dairies, food distribution gets underway in time for the city dweller's daily breakfast and for the housewife's early morning shopping trip to the grocery store. Late stragglers of last night's entertainment in the bright light sections of the city intermingle at the snack bar with the drivers engaged in various delivery services.

In the very early morning hours, the newspaper is "put to bed" (made ready for printing); it will greet the city dweller at the breakfast table. Men and women gainfully employed in the entertainment industries relax after their hours of most intensive work. Policemen and firemen guard the safety of the sleeping. The prowler and criminal seek the shelter of darkness for their exploitative ventures.

Forenoon. As the city awakes, successive waves of the urban labor force move to their places of work. Their hours of work are staggered according to social status. The higher status groups find the lower status groups already at work at time of their arrival.

The daily population movements to place of work are not entirely centripetal. Industrial workers may have to move toward plant sites at the city outskirts. To the extent that they are residentially located at central areas of urban slum and blight, their journey to work takes them on rapid transit lines in a direction opposite to the predominant stream of those gainfully employed in the central business district yet housed in outlying residential areas.[11]

From 8 A.M. to 10 A.M., arrival at work is predominantly an inner city phenomenon. Industrial workers, the service industries, and the janitors are succeeded by the lower ranks of white collar laborers. Business executives and professionals follow later in their wake. On

---

[10] See Calvin F. Schmid, *Social Trends in Seattle*. Seattle: The University of Washington Press, 1944, pp. 56-58.

[11] "In large towns which attract masses of labor from outlying suburbs, there are at the same time centrifugal movements." Kate K. Liepmann, *op. cit.*, p. 4.

the commuter trains from suburbs to the downtown area, the social composition of the traveling populations changes from hour to hour.

At the heels of the urban labor force — and overlapping it — follows a thinner stream of morning shoppers attracted to the downtown business district. When the shoppers arrive, the city is thoroughly at work in manufacturing plants and offices, department stores, railroad stations, and hotels. There is a lull in the late forenoon in the demand upon the services of the intra-urban transportation system. The city population has more or less settled down at the location of its daytime activities.

Luncheon. The length of urban commuting distances has affected both the hours of work and the eating habits of the city dweller. At present, lunch is typically taken in close proximity to the place of work. A short period of time is allowed for luncheon; this arrangement pleases the urban commuter, who prefers the advantage of early closing hours that enable him to return sooner to his family domicile.[12]

A brief and hectic reshuffling of the downtown population takes place while the noonhour passes by. Orders are shouted in crowded eating places. The luxury of taking a leisurely noon meal in an uncongested and quiet environment is reserved to the upper strata of the downtown labor force. The business executive may have earned the privilege of returning to work later than the people that work under him, just as he is permitted to arrive later at the job in the morning.

Afternoon. In the afternoon hours, the downtown labor force starts to scatter, while the central city is invaded by the pleasure-seeking population. Between closing hours and train time, members of the labor force may temporarily turn into shoppers or pleasure seekers. Certain goods are better and more cheaply available in the central shopping district; others are not at all obtainable in either the neighborhood shopping district or the satellite loop. A cup of coffee or a cocktail at the downtown bar may break the tension of the working day.

The service industries are now rushing deliveries to their cus-

---

12 "The hours 9:00 to 5:00, interrupted by an hour for lunch usually between 12:00 and 1:00, from Monday to Saturday noon, represents the standard work time for the gainfully employed." George A. Lundberg, Mirra Komarovsky, and Mary Alice McInerny, *Leisure. A Suburban Study*. New York: Columbia University Press, 1934, p. 95.

tomers, to be enjoyed during the evening when the city dweller calls his time his own and plunges into the world of his private life. Food and clothes arrive at the door-step of the city home.

Commuter trains are loaded to capacity. After hours of slack business, the rapid transit lines now have to accommodate not only the returning labor force but many of the returning shoppers. Nor is the return of the labor force as widely spread in time as its arrival at work in the morning.

Now, the downtown entertainment industries prepare for the rush of evening activities. Night workers converge upon the inner city. The restaurant business gets ready for dinner. Supplies arrive, and managers check up on the arriving service personnel. Visitors to the city start arriving from out of town, and the tourists — returned from a day of sightseeing — are getting ready in their hotel rooms for the evening spree.

At dinner time, people are most closely distributed at their respective places of residence. The visitors have the downtown area almost to themselves.

Evening. Immediately after dinner, residential location of the urban population is again reshuffled. Family members, particularly a large segment of the young adults and adolescents, leave the family home in all directions. The urban population divides into that section which intends to spend the evening with quiet relaxation at home, and that section which engages in specialized leisure time activities outside the home. Of such leisure time activities there is a great variety.[13] There are opportunities for specialized training after working hours. There are also opportunities for commercial entertainment, for the pursuit of specialized hobbies, and for activities of voluntary associations.

From the residential districts of the city, a stream of commuters much smaller than that of the morning hours moves in the direction of recreational and associational activities. Many of these activities are not located downtown. There may be movie theaters located in various directions from the individual family home. There may even be one within walking distance.

Bowling alleys, skating rinks, and movie theaters attract a sufficient number of customers in all urban areas outside the central amusement district. The same, of course, is true for taverns and

---

[13] Chapters 11 and 12.

poolrooms. The centrally located establishments of the entertainment industry cater to less frequent need for entertainment and those of a highly specialized type, such as concerts and the legitimate theater. These needs depend upon a larger urban recruitment area.

In the late evening, people move back toward their residences, transportation peaks coinciding with the standardized closing times of entertainment facilities. Gradually, the city goes to sleep.

Fluctuations. The movement of the city population is, of course, subject to weekly and seasonal fluctuations. On Saturdays, the population that goes to work is reduced by the number of those who enjoy the privilege of a five-day work week. The rest of the urban labor force returns home by noon. In the afternoon, shopping districts are more crowded than usual, as are places of entertainment. In the evening hours, the entertainment industries attract larger crowds than at any other time during the week. Empirical investigations would probably reveal further — though less conspicuous — variations for the other days of the week.[14]

In the summertime, centripetal movement in search of leisure time activities coincides with a centrifugal movement. Outdoor recreation located at the urban fringe pulls crowds toward picnic grounds and bathing beaches. In or near the natural recreational areas, facilities such as movies, fair grounds, eating places, and night clubs are provided. In the summertime, the central entertainment district of the city attracts tourists from abroad and fulfills nationwide and, possibly, international functions.

THE URBAN FABRIC IN INDIVIDUAL PERSPECTIVE

Individual Selection. If the city is made up of the people that live in it,[15] it must be viewed as an area in which many people move around to meet for various purposes and different social groupings. They move and combine with different social purposes in mind. Individually, they oscillate between family functions and occupational functions, between residence and place of work. They conjoin in recreational groups as audiences of the entertainment industry, as play groups or as civic groups, as action committees or as discussion groups. Urban construction is geared to serve these

---

[14] For weekday variations in leisure and non-leisure activities, see George A. Lundberg, Mirra Komarovsky, and Mary Alice McInerny, *op. cit.*, pp. 90-91.

[15] See Henry S. Churchill, *The City is the People.* New York: Reynal & Hitchcock, 1945.

various functions of social interaction and, consequently, determines the direction of such intra-urban movements.

It is interesting to trace the particular movements of isolated individuals through the urban fabric, or to establish family contact patterns that indicate how the family group through its various members enters into different social relations with different parts of the city. As individual or family experience, the city is composed of innumerable subjective patterns cut selectively into the urban fabric.[16]

The city dweller enjoys the privilege of free choice with regard to the social relationships he wants to cultivate and those he wants to neglect. He enjoys, in this respect, an advantage over the farmer and the small town dweller, who are more or less bound to accept social relationships on the bases of geographical proximity.[17]

In looking at the city through the eyes of the individual participant, we recognize an important and characteristic aspect of urban life. The city dweller has an opportunity to pick and choose. He has the opportunity to choose his friends, the activities he wants to engage in, and the type of urban construction that he wants to make use of in the pursuit of his daily routines.

The urban fabric is primarily a social fabric, and as such is of exceedingly complex composition. It is difficult enough to follow the total stream of intra-urban movements within the city environment. No attempt has been made to record individual movements in order to reconstruct schematically the urban fabric from its most elementary units.

Contact Areas. In the perspective of the individual city dweller, certain parts of the urban environment are highlighted as areas of more or less intensive contact. These contact areas spread out in the immediate vicinity of his residence, his place of work, the educational institutions he attends, his places of recreation, the residences of his friends and relatives, and places of civic participation such as church, service club, and other voluntary associations. The desire

---

16 A hypothetical case of a family contact pattern will be found in *Patterns and People*. Kansas City, Mo.: City Plan Commission, 1944, p. 3.

17 "The city offers opportunities to select social contacts from a large number of people and facilities gathered in the urban environment and connected by convenient and rapid means of transportation. These conditions permit the city dweller to pick and choose the social relations he wants to bother with. . . . He enjoys the freedom of choice." Svend Riemer, "Villagers in Metropolis?" *British Journal of Sociology* (March, 1951), p. 31-43.

for economy in movement places a premium on contact patterns which place several of these contact areas in close proximity to each other, or which make them overlap entirely.

Individual contact patterns differ on the basis of subjective inclinations, recreational preferences, occupational ambitions, and attitudes

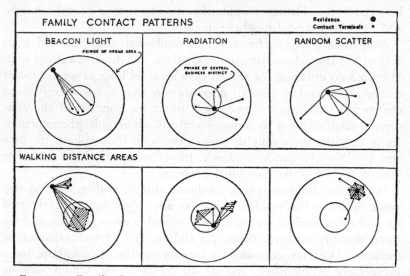

FIGURE 9. Family Contact Patterns. From: Svend Riemer, "Villagers in Metropolis," *The British Journal of Sociology*, Vol. II, No. 1 (March, 1951), p. 38.

toward the associational life of the urban community. They are also extremely dynamic. While an individual grows up and extends his interests, his urban contact pattern extends farther into different city areas. In old age, shrinking interests restrict the urban area in which the individual still wants to get around.

The city dweller is conscious of participation in different contact areas where he sustains more or less intensive and more or less frequent social relations.[18] The consciousness of being part of such an

---

[18] "Walking distance areas tend to be of either of the five following types:
1. Residential,
2. occupational,
3. educational,
4. commercial, or
5. associational."
Svend Riemer, "Villagers in Metropolis?" *loc. cit.*

area helps to constitute it as a social unit. Without any "feeling of belonging," there would be small social interest in these city areas.

NEIGHBORHOODS

From the viewpoint of individual experience, we shall distinguish between (1) residential neighborhoods, (2) roving neighborhoods, and (3) occupational neighborhoods.[19]

Residential Neighborhoods. The residential neighborhood consists of the immediate surroundings of the individual dwelling unit. We need no criterion for the area enclosed, as long as we approach the neighborhood as a social phenomenon, that is, a subjective one changeable from case to case. Still, to tie the concept of the residential neighborhood to some objectively observable phenomenon, let us consider it as roughly coincident with the walking distance area adjoining the family residence. Its perimeter may be extended or limited according to individual propensities.

Within the residential neighborhood, that is, within walking distance of the urban residence, we are apt to encounter services of the following nature: an elementary school, a grocery store, a drug store, possibly a movie theater, a church, and various commercial facilities. We may encounter a laundry, a shoe repair shop, some inexpensive eating place, and an ice cream parlor, which may be directly connected with the drug store. Lack of such facilities within the residential neighborhood imposes severe inconveniences upon everyday life routines. In the newly developed residential areas and in areas with unduly restricted commercial land uses, such deficiencies are not uncommon.[20]

In the modern city, these residential neighborhoods are not necessarily visible in terms or area planning and urban construction. What the residential neighborhood is depends upon individual choice and

---

[19] In this context, *neighboring* is used in a somewhat broader manner than above where the term is set off against that of the natural area and the service area. Only the "residential neighborhood" now under consideration fits entirely the qualification of the neighborhood concept as used above. The reason for the slightly deviating use of terms lies in the somewhat different problems to be dealt with in the analysis of urban environment.

[20] This suburban condition stands in contrast to conditions elsewhere in the city where, however, zoning ordinances are applied to restrict the undesirable effects of commercial land uses. For "zoning" see Arthur M. Weimer and Homer Hoyt, *Principles of Urban Real Estate.* New York: The Ronald Press Company, 1948, pp. 190-199.

propensity. The residential neighborhood of one city dweller may differ from that of his next door neighbor.

Neighborhood planning has encouraged an overlapping of these individual neighboring patterns by carefully premeditated urban construction.[21] Visible barriers, such as major traffic routes or narrow green belts, may surround a residential environment to which neighborhood contacts are to be confined. Services required for everyday living are placed within the "planned residential neighborhood." The plan, however, is confined to physical construction. It remains an open question whether the construction offered develops into the social phenomenon of conjoined residential neighborhood contacts, or whether it will stand as an intended residential neighborhood with actual neighborhood contacts flowing indiscriminately over its edges.

Occupational Neighborhoods. The occupational neighborhood plays a very different part in the life of the city dweller. It is related to his place of work, and to those hours which are spent in the proximity of office building, factory, store, or school building. Here too, shopping facilities are in demand within easy walking distance. In addition, there is need for eating and drinking places not only for purposes of commercially provided consumption, but also to provide opportunities for informal get-togethers between members of the working or the school population.

The city dweller establishes fairly intimate personal relations at his place of work as well as at his place of residence. Different from the small town dweller, he establishes such relations on a basis of choice and selection. Competitive ambitions may alienate the city dweller from his immediate associates on the job and bar close friendship. Still, many casual relations are established on the journey to and from work.

Between the downtown terminal of transportation lines and the entrance that leads to his desk or workshop, the city dweller makes a large number of casual nodding acquaintances that may develop into primary group relations. He avails himself of service facilities that function as home substitutes for the long distance commuter. The tavern may function as a men's club, the tearoom as a ladies' club. The barbershop provides the recuperating influence of daytime grooming. Civic clubs and recreational activities may also be

---

[21] For principles of contemporary neighborhood planning, see Chapter 17.

provided in the proximity of places of gainful urban employment. Length of commuting time has much to do with the development of the occupational neighborhood in the modern city.

Roving Neighborhoods. In between the residential and the occupational neighborhood, the city dweller is inclined to adopt one or several contact areas for intensive cultivation of social relations. We call this phenomenon "roving neighborhood." Its function is derived from a variety of needs. It is warranted to talk in this connection about a "neighborhood" only if several contacts — possibly related to different service areas — are found within easy walking or driving distance of each other.

The roving neighborhood encompasses a city area often much larger than that of the residential neighborhood. It often coincides with the combined service range of several commercial or institutional facilities. These clusters of service facilities may be found around the local high school, the local library, the shopping facilities of the satellite loop, and around localized enterprises of the urban entertainment industry, such as movie theaters, eating places, bars, bowling alleys, skating rinks, and indoor swimming pools.

A special consciousness of neighborhood affiliation is an important factor in molding the roving neighborhood into a social unit. It is often based upon the fact that the same area is similarly used by many other individuals. Another factor is a pleasant combination of relevant construction. Concentrated service facilities are more apt to attract neighborhood loyalties than arbitrarily scattered facilities. The local high school, for example, is very likely to attract its students for other than educational activities into its vicinity, thus forming the basis for a roving neighborhood unit.

Scattered Contacts. Not all urban contacts are combined with others in areas of intensive neighboring. For visits of personal friends or relatives, for specialized hobbies and leisure time activities, for the use of specialized educational facilities, and in the pursuit of civic interests, the city dweller strays far and wide through the entire urban area. He is hampered in his movements only by inadequate means of transportation or commuters' fatigue.

Contacts in the Life Cycle. In the course of his life cycle, the city dweller continuously rearranges the pattern of subjectively significant contact areas. The social contacts of the child are almost completely limited to the residential neighborhood. With the exception of special excursions downtown or to friends and relatives living in different parts of the city, the movements of the child are confined to a small area surrounding the individual family home. Therefore, elementary school facilities ought to be so distributed within the urban fabric that they are available within walking distance of each urban residence.

During high school years, social contacts stretch over a far wider geographical area. The reason is not only the high school student's greater ability to get around by means of private and public transportation, but also the wider geographical service range of the individual high school. The recruitment area of the city high school is much larger than that of the elementary school. Consequently, the high school student comes into contact with many children who are residentially located at more than walking distance. The wider geographical area for high school recruitment leads to the association of the high school student with pupils of diversified background.[22]

The contact area of the adolescent furnishes the foundation for contacts later in life, to be developed by the young adult and the man with full adult responsibilities. Stray friendships may solidfy into participation in voluntary associations. Utilizations of the entertainment facilities of another area may lead to courtship, marriage, and change of residence. Status goals are more consciously pursued in the social contacts of the full grown adult. Trying to make the best possible place for himself within the urban status hierarchy, the adult city dweller tries to establish contacts through which he is able to associate with economically and socially more advanced status groups. He is likely to break off contacts with city dwellers in lower status positions.

In addition, the occupational life of the city dweller leads to the establishment of new contact areas in relation to his place of work. Irrationalities of friendship formation, amorous adventures, or the residential location of relatives occur during the entire life span of the city dweller. They establish individual contacts, or small pockets of contacts, anywhere within the urban fabric.

Advancing age leads to the contraction of the individual or family contact areas, and the development of new contact areas, to be sure, comes sooner or later to a standstill. In later age, only strong occu-

---

[22] For the function of the urban high school in the establishment of "neighboring," see William Brussat, "The Neighborhood as a Function of School and Childhood," *The Journal of Educational Psychology,* Vol. XVII, No. 2, Spring, 1951, pp. 77-79.

pational, recreational, or civic interests allow the individual contact area to protrude beyond the area of previously established social relations. Adolescence and young adulthood are the most expansive phases in the life history of the city dweller.

With growing infirmities, finally, contacts within the city shrink to a minimum comparable only with the contact area of early childhood. The life cycle closes. Occupational contacts are abandoned. Friends and relatives living in other parts of town are visited at increasing intervals of time. Physical incapacitation reduces the effective walking distances of the ageing individual even within the immediate surroundings of the dwelling unit. The contact area finally shrinks to the individual home and the bedroom.

SERVICE AREAS

Distribution of Service Facilities. The urban fabric has two aspects. Subjectively, it has to be evaluated with the circulation of urban populations, with their individual contact areas, in mind. Objectively, it has to be viewed with regard to the spatial distribution of urban service facilities.

Transportation is the means by which subjective needs and objective facilities find themselves connected. A city is well developed or planned, if needed urban construction is placed within the range of easy access to that section of the population which wants to make use of it.

Occupational Facilities. Of foremost importance to the city dweller is easy access to the labor market, to those parts of the city where he can engage in gainful employment. Until recently, this meant primarily the accessibility of rapid transit lines to carry the individual city dweller from his place of residence to his place of work in the downtown area where both commercial and industrial activities were concentrated. Residential land values, under the circumstances, were greatly dependent upon the extension of public means of transportation. Along the course of rapid transit lines, residential housing shot far out into the periphery of the city, leaving a vacuum of open farm lands between the axial spokes of public means of transportation.[23]

Industrial plant location at the outskirts of the city has complicated the problem of commuting between place of work and place of resi-

---

[23] See Fig. 5, p. 107.

dence. Housing of industrial workers and some white collar labor
has found new advantages in location close to peripheral factory
sites. Such housing must be considered undesirable for two reasons:
(1) a high labor turnover, and (2) the gainful employment of more
than one member of the family.[24]

With a change of job, a once favorable residential location may
well turn into a gross liability. At a peripheral location, the home of
the industrial laborer is close to one or a limited number of factories
only. If interested in a change of position, the industrial laborer may
find himself obliged to travel far to another factory for work.

If the place of work of more than one family member has to be
considered, peripheral residential location offers similar disadvantages. Conditions close to the peripheral factory are seldom good for
full family employment. Conflicts also arise between residential propinquity to place of work and residential distance from educational
and recreational facilities.

White collor laborers share in this dilemma to a lesser extent. Their
places of work are still predominantly located in the central business
district, if not more conveniently in some nearby satellite loop.
Downtown transportation facilities tend to develop in close relationship to residential expansion. Thus, only the inhabitant of relatively
recent real estate developments is likely to suffer from inadequate
access to downtown commuting services.

As our cities grow, loss of commuting time gains importance as a
factor in the choice of urban residential location. In the urban fabric,
as it exists today, this frequently places a dilemma before the city
dweller. He may have to choose between more adequate, more recent, and more desirably located family housing in the outskirts of
the city, and less adequate quarters closer to his place of work in
residential areas built up at a much earlier date.[25]

Commercial Facilities. As a consumer, the city dweller is dependent upon the service range of commercial facilities located at various
distances from his family home. For the location of shopping facilities within the urban fabric, a simple principle prevails. High price
and rare occasions for purchase make it mandatory for commercial

---

[24] For a considerate discussion of the disadvantages of peripheral and close-
to-factory housing, see Kate K. Liepmann, *op. cit.*, pp. 98-103.

[25] For a popular discussion of this problem, see Svend Riemer, "To Remodel
or Build a New Home?" *The American Home* (January, 1946).

enterprise to be so located within the city that a relatively large area of potential consumers will be equally well serviced.

Specialty shopping will therefore most frequently be located in the central part of the city upon which the rapid transit lines converge, piercing through all residential areas.[26] Some specialty trade, particularly if it is dependent upon a large display area, will find location in the outer ring of the built-up city that is accessible to motor traffic on spacious belt-line highways, and can operate at lower cost due to less intensive competition for land uses in this environment. Dependent upon motor transportation, this specialty shopping belt at the outskirts is a relatively recent development. It does not cater to income levels below the range of car ownership.

The service range of the local shopping area is much more limited. Its recruitment area may be limited to walking distance. In outlying residential areas, where car ownership is taken for granted, it may extend further to a short driving distance. Repetitive needs of daily or weekly shopping within the local area make up for the limited number of potential consumers. The total amount of purchasing power carried to the local drug store and grocery store, although derived from a summation of relatively small individual purchases, suffices to support the economic enterprise at profit.

Distributed all over the urban fabric are shopping districts that are larger and more specialized, and cater to a wider recruitment area than do those found within walking distance. These shopping areas are of more than local importance and yet not sufficiently specialized and centrally located to draw consumers from all of the city. All over the city, these shopping areas are in competition with each other. They carry on about the same kind of trade. Degree of specialization increases with the size of the shopping center. The reason is the need for larger recruitment areas where sales are limited to rarer circumstances in the life of the individual city family.

The following commercial areas for specialty trading have been localized in the ecological pattern of New York City:

garments
theaters

[26] See Inez K. Rolph, "The Population Pattern in Relation to Retail Buying," *The American Journal of Sociology*, Vol. XXXVIII, No. 3 (November, 1932), Noel P. Gist and L. A. Halbert, *Urban Society*. New York: Thomas Y. Crowell Company, 1948, pp. 109-119; and Walter Firey, *Land Use in Central Boston*. Cambridge: Harvard University Press, 1947, Chapter VI, pp. 229-261.

automobiles
style
art
flowers
publishing
meat
wholesaling
machinery
produce
insurance
cotton textiles
leather
finance
fish
commodities

See: "A Baedecker of Business in New York," *Fortune*, July, 1939, p. 108 ff.

Most city dwellers make use of more than one of these shopping areas. Because trade attracts trade, there is a cumulative tendency in the development of these shopping centers. Shoppers drawn into a commercial district for some definite purchase may be induced, by displays or simply by occasions that offer themselves in the same store, to spend their money for other purposes. In the shopping area, therefore, the commercial value of available property is measured by the number of pedestrians passing by in the course of the average day or week.[27]

In the downtown shopping area, a wide array of random shopping opportunities is added to specialty shopping facilities. Excluding only daily shopping needs, practically all purchases can be negotiated in this environment which attracts people for the half-day or all-day shopping trip. The department store in itself aims at comprehensive coverage. It is supplemented by small retail stores of endless variety.

An interesting phenomenon observed at the fringes of the down-

---

[27] "Frequency of purchase affects the importance of convenience. Other things being equal, the greater the frequency, the more important the convenience of location." Richard U. Ratcliff, *Urban Land Economics*. New York: McGraw-Hill Book Company, Inc., 1949, p. 379. One of the best discussions of retail location will be found on pp. 376-384.

town shopping district is the concentration of a certain type of specialty shopping within relatively limited areas. Examples in case are the second-hand book stores, the flower markets, or the furriers' section in New York City. Contrary to retail grocery and drug stores which are sufficiently spaced not to ruin each other in competition, these specialty stores are concentrated in such a manner as to provide the specialty shopper a greater variety of shopping opportunities.

Educational Facilities. The distribution of the public school system over the city area is another point of concern to the city dweller. The service range of the elementary school should be limited to walking distance. Its service range may be extended by school bus or by means of public transportation, neither of which is quite satisfactory for children's needs.

High school attendance is drawn from a wider radius of family housing. City finances cannot afford to make high school services available within walking distance of all urban residences. Public means of transportation have to be relied upon to cover the distance between residence and school building. Needless to say, certain residential areas find themselves placed more advantageously than others.

Training on the college level of instruction may not be available at all within the city area. If it is, location is rarely chosen with the intra-urban transportation problem in mind. The city college may be close to the downtown business district upon which the rapid transit lines converge from all residential areas. Elaborate campus construction, on the other hand, is predicated on a spacious layout more suitably placed where land values are relatively low. Moreover, the ivory tower of academic learning is better accommodated at a distance from the hustle and bustle of the downtown business district. Under the circumstances, the university is not often easily accessible to all city dwellers and their children.

Specialized educational facilities, such as occupational schools, art schools, and adult educational institutions tend to be placed in the central part of town, where they are reached with relative ease from all residential sections, or where they can be attended after working hours by the population gainfully employed in the central city.

Recreational Facilities. Recreational facilities in our large cities are rarely spaced so that their services spread equitably to all sections of the residential population. In the past, the location of parks has been left to historical accident and peculiarities of topographical conditions. Ravines, steep lake sides, and swamps unsuitable for residential or other urban construction were superficially landscaped and used as parkland. The location of such parks was not necessarily amenable to best public usage.

Parks and playgrounds have been called the "lungs of the city." Attention has been given to the occurrence of green spots in the city at not too great distance from each other. Parks and playgrounds serve many different recreational functions. Therefore, serious consideration must be given to the recreational equipment made available in the park areas distributed through the urban fabric. Playgrounds for children of preschool age are unsuitable for the relaxation of the aged and the team play of adolescents. The beaches, in the summertime, attract populations from great distances, while the playground for children of nursery school age serves only a limited residential area within walking distance. If the differential uses of the urban green areas are considered, few cities even approximate an equitable distribution of services.[28]

The distribution of commercial recreation follows very much the pattern discussed for commercial services in general. The central business district is the climax area, with the roadhouse area in the peripheral belt as a secondary zone for recreation.[29] Less specialized and more frequently utilized services are distributed in more or less concentrated clusters over the entire city area. Commercial entertainment seems to follow in the wake of commercial trade. At various distances from the individual family home in the city, commercial facilities are available. Peripheral residential areas suffer from long commuting distances to the specialized entertainment facilities of the central bright light district. The central residential areas, on the other hand, suffer from lack of access to outdoor recreational facilities.

NATURAL AREAS — RECONSIDERED

Equilibrium in the Urban Fabric. The push and pull of preferences as supported by purchasing power (effective demands) tend to mold the urban fabric in such a manner as to relate social needs and

---

[28] See Harold MacLean Lewis, *op. cit.*, Chapter 10, "Parks and Recreational Facilities," pp. 195-214.

[29] See pp. 96-98.

urban construction to each other at a minimum of transportation distances. Automatic adjustment processes or city planning must establish some total equilibrium, some optimum spatial relationship between individual contact areas and the service ranges of urban institutions.

The task is infinitely complex due to the many factors involved. Nor will it ever be finished, because dynamic changes are constantly occurring in the urban environment. Changes both in preferences and in urban construction necessitate immediately a process of individual as well as institutional readjustment.

Clustering of Contacts and Services. Natural areas develop wherever a cluster of related needs for contact impinges upon a residential area, and where frequent visiting makes residential propinquity desirable for certain families. Thus the ethnic group and the criminal underworld pull together, due to the frequency of personal contacts within the group. In the single men's district downtown, specialized services catering to the needs of this population have their only chance for economic survival. Within this concentrated settlement of a very unique population, needed facilities can be held available at distances requiring none but pedestrian travel.

Populations of similar status tend to locate in close proximity to each other because opportunities for the establishment of friendships and for the active participation in the associational life in a relatively homogeneous residential section are thus increased. At the same income level, similar commercial, institutional, and recreational needs promise better service. Generally, special needs are better serviced in the relatively homogeneous residential environment. Status symbols are not the only reasons for the segregation of homogeneous populations.[30]

The Total Picture. Under the impact of existing and extending services and the changing preferences of the population, the entire urban fabric finds itself continuously in a state of flux. Residential location of the individual city dweller is carefully placed between different services provided commercially or publicly in the city. Once established, residential location in its turn attracts certain types of services.

Demand for space projects both residences and services far into the periphery of the built-up urban area. After having pulled apart

---

[30] For status and segregation, see pp. 309-315.

in the search for new building space, the urban population has to be pulled together again by means of artificial transportation, by rapid transit lines or motor traffic and a convenient highway system. The urban fabric extends or shrinks with the social needs of its population. But previous investment in urban construction tends to prejudice future developments. Detailed urban developments can be fully understood only on the basis of urban history.

SELECTED READINGS

1. *Highways in our National Life. A Symposium.* Princeton: Princeton University Press, 1950, pp. 66-163, 201-325, 414-475.

2. Henry S. Churchill, *The City is the People.* New York: Reynal & Hitchcock, 1945, pp. 1-186.

3. George A. Lundberg, Mirra Komarovsky, and Mary A. McInery, *Leisure. A Suburban Study.* New York: Columbia University Press, 1934, pp. 1-378.

4. Kate K. Liepmann, *The Journey to Work. Its Significance for Industries and Community Life.* New York: Oxford University Press, 1944, pp. 3-110, 191-194.

5. Richard U. Ratcliff, *Urban Land Economics.* New York: McGraw-Hill Book Company, Inc., 1949, pp. 1-145, 368-405.

PROBLEMS

1. *Recording and Design of Family Contact Patterns.* Select three families with different residential location in your community. Make sure that all members of each family are willing to co-operate with you and to give some time to the following project:

It will be your task to ascertain as completely and as exactly as possible the addresses which are important to all members of these families for contacts in connection with occupational, educational, commercial (shopping), recreational, church, associational, and informal social activities. You may limit yourself to the discussion of activities that have actually occurred during the last six months.

Secure a base map of your community. By the use of different colors or patterns of design you will then make visible the contact patterns of these individual families.

Discuss apparent differences and analyze the advantages and disadvantages of different residential location on the basis of the information gained.

2. *Advantages and Disadvantages of Peripheral Residential Location.* Peripheral residential location has been recommended and has been

deemed undesirable for various reasons. Consult Kate K. Liepmann's *Journey to Work,* and *Leisure,* by Lundberg, Komarovsky, and McInery. In reading these two books, collect arguments and quotations either in favor of or against peripheral residential location. Then discuss the specific needs and preferences for which peripheral residential location is either to be desired or avoided. Close your argument with a recommendation for general planning and building policies.

3. *Highway Planning or Relocation of Urban Construction.* City planning is a matter of establishing easy contact between the people and the type of urban construction they need. People, as a matter of fact, move from building to building for various purposes. To avoid waste movement, buildings can either be placed close to each other or connected by means of transportation. The alternative is not always clearly perceived. Highways often connect land uses which should not be found in their present locations in the first place. Urban construction is clustered that need not be as long as the different land uses are connected by convenient transportation.

Consult *Highways in our National Life.* Read all contributions related to problems of contemporary urban planning.

Report instances in which highway construction may substitute for costly relocation projects and instances in which highway construction could be made superfluous by relocation of private, public, commercial urban construction. Discuss the place for highway planning in the general field of city planning.

PART III

Urban Personality

CHAPTER 8

City Ways

THE CITY AND HUMAN NATURE

The Social Climate. Life in the city has a profound influence upon human nature.[1] This influence asserts itself as a cultural, not a biological, fact. We have no reliable information about the effects of insufficient sunlight and gasoline poisoning upon the health of the city dweller.[2] We do know that his personality changes under the impact of the social conditions to which he is exposed.

The city dweller associates with a much larger number of people than he can get closely acquainted with. Therefore, he must limit his contacts strictly to the business at hand. He deals with his boss as a boss, with the newspaper boy as a newspaper boy.

Small town people, villagers, and farmers look upon each other in a very different manner. The small town business man is known to his patrons also as a family man, a member of church and service club, a member of the local P.T.A., the fire brigade, and so forth. In the small town, the same people are tied to each other through many overlapping relationships.[3]

---

[1] The most systematic analysis of urban attitudes available in American publications, will be found in Louis Wirth, "Urbanism as a Way of Life," *The American Journal of Sociology*, Vol. XLIV, No. 1 (July, 1938), pp. 1-24.

[2] A discussion of the physical injuries to the human constitution through metropolitan living conditions is offered in Willy Hellpach, *Mensch und Volk der Grosstadt*. Stuttgart: Ferdinand Enke Verlag, 1939. See particularly Part II, "Psychophysik des Grosstadtdaseins," p. 36-67.

[3] See Granville Hicks, *Small Town*. New York: The Macmillan Company, 1947. For a description of overlapping institutional and personal relations in the small town, see Chapters VII and VIII, pp. 133-194.

Life in the city is characterized by a strange and paradoxical kind of anonymity. In spite of more numerous social contacts in the city, the individual city dweller remains unknown as a full personality to most of the people with whom he deals. He is known to his associates only with regard to that specialized, that segmentalized, that partial function with which their relationship is concerned.

How does this condition affect the personality of the city dweller? What sort of people are the city dwellers and in what respects do they differ from people with a different background? If we want to understand the place of the modern city in civilization we cannot neglect the socio-psychological aspects of city life which mold the human agent in this environment. After all, "the city is the people." [4]

Misunderstandings. The occasional visitor to the big city notices that city people behave differently. He resents his own clumsiness in finding his way on, let us say, Manhattan Island; he resents his inability to understand the many conventions, the small signs and gestures by which the milling city crowds find their way more conveniently around each other, by which they push their way effectively through railroad stations and eating places, through lines waiting at the box office or at the ball park.

It takes special training to move successfully through the urban environment. It does not necessarily take more intelligence. Yet, by comparison the occasional visitor appears lacking in intelligence to himself as well as to others.

We talk about the "country hick" and the "city slicker." These very terms carry connotations of mutual envy, contempt, and resentment. Actually, these stereotypes are tied not to individual differences but to different ways of life that impinge upon the personality formation of either city dweller or small town boy. Personal misunderstanding and social tension between these different sections of our society can be overcome only by realization of the causes of these differences.

At a first glance, the city dweller seems to be mentally more alert and smarter. This is particularly true if you meet him on the paved sidewalk of the metropolis. Whenever, as a vacationer, he finds his way to the farm, it is the country boy's turn to feel superior.

The differences between the urban and the rural personality, of

---

[4] See Henry Churchill, *The City Is The People.* New York: Reynal & Hitchcock, 1945.

course, go deeper than that. City and small town folks are distinguished not only by different techniques of living; their basic attitudes toward life are at variance with each other for reasons that we shall discuss presently.

ECONOMY OF HUMAN INTERACTION

Numbers. City behavior is dictated by a pressing need for economy in human interaction. The sheer quantity of interpersonal contacts experienced from day to day by the city dweller has a distinct influence upon the quality of these contacts.[5] They become more superficial. They are limited in a businesslike fashion to the problem at hand.

Personal contacts in the city are facilitated by highly standardized means of communication such as signals (traffic signals, for example), gestures, slogans, or formulas by which they understand each other without delay. This need for economy in urban human interaction shall be discussed in relation to these sociological concepts developed for the interpretation of the situation: (1) segmentalization, (2) stereotypes, (3) automatization, and (4) cosmopolitanism.

Every one of these concepts furnishes a slightly different approach to the analysis of urban attitudes. They are closely related to each other and somewhat overlapping in content.

Segmentalization. Urban dwellers associate with each other in partial roles which truly split the individual into a large number of different segments, each one applying to a select group of people or to distinct types of situation.[6]

In the course of his daily activities, the urban dweller is forced to participate in a great number of social groups. We call these groups

---

[5] "Increasing the number of inhabitants in a settlement beyond a certain limit will affect the relationships between them and the character of the city." Louis Wirth, *op. cit.*, pp. 10-11.

[6] "There arise numerous associations (in the city) on the basis of specialized interests differentiated out of the total community life. The city man substitutes a social life in associations for the community life which has lost its social effectiveness. . . . The association touches only certain aspects of his personality, demands only a limited participation, and leaves him free to enter into innumerable other associations," Nicholas J. Spykman, "A Social Philosophy of the City," in Ernest W. Burgess, editor, *The Urban Community*. Chicago: The University of Chicago Press, 1926, pp. 56-57.

"Characteristically, urbanites meet one another in highly segmental roles." Louis Wirth, *op. cit.*, p. 12.

secondary groups, if they function for a particular purpose and to the exclusion of other purposes.[7] The secondary group is seen in juxtaposition to the primary group, which is characterized by intimate and all-around acquaintance of all members in the group.[8] In the city such primary group relations prevail only in the family group and among close friends.

Elsewhere, the city dweller applies the short cut of specialization to social relationships. He deals with the barber as a barber only; he expects the barber to cut his hair and to give him a shave, and he expects him to do it well. He is not worried about the barber's family life, nor is he seriously (for other than conversational purposes) interested in the hobbies of the barber. The same holds true for other social relationships. The umpire at the baseball game may be the man to throw pop bottles at; the minister is the man to listen to once a week and to shake hands with at the end of the service; the bus driver, the salesman in the grocery store, the boss, and the stenographer, all have their own pidgeonholes in this scheme of affairs.

Social relations in the city are of a one-sided nature, although they are very intensive with regard to the segment of personality involved at any given time. It is not quite correct to say that these contacts are superficial. Contacts are intensive, but they are partial. It is certainly true that they do not fulfill the human need for personal relations which permit the sharing of the entire range of individual activities and ambitions with others, for contacts that permit complete identification, the giving and receiving of moral support.

Role Switching. Adjustment to the urban way of life puts a severe

[7] "The embodiment of rational thought is the tool, the machine, in which all the parts are manifestly designed to achieve a perfectly intelligible end. . . . The mentality of the modern man . . . is based upon the machine, and upon the application of science to all the interests of life — to education, to advertising, and, presently, perhaps to politics." Robert E. Park, "Magic, Mentality, and City Life," in Robert E. Park, Ernest W. Burgess, and Roderick D. McKenzie, *The City*. Chicago: The University of Chicago Press, 1925, p. 130.

"The growth of cities has been accompanied by the substitution of indirect, 'secondary,' for direct, face-to-face, 'primary' relations in the associations of individuals in the community." Robert E. Park, "The City: Suggestions for the Investigation of Human Behavior in the Urban Environment," in Robert E. Park, Ernest W. Burgess, and Roderick D. McKenzie, *op. cit.*, p. 23.

[8] About the primary group, see Richard T. La Piere and Paul R. Farnsworth, *Social Psychology*. New York: McGraw-Hill Book Company, Inc., 1936, pp. 222-226.

strain upon the individual.[9] He stands alone in the task of integrating a variety of social roles into a well-rounded whole that gives consistency to his behavior and grants the experience of self-identification. He has to learn to switch between these different roles as the situation demands.

He may have to treat his boss as a superior at one time, and as a social equal at another. He has to give himself to devotion in church, to intellectual concentration at work, to rooting at the football game, and to merrymaking at the cocktail party. His personality seems to be pulled apart. Great flexibility is demanded of him. He is threatened with the danger of losing himself in the turmoil of urban living.[10]

Stereotypes. Casual and varied contacts in the urban environment require quick orientation. The city dweller knows little about the many people with whom he associates during the course of the day. He is not familiar with their backgrounds. He does not know whether they are aggressive or friendly, whether they are willing to practice fair play or whether they are carrying chips on their shoulders. The need for quick orientation introduces another element into urban social relations: the use of stereotypes, which are snap judgments of personality.[11]

Stereotyped ideas about other people are, in the city environment, necessarily based upon relatively scant information. They have to be based upon behavior that can be observed rather than motivation and underlying sentiment. Appearance will be more important than character and emotional attributes. We all develop our own personal skill in dealing differently with the tough or the meek, the friendly or the officious individual. We find out by experience how the taxi driver, the man behind the counter in the post office, the business executive, or the janitor ought to be treated.

---

[9] "Demoralization (in the city) is the result of the formation of experience complexes which are nevertheless not integrated or organized among themselves sufficiently to secure behavior reactions corresponding with reality or with existing social values." William I. Thomas, "Personality in the Urban Environment," in Ernest W. Burgess, *op. cit.*, p. 47.

[10] For the "split personality," see Richard T. La Piere and Paul R. Farnsworth, *op. cit.*, p. 350.

[11] For the common use of stereotypes, and the dangers involved in their use, see Walter Lippmann, *Public Opinion*. New York: Pelican Books, 1946, Part III, "Stereotypes," pp. 59-117.

These stereotypes tend to be organized around crude social classifications. The rules of etiquette accepted by the experienced city dweller are oriented at occupational and income differences which express themselves in dress and appearance.

Further sophistication demands an understanding of different situations. We have to learn to distinguish between the executive who is our boss and the executive of a store in which we appear as consumers and patrons. If we learn, in addition, to size up people quickly as to their individual reaction patterns, their affability or hardboiled aggressiveness, we are well on the way to success in an environment where speedy reactions in dealing with strangers are at a premium.

Automatization. A great deal of urban behavior is guided through automatic controls.[12] To adhere to formalized general rules may become a matter of survival. If the city dweller does not stay on the right side of the metropolitan sidewalk, people will bump into him relentlessly. Nor will they feel grief for anybody who gets killed while jay-walking. As a participant in urban living, the city dweller is expected to follow a set of conventionalized rules.

The traffic lights at the street corner facilitate safe crossing. The watch in his pocket guarantees that the city dweller will not miss the show for which he has bought a ticket in advance. Nobody can wait for him. There are too many people involved. They have to be co-ordinated in some impersonal manner. If somebody whistles for a taxi, it means that he wants to hire it. If somebody asks a girl for her telephone number, it is a sign of personal interest, and if she gives it she should accept a date in the near future.

Fixed meanings are attached to gestures, words, and other means of communication. They stand as standardized symbols for intended interaction. The city dweller is asking for trouble if he refuses to accept the code that translates his gestures into commitment.

In business, the adherence to conventional communications is a must for economic survival. Observe the stock market, where certain gestures are accepted as definite indications that certain goods or bonds are either "sold" or "bought." The number of daily transactions on the stock market requires the automatization of communication.

---

[12] "Competition (in the city) and formal control mechanisms furnish the substitutes for the bonds of solidarity that are relied upon to hold a folk society together." Louis Wirth, *op. cit.*, p. 11.

Cosmopolitanism. The strain of social contacts in the city environment is eased by the avoidance of emotional involvement. Cosmopolitanism implies just that. There are other terms to refer to this same urban attitude. We talk about a blasé outlook on life, about urbanity, and about the impersonality of urban social relations.[13]

Emotionally, the city dweller lives in a hardened shell. As a matter of psychological survival, he has to abstain from close identification with all those people he meets during the course of the day. Yet fatigue and weariness in human interaction are not only a matter of numbers, but also of heterogenity. The city dweller finds himself surrounded by so many different types of people that his technique of stereotyping will fail him in developing an attitude of deep understanding sympathy.

Without some measure of indifference, it would be impossible for the city dweller not to be confused by the multiplicity of personalities and situations through which he has to steer the course of his life. This indifference is forced upon him. With an air of indifference, he learns to take many things and people for granted.

In the city, many peculiar people find their way to each other in mutual understanding. In a small town environment, they might be considered as strange individuals. In our large cities, like-minded deviants have a chance to cluster together and give sympathy in their own circle. They associate with each other and re-inforce their own peculiarities. There are drinkers and homosexuals, stamp collectors and kleptomaniacs. They become group conscious and meet the outside world with some confidence.

The city dweller has to get used to these people. He has to get used to the fact that it takes many kinds of people to make a world. He has to learn to accept quaint and unusual behavior without necessarily condoning it. Freedom rules in the city. Many minorities are entitled to express themselves and to organize in the pursuit of their ways of life. In the city, differences are more frankly expressed, and there is little desire to have the stamp of conformity placed upon all of them. The city dweller must learn to live with people who abide by different creeds.

The in-group with whom the individual feels identified by bonds

---

13 "The superficiality, the anonymity, and the transitory character of urban social relations make intelligible, also, the sophistication and the rationality generally ascribed to city-dwellers." *Ibid.,* p. 12.

of loyalty or community of interests does not encompass all inhabitants of the city. Relatively cohesive are the clusters of relatively
like-minded people. The social world beyond such clusters, or in-
groups,[14] is not necessarily the object of outright hostility. On the
contrary, different types of people are in need of each other in the
city environment. They work with each other and for each other,
albeit in a somewhat detached manner.

Deviant behavior may thus be taken for granted. The truly cosmopolitan individual is not shocked by it as the small town person
might be.[15] In the typical city dweller, the core of personality is
deeply imbedded in many layers of relatively superficial concern
with his immediate social environment.[16] Many casual social contacts
make it necessary for the city person to develop an ability to get
along with others with a minimum of friction.

A shell of indifference keeps the city dweller relatively invulner-
able as he goes through his daily routines, as he meets people and
loses contact with them forever, as faces appear on his horizon and
fade back into the milling crowds.

Urban Freedom. So far we have not dealt with the positive aspects
of the urban way of life. Our intellectual tradition tends to ignore
them. Many city people are small towners by origin, and inclined to
nostaligic contemplation of the past. Others have lost younger
family members to the lures of the city and consider the attractions
of city life demoralizing and somehow subversive. Others come to
the large cities as visitors and get a skewed perspective on the urban

---

[14] "The member of a primitive, relatively stable society will have a fairly
consistent set of person-to-person attitudes. He will probably classify people
into two contrasting groups — friends and enemies. . . . These two categories
and the people who enter each are culturally determined. The members of his
village or tribe are friends; they belong to his 'in-group.' But all the members
of some other group are his traditional enemies; they constitute his 'out-
group.' " Richard T. La Piere and Paul R. Farnsworth, *op. cit.*, pp. 222-223.

[15] "The metropolite is an individualist, a relativist, and a formalist in all
aspects of moral life. He substitutes 'good manners' for personal sympathy and
'correct behavior' for 'old-fashioned morality.' He refuses to accept the moral
code as fixed for all eternity, and reserves the right to design his own norms
of conduct." Nicholas J. Spykman, *op. cit.*, p. 60.

[16] "The individual's status is determined to a considerable degree by conventional signs — by fashion and 'front' — and the art of life is largely reduced
to skating on thin surfaces and a scrupulous study of style and manners."
Robert E. Park, *op. cit.*, p. 40.

way of life. Many books about the evils of the city have been written by indignant outsiders or disappointed renegades.[17]

Mankind has gained freedom and power under urban living conditions. The Middle Ages proclaimed that "stadtluft macht frei" (city air makes free). This statement referred to legal committments contained in the city charter. Living for a year and a day in the city literally made a free man out of the serf.

Today we are not beset by the fetters of feudalism but the city still holds the key to certain freedoms. The economy of human interaction, as described above, frees energies for specialized pursuits and breaks the fetters of tradition. Acceptance of change and the search for improvements is made of an urban clay. The individual is left free in his accommodation to social change. He is not hampered by the opinions of his neighbors. The strain to conform is replaced by the strain experienced in the adjustment to new technical and social instrumentalities.

The city dweller, at his best, is a specialist. He may have to sacrifice the full life, the well-rounded life, but specialization makes him free to put his shoulder effectively to the cart of modern civilization. The city is not the best place for comfort and security. It is a place for co-operation and teamwork, for pioneering effort and the dedication to specialized pursuits. City life involves many sacrifices, but it also releases potentialities that would lie unused under more stable living conditions.

Discrepancy Between Physical and Social Distance

In the city, physical and social distance do not coincide. Thousands and even millions of people move around each other within a very limited space, but they remain remote from each other socially. In spite of its milling crowds, the city can be one of the loneliest places.

Anonymity. In this urban environment, individuals remain anonymous to most people with whom they establish casual contacts during the course of the day. Their personalities remain unknown. Only a part of it, a segment of it function in most social situations.

---

[17] For the small town background of "social pathologists" and their critical views of modern urban civilization, see C. Wright Mills, "The Professional Ideology of Social Pathologists," *The American Journal of Sociology*, Vol. XLIX, No. 2 (September, 1943), pp. 165-180.

Whether casual, as with the newspaper boy, the druggist, or the milkman, or intensive and specialized, as with colleagues and with the boss, urban contacts will seldom make it possible for the city dweller to have his full personality recognized. He may feel like a cog in a machine. As such, there is a place for him. As a person in his own right, few or none may care about him.

No wonder we talk about "hiding in a crowd." As an individual the city dweller may find himself lost in the city. The urban family with its insistence upon companionship fills an important need by making up for the loss of other intimate social contacts.[18]

Passive Entertainment. Nor does the pattern of urban recreation overcome this condition. It is shaped to satisfy the desire for diversion on the part of large urban crowds that have no close acquaintance with each other and do not wish to establish such acquaintance.

Recreation often follows the line of passive entertainment in which large numbers of people participate by making themselves part of an audience. They may be crammed into a movie house. They may sit elbow to elbow and suffer from inadequate ventilation. Yet they do not get into social contact with each other. Their reactions may run parallel and reinforce each other as they laugh or cry; but they laugh and cry about something that is carried to them from the outside. There may be embarrassment as they leave and realize that they have shared their experiences with others.

Deviants. The anonymity of urban living attracts certain individuals and groups of individuals. The criminal seeks his field of activity in urban crowds because they offer opportunities for financial gain and the security of anonymity. He operates against the unknown sucker, while frequently held to unexpectedly strict standards of decency and fair play in behavior toward his friends.

So-called bohemian groups — artists, writers, students, and actors — also congregate in the city and find its social climate more congenial than that of the small town. In searching for new ways of expression, in searching for original truths uninfluenced by the wisdom of their elders, they shun an environment that holds them confined within the fetters of tradition. They seek refuge where they can remain anonymous. They seek the freedom of the city.

Group Loyalties. There is no relation between proximity in space and intimacy in urban social relations. This rule is not without ex-

---

[18] For the urban family and its functions, see Chapter 10.

ceptions. Immigrant groups have a tendency toward clustering within a few square blocks. They give expression, thereby, to the existence of mutual loyalties.

In the North End of Boston and the "Little Sicilies" of other large cities, Italian immigrant groups remain huddled close together in space, and provide themselves with an environment that physically and visibly protects them against the outside world. The housewives of the near North End in Boston talk about "going to America" when they visit the downtown shopping district.[19] This exception confirms the rule of prevailing urban anonymity. We are confronted here with a residue of village living.

As the process of Americanization proceeds, the younger generation leaves the settlement of the ethnic group and merges into the heterogeneous city population. These younger people leave the "village" and move to the city where they reside as individuals and where residential clustering has been abandoned for an urban way of life.[20]

Exploitation. Anonymous and segmentalized relationships easily turn into exploitative relations. Where personal loyalties have been relinquished, the struggle for success becomes highly individualized. Beyond strict adherence to the rules of the game, the city dweller is not committed to commiseration with his fellow man.

The same rules and conventions apply to everybody. To that extent the denizens of metropolis are bound to each other. But they remain unconcerned with the effects of an anonymous competition upon other human beings.

Gambling as well as the stock market have their home in the city. Property easily changes hands in the search for profit. In these endeavors, the city dweller stretches his hands out for nationwide and worldwide economic transactions. Space is not of the essence. In his struggle for success, however, he stands alone against the world.

---

[19] "One of the greatest surprises of my life . . . is to hear from time to time, especially from Italian women who have lived in America for years, a statement like this: 'I have been down to America today,' meaning that they have gone a few blocks outside the district of the Italian colony." Quoted in Walter Firey, *Land Use in Central Boston.* Cambridge: Harvard University Press, 1947, p. 211.

[20] For the exodus of the younger immigrant generation, see Walter Firey, *op. cit.*, p. 191: "Three broad reaction patterns may be discerned among the younger Italians: (a) the in-group reaction; (b) the rebel reaction; and (c) the apathetic reaction."

The Curse of Standardization

The city dweller is more exposed to the influence of standardization than other contemporaries. The many different people that flow into the confines of the city area put on a somewhat similar veneer.

Ethnic distinctions tend to be sloughed off. Beards are cut off. Foreign dress and peculiar tastes fall by the wayside. Even the gestures of the city dweller gradually mold themselves into a more or less unified pattern. Gesticulating Italians will be found only within the refuge of their own neighborhood, and the stolid reserve of the Scandinavian loosens up in the swirl of the downtown shopping center.

Mass-Fabrication. Mass-fabrication aids standardization. The trend toward mass-fabrication reaches back to the very dawn of the industrialization process.[21] It is based upon a process of production that takes advantage of the efficiencies of a division of labor.

The improved standard of living in our urban civilization is achieved at a cost. It is achieved through the sacrifice of individualized services and the sacrifice of those consumer goods catering to individual tastes. Only to the extent that the modern consumer is willing to submit to the limited choice between highly standardized products can he get them more cheaply and in greater quantity. The stamp of standardization is placed upon our food supply as well as our clothing, our housing preferences, and our entertainment pattern.[22]

Trademarks hold the attention of the housewife shopping in the grocery store. Bread comes in a package; and there are no local varieties because it is produced so cheaply that the local baker is unable to compete. Complicated machinery has replaced production by hand; and this machinery can be purchased only where a large regional or national market makes its amortization possible. On this large market, production aims at the best possible compromise be-

---

[21] In his "Anonymous History" of mechanization, Siegfried Giedion refers to numerous inventions in the service of efficient production that date back far into the early 18th century. See his *Mechanization Takes Command*. New York: Oxford University Press, 1948, particularly Part I, "Anonymous History," pp. 2-11.

[22] "The fullest exploitation of the possibilities of the division of labor and mass production . . . is possible only with standardization of processes and products." Louis Wirth, *op. cit.*, p. 17.

tweeen the tastes of large masses of consumers. Spice and flavor and highly individualized distinction has to be sacrificed because it may be annoying to some. Standardization encourages the production of neutral products, inoffensive to all, though flavorless, dull, and uninteresting:

The production of bread has proceeded through the entire sequence from craft to mass production. It has become whiter in the process and free from impurities. Nutritious values have been eliminated as undesirable irritants. For a select market, they were retained in the Graham bread, the production of which began at the time of the back-to-the-crafts movement of the 19th century.[23] Most consumers prefer the flavorless wheat bread of even texture, with a minimum of crust and of a consistency that preserves the illusion of freshness for more than a day.

Cigarettes have reached a similar dead-end of standardized consumer preferences. It is impossible to tell different brands from each other when blindfolded. Wieners vary little in taste, either with the seasons nor with the regions in which they are produced. Bacon comes in a standard package. Butter, milk, and eggs are held within the confines of standardized tastes, with regard both to flavor and appearance. Standardized soups are served at all counters on a nationwide basis.

Mechanical Equipment. The advantages of standardized parts in individually owned machinery are obvious. The ease of repair work on the Model-T Ford became known all over the world. Conventional tastes with regard to household gadgets level off to such an extent that it is scarcely possible for competing industries to vary much from the standard conception of what the gadget should look like.

A safety razor that does not look to the consumer like a safety razor has little chance for mass production. It will find itself squeezed out of the standardized urban market. The same holds true for vacuum cleaners and toasters, for the kitchen sink and the house itself. The market follows the taste of the average consumer.[24]

Neutral Tastes. The advantages of mass production are not the

---

[23] See Siegfried Giedion, *op. cit.*, "Mechanization and Organic Substance: Bread," pp. 169-208.

[24] *Ibid.*, Part VI, "Mechanization Encounters the Household," pp. 512-627.

only cause for the standardization of consumer goods. Consumer tastes in the modern city are, in fact, quite uniform.

City tastes travel the line of least resistance and encourage the producer to aim at qualities in his product that are generally acceptable, inoffensive, and void of any uniqueness that might keep some buyers from his market. Individual discrimination and taste are not strongly developed. As long as there is nothing in the product that is obviously unpleasant, he accepts it with ease. Consequently, he gets a product that is neither outstandingly good nor apt to arouse any displeasure. The virtues of the standardized consumer product of modern urban civilization are negative.

Lowbrow and Highbrow. In the city, there exist side by side a low "culture" and a high "culture" ("culture" here is used in the popular sense): the "culture" of the specialist and that of the undiscriminating urban consumer.[25] The sophisticated may manage to keep up with the advance of more than one of the contemporary esthetic pursuits. Most city dwellers do not "keep up" in any of the arts. They would have to devote considerable time to the development of their sensibilities. They tend to drift into less demanding activities.

Low "culture," aims at the lowest common denominator of the urban populace. Nobody is excluded. It stirs simple sensations and directs itself to a consumer in a state of passive relaxation. Music becomes background music, and art deteriorates to decoration.

High "culture," on the other hand, aims at a select group of followers who have disciplined their tastes to the point of discriminating enjoyment, to the point where they understand what the artist or the musician is trying to do and whether he is doing it well.

Low culture predominates in the contemporary urban scene. But, high culture also reaches an unprecedented pitch in the city, the only population settlement large enough to collect a sufficient number of connoisseurs to provide the creative artist with a livelihood.[26]

---

[25] The truly ancient origin of this split in urban culture is indicated by the following quotation:

"To the intellectual development of the literate section of a population carrying an urban culture may be given the designation the high intellectual tradition; to the intellectual development of the illiterate section may be given the designation the low intellectual tradition." Ralph Turner, *The Great Cultural Traditions.* Volume I, *The Ancient Cities,* New York: McGraw-Hill Book Company, Inc., 1941, p. 269.

[26] See also Chapters 11 and 12.

Vulgarization. In the arts, our cities are the centers of innovation and esthetic creation, but they form likewise the bulwark of resistance against "cultural" advancement. The artist, far ahead of his time, mingles on the urban asphalt with the opportunist of show-business, who caters to the lowest common denominator of contemporary taste. Objects of low culture are mass-produced. Advertisements and the juke-box stimulate the senses of the city dweller painlessly and without a challenge to effort. After a day in the office or at the factory, he is only too willing to let himself be lulled to sleep, emotionally, artistically, and literally. Vulgar habits of consumption are indeed habit forming.

The products of urban low culture engulf the city dweller from dawn to dusk. Their enjoyment is effortless and yet slightly stimulating. Office and factory workers indulge in popular song and dance and illustration as a pleasant background to the work of the day. Such habits build up resistance to active participation in the pursuit of the arts. The professional artist who is trained to devote his entire lifetime to one means of expression is so far ahead of all but the equally specialized connoisseurs that he loses contact with the majority of the urban population.

THE TENSION OF URBANISM

Challenge. Unusual tensions prevail in the artificial environment of the modern city. City life is stimulating and interesting, but it also causes weariness and fatigue. A complicated system of social organization enables the city dweller to reach beyond the individual human achievement in the implementation of new efficiencies and the creation of new comforts of living. He does in co-operation what he could not possibly do alone. He uses machines to increase his productivity.

In order to do so he has to make himself subservient to the machine. He has to consent to make himself part of a complicated social machinery. In accepting division of labor, he has to accept the stultifying consequences that go with it. The city dweller becomes one-sided.

Resistance. From early beginnings, city life has been accompanied by attempts to escape its undesirable aspects without relinquishing the improved standard of living produced by human co-operation in large urban settlements.

The wealthy always retained their country estates. They built their summer homes outside the fortified walls of the medieval city.[27] After the invention of gunpowder had made these fortifications useless, they left the inner city for good and escaped back to natural surroundings. At the beginning of the industrialization process, the French court withdrew from Paris and sought refuge in the artificial suburban parklands of Versailles. Improved means of transportation encouraged less well-to-do classes to leave the congested areas of central urban settlement. The flight to the suburbs has not abated yet.[28]

There are other reactions to undesirable aspects of city living. Physical exercise and sports, bathing, and swimming in the open air became recognized in the 19th century as necessary compensations for the sedentary and otherwise unnatural life in the big city. Interest in nature originates in the city with the force of social movement.[29] Today occasional relaxation in a natural environment has become part of the urban way of life.

It would appear as if man, in the metropolis, were straining his powers to the limits of his own capacity. As a way of life, the city presents a challenge, not a haven of accomplishment. Not all city dwellers do accept the challenge. Some try to live up to it, but most of them remain indifferent.

SELECTED READINGS

1. Louis Wirth, "Urbanism as a Way of Life," *The American Journal of Sociology*, Vol. XLIV, No. 1 (July, 1938), pp. 1-24.

2. Robert E. Park, Ernest W. Burgess, and Roderick D. McKenzie, *The City*. Chicago: The University of Chicago Press, 1925, pp. 1-46, pp. 80-160.

3. Ernest W. Burgess, editor, *The Urban Community*. Chicago: The University of Chicago Press, 1926, pp. 3-646.

---

[27] For the summer cottage of the medieval city dweller (Gartenhaus) outside the city walls, see Alwin Schultz, *Deutsches Leben im XIV und XV Jahrhundert*. Prag, Wien, Leipzig: Grosse Ausgabe. F. Tempsky, 1892, p. 128.

[28] See Chauncy D. Harris, "Suburbs," *The American Journal of Sociology*, Vol. XLIX, No. 1 (July, 1943), pp. 1-13.

[29] The zest for "regeneration" in the city is discussed in Siegfried Giedion, *op. cit.*, pp. 628-712. See his discussion of the history of the bath in urban civilization, particularly the section, "Hydropathy and the Return to Nature," pp. 660-662.

4. Walter Lippman, *Public Opinion*. New York: Penguin Books, 1946, pp. 1-316.

5. Granville Hicks, *Small Town*. New York: The Macmillan Company, 1947, pp. 3-276.

6. Siegfried Giedion, *Mechanization Takes Command*. New York: Oxford University Press, 1948, pp. 2-256, 389-712.

PROBLEMS

1. *Check on Stereotypes.* Select three urban stereotypes, such as the salesman, the teacher, the businessman, the coed, or the landlady. Ask for the opinions of 20 of your fellow students about these stereotypes. Try to develop as accurate a conception as possible about the following assumed attributes of the stereotypes:

   1. appearance
   2. gestures
   3. attitudes toward people
   4. attitudes toward business
   5. social participation
   6. family attitudes
   7. expected behavior at anonymous encounter in the city

   What are the traits of the individual stereotypes that appear in more than ten, and those that appear in all or practically all of your interviews? Define the three stereotypes in terms of these interview results.

   Check carefully with three individual representatives of the social groups to whom the stereotypes pertain about the presence or absence of stereotyped attributes.

   Discuss coincidence or lack of coincidence of stereotyped and actual attributes.

   Discuss the possible derivation of those stereotyped attributes that do not happen to be present in the actual cases investigated. Are your cases likely to be exceptional cases, or are the stereotyped attributes based upon selective judgment?

   Have you any reflections on the discussion of stereotypes in this chapter or in Walter Lippmann's *Public Opinion*, on pp. 59-117?

2. *Check on Anonymity.* Select from among your fellow students ten with a background of residence predominantly in an urban community of 50,000 population or more, and ten with a background of residence predominantly in a small urban community of 25,000 population or less (not farms).

   Obtain answers to the following questions from these two groups of interviewees: (1) How many people know your birthday, and who are they? (Insist upon an exhaustive list.); (2) How many homes in the residential block in which you live have you ever entered? (Consider all but commercial purposes for such intrusion.)

Comment on any noticeable differences between the two groups. Pay attention to the types of people who know a person's birthday, their residential location in relation to that of the interviewee, and the clustering or spread of homes entered in either of the two environments.

Consult references to Chapter 8 for materials about rural-urban differences. Can you hypothetically correct some of our assumptions about the rural-urban differences? Have you any questions that should be clarified by further research? Or do you feel that even your very fragmentary research encourages you to change your ideas or to perfect your reasoning about the occurrence of anonymity in the metropolitan or the small town environment?

If possible, point out different qualitative aspects with regard to the structure of intimate acquaintance in either environment.

3. *Standardization of Urban Consumer Habits.* Write an essay based on different types of information available about standardization of consumer habits in the modern city.

For technological backgrounds, see Siegfried Giedion, *Mechanization Takes Command.* New York: Oxford University Press, 1948.

For statistical information, see *Recent Social Trends.* New York: McGraw-Hill Book Company, Inc., 1933.

For socio-psychological information, see David Riesman, *The Lonely Crowd.* New Haven: Yale University Press, 1950.

Discuss advantages and disadvantages of standardization of consumer habits. What trends do you expect for the future? Why? Consider the resistance to standardization and its effectiveness.

CHAPTER 9

Man in the City

INDIVIDUALIZATION AND SOCIALIZATION IN THE CITY

Pre-Urban Social Control. The city is the home of the criminal. It is also the home of the genius. Both the criminal and the genius have one thing in common: neither of them adheres too strictly to traditional rules of behavior.

In pre-urban society, social behavior was molded by custom. The child observed the behavior of its elders, and thus learned to accept and expect traditional ways of doing things. In pre-urban society, the child made traditional behavior part of his own personality. These pre-urban societies were far from "primitive," although they have frequently been called so. In some respects they were more complex than the modern city.[1]

If they were not necessarily more primitive than society in the modern city, pre-urban societies were and are certainly more stable. If social change occurred, it was forced upon society from the outside either through change in natural environmental conditions (such as climate and natural resources) or through invasion by and interaction with other societies. Pre-urban society stood in lack of

---

[1] In pre-urban societies, family and kinship structures tend to be much more elaborate, more complex than in modern society. See Don Martindale, "The Variety of the Human Family," in Howard Becker and Reuben Hill, editors, *Family Marriage and Parenthood.* Boston: D. C. Heath and Company, 1948, pp. 50-83.

principles of social organization that would promote change or provide its members with any conception of progress.[2]

Stability in pre-urban society was guaranteed by a process of socialization through which the child grew into an awareness of how he ought to behave in all situations that he might be confronted with in the course of his life time, in the fullfilment of parental, occupational, religious, and civic obligations. Social learning was a matter of concrete conditioning. Deviant behavior, under the circumstances, required an unusual amount of intiative, imagination, drive, and independence.

Urban Social Control. In the modern city, social behavior is not anarchic. It is not completely open to individual choice and preference. Even in the modern metropolis, social behavior is steered by folkways, mores, and legislation into a framework that keeps urban society from lapsing into a complete state of chaos.

The fetters of custom have, however, been relaxed in several ways. Within the sphere of commercial and industrial activities, change is encouraged. Still, such change is kept within a framework of business ethics and commercial law which discriminates between fair and unfair competition. This framework consists of rules within which individual initiative is allowed to unfold. Our economic institutions, moreover, direct the activities of the entrepreneur through profit incentives.

The freedom of the city pertains primarily to the private lives of the urban population. Anonymity in the urban environment relaxes the pressure of custom. Still, even in the private lives of the city dwellers, some conformity of social behavior is achieved through social pressures. They originate in two ways: through law and through economic ambition.[3]

Law circumscribes the borderlines of permissible behavior. Such law protects the individual city dweller against violations of his per-

---

[2] "Behavior in the folk society is highly conventional. Custom fixes the rights and duties of individuals, and knowledge is not critically examined or objectively and systematically formulated. . . ."

"Behavior in the folk society is traditional, spontaneous, and uncritical, . . . what one man does is very much the same as what another man does, and . . . the patterns of conduct are clear and remain constant throughout the generations." Robert Redfield, "The Folk Society," *The American Journal of Sociology*, Vol. LII, No. 4 (January, 1947), pp. 300, 302.

[3] See also Chapters 13 and 14.

sonal rights. It protects the community against behavior not sanctioned by its mores. Within the limits of permissible behavior, the law leaves the individual free to do as he pleases.

In the small American town, it is economically rewarding to adhere to prevailing standards of "respectability." [4] The notion of respectability may refer to many different situations. It may determine the manner in which visitors are received at home, or whether or not one may have a divorce. It may require the individual to belong to some church, to see that the children behave more or less like the other children in the community, to refrain from drinking, or not to be too different with regard to dress, and style of home, thought, speech, and mannerisms.

Economic pressures achieve conformity of behavior in either a direct or an indirect manner. In the United States, the small town environment is known for strict social control applied to all members of the community. Because small town people live close together and know each other well, they are more vulnerable to informal means of social control such as gossip and ridicule, slander and defamation. More direct economic pressures are also brought to bear upon the small town dweller. Teachers, ministers, and other public servants endanger their positions if their children do not behave acceptably in the community. Businessmen risk the loss of patronage if they do not conform to acceptable standards of social behavior.

In the large city, the superficiality of social contacts in the work situation lowers the risk of direct and increases the importance of indirect economic pressures. As responsibility on the job increases, the individual is expected to conduct himself somewhat differently. Just as the top sergeant is supposed to change into a "gentleman" when he earns his commission, the business executive is expected to carry a different demeanor than the clerk in a subordinate position. He may be expected to live in a different part of town, drive a more expensive car, and wear more expensive clothes. Familiarity with the clerical staff turns into aloofness, subservience to superiors turns

---

[4] "Small town and village people are made to conform to socially approved behavior by the inescapability of economic pressures." Svend Riemer, "Villagers in Metropolis," *The British Journal of Sociology*, Vol. II, No. 1 (March, 1951), pp. 31-43.

into friendly familiarity. Early display of the social graces demanded from a man of a higher position invites promotion.

Freedom of the City. In his private life, however, the city dweller more easily than the small town dweller is able to submerge into relative freedom. Still, occasional entertaining throws his home open to inspection by his business associates. The social assets of belonging to the right country club, the right church, and the right service club, and participation in charities are ignored only at the cost of economic loss.

Within the borderlines of the law, complete freedom, even within the city, offers itself only to those indifferent to opportunities for

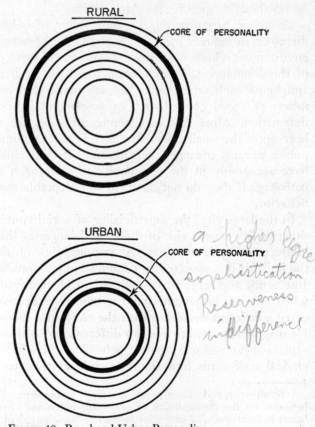

a higher degree
sophistication
Reserveness
indifference

FIGURE 10. Rural and Urban Personality
Core. From an idea by Kurt Lewin.

economic advancement. Relative freedom is obtained by all citizens with regard to the less conspicuous aspects of their private lives.

These conditions of urban freedom promote an attitude very different from that prevailing in non-urban societies.[5] The city dweller has to observe the rules of the game as long as he participates in the competitive occupational life of the city, but he is not chained to any one job. Nor is the etiquette of urban private living as binding as moral principle. It is certainly not as binding as the customs based on superstition in pre-urban society.

In adjusting to different social environments, the city dweller finds himself accepting different rules of social behavior as he goes along. Social pressures are limited to specific social contacts. From such contacts the city dweller may withdraw if he pleases. He has free choice with regard to the contacts he will seek.

Man feels more independent in the large city. Whatever social rules he adheres to are self-imposed, a token payment based on the city-dweller's own choice of wanting to participate in certain group activities. The city dweller commits himself voluntarily to a given set of folkways. They are not forcefully imposed upon him from without.

The core of urban personality withdraws behind many layers of highly standardized behavior by which the individual bids for group acceptance.[6] In the anonymous urban crowd, he moves under the acceptance of prevailing rules of urbanity, with formal politeness rather than consideration for his fellowman, with superficial chumminess rather than true familiarity, with purposes of expedient communication rather than moral principle in mind. While plunging with ease into numerous though superficial social contacts, the city dweller withholds part of himself. The urban environment permits him to submit only to a highly segmentalized process of socialization.

---

5 "Involved in an analysis of human behavior are three sets of factors: the social situation to which the person must adjust, the wishes of the person, and the attitudes of the person — constellated about certain objects and situations, and integrated into personality patterns." Harvey W. Zorbaugh, "The Dweller in Furnished Rooms: An Urban Type. *Proceedings* of the American Sociological Society. Vol. XX. Chicago: The University of Chicago Press, 1925, pp. 83-84.

6 The notion of "personality core" is used here as it is used in Kurt Lewin, "Some Socio-Psychological Differences between the United States and Germany," *Character and Personality*, Vol. IV (June, 1936), pp. 265-293. The United States-Germany continuum is easily transferred to the urban-rural continuum.

The Core of Urban Personality. The inner core of the city dweller's personality is not structured in terms of specific definitions of specific situations. Nothing in the core of his personality tells the city dweller how to behave at a football game or how to buy a suit of clothes in the department store. The city dweller is trained to behave correctly in all situations by way of ad hoc adjustments, that is, by direct conditioning at the scene of action, a process of conditioning that remains ever dependent upon the stimulus of the situation to which he exposes himself.

The "core" of personality can be defined for our purposes as those persistent attitudes which apply to all situations indiscriminately.[7] They determine whether a person will attack a certain task aggressively and with self-confidence, or timidly and with fear of failure. They do not tell him how to behave at a business conference or at a prayer meeting. The form of behavior, not its content, is carried by the core of the personality. The personality core in the city dweller is withdrawn behind numerous layers of surface-conditioned behavior.

Persistent individual traits deeply imbedded in the core of the personality are of relatively limited importance for the city dweller and his social adjustment. In the anonymous urban environment, social control in diverse situations is greatly limited to overt behavior. The individual city dweller finds specific definitions of specific situations indicated in his environment. The acceptance of prevailing standards of behavior in the office, in the factory, in the play group, or on the school grounds is the criterion by which his social success is determined. Nobody much cares at what costs of internal frustration such conformity is achieved.

The urban process of socialization leaves the individual relatively independent. While the city dweller moves through many fleeting situations, few people follow his shifting adjustments consistently enough to be interested in the core of his personality. The emphasis of the urban environment is upon social content rather than psychological form, upon the correct definition of the situation rather than upon desirable personality traits. The emphasis is upon etiquette rather than morals.

---

[7] These persistent attitudes correspond roughly to what other writers discuss as "psychogenic traits." See Ernest W. Burgess and Harvey J. Locke, *The Family.* New York: American Book Company, 1945, pp. 243-245.

Culture Conflict in the City

Conflicting Standards. The city dweller participates in the activities of many different groups and finds himself exposed to many different social situations. For successful participation in such group activities, he has to submit to accepted standards of behavior. Difficulties arise when the city dweller moves between different groups and situations. He may lose his orientation and apply the wrong standards of behavior to the wrong situation. If this happens to him, we call him maladjusted due to culture conflict.[8]

For examples of culture conflict, we do not have to go far. Consider the young man who carries barroom behavior into a church supper, or the girl brought up in the sedate and restrained environment of small town sewing circles who finds it impossible to join wholeheartedly in the fun of a college beer party.

Such culture conflict, to be sure, does not cause consequences worse than embarrassment. Such deviant behavior makes the city dweller an object of either ridicule or contempt. The resulting maladjustment may be slight, yet all elements of true culture conflict are present in these everyday situations.

Symptoms of Maladjustment. The consequences of culture conflict may, of course, lead to seriously damaging maladjustment. Culture conflict can be the origin of crime and delinquency, of neurosis, and of more serious mental disorders.[9] It has been the cause of divorce and family disorganization.[10]

Many symptoms of social and individual disorganization increase as we move from the non-urban to the urban environment, and as we move from urban communities of smaller size to urban communities of larger size.[11] In recording these conditions, we are limited to

[8] See Thorsten Sellin, *Culture Conflict and Crime*. New York: Social Science Research Council, 1938.

[9] Social disorganization in general has been defined as a "decrease of the influence of existing social rules of behavior upon individual members of the group." William I. Thomas and Florian Znaniecki, *The Polish Peasant in Europe and America*. New York: Alfred A. Knopf, 1918, Part II, p. 1128.

[10] "Similiarity of cultural background is favorable, and dissimilarity, if sufficiently great, is unfavorable to adjustment in marriage." Ernest W. Burgess and Harvey J. Locke, *The Family*. New York: American Book Company, 1945, p. 466.

[11] "It is probably a valid generalization that the incidence of crime is higher in large cities than in small communities or rural areas." Noel P. Gist and L. A. Halbert, *Urban Society*. New York: Thomas Y. Crowell Company, 1948, p. 347. See the discussion of "Crime Rates and Size of Community," pp. 347-349.

readily available census data. The rural-urban-metropolitan continuum of social disorganization, however, is statistically so convincing [12] that we may assume that the balance sheet of the city is unfavorably loaded even with conditions of individual and social disorganization less systematically recorded.

Nervous ailments not requiring institutional treatment are probably more frequent in the city as compared to the country, more frequent in the large as compared to the small city. Exploitative behavior not open to legal prosecution is probably more prevalent in the city than the country. The reason for these greater frequencies of individual and social disorganization in the city is related to the greater chance for experiences of culture conflict in the life of the city dweller.

TABLE XII

SPECIFIC CRIME RATES BY COMMUNITY SIZE

U.S.A. 1948

Offense	Over 250,000	100,000-250,000	50,000-100,000	25,000-50,000	10,000-25,000	Under 10,000
Murder	7.28	6.98	6.16	3.92	3.98	3.98
Manslaughter	5.11	5.06	3.42	2.97	1.84	2.14
Rape	16.81	11.54	9.38	7.63	6.65	9.11
Robbery	82.4	61.2	44.4	28.7	22.1	23.1
Assault	97.3	69.2	86.9	60.2	45.5	35.3
Burglary	464.9	489.3	417.3	343.7	276.7	245.4
Larceny	1037.8	1156.1	1053.5	1004.0	852.5	650.8
Auto Theft	184.0	212.8	172.6	152.3	119.7	100.0

Source: Uniform Crime Reports. F.B.I. U.S. Government Printing Office, 1949. XIX (2): 78.

The Nature of Maladjustment. What is maladjustment? [13] We need definite criteria to distinguish between one type of behavior as an indication of maladjustment, and another type of behavior as an indication of perfect adjustment.

[12] For a systematic account of specifically urban characteristics and many of these symptoms of social disorganization, see *Our Cities.* National Resources Committee. Washington, D.C.: U.S. Government Printing Office, June, 1937. See the section on "The Urban Way of Life," pp. 7-24.

[13] Technically, maladjustment occurs where social attitudes and social values fail to coincide. See William I. Thomas and Florian Znaniecki, *op. cit.,* "Methodological Note," pp. 1-86.

Technically, social maladjustment may be found in lack of conformity to socially accepted behavior. Social maladjustment is thus a relative concept (relative to environment). Still, we need a firm point from which to judge. Our judgment is bound to falter due to the co-existence of conflicting values in the urban environment. What is considered maladjustment from one point of view, may be considered perfect adjustment from another.

We sometimes hesitate to call boys growing up in the crime-infested slum environment maladajusted, even if they acquire long delinquency records. On the other hand, the boy who never runs into conflict with the law would be considered a deviant in this environment. The "well adjusted" boy appears to be really maladjusted, and vice versa.

The paradox results from the fact that different standards are applied in the definition of maladjustment. The difficulty is semantic, not real.[14]

In the city different standards of behavior prevail in different environments. We therefore have to make a choice of the standards we want to apply.

Considering the relativity of standards of behavior in the urban environment, we decide to define as maladjusted all behavior that runs afoul of the law. Full adjustment to urban living, however, requires more. We must ask of the well adjusted city dweller, moreover, that he be able to move efficiently and successfully in the environment of which he chooses to make himself a part. Within the limits of the law, we probably are not wrong in judging an individual's adjustment by the conformity of his behavior to the behavior accepted and approved by the group of which he is — by either circumstance or choice — a part.

Lack of Flexible Readjustment. Culture conflict causes maladjustment because human beings are not completely flexible in changing their behavior as they move from one environment to another. They carry with them the behavior routines to which they have become accustomed in the past. For perfect adjustment, previous conditioning would have to be abandoned completely as an individual steps from one environment into another that places different demands upon him. For reasons which the sociologist is not called upon to explain, this ideal condition is rarely achieved.

---

[14] The difficulty originated from lack of clear definitions. The term "maladjustment" is used to designate two different phenomena.

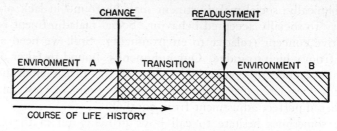

FIGURE 11. Environmental Conflict.

In the daily life of the city dweller, a certain amount of carry-over can be observed as he moves from one environment to another, as he finds himself challenged to exchange one segment of his "personality" for another.[15] The downtown clerk appears frowning, officious, and pre-occupied at the family dinner table. It takes him some time to relax sufficiently to meet the demands of a very different social role than the one he played in preceding hours. From a subservient clerk he is expected to change into a respect-demanding family father. This same clerk may forget himself in his behavior toward his boss at the office, if at a preceding luncheon meeting he associated with the same man in the back-slapping good fellowship of the service club.

The city environment is beset with innumerable occasions for such transitions that have to be made in adjustment to different surroundings. The city dweller is more exposed to such experiences than the non-urban individual because both environmental differences and social mobility are more pronounced in the city.[16]

---

[15] "The multiplication of persons in a state of interaction under conditions which make their contact as full personalities impossible produces that segmentalization of human relationships which has sometimes been seized upon by students of the mental life of the cities as an explanation of the 'schizoid' character of urban personality." Louis Wirth, "Urbanism as a Way of Life," *American Journal of Sociology*, XLIV, No. 1 (July, 1938), p. 12.

[16] "Transportation and communication have affected . . . what I have called the 'mobilization of the individual man.' They have multiplied the opportunities of the individual man for contact and for associations with his fellows, but they have made these contacts and associations more transitory, and less stable." Robert E. Park, "The City: Suggestions for the Investigation of Human Behavior in the Urban Environment," in Robert E. Park, Ernest W. Burgess, and Roderick D. McKenzie, *The City*. Chicago: The University of Chicago Press, 1925, p. 40.

The effects of culture conflict are more penetrating not only where the daily course of regular activities is involved, but where the entire life routine is transferred from one subculture to another, or where the entire life routine is suspended between two conflicting subcultures.

Subcultures. It is difficult to distinguish between merely situational conflicts and culture conflict proper. Both of them place a strain upon the individual city dweller. We are more inclined to talk about conflicting cultures where all facets of a way of life that has a chance for independent survival are concerned.

No two comprehensive culture patterns co-exist within the modern city. It is possible, however, to talk about subcultures in the city, that are *relatively* independent of each other. They have to fit themselves into our modern industrialized society. Yet, while all occupational activities have to be closely co-ordinated, relatively self-contained spheres of private life may well exist side by side.

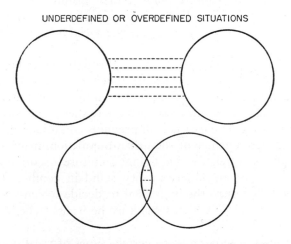

UNDERDEFINED OR OVERDEFINED SITUATIONS

FIGURE 12. Two Types of Culture Conflict. The second alternative is typical for the environment of the modern city. It permits irresponsible choice between the obligation stipulated by either subculture, it may lead to outright error in the definition of the situation, or it may affect the individual through emotional involvement in conflicting loyalties.

The distinction between different urban subcultures, however, is fuzzy at the edges. For precise delineation we have to resort to arbitrary criteria. The individual ethnic group blends gradually into other ethnic subcultures and into the subcultures provided by status and income divisions in the highly Americanized population.[17]

Definition of the Situation. Culture conflict is based upon subjective experience. Internalized within the individual, severe culture conflict such as that prone to develop in a clash of the values of a preliterate Navajo culture and modern American society may become a very real thing, although the total cultures as such do not run into hostile conflict with each other. We are not concerned with a situation in which different types of social organization compete with each other. Yet, individuals intermingle in the modern city whose social behavior has entirely or in part been conditioned in a different cultural environment.

The effects of culture conflict upon the individual may be either external or internal. Culture conflict may manifest itself in either lack of conformity of social behavior, or in internal tension and suffering which may indirectly influence the social behavior of the city dweller.

Culture conflict originates typically through contradictory definitions of the same situation. The city dweller is exposed to different values, which may have their ground in different cultures or subcultures. Several subcultures may have left their traces in the personality of the city dweller through previous conditioning processes.

Due to the heterogenity of the urban population, many situations are over-defined; often the immigrant's culture of origin and the culture of the modern American city stand in conflict with each other. It may be left to the individual to decide which situation he wants to accept and by which subculture he wants to be blamed for non-conformity.

This condition is in contrast to certain types of rural disorganization where the influences of a stable peasant society have lost their hold upon a population that has not as yet been touched by the constructive influences of social organization developed in the wake

---

[17] See George S. Hill, "The Use of the Culture Area Concept in Social Research," *The American Journal of Sociology*, Vol. XLVII, No. 1 (July, 1941), pp. 39-47.

of the industrialization process.[18] Under the circumstances, many social situations remain completely undefined, or "unstructured." [19]

MECHANISMS OF MALADJUSTMENT

Different Lines of Causation. Over-defined situations cause culture conflict in the modern city. But why? How, exactly, do overlapping definitions of the situation lead to social disorganization or to symtoms of individual maladjustment?

Exposed to culture conflict, the city dweller may encounter difficulties of social adjustment in three distinctly different ways. He may behave inadequately, (1) due to error, where a type of behavior is applied which is not accepted as a means to cope with the situation at hand, (2) due to inner tension, processes of internal maladjustment which make it impossible for the city dweller to deal expediently with the situation at hand, or (3) due to the egotistical pursuit of individual advantage causing the elements of conflicting culture patterns to be arbitrarily used to rationalize exploitative behavior.

Error. Crime due to outright error in the choice of conduct is illustrated by the following case:[20]

During the summer months, a song writer of renown is granted the privilege of using the home of his respectable middle class friends. He accepts the offer and, within the course of a few months, gives in this city home one riotous party after another for his friends. Late one night the financial resources of this group are sufficiently depleted to make impossible the continuation of a drinking bout that is pleasantly under way. They roll up the living room carpet and

---

[18] See William I. Thomas and Florian Znaniecki, *op. cit.*, pp. 1127-1300.

[19] The conception of a "social vacuum," hinted at in the text, is of course acceptable only as a borderline concept. W. I. Thomas and Florian Znaniecki deal with rural social disorganization in terms of an "overdefined" situation. The peasant culture and modern urban civilization are both impinging upon the immigrants to this country. Still, this writer feels that some phenomena of disorganization, such as the disruption of family loyalties and the crude egotistical exploitation of all social relationships, might be understood better through the complete absence of either traditional or modern social controls, rather than through their overlapping. For an example of such conditions, see Svend Riemer, "A Research Note on Incest," *The American Journal of Sociology*, Vol. XLV, No. 4 (January, 1940), pp. 566-575.

[20] From clinical experience in the prison clinic on Langholmen, Stockholm, Sweden.

take it to the pawnbroker. With the proceeds of this venture they merrily continue their party.

Nothing untoward would result from such actions, were it not for an unexpected lack of a "sense of humor" on the part of the middle class hosts. They go to the police and have the song writer arrested for theft. "Bohemian" standards of behavior, in this instance, clash with the standards of conduct expected by a respectable middle class family. What might be laughed off as a bad practical joke within the group is considered crime and treated as such by people with different standards.

Emotional Involvement. More indirect processes of emotional involvement must be blamed for other types of urban delinquency and crime. A social group particularly prone to enter into careers of delinquency and crime is the first American born generation, which, in the immigrant settlements of our large cities, totters somewhat haplessly back and forth between the old-world culture, represented by their parents, and standards of the American way of life, as represented by their school teachers.[21]

It would be wrong to blame such crime and delinquency upon the lack of knowledge of American laws, or to consider it the result of uncertain loyalties. Some juvenile delinquents, in this environment, are prone to act aggressively on a neurotic basis. Continuously exposed to conflicting demands upon their behavior by either parents, teachers, or schoolmates, the process of personality integration is sufficiently thwarted to lead to indiscriminate outbursts of hostile behavior.

Some delinquents, in this environment, steal "for kicks." They appear irrationally destructive and prone to commit crime that does not do them any good, crime that results from the inner conflict between alternately accepted and rejected authorities. Deep-seated personality dynamics have to be taken into consideration here to explain these processes of crime causation.

Crime and delinquency are not the only symptoms of maladjustment produced in this manner. The consequences of culture conflict

---

[21] "The second generation of immigrants has been generally believed to be more criminalistic than their foreign-born parents and also more criminalistic than the native whites of native parentage." Edwin H. Sutherland, *Principles of Criminology*. New York: J. B. Lippincott Company, 1939, p. 126.

The above assertion is not left without qualification, but it seems possible to explain the exceptions by special circumstances.

may well be arrested at the level of neurosis.[22] Thus, maladjustment may not cause more than internal suffering, occupational inefficiencies, and inadequacies. Culture conflicts keep some of these people from functioning well as family members and in the fulfillment of their civic and occupational duties.

Exploitation. Culture conflict can also be turned into an efficient means of exploitation.

Any internally consistent culture pattern imposes duties upon its members and grants them certain privileges, according to social and family position. Exposed to the impact of different social values, the individual is tempted to accept, by way of inconsistent choice, the privileges wherever they are offered and to refute corresponding obligations under reference to that value system by which they are not demanded.

The immigrant father may demand from his children that subservient respect which, according to old-world standards, is his due. He may fail, on the other hand, to live up to corresponding obligations of protecting all members of the extended family against economic insecurities. The young married man may encourage his wife to contribute, at least temporarily, to the family income by some kind of gainful employment. Simultaneously, he may expect to remain free as he was when he was the only breadwinner. Immigrant children are not unlikely to make cunning use of avoidance techniques.[23] They may refer to demands of parental authority when they conflict with the demands of the school system, while referring to school authorities in order to escape domestic obligations.

In an area of culture conflict, the city dweller is left to pick and choose between obligations and privileges that impinge upon him from different value systems. Wanting to eat his cake and have it too, he may endeavor to gain maximum advantages in his choices.

ANTI-SOCIAL ORGANIZATION

Gang Formation. Where the experience of culture conflict be-

---

[22] See Karen Horney, *The Neurotic Personality in Our Time*. New York: W. W. Norton and Company, 1937.

[23] Parent-avoidance techniques (in the Polish immigrant community) are easily acquired because of the parents' halting use of English and the fact that both parents, typically, work in the local factory." Arnold W. Green, "The Middle Class Male Child and Neurosis," *American Sociological Review*, Vol. 11, No. 1 (February, 1946), p. 33.

comes a mass phenomenon, as it does in the modern city, we observe a tendency toward a spontaneous structuring of individualized and socially amorphous masses, a tendency of "gang-formation." [24]

In an area of culture conflict the city dweller is likely to find himself without binding attachment to any one of the different overlapping value systems. In choosing between kinds of etiquette, he achieves a degree of emancipation which leaves him — within the limits of the law — to do more or less as he pleases.

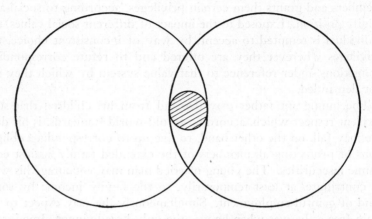

FIGURE 13. Anti-social Organization. In an area of overlapping sub-cultures, tendencies toward gang formation or similar voluntary associations arise. These organizations may be considered anti-social in the light of either sub-culture.

Within the chaos of culture conflict areas in the city, where definitions of the situation are in competition with each other and thus lose their hold upon the individuals, the crystallization of a very elementary type of new social organization occurs. Gang-formation finds a fertile soil. It satisfies the individual's yearning for escape from freedom.[25] It puts the stamp of socially approved or disapproved behavior upon an environment and a range of activities within which the individual otherwise would be left to shift for himself.

Adolescent Gangs. Gang-formation is particularly rampant in adolescence because our adolescents find themselves temporarily

---

[24] Frederick M. Thrasher, *The Gang.* Chicago: The University of Chicago Press, 1927.

[25] See Erich Fromm, *Escape from Freedom.* New York: Farrar & Rinehart, Inc., 1941.

operating in a socially unstructured field. While gradually escaping from parental authority, they are not as yet hamstrung by the fetters of social approval or disapproval to which they must submit in their struggle for acceptance in adult society, in their struggle for occupational and status advancement. Exposed to two competing standards of conduct, they forge themselves spontaneously into a pattern of organization that does not borrow its claim to authority from either parental approval, school sanction, or patterns of social success.

We accept the tendency toward gang-formation in an unstructured social field as an elementary sociological fact We can assume that gang-formation is the result of a demand for socialization, however primitive, in an otherwise not well socialized environment.

Gang-formation is strongest in those areas of the city most exposed to culture conflict. In every part of the city, to be sure, adolescents tend to form gangs. They willingly submit to gang rule. Yet, where internally consistent culture patterns reach out for the growing individual both from the side of parental guidance and from the side of adult society, the socializing function of the gang is limited to matters of recreation and of sociability for its own sake.

Gang structures are absorbed within the activities of boys' and girls' clubs, within the mutual give and take of athletic teams, church groups, debating societies, and so forth. The boy scouts and the campfire girls, sororities, and fraternities permit the constructive aspects of gang-formation to operate within their highly institutionalized framework.[26] In the urban area of culture conflict, gangs as well as individuals are more or less left to shift for themselves. Youth services may try to penetrate into this environment. Yet, they are not always successful in making their services acceptable to groups that are exposed not only to the transition period of adolescence but also to the conflicting demands of different cultures.

Adult Gangs. In our cities there is some carry-over of adolescent gang activities into adult life. Problems of social disorganization may arise where such gang activities extend beyond the leisure time activities of a certain group. This does occur in the environment of the professional criminal, the "gangster." [27]

---

[26] For the nature of social institutions, see Chapter 14.

[27] The terminology applied to such group formation may differ. "The working group of professional thieves is known as a mob. troupe. or outfit." Edwin H. Sutherland, *The Professional Thief.* Chicago: The University of Chicago Press, 1937, p. 27. The structure of the criminal mob is analyzed in Chapter II, pp. 27-42.

In areas of culture conflict, the individual growing into adulthood is often delayed in his adjustment to the dominant structures of occupational and social activities Both immigrant culture and modern urban society may claim the individual's loyalties in conflicting demands upon his behavior. For many of the individuals, a solution is found in strict separation between the private and the public spheres of their lives, between leisure time and time devoted to gainful employment. More consistent personality integration is accomplished in adult gang activities that integrate ethnic traditions and modern American standards of behavior.

Within the adult gang, the offspring from our immigrant communities has an opportunity of retaining informal social contact with other members of the same ethnic group, or with members of other ethnic groups similarly exposed to culture conflict. They are joined, furthermore, by individuals in the slum environment who — for personal reasons of emotional maladjustment or economic failure — have severed their relations with more homogeneous and more highly Americanized urban environments.

These adult groups provide opportunities for economic advancement from which — due to their ethnic status — their members are otherwise excluded. In the pursuit of economic gain, such gangs do not hesitate to engage in illegal activities. They are made subservient to political purposes and are not resistant to bribery and corruption. These outlets — in spite of some carryover from adolescent delinquency — are chosen because of the lack of other outlets.

In his isolation, then, the urban individual is prone to submit to a process of socialization that favors a principle of social organization incongruent with otherwise accepted social and business relations.[28] Certain affinities exist between this type of gang-formation and fascism, both being dependent upon the breakdown of predominant (manifest)[29] social structures, individual isolation, and culture conflict.

Gang Structure. The individual in gangland considers himself only secondarily an integral part of the larger urban community. He may live his private life within the boundaries of the law. He may

[28] See pp. 240-241.

[29] For manifest and latent function, see Robert K. Merton, *Social Theory and Social Structure*. Glencoe, Ill.: The Free Press, 1949, Chapter I, "Manifest and Latent Functions," pp. 21-81.

gain his livelihood within the framework of approved business channels. His interests may be represented by government, public institutions, and voluntary associations, such as trade unions, political parties, pressure groups, and so forth.

Yet, the member of the gang regards the larger community and its institutions from a different viewpoint than the ordinary citizen. Not bound to the urban community at large by strong bonds of loyalty, he is prone to consider it a field open to exploitation by himself and the other members of his gang. Indifference to existing social, business, and governmental institutions may give way to outright hostility in case of conflicting interests. In gangland, the officers of law enforcement are the object of hatred and contempt.

Within the gang itself, mutual loyalties attain an intensity rarely matched by other social groups in the urban environment. There are few qualifications to in-group loyalties. In principle, there are none. The struggle for gang leadership may insert an element of insecurity into an otherwise exceedingly cohesive group. Frustrated ambitions to obtain leadership may cause a break with in-group loyalties.

Leadership in adolescent as well as adult gangs rests often upon the command of physical power. In the adolescent gang, a pecking order of physical prowess is established and crowned by a leader who holds his position because he is able to beat up any other member of the gang. There are some exceptions to this rule; for example, when intelligence, daring, or popularity is used in the manipulation of social relations within the gang. In other exceptional cases, the one-sex composition of the gang may be disrupted by the participation of a female. Where this occurs, the female may achieve a position of supreme leadership.[30]

In the adult criminal gang, physical strength as a qualification for leadership is often replaced by access to other means of physical power. The gun, the bodyguard, and the daring to kill step in where gang activities cannot constantly be endangered by personality shifts in positions of central control. The more complex adult gang activities become, the more elaborate is the machinery of power that holds it together. The more important relationships with outside groups become, the greater is the tendency to place leadership at the

---

[30] See Frederick M. Thrasher, *The Gang*. Chicago: The University of Chicago Press, 1927, Chapter XIII, "Sex in the Gang," pp. 221-246.

foot of organizational ability and to secure the permanence of such leadership through indirect means of physical control.[31]

INSANITY IN THE CITY

Urban Stress. Another reaction to culture conflict in the city is withdrawal into insanity. Lack of opportunities to establish desirable and satisfying social contacts in the heterogeneous environment of urban culture conflict may lead to fictitious processes of adjustment within the "pseudo-community" of psychotic derivation.[32] Neurotic as well as psychotic ailments have been attributed to stresses inherent in the urban way of life.[33]

Discussions of the neurotic personality most frequently focus upon the modern urban personalitiy[34] The internalization of controls — in the form of self-imposed inhibitions — places particularly strenuous demands upon the city dweller, who is constantly and at close range rubbing elbows with his fellow men.

In addition to the number, the great variety of social contacts in the city causes strain. It is not based upon the severity of restrictions as such or upon the inescapability of having to adjust constantly with little opportunity for relaxation. It is a strain inherent in the need for constant role-switching.

The city has been blamed for mental disorders originating from severe conflicts between the id and the super-ego (neuroses), and also for disturbances in personality organization, with consequent loss of contact with reality (psychoses).

Neuroses. Whether neuroses are more frequent in the city than in non-urban areas has never been fully ascertained. Attempts to do so are beset by the difficulty of discriminating between the actual occurrence of neuroses and the extent to which they come to the attention of our medical services. Better urban health services are bound to lead to more abundant treatment of neurotic ailments. Different attitudes of potential patients must also be taken into consid-

---

[31] See *The Autobiography of Lincoln Steffens.* New York: Harcourt, Brace and Company, 1931, Chapter VIII, "Political and Financial," pp. 231-238. Consult also the description of individual bosses of city machines (see index under 'boss').

[32] See Norman Cameron, "The Paranoid Pseudo-Community," *American Journal of Sociology*, XLIX, No. 1 (July, 1943), pp. 32-38.

[33] See H. Warren Dunham, "Current Status of Ecological Research in Mental Disorders," *Social Forces*, Vol. 25, No. 3 (March, 1947), pp. 321-326.

[34] See Karen Horney, *op. cit.*

eration. The city dweller is more likely than the small town person and the farmer to avail himself of psychiatric help.

The claim that city life produces a higher rate of neuroses than the non-urban environment remains at the present time within the realm of conjecture. Still, this conjecture probably coincides with actual conditions. In assuming a close relationship between city life and the formation of neuroses, we consider the stresses exerted upon the city dweller through a life of intense competition, a high degree of social mobility, and frequent and varied culture conflicts.

Psychoses. The spread of psychoses in the urban environment has been ascertained with more accuracy than that of neurotic behavior. Careful investigation permits even a breakdown into different types of psychoses.[35] The occurrence of schizophrenia is more frequent in the center than in the periphery of the city.

This is the type of psychosis associated superficially with a "split personality." It is accompanied by the loss of self-identification. The individual afflicted loses the ability to place experiences in proper relationship to each other and to his personal concerns. Everything seems to be of equal importance, whether it be the fly running up the wallpaper or the child dying of diphtheria. Personal experiences remain unstructured. Considering the haste with which multitudinous but shallow experiences follow upon each other in the life of the city dweller, the symptoms of schizophrenic psychoses appear indeed to be expressive of the urban way of life.

The symptoms of schizophrenic psychoses resemble exaggerations of widespread urban attitudes.[36] Such similarity, however, does not establish a relationship of cause and effect.

There can be no doubt about the concentration of schizophrenic afflictions in the areas surrounding the central business district, within the inner Area of Transition. Scientific comparisons of rates of schizophrenic conditions between city and country, on the other hand, are not available. Therefore, even the most elaborate statements about similarities between urban life and this type of psychosis rest on not much more than spurious argument. The reasons for the

[35] See R. E. L. Faris and H. W. Dunham, *Mental Disorders in Urban Areas.* Chicago: The University of Chicago Press, 1939.

[36] "The so-called 'split personality' is but an extreme manifestation of this exceedingly commonplace technique by which the individual can avoid the tensions which are caused by conflicting life experiences." Richard T. LaPiere and Paul R. Farnsworth, *Social Psychology.* New York: McGraw-Hill Book Company, Inc., 1936, p. 350.

clustering of schizophrenia close to the central business district are also far from known. Two lines of reasoning may explain the well established fact. It could be that (1) schizophrenia is produced by living conditions in the central slum environment, or that (2) schizophrenic individuals are attracted to this area because their personality needs are here best accommodated.

Whatever the line of cause and effect, some such relationship is likely to exist. It is not possible to say with assurance, however, that schizophrenia is a type of insanity that typically originates in the city.

THE MARGINAL MAN IN THE CITY

Genius. Modern science is no longer committed to the idea that insanity and genius are psychologically related to each other.[37] Still, the criminal, the insane, and the genius make their homes more often in the city than elsewhere. The question remains whether all these one-sided distributions can be attributed to a special attractiveness of urban living conditions.

The term "genius" has been used to cover a wide range of personal qualities and social achievements. Genius has been associated with divine inspiration; it has been associated with unique personality qualities not attached to any measurable personality attributes.

Today the social scientist most often talks about genius in terms of the higher ranges of test intelligence.[38] The social scientist places more emphasis upon measurable performance of intelligence than is customary in common usage of the term genius. Other scientists consider outstanding achievement as an indication of genius. Thus, a social component is added to the concept. High intelligence is not always considered enough to define an individual as a genius. Important contributions to our culture are required to justify the designation.[39]

The genius is expected not only to adjust to existing conditions, to

---

[37] See Cesare Lombroso, *The Man of Genius.* New York: Charles Scribner's Sons, undated. Although the English title of this publication does not indicate it, the entire book is devoted to a discussion of the avowed relationship between genius and insanity.

[38] For the definition of test intelligence, see William F. Ogburn and Meyer F. Nimkoff, *Sociology.* New York: Houghton Mifflin Company, 1940, p. 90. See also the 1950 edition of the same publication, p. 204 ff.

[39] "The social component in general intelligence should be kept in mind by the reader in estimating the importance of intelligence for personality." William F. Ogburn and Meyer F. Nimkoff, *op. cit.*, p. 148.

support desirable trends of progress, or to rise to unequalled heights
of specialized performance, he is expected to make some "creative"
contribution, to move on his own and not entirely as the outcome
of social conditioning. The personality of the genius is thus considered more than a medium that gathers social influences and carries
them effectively into vocational and avocational activities. He carries the challenge of new tasks to the social environment in which
he finds himself anchored.

Such definition of genius makes its appearance greatly dependent
upon social opportunity. A fairly even distribution of this phenomenon in history would have to be expected were it to be considered an attribute inherent in the physical constitution of man.
But genius appears in human history quite sporadically, in dense
concentrations in some periods and locations and very sparsely
spread in others. The phenomenon of genius seems dependent upon
specific social outlets.[40]

If in some manner [41] we pin the concept of genius down to something that can be observed empirically and systematically recorded,
we shall find a preponderance of it in the city.[42]

But the location of men with outstanding merits in the modern
city does not in itself credit the urban environment with having

---

"In ranking geniuses we evidently do not rank them according to intrinsic
ability, which we have little means of estimating as such; rather, they appear
to us as the composite product of personal superiority and cultural influence."
A. L. Kroeber, *Configuration of Culture Growth*. Berkeley and Los Angeles:
University of California Press, 1944, p. 15.

[40] This argument is well developed in A. L. Kroeber, *op. cit.*, section on
"Genius," pp. 7-16.

[41] Unfortunately, the following contributions have not been applied to the
rural-urban differential:
Joseph Schneider, "Social Class, Historical Circumstances and Fame," *The
American Journal of Sociology*, Vol. XLIII, No. 1 (July, 1937), pp. 37-56;
"The Cultural Situation as a Condition for the Achievement of Fame," *Ameri-
can Sociological Review*, Vol. 2 No. 4 (August, 1937), pp. 480-491; and "The
Definition of Eminence and the Social Origins of Famous English Men of
Genius," *American Sociological Review*, Vol. 3, No. 6 (December, 1938), pp.
834-849.
The feudal as well as the urban upper classes stand out as most productive
of genius.

[42] Urban background is associated with higher test-intelligence than rural
background. See Noel P. Gist and Carroll D. Clark, "Intelligence as a Selective
Factor in Rural-Urban Migrations," *The American Journal of Sociology*, Vol.
XLIV, No. 1 (July, 1938), pp. 36-58. See also Frank S. Freeman, *Theory and
Practice of Psychological Testing*. New York: Henry Holt and Company,
1950, p. 478.

produced genius. We must apply the same reasoning we applied to the concentration of insanity and criminal behavior in the city. Genius may be more prevalent in the city because the city dweller is more stimulated to make outstanding cultural contributions, but it may also be that individuals with potentialities for such outstanding contributions are attracted to the urban environment.

There is little reason to question the contention that present differential migrations tend to draw from the urban hinterland (the small town and the farm) more individuals in the higher than in the lower intelligence brackets.[43]

Freedom for Social Change. Whether genius is grown in the city or attracted to the city, the urban environment is congenial to outstanding historical contributions productive of social change.[44] Paradoxically, we find the basis for outstanding economic, social, and cultural contributions in the same urban environment that accounts for high rates of delinquency, crime, insanity, divorce, suicide, and other symptoms of social disorganization. The freedom of urban living is equally conducive to the constructive and the destructive tendencies in modern civilization.

The freedom of urban living is due to the prevalence of culture conflict and the relative anonymity of urban existence.

Within the limits of the law, the city dweller is free to pick and choose between different values and different standards of behavior. He is challenged, as a matter of fact, to arrive at some sort of personal integration of values and standards within the urban chaos of coexisting and overlapping standards appealing simultaneously to the individual. The opportunity for such choice grants otherwise un-

---

[43] For city-ward migration differentiated according to intelligence, see pp. 81 ff.

[44] "Cities, and particularly the great cities, are in unstable equilibrium. The result is that the vast casual and mobile aggregations which constitute our urban populations are in a state of perpetual agitation, swept by every new wind of doctrine, subject to constant alarms, and in consequence the community is in a chronic condition of crisis."

"In a small community it is the normal man, the man without eccentricity or genius, who seems most likely to succeed. The small community often tolerates eccentricity. The city, on the contrary, rewards it."

"The reason the modern man is a more rational animal than his more primitive ancestor is possibly because he lives in a city, where most of the interests and values of life have been rationalized, reduced to measurable units, and even made objects of barter and sale." Robert E. Park, in various contributions to Robert E. Park, Ernest W. Burgess, and Roderick D. McKenzie, *op. cit.*, pp. 22, 41, and 130.

equalled freedom to the city dweller; therein lies his privilege. The task of choosing and the task of developing an internally consistent pattern of standards for his personal orientation, on the other hand, places upon the city dweller an elsewhere unequalled burden of individual responsibility; therein lies an unusual challenge.

Marginal Existence. The modern city dweller fits well the conception of the "marginal man" located at the fringe of different cultures or subcultures.[45] He enjoys individual freedom from committment to any encompassing value system. At the same time, he has little guidance for the orientation of his social life. Social experimentation is forced upon him.

In the thin air of anonymous living, the urban individual is given a chance to define and redefine for himself, for his immediate associates, and for the large audience of the urban public the reason for his existence and the desirability or undesirability of prevailing social trends. He is challenged to improve existing social conditions.

SELECTED READINGS

1. Kurt Lewin, "Some Social-Psychological Differences between the United States and Germany," *Character and Personality*, Vol. IV (June, 1936), pp. 265-293.
2. W. I. Thomas and Florian Znaniecki, *The Polish Peasant in Europe and America.* New York: Alfred A. Knopf, 1918, pp. 1-302.
3. Edwin H. Sutherland, *The Professional Thief.* Chicago: The University of Chicago Press, 1937, pp. 3-231.
4. Karen Horney, *The Neurotic Personality in Our Time.* New York: W. W. Norton and Company, 1937, pp. 13-290.
5. Frederick M. Thrasher, *The Gang.* Chicago: The University of Chicago Press, 1936, pp. 3-553.

PROBLEMS

1. *Culture Conflict in Different Immigrant Communities.* Consult the following sources: William I. Thomas and Florian Znaniecki, *The Polish Peasant in Europe and America.* New York: Alfred A. Knopf, 1918, Part III, "Organization and Disorganization in America," pp. 1467-1827; William Foote Whyte, *Street Corner Society.* Chicago: The University of Chicago Press, 1943, pp. 2-276; and Walter Firey, *Land Use in Central Boston.* Cambridge: Harvard University Press, 1947, Chapter V, "The Influence of Localized Social Solidarity Upon Land Use: The North End," pp. 170-225.

---

[45] "To describe such an individual, who lives in a cultural no man's land, the phrase marginal man has been proposed." William F. Ogburn and Meyer F. Nimkoff, *op. cit.*, p. 387.

All these sources deal with the adjustment of different immigrant groups to the culture of the modern American city. It is your task to compare the adjustment difficulties arising in the Polish and Italian immigrant communities. The Polish immigrant community is discussed in the first source, the Italian immigrant community is discussed in the publications by Whyte and Firey. What are the similarities? What are the differences? Discuss symptoms of the generations conflict.

To improve your paper, you may want to go further and use other theoretical or empirical publications that will help you answer the intriguing questions of what the causes for the differences might be, or why the differences are not greater than you found them.

2. *Appraisal of Your Own Marginality.* It is your task to analyze your own life history, your present social contacts, your ambitions for future social advancement and your social background with the purpose of discovering sources of behavior conflict. State clearly with regard to what situations different environmental influences are dictating different behavior to you.

Arrange your essay either along the lines of an array of situations, such as relations with friends, relations with members of the opposite sex, studies, occupational life, or recreational life; or arrange the essay according to environmental influences (subcultures impinging upon your life history), such as parental family, school friends, educational or occupational contacts, acquaintances who have impressed you, or reading matter.

On the basis of your detailed discussion, define your position in society, and indicate major and minor potential conflicts and your individual solution to the ensuing adjustment problem.

3. *Affinity Between Insanity and the Urban Way of Life.* Study carefully all sources quoted in this chapter with regard to the spread of insanity and with regard to urban personality patterns. Consult with particular care Kurt Lewin, "Some Socio-Psychological Differences Between the United States and Germany," *Character and Personality,* Vol. IV (June, 1936), pp. 265-293; Louis Wirth, "Urbanism as a Way of Life," *The American Journal of Sociology,* Vol. XLIV, No. 1 (July, 1938), pp. 1-24; and Karen Horney, *The Neurotic Personality in Our Time.* New York: W. W. Norton and Company, 1937, pp. 13-290. Abstract quotations from these different publications, and others from further references offered in this chapter, and arrange them in juxtaposition to make apparent the similarity of urban personality traits and certain neurotic and psychotic conditions.

With the understanding of the problem gained, discuss the distribution of different types of insanity in the city, as described in R. E. L. Faris and H. W. Dunham, *Mental Disorder in Urban Areas.* Chicago: The University of Chicago Press, 1939.

CHAPTER 10

The Family in the City

Urban Families. In the city, the family has been freed from the close interrelationship with economic, social, and political affairs that characterized pre-urban society. In pre-urban society, family position determined the manner in which the individual was to participate in the productive life of the community, religious ceremonies, and affairs of state. The mass society of the large modern city concerns itself with individuals according to personal qualities rather than family background.

The modern urban family has lost in economic function. Individual members stray from the family for various purposes of participation in specialized urban activities. Urban industry and commerce grant gainful employment to the isolated individual. Participation in the associational life of the city is similarly individualized. The welfare and relief institutions of the city concern themselves to a large extent with individual rather than joint family needs.

In the urban environment, the large consanguinal family [1] has loosened its hold upon its individual members. It has been replaced by the small family group of parents and immediate offspring. Pushed into the background of private urban living, however, even

---

[1] The consanguinal family includes even remote blood relations. Some sociologists prefer to talk about the large family system. There are many different types of consanguinal families.

231

the small family group in the city is endangered by the impact of conflicting loyalties and individual interests.[2]

The question arises whether social change in the city does not lead to individualization so extreme that it approximates a state of complete family disorganization.[3] Rising rates of divorce and delinquency in the urban environment point in that direction. Nevertheless, careful consideration of the change of urban family functions does not permit us to share such pessimistic views.

Romance. Individual interests, to be sure, assert themselves in the urban environment. In the courtship period of the family life cycle, these individualistic tendencies are expressed in the strong emphasis on "romance" as an intense individual experience.

The delicate flower of romance is far from allergic to the city pavement. Romantic love, in modern civilization, finds its most forceful expression in the urban environment.

Romantic love anywhere remains essentially unfulfilled.[4] It consists of yearning rather than physical enjoyment. It feeds on obstacles and frustrations. Historically, romantic love traces its origins to a period which cultivated an emotion of frustrated desire. The troubadours worshipped at the altar of a love object that was, in principle, unobtainable. They directed their songs to the hostess of the castle in which they dwelled. To the lord of the castle they were bound in loyalty and homage. The latter's wife, of course, was inviolate to anything but spiritual adoration.[5]

---

[2] "The concept of familism . . . signifies that the interest of the family as a group is paramount to the interests of its individual members. The concept of individualism by contrast means that the continuity and welfare of the family is no longer the chief social aim but rather the personality development of its members." Ernest W. Burgess and Harvey J. Locke, *The Family.* New York: American Book Company, 1945, p. 527.

[3] "The very continuation of our culture seems to be inextricably associated with this nihilism in family behavior."

"That the family of the immediate future will move further toward atomism seems highly probable." Carle C. Zimmerman, *Family and Civilization.* New York: Harper & Brothers, 1947, pp. 797, 806.

[4] For the prototype of romantic love, see Denis de Rougemont, *Love in the Western World.* New York: Harcourt, Brace and Company, 1940, Book I, "The Tristan Myth," pp. 3-49.

[5] "One of the great efforts of the twelfth century troubadours, self-conscious exponents of love, was to lengthen the period of love's probation. . . ."

". . . the Court of Love in Provence decreed that the object of love must be married; hence she was inviolate to her true lover. Yearning supplanted carnal conversation: the chivalrous lover, if he wished to keep his lady, ran away from her." Lewis Mumford, *The Condition of Man.* New York: Harcourt, Brace and Company, 1944, pp. 113, 114.

A peculiar revival of romantic sentiment took place at the beginning of the industrialization period.[6] It was inspired by the gradual breakdown of fixed class lines. Intermarriage occurred between ever widening levels of social stratification. The nobleman yearned for the baker's daughter. The tutor and teacher fell "hopelessly" in love with the baroness. The peasant's son longed for the city girl, and the son of the wealthy merchant gave his heart to the ballerina. Love ventured beyond accepted boundaries and grew in intensity as it dared to be "unconventional."

Love at a Social Distance. Romantic sentiment as a mode of experience penetrates into the modern city environment. Advertisements, movie pictures, hit songs and comic strips surround us with an endless elaboration upon the theme of romantic entanglement.

In the course of centuries, artistic elaborations upon the theme of romance have lost their novelty, have become trite and often vulgarized. Romance, today, is frequently replaced by direct sex appeal. We are continuously stimulated, and our attention is continuously captured by allusions to the fact that there are two sexes in this world. Superimposed upon this elemental fact is the promise of unprecedented and unique emotional experience. Modern fiction likes to dwell upon love at first sight. It would appear as if the haste of city living had condensed years of romantic adoration from afar, the close identification of two people who have grown to love each other, into the fleeting moment of first recognition. The bobby-soxer waits for the lightning to strike, yet wonders with each passing experience whether this "is really it." Love at first sight and love of the "only one" are notions well established in contemporary folkways.[7]

Tension and seemingly insurmountable obstacles are necessary prerequisites for the development of a feeling of romantic love. Yearning has to precede anything more elaborate than mere physical thrill.[8] The modern city environment provides fertile soil for the development of romantic sentiment. The obstacle is the invisible social distance that separates all urbanites from each other as they

---

[6] See Lewis Mumford, *op. cit.*, Chapter VIII, "The Insurgence of Romanticism," pp. 265-300.

[7] The social origin of these notions cannot be reliably accounted for.

[8] For the process of crystallization as a prerequisite for romantic love, see Marie Henri Beyle, *On Love*. New York: Liveright Publishing Corporation, 1947, particularly pages 1-34 and 359-371.

meet in the downtown business district. They wear invisible masks. They pose as stereotypes. They wear alluring clothes to impress each other and to arouse sexual desire. In dealing with each other face to face they hide behind the deadpan of urban "sophistication."

The ever present chance to shatter the wall of social distance that separates from each other the pretty girls and the handsome boys who mill around almost at touching distance keeps erotic stimulation at a peak. The high school boy yearns for the waitress at the drug store. The tired attorney imbues the hat-check girl with qualities she never possessed. The stenographer dreams about her boss as a real person, and the king forsakes an empire for the woman he loves.

Tension. Our fiction, in magizines and in good books and bad, amply illustrates the fascination which the theme of romantic love holds for the city dweller. Of course, romantic love might well be cultivated because — being based on conflict — it always makes a good story. Romance might be considered an interesting theme in any type of literature. It may be considered an eternal theme for fictional elaboration.

Yet we cannot overlook the unusually keen and widespread interest in unhappy love, in courtship difficulties, and the interest in yearning as an end in itself in the love literature of our times. Death and suicide have always been essential props in the stage setting of romantic entanglement. Why does this peculiar type of lovemaking hold our interest today? It preoccupies people to the exclusion of other types of love relationships. Our interest wanes as conflict straightens out, as the couple approaches that blissfull stage where they "live happily ever after." We indulge in the embellishment of tension and yearning rather than the consummation of a happy family life.

Of recent, the romantic plot has become well worn. It has become standardized in contemporary mass fiction. Modern fiction serves the purpose of vicarious satisfaction. Modern escape literature is not read for the sake of curiosity, to gain knowledge about what happened or might have happened to other people. The reader identifies with the hero and lives vicariously through a sequence of exciting events that stand in contrast to the drab monotony of his own life. A reaction against the dull and safe routines of his own life arouse the interest of the city dweller in romance. The reader's emotional identification with the hero or the heroine likewise explains the stereotyped happy ending.[9]

A significant change of emphasis has taken place in the stereotyped plot of modern romantic literature. Our interest has somewhat shifted from yearning as an end in itself to the moment when boy and girl abandon stereotyped behavior, throwing their social roles overboard, dismiss the "line" of preliminary flirtation as false and dishonest, find themselves in each other's arms, and become aware of what they may well call love at first sight.

The uniqueness and the explosive force of the experience is due to contrast with attitudes otherwise rampant in the anonymous urban environment. After leaving their parental families, they have never revealed themselves as full personalities. They have grown adult by learning to play the different roles demanded from them in the different environments through which they moved.

In love, as they know it, modern city dwellers regain their identity as full personalities. The desire for romantic love covers a bitter need for self-realization that develops in the impersonal atmosphere of the modern city.

Romantic love was first noted in Western civilization by the troubadours.[10] From there it filtered down to less elevated social strata. It was emulated by burghers and peasents, not without change of function. It gained new emphasis at the beginning of the industrialization process. For all that, it could well be a dead custom today, were it not for an unusual susceptibility of the modern city environment to this pattern of courtship and lovemaking. It offers adventure in a world of monotonous routines and it satisfies the need for self-realization of the urban personality with all its fragmentalized roles combined.

Unconventionality. Romantic love is often confused with physical love.[11] This misunderstanding is the outcome of its association with

---

[9] For "vicarious living" in the enjoyment of urban leisure, see pp. 283 ff.

[10] "Here (among the troubadours) the cult of love was associated with the heresy of Catharism, an offspring of Manichean religion which had been preserved in the mountains of Bulgaria and reappeared in the South of France to present a bold, confident challenge to Christianity." Lewis Mumford, *op. cit.*, p. 113. Others refer to an origin from Near Eastern culture traits with which the European nobility came into contact during the crusades.

[11] "The popular philosophy of romantic love was always more or less tempered by common sense. But certain social reformers and advanced thinkers carried this doctrine to its logical extreme of 'free love.'" Ernest W. Burgess and Harvey J. Locke, *op. cit.*, p. 370.

lack of conventionality. Romantic tension thrives on barriers that impede the fulfillment of love. These barriers, not insurmountable but hard to overcome, are set by way of ethnic and status segregations that inhibit intermarriage. More fundamental are the barriers set in modern society against the uninhibited expression of the sex urge on the part of unmarried adults.

Thus, romance is often made the excuse for illicit sex relations. This presents a contemporary vulgarization of the concept of romantic love. At this point, romance is in danger of defeating its own end. It thrives on frustration and sublimation. The fulfillment of physical desire may create enjoyment or happiness; it is the death of romantic love.

Emotional Efficiency. There is still another component in the susceptibility of modern society to romantic love. Courtship has emancipated itself from being part of a process that leads unrelentingly to marriage and child raising.[12] Courtship, like other specialized activities, has become an end in itself. In the modern city, it has become part of the entertainment pattern of physically mature but unmarried adults.

Romance or the play at romance promises greatest emotional rewards in the relationship between the two sexes. Through adherence to romantic love patterns a maximum of thrills is obtained from flirtatious entanglements which do not lead all the way to the wedding march.

INDIVIDUALIZATION

Single Status. The family is a latecomer to the urban environment. Many of our cities were founded by single men; the demand for women remained for a long time in excess of the available supply.

The lack of emphasis upon family living in the city must partly be attributed to the fact that city-ward migration has been predominantly a migration of single persons, whether male or female.[13]

---

[12] "Courtship may be defined as the set of processes of association among the unmarried from which, in time, permanent matings usually emerge." Willard Waller, "The Rating and Dating Complex," *American Sociological Review*, Vol. 2, No. 5 (October, 1937), pp. 727-734.

[13] "Available evidence leads us to conclude that the bulk of the migrants are single persons. For one thing, the youthful character of the migrant probably means that the majority leave before taking a spouse." Noel P. Gist and L. A. Halbert, *Urban Society.* New York: Thomas Y. Crowell Company, 1948, p. 254.

While the new arrivals have generally been of marriageable age, they were bound to spend years after their arrival in the metropolis in adjustment to a new way of life. During this period of adjustment these people had to remain flexible, and therefore preferably single.

Even in later phases of urban acculturation, individual interests come first, and family interests second. For many immigrants, arrival in the large American city establishes their first contact with a society dominated by industry rather than agriculture. The transition from peasant family life to a mode of existence supported economically by individual wage earners has shown its atomizing effects even where the process was drawn out over several generations.

The Family Boss. In the city, production and consumption fall apart. The breadwinner gains unique prestige in the family, if he finds himself to be the only one who "brings home the bacon." Children turn from assets into liabilities. As the work of women is increasingly replaced by commercial and public city services, these women are easily looked upon as a luxurious household equipment for those who can afford it.[14]

In predominantly agricultural regions of the European continent waves of law suits, haggling over property arrangements and responsibilities for support, swept the countryside for several decades after landholdings had been regrouped into individual lots, and after the development of scattered industries had made a breadwinner of the husband, a recipient of wages paid to him individually. The patriarch was transformed into the boss of the household who could wield his powers with little restraint.

The immigrant carried the same process into the American city. Family loyalties and responsibilities, formerly upheld by deeply ingrained traditions, dissolve readily in an environment that binds the individual worker with only temporary employment contracts. For the family to survive under such circumstances, it had to be put on a new basis.

Rural Traditions. From its early origins, the city family had the difficult task of finding a new rationale for its very existence. Unfortunately, this task has never been clearly perceived. Rural

---

[14] See Ernest W. Burgess and Harvey J. Locke, *op. cit.*, Section on "Changing Family Functions," pp. 501-511.

family traditions have survived haphazardly in an environment to which they were ill fitted. Most writers in the family field fall for the temptation of considering the urban family as a degenerate offspring of its agrarian ancestor. Under this perspective, attention is focused on the negative aspects of urban family living.[15]

We tend to deplore the fact that certain family functions have been lost, and we regret that certain rural traditions have perished. We may recognize that the urban family is a consumption rather than a production unit. Still, we are not enthusiastic about the consequences. Each household task, such as food preservation, laundering, nursery school education, and recreational supervision of children, that is taken out of the individual home is relinquished with a feeling of guilt and moral indignation.[16]

City Functions. In the city, the family has ceased to be considered an end in itself. It is not taken for granted any more. The family is considered in the light of ulterior purposes to which it can be made subservient.

Different arguments have been offered for the retention of traditional family values in the city environment. The needs for urban reproduction have been stressed, for either economic, psychological, or nationalistic purposes. There is the argument that makes the family an agency for mutual insurance, all members dividing the risks of unemployment or unemployability, the younger and the older members of the family being supported by those with earning power. Family formation, just like home ownership, has been praised for its stabilizing effects. Family responsibilities are said to retain the venturesome, the dissatisfied employee, the striker, or the career man in location once they have settled down. Such responsibilities prevent the city dweller from changing his job, from risk-

---

[15] "There can be three main family types. One is the trustee family which has the most power, the widest field of action, and the greatest amount of social control. The completely opposite type is the atomistic family, which has the least power and the smallest possible field of action. An intermediate type is the domestic family, in which the balance of power is distributed between the family and other agencies." Carle C. Zimmerman, *op. cit.*, p. 125.

[16] "The opinion is repeatedly expressed (among the Puritans) that men, or at least some men, will grow conceited and otherwise sinful if they are allowed to enjoy life too much." Svend Ranulf, *Moral Indignation and Middle Class Psychology.* Copenhagen: Levin & Munksgaard, 1938, p. 67.

ing unemployment, and from excessive absenteeism. The family man is assumed to be the best and most reliable citizen.[17]

The family has also been recommended as the cornerstone of individual happiness. Individual happiness is considered a criterion for successful marriage. Under the impact of industrialization and urbanization, the modern family has changed from a social institution to a more informal human relationship upheld by the delight in intimate companionship and advantages of mutual assistance. A trend is perceived from "familism" to "individualism," and the interests of individual family members are held to be more important than the interests of the family group as such. This tendency toward an individualization of interests finds its supreme expression in the urban family.[18]

In the service of individual happiness, the modern family has been re-evaluated. Marriage, under the circumstances, is no longer considered by many as an unshakable sacrament. Its worth is made dependent upon its performance. Divorces have never been approved of, but under certain conditions the urbanite is willing to accept divorce as an alternative preferable to unhappy marriage. The urban family is seen under a "secular" perspective. Its worth is not anchored in absolute values. It is appreciated according to its effect upon the participant members.

Functional Separation. Urban living separates the different members of the family during the major part of their waking hours. Occupational and educational activities isolate family members from each other. In the factory or in the office, in school or on the playground, adults as well as children have to fight for their own individual acceptance. Family living has been relegated to the sphere of private consumption and relaxation.

The urban family does not participate as such in the process of work and production. The individual by himself makes his contribution to the production process of our urbanized society. The

---

[17] A complete and systematic argument in favor of large families, an argument not based upon tradition but upon an understanding of social effects, has been offered in Alva Myrdal, *Nation and Family.* New York: Harper & Brothers, 1941.

Gunnar Myrdal, *Population: A Problem for Democracy.* Cambridge: Harvard University Press, 1940.

[18] See Ernest W. Burgess and Harvey J. Locke, *op. cit.,* Chapter IV, "The Urban Family," pp. 113-147.

family may or may not stand by in faithful loyalty. Individualization is promoted by the gap between everyday experiences of the different members of the family group.

In both work and leisure, parents and children may associate with very different groups of people. The father may go around with other factory workers, but the daughter may have most of her social contacts with the boys and girls of the white collar group downtown. The father may stick to his countrymen, although his son has learned in high school to get along with all sorts of people.[19] Ethnic and status barriers put their stamp most irrevocably upon the mother, who remains the last pillar of complete family solidarity within the confines of a separated residential environment.

A conflict between the different generations originates from the advance of modern education. At times, parents and children literally do not speak the same language. Even where the linguistic barriers of the ethnic group are not involved, the modern school promotes new and different attitudes towards practices of citizenship, towards group and family loyalties. The attitudes of the modern school child toward problems of nutrition, toward work and expenditures, toward family formation, and toward sex and child raising, will probably be different from those of his parents, who received their training 30 or 40 years ago.

Individualization may be looked upon as the price we have to pay for efficiency and progress. Family relations in the city are apt to give way to a type of social organization which places the individual — in processes of learning, work, and play — where he best fits. And that often places him apart from his family group.

AGE GROUP CULTURES

Substitute Group Shelter. Complete individualization is hard to accept. The shelter of group life is sought as a means of gaining approval and encouragement.[20] It provides a medium for self-expression in leadership, co-operation, and competition. In the city, the family no longer satisfies these basic desires. Consequently, a spontaneous formation of group life has taken place which unites the

---

19 See William Brussat, "The Neighborhood as a Function of School and Childhood," *The Journal of Educational Sociology*, Vol. XVII, No. 2, Spring, 1951, pp. 77-79.
20 See above pp. 219 ff.

members of different sexes and different age groups with each other in bonds of loyalty and by means of informal association.

Age and sex group cultures flourish in the city environment. The phenomenon is not exclusively a part of city living. There are age group cultures in preliterate and pre-urban societies. In relation to our immediate social past, however, the clinging together of age and sex groups in more or less informal recreational pursuits, must be considered an urban departure from existing customs.[21]

Modern urban age and sex group formation is not based on tradition. It conflicts, as a matter of fact, with a way of life which places family loyalties and family pursuits in the very center of private living.

The Play Group. As the first of these urban subcultures, we have to consider the play group of the preschool child. It is not segregated by sex, although the interference of adults tends to discourage the association of their sons with the little girls in the neighborhood.

Parental concern with these play group activities shows that they are more than social get-togethers. The modern city dweller does not only want to make sure that his children get to know other children with the right type of parents. He does not limit his worries to bad words and bad habits. Play group activities are looked upon as a first station in the process of socialization through which the child detaches himself step by step from the family group and learns to stand on his own feet [22]

Parents have learned to look at the play group through the eyes of the child. It is not meant anymore as a place to develop correct manners, or to relax from them. It is considered a small universe that carries its own dignity and imposes its own tribulations upon the

---

[21] For an important exception for age group control over courtship processes in certain European peasant regions, see K. Robert V. Wikman, *Die Einleitung der Ehe*. Abo, Finland: Abo Akademi, 1937.

[22] "The important early steps in bringing up a child to be sociable and popular are: not fussing over him in his first years; letting him be around with other children his size from the age of a year; allowing him freedom to develop independence; the fewest changes possible in where the family lives and where he goes to school; letting him, as far as possible, dress like, talk like, play like, have the same allowance and other privileges as the other average children in the neighborhood, even if you don't approve of the way they are brought up." Benjamin Spock, *The Pocket Book of Baby and Child Care.* New York: Pocket Books, Inc., 1946, p. 313.

participant members. Play group activities initiate the process of social weaning.

To allow the play group to fulfill this function, the child is left to his own devices, whether the youngsters sling mud or drown the kitten in the watering can. What many parents want to know is whether in all these sundry activities their children establish themselves as "leaders" or as "followers," whether they tend to cooperate or to go their own ways, whether they are considerate or unduly aggressive. Content of activities is of less concern than the form of participation.[23] The individual pattern of association, we assume, will later transfer itself to the type of play and work demanded from the child as it grows into adulthood. Play group activities are judged by the opportunities they offer the child to express himself and to develop self-reliance.

Early School Years. During the early years of school, children are beset by so many new influences that the tendency to age group formation reaches a low ebb. The children have to establish individual relationships with their teachers. This may cause considerable internal conflict if there is a clash between home values and school values. There are occasions for more formal association with their schoolmates at birthday and other parties. They learn to evaluate their playmates by standards of social acceptability. Temporarily, the child goes his own individual way in absorbing these different influences and making his own individual choices.

Teen-Age Culture. This lasts until the teen-age culture claims the child as a loyal member. The teen-age culture is closely related to the tendency of gang-formation among adolescents and young unmarried adults.[24] Biologically mature, yet socially still dependent, the individual finds himself temporarily in a no-man's-land as far as family living is concerned. Emotionally, he has not quite freed himself as yet from dependence on members of the parental family.

---

[23] "The psychogenic traits . . . include tendencies to extroversion or introversion, dominance or submission, optimism or pessimism, emotional dependence or independence, self-confidence or lack of confidence in self, and egocentrism or sociocentrism." Ernest W. Burgess and Harvey J. Locke, *op. cit.,* p. 244.

[24] "From the age of 13 or 14, most girls and boys are preoccupied with social activities and social experimentation. This is their most important business." Robert J. Havighurst, *Developmental Tasks and Education.* New York: Longmans, Green and Co., 1950, p. 34.

Nor has he settled down as yet to forming a family of his own. Spontaneous formation of cliques and gangs occurs to satisfy the ever present demand for social contact.

In the modern city the need for self-expression unimpeded by parental supervision is accentuated by the rapid progress of education. The city high school fills the important function of bringing the city child into contact with other children of different backgrounds. City children thus face the necessity of making an adjustment to the cosmopolitan urban community. They do not necessarily share this experience with their parents, who may withdraw into the refuge of an ethnic neighborhood, or a neighborhood segregated along lines of status or economic success.

Thrown back upon their own resources, these teen agers develop a subculture of their own. The manifestations of the teen-age culture are frequently but insincerely reported in current magazine literature. In a coeducational environment, social get-togethers are centered around the first flirtatious approaches of the two sexes to each other. They go to dances and picnics, to camps and parties. The relationship of the two sexes covers the entire range from chummy friendship to romantic love, from necking and petting to occasional intimate sex behavior.[25] Their dress varies from blue jeans to evening dress, from tee shirt to dinner jacket.

In many ways, symbolic expression is given to self-consciousness and a desire for independence on the part of this age group. In dress and manner, in speech and gestures, the teen agers assert themselves as being different from the traditional world of adults.

Fads are rampant in the teen-age group. They come and go. Wooden shoes are clattering through the halls one year. The next year, both boys and girls will sneak around in moccassins. Wearing a zoot suit is one way of showing the world and your parents that your loyalties are shifting toward the values asserted in your own age group. Smoking a pipe and speaking teen-age slang is another.

Adult Age and Sex Groups. Specialized sex and age cultures are not quite as prolific in the higher age ranges, but they do exist.

---

[25] See Alfred C. Kinsey, Wardell B. Pomeroy, and Clyde E. Martin, *Sexual Behavior in the Human Male.* Philadelphia: W. B. Saunders Company, 1948, p. 182.

Specialized age and sex cultures of adults are more frequent in the middle class environment than elsewhere.[26]

The flapper culture is a case in point. It developed during the 1920's among unmarried females, young adults who came to the city to live apart from their family homes and to make a living as stenographers or in other white collar positions. They cultivated their own food habits, dressed alike, and accommodated themselves in similar types of housing facilities — the boarding house, the rented room or the "bachelor apartment."[27]

The downtown men's club furnishes another example of an urban sex and age group. There are stag dinners and luncheons, with drinks before and after. There is the billiard game or the card game during working hours. There are dinners and visits to the night club financed through the executive's expense account. Again, the manner of dress (white shirt and business suit), social behavior (back-slapping, first names, and name-calling), the telling of jokes, and the way of mixing business with informal sociability are more or less standardized for each professional and business group, for directors and executives, for the young men and the janitors.

Women associate in a different, but equally specialized and standardized fashion. We have to consider such informal undertakings as the shopping trip, the luncheon date at the fashionable department store, and the dessert bridge at the home of the golf widow. We have to consider more formal meetings in connection with church groups, civic clubs, or study circles. Ethnic difference may lead to a preference of either the afternoon tea or the kaffee-klatsch.

Adult sex groups are somewhat subdivided according to age. Some civic clubs tend to attract the younger, others the somewhat older businessmen of the community. Women segregate according to their family status as unmarried, young matrons, or married. The manner in which adult men and women address each other at these informal meetings as "boys" and "girls" leaves no doubt about their origin in earlier age group formations.

---

[26] "In their leisure time pursuits middle-class husbands and their wives have considerable joint participation. Much of the social participation of a couple, however, is by the sexes separately, especially in the lower middle-class." Allison Davis, Burleigh B. Gardner, and Mary R. Gardner, *Deep South*. Chicago: The University of Chicago Press, 1941, p. 102.

[27] See Harvey W. Zorbaugh, *The Dweller in Furnished Rooms*. Publications of the American Sociological Society, Vol. XX, pp. 83-89.

Old Age. With advancing age, group consciousness tends to diminish in our urban culture. The strain of urban living gives cultural prominence to the younger residents of the urban environment. The dignified old timer of the American small town loses in the modern city his elevated status as the carrier of tradition, the hoarder of memories otherwise lost, and the proponent of balanced judgment.[28]

Aging, in the city, is associated with the irrevocable loss of both mental and physical powers. In a world that is set for change and progress, the aged have little to be proud of. Contemplating their fate as individual misfortune, the aged will be the last of the age groups to assert itself by way of spontaneous group formation.[29]

STRATIFICATION

Status Differences. Talking about *the* urban American family involves a crude generalization. There are many different types of urban families.

This is partly due to internal and external migration gains through which the city constantly faces the need for assimilation of different cultural backgrounds. It is due also to social stratification which has permitted the development of highly divergent family cultures in our urban upper, middle, and lower classes.[30]

Upper Class Families. In the upper class, family ties encompass the entire lineage group. Only those who for generations have resided in the community under comfortable financial circumstances can pride themselves on truly belonging to the local upper class. Historical affiliation rather than wealth decides membership in an upper class that is conscious of its prestige.

In this upper class environment, the family comprises the large consanguinal group. This is an exception to otherwise prevailing urban conditions which place emphasis upon the small conjugal group consisting only of parents and their immediate offspring. Under the circumstances, prestige and power in the upper class

---

[28] See Granville Hicks, *Small Town.* New York: The Macmillan Company, 1947, pp. 86-87.

[29] "The problem of participation in groups outside the house is acute for many old people." Ruth Shonle Cavan, *Old Age in a City of 100,000.* Illinois Academy of Science Transactions, Vol. 40, 1947, pp. 166-167.

[30] See Allison Davis, Burleigh B. Gardner, and Mary R. Gardner, *op. cit.,* Chapters IV-VI, pp. 84-136.

family are wielded according to position in the succession of generations. The older generations — being closer to the historical past and carriers of valuable memories — are met with respect and deference. The dowager rules the roost over the younger male members of the large family group, although these men may be the main breadwinners and the administrators of family property.[31]

Middle Class Families. In the urban middle classes, very close-knit ties exist between the members of the small conjugal family. Parents identify with their children and the children's social advancement. Family living in all its facets is made (more than in either the upper or the lower classes) subservient to the struggle for economic gain and social prestige. Parents are concerned with the social composition of the child's play group and, later on, with its dating and courtship practices. Although children may resist successfully, attempts are made to arrange marriages that promise advancement in social prestige.

The family home is also made instrumental to the advancement of career and social prestige in the community. The boss and the business friends are entertained at formal dinners. Otherwise, the family's social contacts are to a large extent pursued on a one-sex basis.

Family members spread out to join the best clubs within reach of their social prestige and let it be known that they have done so. The children's education is closely watched and early signs of talent and outstanding performance recorded with satisfaction. Children are urged to move ahead, to make a place for themselves in the competition for grades, degrees, and scholarships.

The older people do not occupy a very enviable position in the middle class family. Unless they have provided by home ownership, savings, and old age insurance for their livelihood in the final unproductive stages of their lives, they have to move in with their children. Here they are considered an economical liability which duty imposes upon the younger couple.[32]

Lower Class Families. Individualization is most advanced in the lower class urban family. Mutual identification is at a minimum. There is little interest in the social, economic, or educational achievements of the children. The two sexes are almost completely segregated from each other in their leisure time activities.

---

[31] *Ibid.*, Chapter IV, "The White Upper-Class Family," pp. 84-99.
[32] *Ibid.*, Chapter V, "The White Middle-Class Family," pp. 100-117.

In the lower class home, the husband is more decidedly the boss than in the middle class family in which the household carries functions of semi-official family representation. He will not be told to wipe his feet or where to hang his hat. Marriage is a contract for mutual convenience on the part of husband and wife. The husband fulfills his end of the bargain if he brings most of his paycheck home. The wife makes her contribution by putting breakfast and supper on the table.

Children leave their home early to embark on individual careers. The fire of their ambition is not as eagerly fanned as in the middle class environment. As they move away from their families, they tend to lose contacts with parents as well as siblings. As adults, they have to stand on their own feet or to join with appropriate mates to take care of their housekeeping demands.[33]

HETEROGENEITY

Culture Conflict. Culture conflict besets the city family more than that of any other contemporary environment. Diverse backgrounds, different income levels, and different occupational experiences allow different patterns of family living to exist side by side.

Diversified family traditions flourish in the shelter of ethnic groups in more or less contiguous neighborhood units. Such traditions may be enforced by voluntary associations sponsored by either church or nationality groups, by civic clubs, historical societies or by cults and religious denominations.

In the city there is sufficient opportunity for intermingling to cause confusion and conflict when and where these different traditions come into contact with each other. Conflicts between different family traditions occur through intermarriage and in the course of preceding courtship. In the cosmopolitan environment of the large modern city, there are, in principle, no barriers to intermarriage. In practice, marriages between like people are encouraged and marriagable individuals safeguarded against contacts with members of the opposite sex who do not "belong."

---

[33] *Ibid.*, Chapter VI, "The White Lower-Class Family," pp. 118-136.
See also St. Clair Drake and Horace R. Cayton, *Black Metropolis*. New York: Harcourt, Brace and Company, 1945, "The Hazards of Marriage," pp. 581-588.

Marital Conflict. The fusion of different family traditions in marriage causes difficulties of marital adjustment.[34] We have seen how different social experiences at different phases of the individual life cycle furnish a background for personal maladjustment.[35] In marriage, the target area for culture conflict is widened.

The early childhood experiences and the later social experiences of two different individuals are brought into most intimate contact in marriage. Expectations with regard to the roles of husband, wife, or children within the family do not necessarily coincide.

Due in part to such conflicts, divorce rates are higher in the large city than in smaller communities. Due to such conflicts, young people in the city are more prone to rebel against parental authority and to drift into juvenile delinquency.

Matchmaking and Emancipation. The supervision of urban courtship practices by the older generation is an uphill fight. Young marriagable adults tend to emancipate themselves from ethnic prejudices. The democratic way of life in the city and the appreciation of personality on its own merits, as promoted in our educational institutions, counteract attempts of the older generation to preserve endogamy within the confines of the ethnic group. Manifestations of barriers to free association between the two sexes are found in the social activities of church and ethnic groups, in restricted home entertaining, in the choice of playmates for the child at an early age, and in the careful selection of schools that will not expose the child to undesirable heterogeneous contacts.

The outcome of such push and pull is often duplicity in the relations between the two sexes. For each particular group, there are the "good" girls and the "bad"; the former being considered marriageable, the latter exploitable at best. Formal dates may be avoided because they involve contacts with the parents and establish "serious intentions." Only girls who do not belong to the in-group can be dated without commitments. There is no lack of opportunity for clandestine meetings in the downtown entertainment district.[36]

"Dating," in the city, is not necessarily related to courtship and

---

[34] See Judson T. Landis and Mary G. Landis, *Building a Successful Marriage.* New York: Prentice-Hall, Inc., 1948, Chapter VII, "Mixed Marriages," pp. 132-163.

[35] See p. 214.

[36] See William Foote Whyte, "A Slum Sex-Code," *The American Journal of Sociology,* Vol. XLIX, No. 1 (July, 1943), pp. 24-31.

later marriage. It establishes itself independently from later steps toward marriage as part of the urban entertainment pattern. The noncommittal character of such associations stimulates the participant members to make the most of the immediate situation, to engage in that "barter of thrills" of which the sociologists of the family have written.[37]

In-Law Trouble. The small conjugal family in the city is bound to suffer from in-law troubles unequaled in more homogeneous environment. Maternal and paternal grandparents not only interfere with marital adjustment by enforcing and exploiting psychological relationships that have been formed in early childhood,[38] they represent different value systems and make themselves the defenders of family traditions which are not necessarily shared by both husband and wife.

Different family traditions, ingrained during long years of childhood, are not as easily abandoned in later married life as during the few years of unmarried adulthood which are often passed in a temporary state of rebellion. As responsibilities of full family living close in around the young city dweller, he is apt to remind himself of how "things were done at home." This memory may have been suppressed during the courtship period.

Downtown Separation. Even after family formation, heterogeneity of urban contacts presents an ever present danger to the permanence of family life. In the world of downtown business, the husband associates with members of both sexes. This downtown world presents a subculture of its own. It establishes a peculiar system of loyalties, not exclusively of a business nature.

Encouragement and consolation, affection and flirtation are more easily provided by fellow workers in the office than by the wife engaged in child raising activities far off in the dormitory suburb. Many permanent attachments develop under these circumstances. These attachments may become serious enough to carry conflict into the small family group.

---

[37] "The value judgment which many lay persons and even some trained sociologists pass upon thrill-seeking arises from the organizational mores of the family — from the fact that energy is dissipated in thrills which is supposed to do the work of the world, i.e., to get people safely married." Willard Waller, *op. cit.*, p. 728.

[38] See Harriet R. Mowrer "Getting Along in Marriage," in Howard Becker and Reuben Hill, editors, *Family Marriage and Parenthoood.* Boston: D. C. Heath and Company, 1948, pp. 341-365.

FAMILY TYPES ON THE CITY GRADIENT

Patriarchy and Matriarchy. We observe some regularity with regard to the distribution of different family types within the city. Upon a gradient drawn from the city center, penetrating the built-up zones and stretching in a straight line into the urban circumference, the family patterns have been found to change gradually from extreme patriarchy to extreme matriarchy.[39]

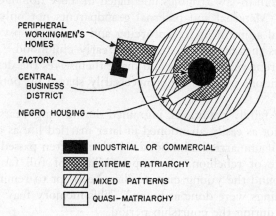

FIGURE 14. Family Types on the City Gradient.

If we consider only the extreme poles of this sequence, our attention is called to the immigrant family in the central slum environment at one end of the continuum, and to the dormitory suburb at the other where fathers are absent during most of the waking hours.

Patriarchy and matriarchy in the urban class sequence:

I. Lower Class: Marriage for purposes of expedient and convenient domestic relations.

The father has absolute power with regard to major and minor decisions.

He determines the expenditure pattern.

He is in no way restricted in his use of the private dwelling unit.

Source of power: threat of withdrawal of funds and separation.

The sexes are separated in recreation.

---

[39] "The zonal organization of the city by distinctive types of inhabitants and institutions has also its characteristic types of urban families." Ernest W. Burgess and Harvey J. Locke, *op. cit.*, p. 116. Consult the entire discussion on pp. 116-134.

II. Middle Class: Marriage for purposes of procreation and advancement of family status.

Division of power between husband and wife.

Decisions in family matters either on the basis of consultation, or on division of spheres of competence.

Sources of the father's power: Income and traditional authority.

Sources of the mother's power: Emancipation and absence of father in dormitory suburb.

The sexes are either joined or separated in recreational activities.

III. Upper Class: Marriage for purpose of continuing family lineage.

Power is relinquished to older generation; the mother may find herself in a stronger power position than the father, depending upon status of her family.

Source of power: Relationship to longest line of ancestors resident in community.

The sexes are typically joined in recreational activities.

Source: Allison Davis, Burleigh B. Gardner, and Mary R. Gardner: Deep South. The University of Chicago Press. .Chicago, Ill. 1941, pp. 84-136.

Central Zone. To be sure, the immigrant family, in the central slum, is characterized by a high degree of paternal authoritarianism. Here we have a direct carry-over from the European peasant household. More than that: the position of the father as the main breadwinner concentrates economic powers in his hands. The immigrant father enjoys the deference accredited to the household head in the Old World; he also wields the powers connected with an individualized flow of income and individualized rights of property.

In the central zones of urban residences, however, this family pattern finds itself in juxtaposition to the so-called matriarchy of loose and disorganized family groups. Easy and frequent seperations in the Negro group have called attention to family relations which establish a somewhat firmer nucleus of cohesion between the mother and her children. In cases of emergency, support of the children is more likely expected from the mother and her parents than from the father and his parents.

This family pattern of quasi-matriarchy is more closely associated with the in-migrants to our large American cities. In the case of the Negro community, it is to some extent based upon a carry-over from conditions of slavery under which the father was more readily separated from his children than was the mother. This pattern, however, is not limited to the Negro group. We find it wherever family bonds are severed frequently under pressure of economic emergencies. Whether it is warranted to use the term matriarchy for this condition or not, it certainly interferes with the prodominance of patriarchal family living in the central slum environment.

Peripheral Zones. Similarly, it takes a loose definition of the term matriarchy to make it applicable to family living in the dormitory suburb. After all, the father is still a constituent member of the family group. He carries considerable power in relation to all important decisions about matters of finance and education. Yet, the father fades out of the picture of everyday family living.[40]

Continuum? It has been assumed that a gradual transition takes place between the central urban emphasis on patriarchal and the peripheral emphasis on matriarchal family patterns.

Indeed, extreme patriarchy weakens and gradually fades out of the picture as we move toward the residences of increasingly higher income groups in the outlying districts. This can be explained as a secondary effect of several changes that occur in the process. On the one hand, we leave the settlements of first immigrants (foreign-born family heads), as we advance from the slum to the housing of successively higher status groups. Old world patterns of family living are lost in the process of increasing Americanization.

In addition to a gradual approximation of the American way of life, we shift from lower to upper class patterns of family living. We leave an environment where the father's authority remains more or less unquestioned.

In middle class families certain powers are granted to the housewife. Her decisions hold sway with regard to problems of home living. Co-operating in the task of raising their children and advancing them socially, husband and wife in the middle class family present a relatively close-knit team with some restrictions upon the patriarchal prerogatives of the former. In upper class families, prestige within the family group is attached to generation precedence rather than to sex or other conjugal family roles. If, therefore, status rises as we approach the residential sections of the urban periphery, it is warranted to expect patriarchal family traits to disappear.

---

[40] *Ibid.,* "The Suburb and the Matricentric Family," pp. 131-134.

Sex Ratios. The sex ratio tends to decrease as we leave the center and approach the periphery of the modern city.

Single men outnumber single women in downtown residences. This condition has changed somewhat since World War I, by a sizable influx to the city of female labor engaged in white collar positions.[41]

Yet, the composite sex ratio is still relatively high for the entire downtown area, as compared to the suburban residential sections. In the periphery of the city, both the presence of single females as domestic servants and an excess of unmarried females in the resident families keep the sex ratio relatively low. The excess of unmarried females increases with status because the barriers against marriage with members of lower social status are more strictly enforced for women than for men.[42] The derived status of a woman is more vulnerable to a "degrading" intermarriage.

GADGETS

Inventions. The urban family is more receptive to the use of technical inventions than either village or rural families. The willingness, or even eagerness, in the city, to accept new technological devices has set the urban family somewhat apart from that of the non-urban environment.[43]

Outside the city, adherence to traditional ways of doing things makes all new gadgets suspect. They may be considered a means to undermine respect for the way of life of the older generation. Older people, more set in their behavior, are less likely to adjust their ways to opportunities offered by new inventions. In the city, the values of the younger generation predominate. New instrumentalities for everyday living are not only eagerly welcomed, they

[41] "The 'Skid Road' . . . a typical habitat of homeless men — has 756.9 males per 100.0 females. . . . On the other hand, the districts with the highest proportion of females . . . contain typical rooming-house and apartment-house sections toward the center of the city." Calvin F. Schmid, *Social Trends in Seattle.* Seattle: The University of Washington Press, 1944, p. 91.

[42] "North Broadway and the University District (outlying districts) also evidence high ratios of females." *Ibid.,* p. 91.

[43] "The machine-power complex is being diffused outward from the cities into the villages and farming areas with almost dramatic effect." William F. Ogburn, with the assistance of S. C. Gilfillan, "The Influence of Invention and Discovery," in *Recent Social Trends.* New York: McGraw-Hill Book Company, Inc., 1933, p. 128.

achieve importance as symbols for the dividing line between successive generations.

The ready acceptance of inventions in the city is not entirely due to the fact that the centers of trade and commerce are located here. The city family is susceptible to the inroads of new inventions. At that, the urban public is highly selective in the type of inventions which it accepts. Inventions are accepted because they fit urban needs and satisfy an urban conception of comfort. Where they do so, it appears as if they were making social history. It is seldom the invention itself, however, that carries the original impetus to social change.[44]

Inventions such as forms of birth control, the automobile, radio, and television have not by themselves reshaped the urban way of family living. Were it not for a desire to restrict offspring, the invention of various contraceptive devices would have remained without impact upon the urban way of life.[45] Were it not for the need for transportation to contact an ever widening range of urban institutions and family friends, were it not for a tendency toward the formation of independent age group cultures, the automobile would have remained without impact upon urban family customs.[46] Radio has not fullfilled its original promise of drawing the different members of the intimate family circle closer to each other.[47] The same may be expected of television, once it has become less expensive and its original glamor has worn off.

Household Machinery. The same holds true for the invention and dissemination of household machinery intended to ease the burden of household chores in the individual dwelling unit.[48] Inventions

---

[44] See William F. Ogburn, with the assistance of Clark Tibbitts, "The Family and its Functions," in *Recent Social Trends. op. cit.,* pp. 661-708.
"Inventional causes and social effects are intertwined in a process." William F. Ogburn, "The Influence of Invention and Discovery," *op. cit.,* p. 158.
[45] Means of contraceptives were known to various preliterate peoples. Some such means (most likely coitus interruptus) must have been used in wide agricultural regions of the European continent where — due to rules of inheritance — a plurality of male off-spring caused the splitting up of estates and threatened the very livelihood of the family. Birth-control, at that time, was not dependent upon technical inventions.
[46] See William F. Ogburn, "The Influence of Invention and Discovery," *op. cit.,* "Transportation Inventions," pp. 141-144.
[47] "Social Effects of the Radio," *ibid.,* pp. 152-156.
[48] See William F. Ogburn, *The Family and its Functions, op. cit.,* "Household Economic Activities," pp. 664-666.

are called forth by needs. They will not stimulate needs unless these have a root in prevailing urban attitudes and coincide with social developments produced by the urban way of life.

In the modern city, the zest for specialization in work as well as in play puts a premium upon every invention that reduces to a minimum a type of activity, like housework, which runs counter to otherwise prevailing trends toward specialization, division of labor, and rational efficiency.

Some household routines are eliminated from the individual household and transferred to commercial agencies or community services. This has happened to laundry, canning, the baking of bread, and preschool educational activities. The scope of the remaining housework is too limited to permit handling on a large commercial scale. We can only increase the convenience of performance and reduce the amount of time spent at it.

This is the task performed by modern household machinery, which has supplied us with running hot and cold water, with electric lights, with gas or electric stoves, with washing machines, electric mangles, toasters, vacuum cleaners, garbage grinders, and dishwashing machines. From a rural perspective, this trend has been associated with urban idleness and an unwillingness to accept full family responsibilities.

New Urban Family Patterns

Reproduction. Upon the urban family rests the stigma of failing in its main purpose, its own reproduction. With increasing city size the net reproduction rate gradually diminishes. Procreation, to be sure, provides only the raw materials for human achievement. But without these raw materials there is no survival. The modern city is dependent for its continued existence upon constant replenishment from the rural hinterland.

We dealt, in Chapter 3, with the population resources required to guarantee the continued growth and existence of the modern city. We recognized its failure to reproduce and its reliance upon immigration and internal migration for self-perpetuation. We have discussed the reasons for this weakness in the urban social structure.

See also Siegfried Giedion, *Mechanization Takes Command.* New York: Oxford University Press, 1948, "Mechanization Encounters the Household," pp. 512-627.

At this point, we want to call attention to some new, and so far only dimly perceived, urban family patterns which may feed new human raw materials into the modern city.

Urban Family Change. The following statistical findings have bearing upon our argument:

a. The marriage rate has increased persistently for more than half a century. This increase is particularly noticeable in the city environment. Since 1940 this increase has taken a tremendous leap not explainable by war conditions.

b. During the same time, the marriage age has been reduced with equal persistence and with similar concentration upon urban populations.

c. After 1890, the age difference between husband and wife decreased, from about 4 years in 1890 to about 3 years in 1950.

d. After 1939 remarriages increased much more rapidly than first marriages.[49]

e. The increase of the marriage rate was particularly noticeable for the very young age ranges up to the middle 20's and for the ages of 45 and over.

f. The increase of the marriage rate was greater in the urban than the farm environment.

g. Between 1940 and 1950, there was a marked increase in the number of married women in the labor force.

h. According to an official survey in April, 1947, the number of children (under 5 years old) whose mothers were in the labor force had doubled since 1940.[50]

i. The marriage boom occurred largely among educated people, particularly in the age range of 35 years and above.

j. Divorce rates in these years must be considered, to some extent, the outcome of a shift from separations to divorces. To this extent, they do not indicate an increase of unsuccessful marriages.

---

[49] See Paul C. Glick, "First Marriages and Remarriages," *American Sociological Review*, Vol. 14, No. 6 (December, 1949), pp. 726-734.

[50] See *Current Population Reports, Labor Force, Employment Characteristics of Households and Married Couples.* Bureau of the Census. Series P-50, No. 5. Washington, D.C.: U.S. Government Printing Office, May 7, 1948.

TABLE XIII

MARRIAGE RATE 1890 - 1940

In per cent of population 15 years old and over.

Year	Male	Female
1890	53.9	56.8
1900	54.5	57.0
1910	55.8	58.9
1920	59.2	60.6
1930	60.0	61.1
1940	61.2	61.0

MARRIAGE RATE — URBAN AND RURAL 1940

Area	Male	Female
Urban	61.8	58.1
Rural nonfarm	62.7	64.5
Rural farm	58.3	66.3

From: Statistical Abstract of the United States. U.S. Department of Commerce. Washington, D.C., p. 42.

Marriage for Its Own Sake. These facts do not support the gloomy view customarily taken about the urban family. The baby boom of the postwar years, of course, cannot be expected to last. The birth rate continues to decline and family size will probably continue to shrink. But, although the odds for full urban family living do not look too rosy, we cannot overlook the fact that the zest for married living is in the upswing to a surprising extent.

For better or worse, there need not be any more children in the urban family than husband and wife may want to raise. A *Fortune* poll on family problems revealed that the American people are divided 50-50 on the question of whether a young couple with marriage plans should wait for the time when the husband will be able to make a living for both of them or go ahead and marry with the prospect of having the wife contribute to the family income. This poll indicates that public opinion is formed on the assumption that in these young families child bearing should be delayed until economically feasible. Planned parenthood is increasingly approved, particularly in the urban environment.[51]

Companionship. The marriage of younger city people has a somewhat different meaning today than family formation had 100 years ago. It is still a commitment to close co-operation between husband and wife. In the earlier years of marriage, they are more likely to be pulling the same strings, both working for a living and taking care of their household needs together.[52] Companionship is more pronounced where the division of labor between husband and wife is less distinct. They have more leisure time in common. Their needs for relaxation and entertainment coincide more closely than they would if the husband returned fatigued from a busy day downtown to find his wife, after a day of household routines, eager to go downtown for the evening.

These young marriages infringe upon the courtship period. Husband and wife get to know each other while developing a routine for married living. They do not marry only when they are ready to settle down. They gradually settle down while building their marriage. If they fail, there are divorces. If they succeed, they have probably built a solid foundation for child raising.

General Trends. Recent urban family trends do not point in the direction of complete individualization. Not only the young, but also those too old for reproduction tend to marry more than ever before. If they do so, it can only be for companionship and other compensations implied in the relationship between man and wife. The increasing remarriage rate of divorcees points in the same direction. The road of the divorcee, today, leads typically into a new marriage. Our eager search for a successful married life explains

---

[51] See "The Fortune Survey," *Fortune*, Vol. XXXIV, No. 2 (August, 1946), p. 8. More specifically, the following poll results have been reported:
Birth Control Information Should Be:

Available to all adults	60%
Given by doctors to safeguard a patient's health	33%
Available to all married adults	4%
Legally forbidden to all	3%
	100%

Opinion News, August 15th, 1948. Reporting a poll taken from the readers of the *Women's Home Companion.*
[52] See Svend Riemer, "Marriage on the Campus," *American Sociological Review*, Vol. VII, No. 6 (December, 1942), pp. 802-815.

better than drink and delinquency the rising divorce rate of recent decades. Our demands on companionship in marriage have grown. Those failing to have their expectations fulfilled break away, and do so earlier than before, not because they give up more easily but because they want to try again.

The modern city population has learned to appreciate marriage as an end in itself. The purposes of marriage may well conflict with the wider purposes of full family living. In the city, children are no longer the supreme purpose of wedded life. Yet, under the competitive strain of modern city life, the shelter of close companionship between husband and wife is valued as something worthwhile in itself.

SELECTED READINGS

1. Ernest W. Burgess and Harvey J. Locke, *The Family*. New York: American Book Company, 1945, Chapter 4, "The Urban Family," pp. 113-147.

2. Carle C. Zimmerman, *Family and Civilization*. New York: Harper & Brothers, 1947, pp. 90-810.

3. Lewis Mumford, *The Condition of Man*. New York: Harcourt, Brace and Company, 1944, pp. 201-423.

4. Allison Davis, Burleigh R. Gardner, and Mary R. Gardner, *Deep South*. Chicago: The University of Chicago Press, 1941, pp. 84-136.

5. *Recent Social Trends*. New York: McGraw-Hill Book Company, 1933, pp. 122-166, 661-708.

PROBLEMS

1. *Identification of Romance.* The problem is whether "romance" can be identified as a relationship different in quality from love or physical attraction to the opposite sex in general. For the definition of "romance," see pp. 232 ff. and consult Denis de Rougemont, *Love in the Western World*. New York: Harcourt, Brace and Company, 1940; Lewis Mumford, *The Condition of Man*. New York: Harcourt, Brace and Company, 1944; and Marie-Henri Beyle, *On Love*. New York: Liveright Publishing Corporation, 1947.

Select according to your preference 5 novels of the classical tradition of English literature, and analyze the love relationships with regard to the absence or presence of "romance."

See 5 current movies, and analyze the love relationships depicted with regard to the absence or presence of "romance."

Repeat the same procedure for 5 modern mystery stories. Discuss different emphases in the pattern of aim-inhibition in the three media.

Interview informally 10 fellow students with regard to the absence or presence of "romance" in their relationship to the opposite sex.

With the partial insights gained from your investigations in mind, what do you think is the future of "romance?"

2. *Family Class Analysis.* Study intensively Allison Davis, Burleigh B. Gardner, and Mary R. Gardner, *Deep South.* Chicago: The University of Chicago Press, 1941, Chapters IV-VI, pp. 84-136.

In these chapters upper, middle, and lower class patterns of family living are described in a somewhat stereotyped fashion. Accepting the underlying conceptual scheme, analyze the family in which you have grown up with regard to the intermingling of different class patterns of family living. In exceptional cases, you may find your family entirely or almost entirely falling into one of the three categories developed.

Develop a checklist of 10 observational items as criteria for either upper, middle, or lower class membership, to be used in the analysis of family living.

In informal interviews, though guided by the list of your criteria, classify roughly the families of 3 of your good friends at the university or at college with regard to relative class affiliation.

Your project will be improved if your checklist is composed of items that do not reveal your intention of grading class affiliation. Avoid criteria closely related to income: The problem is, after all, to find qualitative differences correlated to stratification based upon amount of income.

3. *Quasi-Matriarchy in the Modern City.* Two types of quasi-matriarchy gain prominence in the modern city. In both cases the importance of the mother in the conduct of family affairs increases in relationship to that of the father.

You will find source materials about one of these types in St. Clair Drake and Horace R. Cayton, *Black Metropolis.* New York: Harcourt, Brace and Company, 1945; and about the other in George A. Lundberg, Mirra Komarovsky, and Mary Alice McInerny, *Leisure. A Suburban Study.* New York: Columbia University Press, 1934.

Have these two types of quasi-matriarchy anything in common with each other? In what respects are they different from each other? Using your theoretical skills, develop clear definitions of the two types, discuss their different origins, and, as stated above, clarify differences and similarities.

How do you assume the two types will affect the future of urban family living?

PART IV

Urban Leisure

CHAPTER 11

Crafts, Sports, and Gambling

Classification. Urban leisure is compensatory to urban work routines. As such, it serves either as an outlet for self-expression, or as a means of energy release. Self-expression in its turn is either repetitive or contrasting with regard to prevailing everyday life routines. Energy release is either regenerative or vicious, that is, wasteful in the long run, although possibly relaxing for the moment.

All urban leisure time activities fall into one or more of the above mentioned categories. Also urban leisure is always somehow related to the most important aspect of urban social organization, namely specialization. All these activities either carry a mood of intense concentration and specialization from the urban work day into urban leisure, or they react violently against this very concentration and specialization.

THE TWOFOLD ORIENTATION OF URBAN LEISURE

Activity	Imitative Aspects	Contrasting Aspects
Spectator Sports	Competition	Drama
Model Airplanes	Concentration, Specialization	Craftsman's Pride
Gambling	Speculation	Chance
Reading	Intellectual Effort	Escape

263

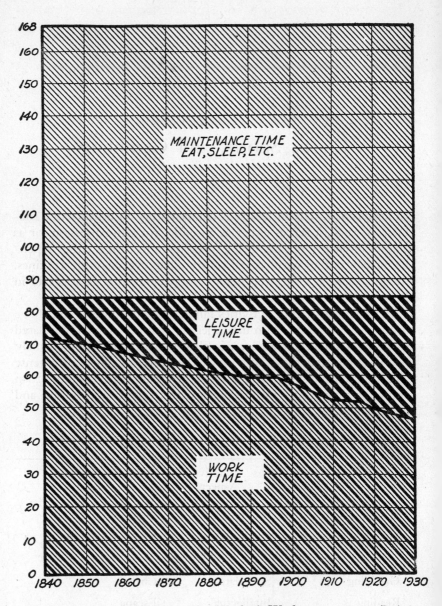

FIGURE 15. Work and Leisure. The Worker's Week over a 90-year Period
From: George A. Lundberg, *Leisure. A Suburban Study*. New York: Columbia
University Press, 1934, p. 5.

The separation between work and leisure becomes more complete and more complex as the modern city grows. Division of labor promotes the division between work and leisure.

Long commuting distances have something to do with this. They infringe upon the meal time arrangements in the urban family. Dinner at noon is replaced by a short luncheon close to the place of work.[1] The comfortable siesta falls by the wayside. Working hours are increasingly concentrated and arranged so as to permit the commuter to withdraw early to the residential district that harbors the leisure time of the city dweller, now even spatially set apart from the environment of his work.

With growing efficiency in urban industry, working hours are continuously reduced.[2] The urbanite lives a double existence. His private life gains a function and a meaning of its own. The weekend, originally limited to the sabbath, is set to begin at Saturday noon. At present the five-day week is accepted by some government agencies as well as by many private employers. The foundation is laid for an urban culture that stands independent of the workaday culture, is relegated to the private sphere of urban living, and is more or less related to urban consumption as an end in itself.

Craft Activities

Slaves of the Machine. Interest in urban leisure is apt to be absorbing. The reason is the city dweller's loss of interest in his occupational pursuits. Efficient performance on the job is often accompanied by fading interest and "loss of meaning." [3] Instead of letting the individual worker switch from one set of performances to another in the completion of the final product, the conveyor belt leaves the individual worker behind to repeat the same job on the next item moving along the production line.

The economies derived from division of labor are well known.

---

[1] "An interesting effect . . . of the distance between home and work is the growth of a catering industry. Establishments catering for the lunches of masses of earners have developed mushroom-like in business centers of all kinds during the last decades." Kate K. Liepmann, *The Journey to Work.* New York: Oxford University Press, 1944, p. 69.

[2] For the relative increase of leisure as compared to working hours between 1840 and 1930, see George A. Lundberg, Mirra Komarovsky, and Mary Alice McInerny, *Leisure. A Suburban Study.* New York: Columbia University Press, 1934, pp. 4-6.

[3] See Hendrik DeMan, *Joy in Work.* Glencoe, Ill.: The Fress Press, 1951.

We know less of their effect upon human beings. Deprived of the use of initiative, paralyzed in the development of diversified skills and unaware of the context in which their automatic muscular and nervous reactions participate in the miracle of modern machine production, modern city dwellers are apt to consider themselves the servants rather than the masters of the machine.

Workmanship. For the experience of human mastery over the physical environment, the city dweller looks to his leisure time activities. There is no place for the conveyor belt in the organization of our leisure time activities.

It would be more efficient to make model airplanes on the production line. But nobody would think of spending his spare hours at a conveyor belt well organized to make bigger, better, and cheaper model airplanes than would otherwise be possible. In leisure time activities, the interest shifts from the product to the process of production. Enjoyment in the process of production is predicated upon the experience of workmanship, an experience which enables the worker to see in the final product a crystallization of a sequence of individual efforts.

In recreational workmanship, efficiency is generally sacrificed to diversification of labor, a tendency contrary to that of specialization and division of labor. The form of leisure time production deviates from the manner in which we meet our material demands for industrial and agricultural products. When leisure is devoted to "making things," such as model airplanes for school children or scooters for smaller children, when animals are raised as pets, and gardens tilled in the backyard, the mode of production is reduced to the craftsman's level. One person does all the jobs consecutively required to complete the final product.

Arts and Crafts Movement. The English Arts and Crafts Movement [4] promoted such active leisure. In the spirit of this movement, recent decades have brought a growing interest in spinning and weaving by hand, in metalworking and the production of handmade furniture. Homespun cloth is appreciated by consumers with

---

[4] "This misuse of machinery (in the production of the machine-made, ornament-imitating handicraft) was what William Morris had in mind when he campaigned against mid-Victorian ugliness and insincerity and tried to revive a genuine spirit of craftsmanship." J. M. Richards, *An Introduction to Modern Architecture*. Harmondsworth, Middlesex, England: Penguin Books, Ltd., 1940, p. 33.

an artistic bent. Crude wood panellings of cedar and knotty pine delight the city dweller in his home with their down-to-earth quality. From machine-made gadgets and the smooth surface of plastics — produced by complicated chemical processes beyond the understanding of the average consumer—the city dweller escapes into an environment which he might have worked with his own hands.

The products of the Arts and Crafts Movement and its imitations in the modern clothing, pottery, and furniture industries are not necessarily made by the consumer himself. They may be commercially produced for a restricted market where they are sold at the additional price required to cover the luxury of relatively inefficient craft production.

Inherent in the creed of the Arts and Crafts Movement is a romantic protest against our modern machine age culture.[5] In handling his own tools, in using simple raw materials found within his region of residence, in building his home with his own hands and applying his own individual skills to supply himself with clothes and equipment, man is supposed to regain the dignity that he is assumed to have lost by submerging under a deluge of machine products.

COMPETITION

Noncompetitive Leisure. Most active urban leisure is somehow competitive. This is so much taken for granted today that we can scarcely imagine how it could be otherwise. Yet in old age and infancy we find leisure time activities that are not competitive in nature.

Before and at nursery school age, there is more interest in expressive than in competitive behavior.

Non-competitive play is more or less confined to those stages of child development characterized by incomplete socialization. As the child begins to orient his activities toward the world of adults, the competitive element superimposes itself even upon activities which under different cultural conditions might have remained random and sufficient unto themselves.[6]

---

[5] For William Morris' struggle to restore the spirit of craftsmanship in the face of the advancing power of machinery, see J. M. Richards, *op. cit.*, p. 56.

[6] "When we see children building with blocks, pretending to be airplanes, learning to skip rope, we're apt to think, in our mixed-up adult way, that these are just amusement." Benjamin Spock, *The Pocket Book of Baby and Child Care.* New York: Pocket Books, Inc., 1946, p. 242.

In old age, beyond the strife for income and social position, activities are again indulged in for other reasons than competitive self-assertion. The old timers tell stories and find relaxation in doing so. There is gossip and story-telling, imaginary and otherwise, and surprises and presents planned long in advance for friends or family members. There are hobbies and crafts employing neglected individual skills, with joy in perfection rather than in economic gain.[7]

Rules of Competition. The bulk of our urban population is engaged in leisure time activities of a competitive nature. They make it possible to excell, to nose out the opponent by either individual skill or luck.

We like to play according to an impersonal framework of rules. Rivalry is cast within a system that distinguishes between permissible and nonpermissible behavior. There may or may not be an umpire, but there must be at least a set of pre-ordained rules to which the player can appeal for "justice."

Such play activities reflect general structures of our social order. Sharp borderlines are drawn between those means by which it is permissible, in business, to make an income at the expense of other businessmen or customers, and those means by which it is not.

Sports. The emphasis upon competition in modern sports cannot be overlooked. Beginning in elementary and high schools, sports are rarely practiced entirely for their own sake, that is, for either plain fun or for the achievement of a feeling of physical well-being. Competitive sports enjoy a larger and a more eager participation than sports designed exclusively for purposes of physical development.

In the Middle Ages hunting was a pastime in which everybody shared co-operatively. The activity was enjoyed in a social manner. It was well known who were the skilled hunters in the party, but hunting was not engaged in with the primary purpose of displaying excellence in physical skills.[8] At the present time, hunting as a

---

[7] "The typical picture is of the old person sitting around or aimlessly puttering at almost useless jobs or restlessly getting into other people's way in trying to help." Ruth Shonle Cavan, *Old Age in a City of 100,000.* Illinois Academy of Science Transactions, Vol. 40, 1947, p. 165.

[8] Even in modern times, the emphasis upon a systematic competition of skills is of relatively recent date:

"The first important development of interest in athletic sports and games occurred in this country in the decades immediately following the Civil War. Prior to that time the emphasis had been upon the German and Swedish

leisure time activity is outdistanced in importance by more specialized sports derived from the more or less composite activity of hunting. Today, horse-racing and shooting have become competitive
sports each in its own right. The breakdown of composite activities into their specialized component parts facilitates competitive
arrangements and hair-trigger decisions about the outcome of the
contest.

The ball games of the Middle Ages have become tightened up
within a framework of strict competitive rules. The process of
rationalization, that is, the establishment of game rules to cover
any playful activity and to submit it to competitive contests, is still
under way.[9] In different countries different sports prevail, due to
natural and cultural conditions which encourage different types of
informal play.[10] In some countries, as informal an activity as hiking
is being broken down into its component parts in walking and map-
reading competitions; it is given a competitive angle which greatly
enhances the interest in this leisure time activity, which makes it a
"sport." [11]

From Rivalry to Competition. The participants in sport's competition are hierarchically arranged, not only on the basis of the
individual meet on the local level, but in relation to regional, nation-

---

systems of gymnastics and calisthenics so widely used in Europe as a means
for physical health and recreation." Jesse F. Steiner, "Recreation and Leisure
Time Activities," in *Recent Social Trends.* New York: McGraw-Hill Book
Company, Inc., 1933, p. 925.

[9] Consider competitions in the dispatch of carrier pidgeons, in the cultivation of garden plants, and also in the plucking of chickens and the husking of
corn, where the competitive arrangement turns the job into a sporting event.

[10] Consider the Rodeo of Western origin, Canadian ice hockey, Scandinavian
interest in skiing that grows out of the use of skis as means of transportation,
and varied competitions in card games that develop on the basis of prevailing
social pastimes.

[11] At the end of the 1930's, a new sport developed in Sweden, called "ori-
entering." It consisted of a combination of map-reading skills and cross-
country running, based on widespread active and passive interests in both
activities. In this country, baseball developed from random play on the empty
city lot.

"In America, baseball was known as early as 1778, when Washington's men
played it at Valley Forge. . . . The earliest known rules of rounders were
printed in William Clarke's *The Boy's Own Book,* London, 1829, which was
reprinted in Boston the same year." *The Encyclopedia Americana.* New York:
Americana Corporation, 1949, Vol. 3, p. 302.

wide, and even worldwide achievements. In this manner, rivalry is set aside in favor of true competition.[12]

Rivalry implies the notion of winning over a specific contestant. The endeavor is concentrated upon coming out first in the contest at hand. In competition, ambition may extend beyond the individual contest in a more abstract manner. Rigid competitive rules make it possible for the contestants to measure their achievements in absolute terms. The time made in the race becomes as important as the outcome of the individual contest. The standing of the individual competitor in the national or worldwide scene is determined by way of absolute measurement.

Records. Such measurement tends to relate to some conventionalized scale. The simplest one is, of course, that of the runner who times himself and who thus calculates his standing in relation to competitors whom he may never see. The crowning glory in a career of sports is the "record," a winning achievement against past and future competitors. The realm of competition is thus extended beyond the range of contemporary competitors.

Records require absolute measurements related to distance and time or to specified achievements with a set of tools the nature of which is specified in detail by recognized sport authorities.[13]

Champions. Some sports, however, do not permit absolute measurement of achievement. The boxer will never know how he ranges among the outstanding contestants in his sport unless he is given a chance to try himself in actual contest. The establishment of a top-ranking class of fighters and the hierarchical arrangement between them is left to the fight management.

In our newspapers and magazines, we frequently read about alleged unfairness or fraud in the evaluation of top-flight competitors and the manner in which they are scheduled to fight against each other. The temptation to such mismanagement is inherent in the fact that an absolute measure of achievement is impossible in some sports. Manipulation in the arrangement of fights at top level com-

---

[12] Rivalry has been discussed as "personalized competition." Competition is characterized by the absence of personal antagonism. See William F. Ogburn and Meyer F. Nimkoff, *Sociology*. New York: Houghton Mifflin Company, 1940, p. 346.

[13] Consider the functions of the American Baseball Commissioner, the Contest Board of the American Automobile Association, the Basketball Association of America, the Billiard Congress of America, the American Bowling Congress, the National Boxing Association, and so forth.

petition, on the other hand, greatly influences the career of the individual boxer during his active years. An ideal situation for exploitation and graft is thus established.

Championship is achieved by participating successfully in a systematically arranged sequence of contests which gradually eliminate the inferior players. On the lonely heights of championship, individual skill might be displayed in exhibitions by the outstanding performer. The billiard champion shoots from one table to another, the chess champion plays "blind," and the accomplished card player shows tricks to an admiring audience.

Professionalism. Championship ends in professionalism; this holds true for sports as well as organized games. The reason is the competitive zest with which leisure time activities are pursued in our times. To many of us sport and games are more important than our occupational activities. Thus we need competent teachers to prepare ourselves for the plunge into local, regional, nationwide or worldwide competition. We need coaches to spur us to new records. The top performer, therefore, has a hard time avoiding the temptation of turning his sport and play into his life work.

The successful football player turns professional. There are those who assert that the average college football player himself must be looked upon as part professional, considering the scholarships he receives and easy employment that is thrown his way on the basis of his physical prowess and skill. The caddy at the golf club longs for nothing more than to become a pro.

At this level, competition is sharpened to a nerve-racking grind. The winter circuit of professional golf tournaments is not only costly to participate in, but trying for both physique and nerves. Professional players are matched at these competitions which establish and re-establish from year to year the hierarchy of the best and the not-quite-so-good. Job and salary hinge upon the excellence in competitive performance. Similarly, the football coach at one of the larger colleges has to win and to go on winning unless he wants to see himself eliminated from his spot-lighted role.

Professionalism is the logical consequence of our delight in top performance, our zest for success in competitive play at all costs. The amateur has little chance to hang on in a competition in which some of the contestants devote all their waking hours to preparation for the contest. The amateur of another day was enabled to devote himself wholeheartedly to his pastimes on the basis of an independent income, as a member of the gentry or the son of a rich father. Today, his role is taken over by the professional who makes a living from sports, who seeks to break records while teaching his sport to less accomplished addicts.

Games. Competitive contests are not limited to the field of sports. As spectator events, they are somewhat more concentrated on physical achievement. Spectator events must direct themselves to the lowest common denominator of interest in a mass audience. For greatest profit, they must appeal to everybody, and it takes little special preparation to enjoy a competition the object of which is to run fastest, to jump farthest, to punch the adversary most effectively, or to toss the ball where the ball ought to be tossed.

On the intellectual level, competition demands a simplification of performance. Competition is more or less naturally guided in the direction of memory display. Competition often takes the form of a quiz. What the Quiz Kids have started, the adult performers on "Information Please" have brought to full "professional" climax. Erudition, in these performances, is atomized. Stray bits of memorabilia are handed around and tucked away in appropriate pidgeonholes. The nationwide audience marvels at a fantastic memory just as the unsophisticated concert goer marvels at the speed with which the pianist is able to run up and down the scales of his instrument.

To increase the audience appeal, memory contests are offered for active participation. The enjoyment consists of checking items on the credit side of the "I knew it all" ledger. Knowledge, thus itemized, becomes measurable and the basis of competitive play. Even so, intellectual endeavor would scarcely have aroused the interest of the many millions who listen to quiz programs, were it not for an element of gambling which, at this point, demands our attention.

GAMBLING

Chance Success. In the modern city there is a kind of gambling to suit every pocketbook. At bingo, lady luck is courted by large middle class audiences while amounts of money far exceeding the surplus purchasing power of the middle class housewife or family provider change hands at the race tracks, and at the sweepstakes and other foreign lotteries. The entire structure of modern competitive sports is overlaid with bets that are placed upon the contestants involved.[14]

The principle of gambling may be conceived as a farcical imitation of the world of modern economic enterprise. There is irony in the fact that success is based on random choice rather than performance or considered speculation. With the turning of the wheel, tickets of fortune are thrown this way and that.[15]

The enjoyment of gambling is not related to a realistic assessment of the actual chances of winning. The thrill of expectation becomes an end in itself.[16] There is even an element of vicarious satisfaction in seeing *another* person win, due to the "human interest" inherent in many urban leisure time activities.[17] We must remember that the idea of luck is unrelated to individual merit and achievement.[18] Predestination, according to Calvinistic doctrine, and not human endeavor is the basis of worldly success. Nowhere in our society is there an indication of indignation at undeserved success.

The hatcheck girl is discovered by the talent scout of the movie industry. She is given the right makeup; she receives speech lessons; she commits herself to a screen personality firmly anchored to some suggestive attitude not yet exploited by show business; and before we know it, out of nowhere a star has arisen. Acting talent may be an incidental advantage. It is no necessary prerequisite of screen success.[19] And yet there is no criticism of the distribution of rewards in show business. Undeserved rewards are applauded rather than criticized in our culture.

The Foil of Contests. A similar attitude supports our gambling enterprises. To avoid legal restrictions, institutionalized gambling is frequently draped in the garb of the contest. The advertising busi-

---

[14] See various references in "Gambling," *The Annals* of the American Academy of Political and Social Science, Vol. 269 (May, 1950).

[15] For a good popular discussion packed with interesting data (the source of which is not always made explicit), see Eric Bender, *Tickets of Fortune*. New York: Modern Age Books, 1938.

[16] The word "gambling" derives, of course, from gaming.

[17] For "human interest," see pp. 283 ff.

[18] For a different interpretation of the relationship between gambling and the "belief in luck," see Thorstein Veblen, *The Theory of the Leisure Class*. New York: The Modern Library, 1934, Chapter XI, "The Belief in Luck," pp. 276-292.

[19] Consider the relationship between box-office success and acting ability with regard to Tarzan and Hopalong Cassidy.

ness avails itself of the tremendous drawing power inherent in the gambling thrill.[20]

Easy contests have been held for years over the radio networks. Give-away programs have bewildered and driven to despair the professional show people. Even the most brilliant talent cannot compete with the enjoyment of gambling. Most gambling, however, is illegal, and so are certain sales practices combined with a stake in anything resembling a lottery. Therefore, the fake contests flourish, and legal battles rage over the question of whether radio give-away programs are to be considered as contests or as lotteries.

There can be no doubt about the immense popularity of the prize contest and its success as an advertising device. That the chances of success are infinitesimal does not influence the situation. The individual contestant is not discouraged if he learns that he finds himself in competition with an ever growing group of semi-professional contest participants who spend their days in libraries digging up information, and who are trained in educational institutions established for the express purpose of preparing the student for contest participation.[21]

The "Fix." The honest gambler, of course, is the exception rather than the rule if honesty means the unwillingness to take advantage of opportunities to influence the outcome of the gamble. The temptation to manipulate the wheel is more than our profit-conscious society can stand. Thus, the "fix" is expected as standard behavior. Rackets which are based upon "fixing" the outcome of a contest that is the object of betting have invaded almost every type of gambling in operation.[22]

There are crooked dice and roulette wheels; there are "fixed" horse races and boxing contests. Even the field of non-professional collegiate sports is occasionally invaded by the racketeer. The victim is the large mass of anonymous suckers. The money is drained from the many gamblers who want to get something for nothing, and who are so intent upon this desire that they do not shrink away

---

[20] See Eric Bender, *op. cit.*, Chapter 10, "Contests, Lotteries, and the Law," pp. 53-60.

[21] *Ibid.*, Chapter 4, "There Are Professionals," pp. 23-27.

[22] "Fifty million adult Americans gamble regularly, butting their heads and dollars against gambling odds and gimmicks that make it impossible for them to win." Ernest E. Blanche, "Gambling Odds Are Gimmicked!" in "Gambling," *op. cit.*, p. 77.

even when they recognize that their chances for undeserved success are tampered with by the criminal underworld. The anonymity of urban living, and the concomitant fact that no man is cheated face to face, undoubtedly come to the assistance of the gambling racket.

STATUS DISPLAY

Conspicuous Consumption. To Thorsten Veblen we owe the concept of conspicuous consumption. It refers to the circumstance that in our urban culture consumer goods are bought for other reasons than the satisfaction of consumer needs. A car is not bought for its speed and operational efficiency. A dress is not bought for the warmth it provides, its durability, or its esthetically pleasing appearance (esthetic appreciation in itself tends to be dependent upon more fundamental values). A new element has entered into the picture. Consumer goods are valued not for their inherent qualities only but as status symbols displayed in a process of "pecuniary emulation." The city dweller wants to display consumer goods that associate him with the highest possible status level to which he can raise his ambitions.[23]

Conspicuous consumption is an urban phenomenon. In the peasant village, there is no reason for ostentation. All members of the community know each other for what they are worth.[24]

The attitude toward clothes changes as soon as the young men and girls are attracted to industrial employment outside their home villages. At their places of employment, these young people are not known. In superficial contacts among the anonymous crowds of the urban community, their prestige is not established any more by their landed wealth and that of their parents. In the anonymous city environment, status for all practical purposes of superficial interaction is improved by dress and consumption patterns associated with a higher status group.

---

[23] See Thorstein Veblen, *op. cit.*, Chapters II, III, and IV ("Pecuniary Emulation," "Conspicuous Leisure," and "Conspicuous Consumption.")

[24] "New needs arose among the members of the younger generation, needs of city products, city pleasures, learning."

"In the consciousness of the peasant who pays absurd prices for a piece of land there is no equivalence possible between land and any other economic value; they are incommensurable with each other." William I. Thomas and Florian Znaniecki, *The Polish Peasant in Europe and America.* New York: Alfred A. Knopf, 1918, pp. 169 and 190.

Symbols of Status. Through conspicuous consumption, the competition for status is extended beyond the occupational spheres of urban life. It reaches into the hours of leisure and into the lives of the unproductive members of the family group.[25]

The purchase of status symbols easily becomes an end in itself.[26] The state of our pocketbooks is known to few of the many people with whom we associate in our daily lives. To many, we are what we appear to be.[27]

Fashion. The bid for apparent status through appearance is most pronounced in the field of fashion. In the earlier phases of the industrialization process, fashion filtered down from the higher strata of society.[28] Novelty, as an individual attention getting device, was more or less reserved to members of the most "fashionable" families. Such novelties, new modes in dress and appearance, were first developed by the leaders of taste and elegance, wealthy people who had sufficient leisure to concern themselves with such matters. Then they were emulated by inferior groups of pretenders. New fashions were thus taken over by the lower status groups, while the upper crust continued to search for new means of distinction.[29]

In this manner, the status of most individuals could be ascertained at any moment by a look at the vintage of fashion they displayed. With regard to durable equipment, such as cars and family housing, this still holds true today. With regard to dress, the situation has somewhat changed.

The course of fashion is not directed any longer by the individual

---

[25] "The end of acquisition and accumulation is conventionally held to be the consumption of the goods accumulated — whether it is consumption directly by the owner of the goods or by the household attached to him and for this purpose identified with him in theory." Thorstein Veblen, *op. cit.*, p. 25.

[26] In Sweden, the taxed income in the higher income brackets is made a matter of public record in a yearly publication available on the book market. Thus, the income declared is at times higher than the actual income — an example of outright purchase of prestige.

[27] For the process of stereotyping, see 191-192.

[28] "Fashions exist not only among the socially elite but also among sharecroppers, Negroes, children, and members of all strata of society." Steuart Henderson Britt, *Social Psychology of Modern Life*. New York: Farrar & Rinehart, Inc., 1941, p. 248.

[29] "We may say . . . that this principle of novelty is another corrollary under the law of conspicuous waste. Obviously, if each garment is permitted to serve for but a brief term, and if none of last season's apparel is carried over and made further use of during the present season, the wasteful expenditure on dress is greatly increased." Thorstein Veblen, *op. cit.*, p. 173.

tailor or the individual member of the smart set in the upper classes. The creation of fashion today lies in the hands of the professional fashion designer. Within the overheated competition of the modern city, the tempo of emulation has increased to such an extent that it isn't possible any more to use "vintage" of dress as a landmark of status. New fashions make their appearance simultaneously at different status levels. The same design elements, the same type of fabrics and the same colors of fashion are made available at the beginning of each season at different price levels to accommodate the pocketbooks of different social strata.

Urban conspicuous consumption in the field of dress has become quite subtle. Symbolic expression of status is inherent, today, in such differences as those between the tailor-made and the ready-to-wear suit, between Harris tweed and domestic tweed, between pigskin and imitation leather. At a superficial glance and with untrained eyes, the appearance of our urban crowds makes it very difficult to distinguish between different status groups. All city people dress, roughly, alike. Therein is mirrored the ease of cosmopolitan contacts in the modern city. That nevertheless great social differences exist between the purchasing potentials of the millionaire and the sales clerk is reflected in a somewhat more underhanded way.

Fads. Fads, as compared to fashions, do not express status. It would be wrong, however, not to consider them as "conspicuous consumption." Fads are not related to the seasonal rhythm of fashions, by which our warehouses are emptied and replenished with new challenges to available purchasing power. They develop with greater irregularity. They also blossom up, reach a climax, and die a slow death. Still, they present a means of conspicuous self-assertion.

Fads are concentrated upon adolescents and young adults.[30] These are conscious of their age group affiliations. They feel set off against the world of their parents and that of their younger sisters and brothers. They feel that they are growing up, yet, they are still rebelling against the world of adulthood that is presented them in a ready-made bundle by the older generation. To express themselves, these age groups resort to shocking or at least startling patterns of consumption. Zoot-suits, blue jeans, old worn out men's shirts, and sloppy sneakers are some of the paraphernalia that have been sported

---

[30] See pp. 242 ff.

in this setting. This is not necessarily a very status-conscious group in terms of adult society. It is cliquish, however, and does not want to let the outsider in.

There is nothing continuous or rhythmical about the fad. A disappearing fad does not have to be replaced by another one. Different fads may exist side by side. But the need for self-assertion in the adolescent group serves as a fountainhead for the spontaneous creation of novelties. New gadgets gain temporary symbolic significance until their symbolic value has become depreciated by imitations in out-group territory.

SELECTED READINGS

See p. 294.

PROBLEMS

See pp. 294-295.

CHAPTER 12

Passive Entertainment, Human Interest, and Escape

PASSIVE ENTERTAINMENT

Audience Participation. The modern city dweller spends a great deal of his leisure time in activities which he shares as a member of an audience. He enjoys much of his leisure as a passive onlooker, as a spectator. In such activities, all active participants can be classed as professional entertainers. The very intensity of highly specialized urban pursuits makes the city dweller want to relax in the role of a merely interested bystander

Even nonproductive activities in the city are pursued with so much consistent effort at perfection that the average citizen has no chance to participate successfully. Participation in competition demands supreme effort. Tied to more or less one-sided occupations during most of his waking hours, the city dweller withdraws from activities that leave him at a disadvantage in comparison with those who make a profession of it. The modern city dweller has much of his fun by proxy. He prefers to identify with skillful performers at play in the arena of modern urban entertainment instead of displaying his own inadequacies.

Increasingly, therefore, urban leisure time activities are transformed into passive entertainment. In this manner, the city dweller finds compensation for the energy-consuming activities of his workday. With his energies at rest, he finds satisfaction by participating vicariously in the activities of the professional performer.

279

Spectators. As active leisure time activities are converted into passive ones, the former participants are divided into a limited number of top performers and a majority of spectators. To be sure, most successful audience sports have developed on a broad basis of active participation. Without an active experience of playing catch on the vacant lot, an experience shared by millions of American youngsters and young adults, the enthusiasm for professional baseball would not be understandable.[1] The same holds true for football, although active participation in this sport is not limited to play at the street corner. It is also promoted through organized educational activities in our high schools and colleges.

Still, a superstructure of commercial mass entertainment overlays a shrinking basis of active participation.[2] The city dweller withdraws early from active participation. He may enter the inactive phase of sports enthusiasm when physically still able to participate, because his own performances are hopelessly outdistanced by achievements on the professional level. In our educational institutions, the instructor's tendency to preoccupy himself with his most promising "material," the tendency to ignore those most in need of physical exercise has been criticized frequently.

Still in the prime of their physical powers,[3] many city dwellers go to baseball and football games instead of playing either tennis or golf themselves. Some do both, but they are in the minority. By and large, the city dweller allows high skills and outstanding physical prowess to perform in front of his eyes. He attaches himself as a fan to some star or some team, he suns himself in the glory of their success. In addition to professionals, we permit our best young people to step into the arena and to participate — for a few years — in the breathtaking competitions of specialized athletes.

---

[1] "The year 1858 marks an important milestone in the early history of baseball. In that year the National Association of Baseball Players, an amateur body, was formed from among the 25 clubs then existing, and uniform rules were adopted. Previously, rules varied according to locality." *The Encyclopedia Americana.* New York: Americana Corporation, 1949, Volume 3, p. 303.

[2] "The most important trend in modern recreation in this country has been the widespread development of commercialized facilities for participation in a large variety of games and sports and other active recreational activities." Jesse F. Steiner, "Recreation and Leisure Time Activities," in *Recent Social Trends.* New York: McGraw-Hill Book Company, 1933, p. 954.

[3] As is well known, the span of active participation for the average athlete is limited to his twenties, possibly reaching into his thirties.

Sports. Most sports have been transformed into spectator events. Basketball is gaining nationwide appeal in the United States, to fill the gap between the football and baseball seasons. The boxing ring attracts the passive sport fans at more erratic intervals.

Tennis matches appeal to a more limited middle and upper class audience, possibly with a country club background and at least occasional active participation. Ice hockey, known in this country almost exclusively as spectator sport, is appreciated for speed and dramatic tension. Golf, table tennis, billiards, badminton, and many other sports appeal to more limited groups of enthusiasts. The audience appeal of many spectator sports depends upon acquaintance with the required performance through some active participation.[4]

Different countries focus the beacon-light of public attention on different sports activities. In England, southern Europe, and South America, the game of soccer plays the same role as an entertainment for large urban masses as do football and baseball in this country.[5] Track sports hold a great attraction for Scandinavian mass audiences. Wrestling and ice hockey have built mass audiences in Sweden and Finland where these sports flourish on a broad basis of local competitions between schools, villages, and industrial teams in the lake-studded winter landscape. The Norwegian proficiency in ski-jumping is well-known.

The Theater. Spectator events are also built around leisure time activities other than sports. Theatrical performances also had their origin in nonprofessional play.[6] At the court of Louis XIV in Paris, the king amused himself and his entourage by amateur performances. The audience was limited; anybody who was anybody was part of the show. The professionalization of the theater is linked to city growth and to the development of large urban audiences. The urban middle classes formed mass audiences entertained by professional show people.

Subsidized by the local court and supported by the ticket-buying public, the repertory theater was a standing feature in the European city of the 19th century. The early theater dramatized some of the personal and social conflicts associated with the Industrial Revolution

---

[4] See also pp. 268 ff.

[5] For the origin of ball games, see *The Encyclopedia Americana*. New York: Americana Corporaton, 1949, Volume 3, pp. 94-96.

[6] See Allardyce Nicoll, *World Drama*. New York: Harcourt, Brace and Company, 1949.

and the process of urbanization.[7] Gradually, the theater lost its educational function. It gave up trying to enlighten, to stir up feelings of protest against the tyrants of the day, the seducers of innocent maidenhood and political suppression.

The theater began to provide entertainment for its own sake. The playwright's concern turned from what he was trying to say to techniques of saying it entertainingly. Wit and theatrical skill replaced the message which, previously, the playwright might have tried to get across. After having turned into a virtuoso writing for applause rather than for artistic expression and education, the playwright waned in importance as compared to the stage personnel with immediate audience contact. The play is reduced to a "vehicle" that permits the actor to display his brilliance.

The Movie. The climax of this development is reached in the modern movie. Movies do not usually aspire to artistic functions.[8] In the movie theater, the city dweller loses himself in a drama without bearing upon his own life situation. Such entertainment is truly passive. The spectator indulges in the luxury of vicariously living a life that is decidedly not his own — or anyone else's, for that matter.

The plot of the modern movie is dramatic and exciting; it is a full life containing love, sex, war, and success. It enables the hero to display his wit and his charm, his physical strength and his reasoning power, and his inimitably successful manner of dealing with members of the opposite sex.

Passive entertainment is not found in the movie alone. Yet, we may doubt that the same void of active participation, coupled with the same intensity of imaginary identification has been reached in any other medium. The modern movie provides the most characteristic urban entertainment feature.

Television, also, permits the audience to identify completely with the happenings on the television screen. Sports audiences may get a thrill from identification with the contestants, the winner, the top flight athlete, the successful football player. To the sports fan, nothing may seem more important than the outcome of a certain

---

[7] Consider Shakespeare in England, Lessing and Schiller in Germany, and Ibsen in Norway.

[8] The production of educational movies does not contradict this statement. For limited audiences, educational movies are produced to fill the gap left by the movie industry that attracts the urban mass audiences.

football game, but the life illusion projected upon the movie screen is missing.

Literature. Books and magazines may carry the city dweller away in illusions almost as compelling as those of the movie screen. To achieve this effect, modern fiction underwent a development similar to that leading from the repertory theater to the movie. Intentions to serve educational or esthetic purposes had to be cancelled.

Modern fiction is not represented by a distinctive flow of anything that might be called the currents of modern literature. There are several literatures,[9] several layers existing side by side and directing themselves at different levels of sophistication. Reading habits and educational achievement decide how much in writing technique and esthetic value, what metaphors, and what language will be tolerable to the individual reader without disturbing him in the process of creating an imaginary dream world.

Interest in writing as an art is limited to a small number of literary connoisseurs. For most of us, literature has come to function as a mechanism of escape, a medium to which we give ourselves passively, with the hope of being guided to a land of fantasy with conditions that are painfully missing in the routines of our everyday life.

It may take comic books or comic strips, mystery stories or short stories in our slick magazines to provide different people with a mechanism for blissful escape.[10] At all levels of education the literature written for the daily consumption of the modern city dweller has ceased to function as a means to improve the mind. It has undertaken to rest it.

HUMAN INTEREST

Social Distance. It is one of the paradoxes of city living that acquaintance with human problems can be held at a minimum in a

---

[9] "Mrs. Q. D. Leavis points out that the eighteenth century peasant who learned to read had to read what the gentry and the university men read; that the nineteenth century readers, on the other hand, are properly spoken of not as 'the public' but as 'publics.' " René Welleck and Austin Warren, *The Theory of Literature*. London: T. Cape, 1949, p. 95.

[10] "In 1933, there was not one comic book openly published in the United States. Today, at a conservative estimate, there are five hundred million yearly; three hundred titles or more, each with an average monthly printing of two hundred thousand copies. From zero to half a billion yearly, in fifteen years — the greatest, fastest literary success the world has ever seen." G. Legman, *Love & Death*. New York: Breaking Point, 1949, p. 29.

densely populated environment. This does not mean that the city dweller does not see or know people. He deals with a tremendously large number of them during every single day of his life in the city. He is limited, however, to highly specialized contacts with his fellow men. He deals with them as teachers or salesmen, as fellow passengers of the suburban transit system, or as professionals assisting him in his medical needs. He deals with them in segmentalized roles, not as human beings.[11]

There are many facets to the personality of the modern city dweller. The point of integration of the many social roles displayed in the modern city is to be found in the needs of the social system, not in the needs of the human individual.

How a system of divergent social roles impinges upon individual experience is the human problem involved in urban living. It is a problem solved behind the surface of social life in the city environment. Society is concerned only with conformity of behavior within each separate sphere of activities. How these activities converge upon the individual, how they combine to leave the individual a full range of self-expression, to leave him satisfied or disgruntled, restless or psychologically at peace with himself, is a problem to which little systematic concern has been devoted.

Interest in Configurations of Roles. "Human interest" arises in the city environment as a concern with the problem of role combination and as a reaction against role specialization. It arises as a spontaneous interest, exploited commercially by the entertainment industry. "Human interest" is accommodated in the daily newspaper which is eager to satisfy a deeply felt need in order to sell itself.[12] In the news, human interest sells, and thereby boosts circulation. The tabloids are bought because their reporting is held to a level where events are reflected in the light of concrete human experience. The

---

11 See Helen MacGill Hughes, *News and the Human Interest Story*. Chicago: The University of Chicago Press, 1940, Chapter V, "Human Interest," pp. 105-125.

12 "In a small community where neighbors know each other such things become the subject of gossip. . . . Now it seems to be a general truth that some adequate vehicle for circulating gossip is found wherever there is a populace emerging into a world wider than the area of oral distribution. Then, if the idea of exploiting this interest presents itself to some enterprising man, he can make a living for himself by selling stories of strange, romantic, sad, or comic personal experiences, which will have for the customers the quality of literature." *Ibid.*, pp. 105-106.

privacy of public personalities is violated. Eyewitness reports wallow in the gory details of human misery. They delight, equally, in jubilant descriptions of the feeling of the man who has achieved the ultimate of his ambition, or the woman who has won the jackpot in a bingo game.

The interest in human interest must be understood as an attempt to scale down social organization to human experience. Human interest satisfies a natural curiosity as to how man fits himself into the superhuman purposes of the modern city. We want to be able to extend our sympathies to all participants in the maze of urban living. We want to be able to identify — as human beings — with the outstanding leaders of the modern city.

Our interest, furthermore, extends to the tremendous variety of divergent human experiences pooled in the modern city. The total organization of the modern city may be hard to understand. Still, we cannot suppress the urge to share in as much as possible of the emotional experience that goes to make up the city as a social universe. "In the large city, everything happens at any given time."[13] We want to participate at least vicariously by extending our sympathy. We want to know how it feels to be on the spot of action. Rape, murder, and suicide are welcome topics, possibly just because we would never be caught as active participants in such extreme behavior.

"Full Experience?" Social organization in the city has become so complicated that the average reader can understand its problems only at the price of considerable concentration, a price he is not willing to pay at the end of a strenuous working day. His attention is reduced to the human interest angle, and he enjoys the ease and freedom with which he can allow himself to look at the lives of others co-operating in the complicated machinery of modern urban life.

In this manner, the city dweller gains a feeling of supplementing the one-sided experiences to which he is exposed at his own work. He gains a glimpse of modern urban life as a full experience.

All performances in the urban environment ·are subjected to specialization. For that reason, our news services tend to treat as unnecessary technicalities much of that information which makes

---

[13] A verbal statement, frequently made by Robert E. Park, and handed down in the Chicago tradition of sociology.

the very life blood of modern urban existence, which is, after all, based on specialization. Reduced to human experience, political, social, and cultural events are not fully apprehended by the urban public.

The city dweller participates as spectator; but he participates in the same manner in which the small town dweller enjoys casual gossip about his neighbors. He wonders how it may feel to be in the shoes of the great man. He wonders how it may feel to fly to a conference in Paris or to throw one's weight around among the staff of a well organized business enterprise, how it may feel to press a button to have the secretaries call for a taxi or order a Pullman berth on the Twentieth Century. He wonders how it may feel to be a movie star who emotes in the embrace of another member of the same guild — and all the time he is losing out in sharing the true experience of all these prominent people, who are probably too concentrated upon their specialized professional tasks to be very concerned with the comforts and tribulations of their everyday lives.

Fans. The fan is a city dweller who dedicates himself to concern with one particular thing or person. Personal fans in the city environment exploit the human interest angle to the extreme. There is a frantic endeavor to overcome the impersonal relationship that prevails between the fan and his idol.[14]

Imaginary personal relations develop between the spectator and the performer in show business. The movie screen is unsurpassed in providing the illusion of intimate personal acquaintance. We all have had our "flirtations" with the movie stars we adore. Imagination shapes an entirely impersonal relationship into an intimate and personal one.[15] The habit first developed in relation to the matinee idol or the movie star is easily extended to other performers, the dashing lecturer to women's clubs, the dancer, and the performer in the world of sports.

There are many objects of adoration to choose from. There are many performers eager — for commercial purposes — to gather fans

---

[14] For the "Interaction of Leader and Audience," see Richard T. LaPiere and Paul R. Farnsworth, *Social Psychology.* New York: McGraw-Hill Book Company, Inc., 1936, pp. 424-425.

[15] "The basis of audience leadership in the theater would seem to consist in providing satisfactory vicarious experience for the individual members. This is ordinarily accomplished by what can best be described as audience identification with the person of hero or heroine." *Ibid.*, p. 420.

around themselves, often on the basis of fan club formation, autographs, hand-shaking, or arrangements for an extensive correspondence with secretarial help.

The Star. The loyalty of the sport fan exceeds the interest in actual contest. He identifies with a certain team and with individual performers. He wants to know about their personal lives. He suffers with them in illness. He delights with them in family happiness as well as love affairs. He commiserates with them as they are penalized for insulting the umpire.

The sports columns are filled with detailed accounts of the private lives of tennis champions, fight heroes and baseball stars. The beacon light of publicity is focused upon any public performer. In his private life, he enjoys the privacy of the proverbial goldfish in his bowl of glass.

The publicity agent finds himself saddled with the job of providing interest-sustaining materials from the private life of his client. If the private life happens to be drab and uneventful, interesting angles have to be produced. Even adverse publicity is better than none.

The star performer has to continue performing even in his own private life. He has no private life, unless he is skillful enough to hide behind the front of the publicity agent who keeps the public on its toes while the star retires to his garden to tend quietly to his roses.

Crime and Accidents. That human interest is vicarious interest, though not always a matter of complete identification, helps to explain the sordid interest in crime and accidents to which the front pages of our daily newspapers bear ample witness.[16] In his life from day to day, the average city dweller is starved for emotional experiences. He may have settled down to a feeling of security in these very routines. Still, his starved emotions crave excitation; and he can enjoy excitment without endangering his own personal security by participating vicariously in the drama of those lives which surround urban existence at its fringes. He finds an emotional outlet in violent criminal action which he would never want to make his own.

---

[16] "The news breaks where some public notice is taken of a condition: at morgues, hosiptals, police courts, bankruptcy hearings, legislative sessions, sales, and the like." Helen MacGill Hughes, *op. cit.,* p. 80.

The city dweller gets satisfaction from reading about the week-end accidents that have passed him by. He is not sufficiently bored to wish for the accident to strike at himself and his family. Nor does he gloat over the fact that he has been spared, thus gaining a positive experience of his own safety. Most typically, enjoyment derives from vicarious emotional experience as such. From suffering to violent aggression, from clandestine love affairs to the loss of a child, the city dweller experiences from day to day the entire range of human emotions by making use of his news services.

IRRATIONALITIES

The prevalence of rational pursuits in the occupational life of the modern city dweller seems to create a desire to break away from the restrictions of carefully regulated behavior during his hours of leisure. When not at work, he enjoys participation in ventures the consequences of which are not strictly calculable. He yearns for surprise and delights in the encounter of unexpected circumstances.

Sneak Previews. This explains the unusual commercial success of the sneak preview offered by the local movie theater.[17] The house is packed, not in spite of the fact that the audience does not know what film is going to be shown, but because of it. It is not a matter of seeing 2 movies instead of 1. Such bargains are offered, with much less financial success, in the theater that shows double features. The sneak preview provides an additional thrill, that of surprise.

Treasure Trips. There are other attempts to exploit the desire for unexpected gratification. Railroad and bus companies feature excursions with no commitments as to destiny. They promise to carry the traveler into some agreeable resort area, but do not tell which one it will be.

With the ticket for a "treasure trip" the traveler buys a surprise. The indefinite goal attracts his interest. An element of gambling is involved in these ventures. The customers are betting on getting something better than expected. Yet the desire to get something for nothing is not predominant. The surprise element in itself offers

---

17 A "sneak preview" carries the presumption that a new movie is sneaked out for a test of audience reaction before being released for commercial distribution. In fact, no testing is ordinarily intended. A movie, later to be shown in the same theater, is added to the evening's fare, thus adding an extra attraction the nature of which is not known in advance to the audience.

relief from the otherwise rationally controlled environment of the city dweller.

Christmas and Exchange of Presents. Even outside the field of commercial entertainment, surprise gratifications are valued highly by the city dweller. This becomes obvious in the manner in which we celebrate Christmas. This festival has, to be sure, other implications than those of giving presents all around. The most highly secularized urban environment is little given to religious observances; but the ritual of giving Christmas presents prevails. Apart from Christmas, there are birthdays and other occasions for the exchange of surprise presents.

Thoroughly irrational is the practice in some clubs, in which the members surprise each other at certain occasions with presents, the purchase price of which is carefully limited. It would be more rational under the circumstances, if every member went out and bought a one-dollar present for himself according to his own preferences. To propose this, however, would imply a complete misunderstanding of the purpose at hand. The surprise element involved is valued as an end in itself. Unpredictability of events has become a desired aspect in our leisure time activities.[18]

The Search for Meaning

Collective and Individual "Meaning." Neither the specialized occupational work of the city dweller nor his isolated private life carries any meaning in itself. Specialized work is meaningful only in its relation to other equally specialized activities. All taken together and well co-ordinated, these various occupational performances add up to something. Taken together, they complete the cycle of productive processes by which we provide ourselves with material goods.

Still, the self-reflecting individual of modern urban society is likely to search for some meaning in his own life history. With a minimum of religious anchorage, without the sophistication required for philosophical self-orientation, and without being endowed with a socializing impulse that justifies the integration of the individual as a mere cog into a complicated social machine, the modern city

---

[18] Reflect upon the surprise element in the plots of stories and shows, audience participation in radio shows, sport events, front page news, gambling, fashion, and so forth.

dweller is looking for such meaning within his own isolated existence. He is not apt to find it.[19]

Systematic Orientation. But what is meaning? Integration of personality is dependent upon some interpretation of the universe and of human existence and purpose. In religion and metaphysics, such integration is found in the dedication to ultimate values. Stripped of religion and metaphysics, the modern city dweller is left to gain the intellectual security of well-rounded self-orientation through pragmatic maxims that guide him through a somewhat disoriented life. Pragmatically, he adopts an attitude toward life instead of developing a philosophy of life.[20] Yet, the zest for systematic orientation remains unappeased.

Life Histories. The city dweller has to search for substitutes that make him feel important. In his leisure time activities he seeks stimuli for day dreams which cast him in parts that give him important influence upon the social life that buzzes around him. The plot of the mystery story or the screen drama gains importance over and above the detailed emotional experiences in which they allow their audiences to share. It is not enough that love and hate, sorrow and joy well over him. It is of consequence that the drama of life in which the city dweller participates by identification is skillfully brought to a happy and harmonious ending.

In the classic novels of modern Western Civilization, as written by Balzac, Dickens, Stendhal, and Tolstoi, to mention only a few names, the entire epic of modern social life is somehow woven around the individual life history. The hero of the novel shares all experiences potentially inherent in his environment. A complicated social structure is made to appear as a stage setting to provide the hero with broad social experience, to provide him with a full life experience from which he emerges a truly educated, wiser man.[21] The confus-

---

[19] For a philosophical expression of this experience, see Franz Adler, "The Social Thought of Jean-Paul Sarte," *The American Journal of Sociology*, Vol. LV, No. 3 (November, 1949), pp. 284-294.

[20] For the contribution of the philosophy of antiquity to this urban need, see p. 12.

[21] One might say that the educational novel (Bildungsroman) of the 19th century would be deprived of one of its basic themes without the interplay of the social classes. What would that literature be without the careers of Lucien de Rupembré in Balzac's novels; without Julien in Stendhal's *The Red and the Black*, without the upright Anton in Freytag's *Soll und Haben*. The family sagas written since the turn of the century penetrate even more deeply into the social structure.

ing vision of a turbulent social life is so described and integrated in the educational novel as to make it meaningful in connection with the hero's life history.

At the beginning of the industrialization process and at earlier stages of modern urbanization, social life was not yet too complicated to be seen in this light. In fiction at least, it was possible to let the individual life history touch upon all aspects of contemporary social life.[22] Nor was it impossible to imagine the individual hero as successful in his personal struggle for wealth and position. Chances for upward social mobility were more abundant than they are today. Social structure and social change could be made to appear as a mere background for individual "success stories."[23]

The serious novelist of modern times has struggled in vain with the difficulty of retaining a semblance of meaningful relationship between social events and the individual life history. Some writers have made an environment rather than an individual person the center of attention in their fiction.[24] Others have moved the lack of meaning in individual existence into the very center of their plot.[25]

Too weary to follow the serious writer in his attempt to present contemporary social experience as a problem, the urban masses have sought refuge with the popular writer who has no message but tries to write books that serve the need of man to feel in harmony with the environment in which he lives, the need to identify — albeit in day dreams — with somebody whose life makes sense, somebody whose life has meaning in that it stands in significant relationship to the surrounding social scene.

Mysteries. The reading of mystery stories is part of the entertainment pattern of the modern city dweller. The structure of the plot is standardized. The social order has been upset by a crime. It is left to the initiative of the righteous individual (the detective) to discover the criminal, to bring him to justice, to compensate the victims, and to delight the innocent bystanders by playing the role of the avenger.

---

[22] This was the intention of Honoré de Balzac's *Human Comedy*, a socially all-encompassing series of novels. A similar intent aimed at the contemporary social scene in the novels of Jules Romain loses form and unity due to the complexity of modern social life.

[23] The Horatio Alger stories, popular in the 1920's, present the typical pattern of the individual success story in a somewhat vulgarized, modern version.

[24] The best example for this type is John Dos Passos' novel *Manhattan Transfer*.

[25] Consider the novels of Franz Kafka, Aldous Huxley, John Dos Passos, and James Joyce.

The modern detective story varies in the choice of the means by which the detective restores the status quo or appeases the aroused citizenry. Sherlock Holmes does not use violence. He uses his wit. He is a student of empirical science and a wizard of deductive reasoning.

Personified in Sherlock Holmes, modern science and modern technological progress stand at the switchboard of events. They triumph victoriously over crime and injustice.

In more recent mystery novels, science no longer holds the center of the stage. The detective is beaten to within an inch of his life, and his physical prowess permits him to indulge in sweet revenge. The reader's vicarious experience of a "meaningful" existence centers around the adventures of a marginal man who is not part of any social matrix in the urban environment, has no parents, does not marry, is not known by his neighbors, and does not necessarily like his employer.[26]

In a mood of loneliness and with an air of cosmopolitan sophistication, the hero of the modern mystery story has the extraordinary ability to submerge in almost any urban scene without being individually conspicuous. With equal ease, he moves in the most formal of social circles and hobnobs with the pimp and the prostitute. The private detective of modern mystery fiction personifies anonymous urban existence. The meaningful integration of the individual life history concentrates on little more than survival in a turbulent urban scene.

Other Escape Literature. The detective story is only the most outstanding example of a prolific escape literature. The urban reader clutches eagerly at any fictionalization of events or personalities that provides him with an opportunity to live a meaningful life, at least in his imagination. There are love stories and stories of occupational success, there is the melodramatic historical novel, and there is the adventure story that takes the hero through the jungle, through wars and dangerous assignments in enemy country, through the crime district of the urban slum, through the mental undergrowth of subconscious yearnings, and through the entanglements of vice and sexual exploitation.

What marks these publications as "bad" literature is the lack of artistic ambition and the unobscured intention to provide food for imaginary wish fulfillment and emotionally satisfying escape from

---

[26] See G. Legman, *op. cit.*, Chapter I, "Institutionalized Lynch," pp. 7-24.

a humdrum existence. This type of literature is available for consumption on all levels of sophistication.

Cults and Creeds. At times the search for meaning becomes more articulate and challenges the city dweller to a higher degree of active participation. His loyalty is demanded by cults and convictions which offer emotionally satisfying interpretations of the intricacies and the seemingly bottomless puzzle of modern life. Where a rational penetration of modern social relations and of modern culture and economy seems outside the range of individual understanding, emotional adjustments offer themselves as a tempting bait.

There is a place, in the city, for cults and religious revivals.[27] They provide landmarks for individual orientation in a world of confusion.

These cults arise on different levels of sophistication and emotional refinement. They cater to the rich as well as to the poor. Similar techniques are used in the Oxford movement that appeals to bewildered intellectuals and people of means and in the tent of the occasional revival meeting. By relinquishing the integrity of objective reasoning, the city dweller finds access to emotional appeasement. He finds his way to an attitude of acceptance in an otherwise anchorless existence.

The above mentioned mechanism is instrumental in shaping certain aspects of modern political life. Fascist parties, particularly, have availed themselves of ritualistic elements in their party ceremonies that make affiliation something other than a matter of enlightened political participation.[28] Rational argument about economic and political affairs is brushed aside by emotional claims to divine revelation or to the inspiration of which "genius" alone is capable.

The individual city dweller will never quite be able to cope with the problem of disentangling intellectually the intricate network of economic and social relations that keeps our urban society functioning. In his political orientation, he finds himself bewildered and suffering from the impact of argument and counter-argument the soundness of which he is unable to test. He accepts with relief a process of indoctrination which appeals to his emotions rather than his reasoning power.

---

[27] See Hadley Cantril, *The Psychology of Social Movements.* New York: John Wiley & Sons, Inc., 1941.

[28] "This entirely irraitonal belief (in National Socialism) will arise in social situations that the average man cannot grasp and understand rationally." Franz Neumann, *Behemoth. The Structure and Practice of National Socialism.* New York: Oxford University Press, 1942, p. 96.

Education. Eager attempts are made to overcome the pitfalls of disoriented urban existence. Education steps in to guide the individual city dweller through the puzzle of urbanized social relations.

In this task, education strikes a different note than otherwise heard in our institutions of higher learning. Education, at this point, is not concerned with specialized occupational training. Adult education has found its unique purpose in the integration of scientific information rather than specialization in some particular field. As the scientist despairs at his growing inability to keep up in more than his own narrow field of specialization, education is challenged to divorce the task of research and professional training from the task of providing a well-rounded view of the scientific universe comprehensible to any one single individual.

Such education may concentrate upon the study of major contributions to the growth of Western Civilization (the hundred great books), or it may be related to citizen participation in self-government or social planning.[29]

SELECTED READINGS

1. Thorstein Veblen, *The Theory of the Leisure Class.* New York: The Modern Library, 1934, pp. 1-400.
2. George A. Lundberg, Mirra Komarovsky, and Mary Alice McInerny, *Leisure. A Suburban Study.* New York: Columbia University Press, 1934, pp. 1-378.
3. Helen MacGill Hughes, *News and the Human Interest Story.* Chicago: The University of Chicago Press, 1940, pp. 1-291.
4. G. Legman, *Love & Death.* New York: Breaking Point, 1949, pp. 7-95.
5. "Gambling," *The Annals* of the American Academy of Political and Social Science, Vol. 269 (May, 1950), pp. 1-149.

PROBLEMS

1. *The Tension of Urban Leisure.* Chapters 11 and 12 indicate a twofold orientation of modern urban leisure: duplication as well as escape from urban occupational patterns. In some leisure time activities, both orientations are inherent simultaneously.

   It is your task to demonstrate this tension inherent in urban leisure. To do so, you are asked to do carefully two things: (1) Place in juxtaposition such patterns of urban leisure that are contrasting

---

[29] For the importance of citizen participaton in social planning, see David E. Lilienthal, *TVA. Democracy on the March.* New York: Pocket Books, Inc., Chapters 9 and 12, pp. 84-101 and 130-137.

with each other; extend the list of contrasting patterns beyond the patterns mentioned in the text. (2) Analyze leisure time activities, and indicate for specific leisure time activities the presence of either duplication of or escape from the prevailing pattern of occupational life. This analysis should be documented as far as possible with factual information. Such information will be found in almanacs, encyclopedias, and publications about various sports and their conduct.

Discuss whether modern leisure is adequately characterized in the above-mentioned manner. If both the absence and the presence of the "business pattern" in modern leisure ar used to detrmine its character, everything would fit anyway. Is there some orientation toward the "business pattern" even where the orientation is one of escape?

2. *Trends of Urban Leisure.* Read Jesse F. Steiner, "Recreation and and Leisure Time Activities," in *Recent Social Trends.* New York: McGraw-Hill Book Company, 1933, pp. 912-957, and George A. Lundberg, Mirra Komarovsky, and Mary Alice McInerny, *Leisure. A Suburban Study.* New York: Columbia University Press, 1934.

The first of these publications gives an indication of experienced and expected trends. The latter studies leisure in the environment of the dormitory suburb that has grown since and is apt to extend further in the future.

Gather more up-to-date information about contemporary leisure time activities and write either an affirmative or a critical essay about the two publications. You will have to answer the question of whether trends indicated in the publications are likely to continue, or are being displaced, and if so, by what other developments.

3. *Changes in the Detective Story.* Read A. Conan Doyle, *The Complete Sherlock Holmes.* New York: Garden City Publishing Company, Inc., 1938; and 10 detective stories published in 1945 or later.

It is your task to describe systematically the social role of the detective as envisaged at the turn of the 20th century and at mid-century. The work of Conan Doyle and the more recent detective stories of your own selection are assumed, for purposes of your task, to be representative of the manner in which this type of literature earlier and today fulfills more or less the same needs. The manner is obviously different today from what it was earlier. To work this out in detail, abstract from both sources descriptions of the detective and his behavior. Consider his procedure of crime detection, his attitude toward people in general, his attitude toward his own function, his relations to the opposite sex, his attitude toward crime, his prevailing moods.

With such material in mind, compare the two types of detectives, and check on the plausibility of a change of function in escape literature as explained in the text. Can you explain this change any other way?

PART V

Urban Social Organization

CHAPTER 13

Social Relations in the City

SOCIAL CONTROL

Types of Urban Control. In the absence of tradition, wide ranges of different means of control stand ready to keep the individual city dweller in line.[1] They are different in nature from the means of control applied in the non-urban environment, where folkways and mores guide the individual through a welter of traditionally accepted and traditionally inacceptable behavior.[2]

In the city, social control is accomplished by either economic pressure, legal restrictions, social pressure, or conventionalization.

Economic pressures, of course, exert their influence only upon those who endeavor to be economically successful. To adhere to prevailing business ethics is not a matter of moral decision to the businessman. He has to keep in step with prevailing standards to retain access to commercial negotiations. To adhere to prevailing business ethics is a matter of economic survival to the businessman.

Cut off from trade negotiations with other producers from whom he purchases his raw materials, cut off from channels of distribution for his final products, or spurned by consumers because of doubtful

---

[1] "To counteract irresponsibility and potential disorder, formal controls tend to be resorted to (in the city). Without rigid adherence to predictable routines a large compact society would scarcely be able to maintain itself. The clock and the traffic signal are symbolic of the basis of our social order in the urban world." Louis Wirth, "Urbanism as a Way of Life," *The American Journal of Sociology*, Vol. XLIV, No. 1 (July, 1938), pp. 15-16.

[2] See Granville Hicks, *Small Town*. New York: The Macmillan Company, 1947, Chapters VI-VIII, pp. 100-194.

production methods or business ethics, the individual urban entrepreneur finds it impossible to operate. Better Business Bureaus in most cities attempt to give institutional implementation to pressures otherwise exerted in a more informal manner. In essence, the Better Business Bureau assumes the function of deciding authoritatively whether prevailing business ethics have been adhered to or not.

We seldom realize that the influence of the law upon the behavior of the city dweller is quite limited. It tends to be broadly restrictive rather than specific and demanding. Most statutory law indicates at what extreme limits the behavior of the individual city dweller will be considered so damaging to urban society that he will be prosecuted by the institutions of law enforcement. The law does not tell the city dweller what to do; it tells him what not to do.

Most social pressure derives its force from underlying economic pressure. It differs from economic and legal restrictions as such by the use of more indirect means of enforcement: snobbery rather than boycott, delay of production rather than dismissal. With regard to both economic and social pressure, however, enforcement places the exposed individual in an economically disadvantageous situation.

If the city dweller behaves so badly that he is excluded from association with the "right" people, he will be restricted also in his business negotiations. If socially not accepted, he may not get promoted to executive positions in which his personal way of life will affect the social prestige of his firm.

The rewards of conformity to social pressure are not entirely reducible to economic gain. They may consist of gains in status and prestige alone. In the last analysis, of course, social status in the modern city is dependent upon income. Actual income, however, is not a matter of public information. To enjoy the influence of and to be the object of that deference customarily granted to positions of high income is reward in itself, even when not accompanied by commensurate purchasing power.[3] Therefore, the behavior of individuals with higher income will be imitated to gain the appearance of affluency.[4]

---

[3] Consider the prestige of members of upper class families, not based on income as much as upon lineage. See Allison Davis, Burleigh B. Gardner, and Mary R. Gardner, *Deep South*. Chicago: The University of Chicago Press, 1941, Chapter IV, "The White Upper-Class Family," pp. 84-99.

[4] In Sweden, where individual income tax declarations are published every year for the upper income brackets, over-declaration occurs frequently for purposes of status promotion.

Still, it is the relationship to economic success that makes social pressures so very effective. They stimulate the ambition to appear wealthy and economically successful. The content of these social pressures varies in different urban environments. It may affect the cleanliness of the "lace-curtain" Irish.[5] It may determine the make of the automobile and the social activities of the business executive who strives for greater responsibilities and a higher salary. Different standards of propriety shade into each other along the ladder of social prestige and economic achievement. At all steps of advancement, specific rules of politeness and manners are accepted as symbols of status. As such they tend to be strictly adhered to.[6]

These social pressures control gestures and form of speech. They may make a person raise his little finger while lifting his teacup, or they may make him refrain from doing so. They may make a journalist at the city desk wear his hat, or they may make a professor take it off when entering the halls of learning. In their influence upon manners, these social pressures come closest to replacing the force of tradition in a non-urban environment. Still, in the large city, opportunities to escape into another urban subculture remain always open. The force of compulsion is not as stringent as the force of tradition in the contemporary small town or in the farming environment. These pressures are not inescapable. In yielding to them, the city dweller bids for economic success in a certain environment.

Conventionalization as a means of social control in the city is reserved to relatively trivial routines of urban living. Conventionalization is a means by which the city dweller moves with a minimum of friction through the anonymous environment of the modern city. It saves energy in the numerous superficial social contacts which life in the modern city entails. Such economy is the force by which conventionalization regenerates itself. Deviant behavior would be cumbersome, and to no purpose.[7]

---

[5] "There is considerably more ritual surrounding the behavior of the immediate family in the middle-class household than is found in the lower class." Allison Davis, Burleigh B. Gardner, and Mary R. Gardner, op. cit., p. 108.

[6] "Manners, we are told, are in part an elaboration of gesture, and in part they are symbolical and conventionalized survivals representing former acts of dominance or of personal service or of personal contact. In large part they are an expression of the relation of status, — a symbolic pantomine of mastery on the one hand and of subservience on the other." Thorstein Veblen, The Theory of the Leisure Class. New York: The Modern Library, 1934, p. 47.

[7] "Wherever large numbers of differently constituted individuals congregate, the process of depersonalization also enters. . . . The fullest exploitation of

To walk on either the right or left side of the street (according to prevailing rules) saves time and conflict. To tip your hat and excuse yourself if you bump into somebody is an expedient way of getting out of trouble. The reasons for conformity to this type of conduct are inherent in the situation itself. Convenience makes appropriate behavior advisable. The structuring of such behavior is based upon expediency and tacit agreement. It is rarely sanctioned by tradition. It may, in some instances, be reinforced by statutory law, such as traffic ordinances.

Co-ordination of Urban Controls. Social control impinges upon the individual city dweller in a much less direct and much less forceful manner than social control in the non-urban environment. The law stakes out broad areas of behavior within which the city dweller is left to shift more or less for himself. Within these borderlines, he is secure against the penalties handled by the institutions of law enforcement.

Urban social control, however, is not limited to the operation of law and law enforcement agencies. To the extent that the city dweller seeks economic success and social prestige, he is subject to all those demands upon his conduct which are backed up by threat of economic failure and loss of social prestige. These demands may express themselves overtly in the course of business negotiations (in employer-employee relations or in sales relations), or they may remain covert, hidden in the realm of manners and informal social relations. In addition, many everyday routines of urban living are forced by convention and tacit agreement into a consistent pattern from which the city dweller may deviate only at the cost of personal inconvenience. Social relations in the city are kept functioning with the help of a unique set of social controls adapted to the preservation of our urban way of life.[8]

the possibilities of the division of labor and mass production . . . is possible only with standardization of processes and products." Louis Wirth, *op. cit.*, p. 17.

[8] "This receding of the community from the actual daily life of the (urban) individual means a weakening of the immediate and spontaneous social restraints and a new form of social controls by means of law. . . . A large sphere of behavior is thus freed from immediate restraint, and in this the individual is allowed an opportunity for differentiation and specialization." Nicholas J. Spykman, "A Social Philosophy of the City," in Ernest W. Burgess, editor, *The Urban Community.* Chicago: The University of Chicago Press, 1926, p. 56.

ECONOMIC RELATIONS

Impersonalized Competition. Social relations in the city are closely tied to the basic structures of our economic life. Economic values are placed above all others in the modern urban community. The large populations congregated in our modern cities, as a matter of fact, invite the type of impersonal relationship that has been the general practice in our culture since the beginning of the industrialization process.[9]

Exploitative relationships restricted by rules of fair competition are well fitted to an environment where the sheer number of people living in close contact with each other hinders the formation of bonds of personal loyalty. There is little resistance to impersonal contacts for exploitative purposes. People are treated not as ends in themselves but as means for economic gain. Competitive rules establish some *modus vivendi,* some way of living together without letting chaos prevail in the motley cosmopolitan crowd.

Competition is impersonal. Unlike rivalry, it does not challenge the city dweller to defeat his fellowman; it challenges him to "beat the system." [10] The relationship of the city dweller toward his fellow man is colored by neither friendliness nor hostility. An atmosphere of emotional detachment or indifference prevails. At the same time, the organization of the urban economy demands some "rules of the game" to co-ordinate all productive efforts in the city without the use of brute force. Such rules are provided by the modern market economy, which reduces all personal relationships to the impersonal common denominator of money.

Other urban cultures have solved the problem of co-ordinating large urban populations through a different *modus vivendi.* Divine or royal authority elsewhere imposed bureaucratic structures upon city populations, thus sustaining the urban way of life.[11] In Western civilization, the competitive market economy has provided the social

---

[9] "The close living together and working together of individuals who have no sentimental ties foster a spirit of competition, aggrandizement, and mutual exploitation." Louis Wirth, *op. cit.,* p. 15.

[10] "When there is a shift in interest from the objects of competition to the competitors themselves, rivalry results. Rivalry is personalized competition." William F. Ogburn and Meyer F. Nimkoff, *Sociology.* New York: Houghton Mifflin Company, 1949, p. 346.

[11] See Chapter 1.

framework without which the development of the large modern city could not have happened.

Rationalization. Tied to the competitive market economy is the trend toward continuous rationalization of the productive process in Western civilization. The profit motive keeps alive the search for more and more efficient means to achieve desired ends in the field of material production. By encouraging the free play of the profit motive, the city has remained unhampered by the fetters of stable tradition. The consequence has been the unprecedented "progress" of our urban communities.

Whether social change is to be conceived as "progress" or as "decline" is, of course, open to subjective evaluation. In a free market society, however, the definition of progress is assumed to result within this society itself and to constitute itself automatically through the operation of free consumers' choice. Such progress is limited to objectives that can be achieved by material production.

Dynamics. Modern economic man has been expected to make the best possible adjustment to existing market circumstances ever since the "free market" was elevated to the status of a guiding principle of modern social organization. He has never had a controlling hand in determining the direction in which these market circumstances were to lead him. Economic change, or progress, has been implemented by anonymously diffused consumer demands, which, during rapid industrial expansion, played the part of benign providence.

New markets, new inventions, and new methods of production and salesmanship have decided whether an important industry was to prosper or deteriorate. The profit incentive has been relied upon to steer economic developments and concomitant social changes. Man, in the city, has never yet faced the responsibility of deciding the trend of current investment from some central control position to arrest economic enterprise that does not benefit the community or to encourage other investment deemed urgently desirable.[12] The city dweller has remained inclined to follow the hidden wisdom of market opportunities.

These economic structures color the attitude of the city dweller

---

[12] For the failure of Nazi attempts in this direction, see Franz Neumann, *Behemoth.* New York: Oxford University Press, 1942 "Profits, Investments, and the 'End of Finance Capitalism,'" pp. 316-327.

and place their imprint upon urban social relations. Rationalization, in the city, tends to be limited to partial and specialized spheres of activity. Efficiency is obtained within the framework of immediate objectives. Just as the businessman is supposed to plan expediently for the most efficient operation of his enterprise without considering the possibility of manipulating existing market conditions, so the city dweller arranges with detached objectivity for the most effective satisfaction of his needs for relief, for entertainment, and for security and other partial objectives. On the other hand, inadequate institutional devices only are available to assess the relative merit of these different objectives.[13]

Urban life is well planned in every detail. As a whole, it moves with a minimum of guidance. It moves in an atmosphere of trust that the total outcome of the many partial, and in themselves expedient, activities in the city cannot be improved upon by willful interference on the part of isolated individuals or social institutions available to accept the responsibility for directive social policies.[14]

Business Cycles. The city dweller knows of his dependence upon economic events beyond the reach of control. Throughout the 19th century, the experience either of poverty and starvation or of prosperity remained unrelated to economic efforts. The economic status of the city dweller did not necessarily improve if he worked harder, nor did it necessarily get worse when he relapsed. Market conditions were more important than anything the individual could do to improve his economic standing.

The city dweller found himself at the mercy of economic fluctuations. He shared this position, of course, with all participants in modern Western civilization; still, he was more helplessly tied to the general course of economic events than the non-urbanite. The small town dweller and the farmer had something to fall back upon whenever the industrial cycle of production and consumption was disrupted. They were closer to a relatively self-sufficient way of living, in which they could produce almost everything they needed

---

[13] For difficulties involved in the attainment of objective standards, see Svend Riemer, "Values and Standards in Research," *The American Journal of Sociology*, Vol. LV, No. 2 (September, 1949), pp. 131-136.

[14] For a strong statement against interference with the "natural," or unplanned, course of events, see Friedrich August von Hayek, *The Road to Serfdom*. Chicago: The University of Chicago Press, 1944.

to stay alive with their families. The city dweller, on the other hand, was confronted with an economic void as soon as he lost his job.

In the 19th century, the business cycle came to be looked upon as a "natural" phenomenon. It was considered natural because it seemed beyond the reach of human control. The business cycle indeed was beyond the reach of human control, due to the lack of concerted planning efforts in an era of autonomous industrial production.

Trade Cycles. The fundamental dependency upon uncontrolled economic events is clearly indicated by the course of isolated trade cycles: [15]

1. The Price of Pork. The price of pork, like the prices of other food products is known to fluctuate in fairly regular cycles. Why is this so? At the production end of this phenomenon we have the farmer who continuously has to make decisions about marketing his pigs as a relatively early date, or investing further in the feeding process and selling them later on as hogs. As the price for pork rises, he is induced to keep his pigs on the farm. With a change in relations for both feed and pork, it pays him to bring more hogs to the market. His decision, however, is shared by innumerable other farmers.

When, finally, those hogs which owe their lives to previous price constellations arrive on the consumers' market all over the country, it appears that they cannot all be absorbed by prevailing demands without a severe cut in price. Production has taken time. During that time, the production of pork was further increased. The market is not too readily cleared of the surplus product.

Under the circumstances, the production of pork is severely reduced by marketing the pigs and refraining from investing in the feeding process that would turn them into hogs. The end result is an undersupply on the consumers' market, an increase in the price for pork, which in turn gets the entire cycle going again.

2. Student Enrollments. A similar mechanism endangers the student's opportunity to make a living after finishing his university studies. Vacancies in white collar positions with the prerequisite of academic training cause salary increases. They are talked about by

[15] See Joseph Schumpeter, *Business Cycles*. New York: McGraw-Hill Book Company, Inc., 1939, Vol. II, Chapter X, "Prices and Quantities of Individual Commodities," pp. 520-543.

the students themselves and those who counsel them in the choice of an academic career.

Consequently, whole age groups of high school students and university freshmen and sophomores let themselves be guided in the choice of their studies by opportunities that seem to be beckoning at the end of their academic training. By the time these increased enrollments appear on the labor market, the situation abruptly changes. The flow of job applicants by far exceeds the need expressed by existing vacancies. The market becomes tight. Positions are hard to get. Years of unemployment may become the lot of the trainee, and salaries may start at lower levels than expected.[16]

The natural reaction on the part of the students is to turn to other fields of study. In this manner, an undersupply of job applicants is again established, and the same cycle is underway again.

Many uncertainties like those discussed above impinge upon the life of the city dweller. He has nowhere to turn to assure himself of fixed living conditions for more than a very limited time. Of even greater impact than special trade cycles is the course of the total business cycle with general fluctuations of money value and labor market.[17]

Considering the central position of our economic relations in the life of the modern city dweller, it is little wonder that he develops a somewhat fatalistic attitude toward his own existence. Things will just happen, things that are completely out of control. The effort of the individual is limited to trying to ride the crest of the wave, whatever that "wave" happens to be at any given time.

War, Inventions, and Monopoly. The feeling of being at the mercy of powers greater than man extends, in the city, beyond the sphere of economic activities proper. War and inventions influence the destiny of human beings without giving them a chance to appeal to greater powers or to correct their own misfortune.[18]

An economic empire may crumble at the mercy of new inventions through which older production methods become rapidly out-

---

[16] See Svend Riemer, *Upward Mobility and Social Stratification.* Published by the State Department of Social Welfare and the Department of Social Science, Columbia University, as a report on Project No. 165-97-6999-6027 conducted under the auspices of the Works Progress Administration, 1937, pp. 31-32.

[17] See Joseph Schumpeter, *op. cit.*, Vol. I, pp. 68-71.

[18] *Ibid.*, Chapters VI and VII, "Historical Outlines," pp. 220-448.

dated. Attempts may be made to corner the market or to retard
the commercial exploitation of some new invention. Wars may destroy the cities of our civilization through shelling or through A- and
H-bombs. Half-hearted attempts may be made to stem the tide of
such destruction through international negotiations, reconciliation
procedures, or other social techniques called for by the situation.
Still, the city dweller is defeated in his basic attitude before he has
made serious attempts to "take arms against a sea of troubles." An
offspring of economic conditions of the 19th century, he does not
rely upon his own ability to change the basic course of economic
and political events.

Monopolies represent attempts to manipulate some of the uncertainties of free competition and price fluctuations on the market.
Instead of setting up institutional devices to deal with the control of
the modern monopolistic business enterprise and turning this instrument of power to the good of the entire community, we tend
to destroy the monopoly and to guard against the regeneration of
monopolistic power. Somehow, the city dweller rejects the responsibility of handling the control of an economic instrument as powerful as the modern monopoly.

Changing Economic Structure. Economic structure changes according to laws inherent in our economic institutions. The growth
of monopolies is the outcome not of shrewd and exploitative business
manipulation but of efficiencies associated with large scale business
enterprise. Once an economic enterprise has grown to sizable proportions in the pursuit of profits, the monopolistic exploitation of
prevailing conditions are too tempting to be passed up.[19]

Economic structure has changed, furthermore, through the development of bureaucratic routines required to administer any large
enterprise with plants and purchasing and sales agencies located in
different communities. White collar jobs have thus increased, while
small business enterprise finds itself squeezed out of the picture on
an international scale.[20] Due to economic changes, also, domestic
service in the city has become rare and dear. The supply of female

---

[19] For the relationship of large enterprise to the formation of monopolies,
see Svend Riemer, *Struktur und Grenzen der statischen Wirtschaftstheorie.
Archiv fuer Sozialwissenschaft und Sozialpolitik,* Vol. 69, Nos. 5, 6 (August,
September, 1933).

[20] See Alfred Meusel, "Middle Class," in the *Encyclopedia of the Social
Sciences.* New York: The Macmillan Company, 1933, Vol. X, pp. 407-415.

agricultural surplus labor is shrinking, and other employment opportunities open up in the city to be filled by this same type of labor.[21]

None of these changes is the outcome of deliberate planning. They impinge upon the life of the city dweller who knows better than to try to combat inescapable developments. Dependency upon prevailing economic conditions leaves the city dweller much less free than he might appear to those who envy him the escape from the controlling force of tradition.

SOCIAL STRUCTURE

Derivative Economic Pressures. Nor is the city dweller completely emancipated in his private life. For the sake of economic success, he has to live up to intricate expectations with regard to his private life and public conduct. Failure to conform involves the risk of finding himself excluded from the competition for economic gain.

Only at the top and bottom levels of economic success do we find the city dweller relatively unencumbered by social pressures. Freedom from social pressure is only for those who refrain from participating in urban competition. The city dweller does not have to consider the opinion of others if his own social position is financially secure. Nor is his environment concerned with his behavior, within the limits of the law, if he is not "running" in the competition for economic advancement, and is resigned to the freedom of being permitted to sleep under a bridge.

Middle Class Controls. The control of social conduct in the urban environment is particularly emphasized in the middle classes. This is the social environment in which standards of consumption are carefully watched by neighbors as well as business associates. This is the environment where participation in church activities and voluntary associations has other purposes than those of worship, entertainment, or the discharge of civic responsibilities.[22]

---

[21] For the declining numerical importance of "Domestic and Personal Service" in the gainful employment of women, see S. P. Breckinridge, "The Activities of Women outside the Home," in *Recent Social Trends in the United States.* New York: McGraw-Hill Book Company, Inc., 1933, pp. 709-750. See particularly the graph on p. 717.

[22] "While significant and necessary, the economic factors are not sufficient to predict where a particular family or individual will be or to explain com-

The associational life in this environment obtains secondary function as an indicator of status. The entire ladder of social advancement is here covered with an associational framework fitted to any level of achievement, a framework of clubs and cliques that will lend itself to the promotion of advancement outside the sphere of occupational activities proper.

Pervasive Middle Class Structure. The "middle class" covers a wide range of contemporary urban populations.[23] At the top levels of social stratification we can eliminate from the definition of the middle classes all those individuals and groups who are securely located for generations to come in the upper income strata. General economic insecurity, the increase of absentee ownership, and the growth of managerial influence in business affairs limit secure membership in the upper classes to an infinitesimal section of the population only.[24]

At the base of the social pyramid, on the other hand, we can eliminate from the middle classes those sections of the population entirely without vested interest in property and completely insecure in facing the economic uncertainties of depression and unemployment. With the organization of labor to provide economic security on a collective basis, strictly lower class attributes become extremely rare, even in the lower income groups. They are the exception rather than the rule. Nor is it possible to consider manual industrial labor as outside the economic struggle for status advancement. Home ownership is widespread among industrial laborers, and educational facilities are used to an ever increasing extent, thus promising status advancement at least for later generations of the individual family.

---

pletely the phenomena of social class. Something more than a large income is necessary for high social position. Money must be translated into socially approved behavior and possessions, and they in turn must be translated into intimate participation with, and acceptance by, members of a superior class." W. Lloyd Warner, Marchia Meeker, Kenneth Eells, *Social Class in America.* Chicago: Science Research Associates, Inc., 1949, p. 21.

23 "Zahn, after eliminating all employees of upper rank and all representatives of the industrial and agricultural middle class, estimates that the economic stratum at the top of the hierarchy constitutes about 15 of the total gainfully employed population." Svend Riemer, *op. cit.,* pp. 11-12.

See also Friedrich Zahn, "Wirtschaftsaufbau in Deutschland," in *Handwörterbuch der Staatswissenschaften.* 4th Edition, Supplement. Jena: 1929, p. 986.

24 See James Burnham, *The Managerial Revolution.* New York: The John Day Company, Inc., 1941.

So considered, only a fraction of the entire population remains outside the influence of middle class values. It leaves only those outside the all-pervasive urban status struggle who are sufficiently secure not to have to worry at all for themselves or for their children and their children's children; and those, on the other hand, who find themselves located at the fringe of modern economic society, those who have resigned completely from ever advancing in social status for lack of opportunities for themselves or for their children and their children's children.

Vertical Mobility. As middle class structures spread in the modern city, consciousness of and the desire for vertical social mobility increases.[25] Channels of social advancement in the city are carefully analyzed, discussed, and exploited for either the current breadwinner of the family or his offspring.

The knowledge of the social scientist about opportunities for advancement, as a matter of fact, lags behind the information made available to members of the younger generation on the basis of informal "experience" and knowledge.[26] Information is more or less systematically gained about occupations in which upward social mobility is possible, in which the individual family may move up several notches in the struggle for status advancement. Talent forges ahead in show business through direct audience appeal and with no consideration of social background. The middle class mother has her daughter take dancing lessons to exploit some outstanding talent or personal appeal. Her boy is encouraged to enter the promising field of television.

Those middle class parents are quite realistic who encourage their children to find work in some expanding industry "to get in on the ground level and to grow with the industry." So are those parents

---

[25] "A steady movement of individuals from one social stratum to another is . . . characteristic of only a limited social sphere, namely, that of the middle classes in their broadest sense. It is of paramount significance for the standard of living as well as for the political and ideological attitudes of these strata that the individual has to stand on his own feet in the struggle for the maintenance of his social position. In fact, this position must be conquered anew by every generation." Svend Riemer, *op. cit.*, p. 35.

[26] In the late 1930's and the 1940's, a group of young social scientists in Chicago did research on occupational opportunities and disseminated the information gained to counseling agencies and educational institutions on a commercial basis.

who realize the opportunities inherent in a career that begins with the study of the law and may well end in high political office. High status and ample economic returns are also associated with a medical career, which, however, is not attainable without considerable investment in education.[27]

Individualization Through Status Struggle. The competition for status in the middle class environment has no little influence upon prevailing social attitudes. Such competition is always concerned with the advancement of the individual and possibly his family; never with the advancement of his social group or the improvement of living conditions for the community as a whole. Competition for status breaks down existing group loyalties. It gives such group loyalties little chance to develop.

We have dealt with the anonymity of urban life that develops simply on the basis of numbers.[28] There is no chance for the city dweller to get to know well all those people he comes into contact with in the daily course of his life. The consequent indifference of the city dweller to his fellow men is greatly reinforced by his struggle for status.

About most city dwellers we can say that at no point of their careers do they relax sufficiently in their struggle for status to accept their economic and social position as permanent. At all points of their career beckons the promise of further advancement. While young, such advancement may be sought on the basis of merit, educational achievement, or skillful manipulation of the job situation. When old, they can hope to advance through seniority and the death of staff members in positions of higher prestige and income.

Preoccupation with individual social advancement makes it hard for the city dweller to develop deep group loyalties. At any stage of his career, he looks forward to new group affiliations at higher status levels accessible to him in the near or far future. He eyes his immediate environment with some suspicion. He fears being permanently committed to an inferior status level if he relaxes and establishes strong personal group ties.

This is why neighbors in the anonymous urban residential environ-

---

[27] See Talcott Parsons, *Essays in Sociological Theory Pure and Applied.* Glencoe, Ill.: The Free Press, 1949, VIII, "Professions and Social Structure," pp. 185-199.

[28] See p. 189.

ment tend to be considered as riff-raff.[29] This is the reason why children are restrained from free contacts with the neighborhood kids. The parents pretend to shrink from contacts with status groups lower than their own. In fact, they try to avoid identification even with neighbors of similar status because they anticipate — every one by himself and simultaneously — to move into some higher income bracket where full social acceptance might be handicapped by previous association.

At times of skyrocketing careers in the 19th century, home ownership tended to be established relatively late in life; so were marriages. Both ventures imply commitments to a way of life tied to a certain status level. At times of rapid and often unexpected and ever-beckoning advancements in the life of the city dweller, he wisely waits before he ties himself to a way of life indicative of certain status. He might buy a home and become associated in his private life with a group of people who will later drag down his status appearance. In the same manner, the "social" accomplishments of women met and married in the early stages of an occupational career might place a blemish upon a man's status appearance when — as an executive charged with considerable responsibilities, and highly salaried — he has to entertain in an environment where women are provided with different social graces and are better educated and "culturally" more refined.[30]

The status struggle of the urban middle classes leaves the individual member of the group quite isolated. The individual city dweller is reluctant to sink firm roots into any social environment from which he might escape by further status advancement. Individual mobility prohibits close indentification with any status level. The social struc-

---

[29] "In due course Herbert grew old enough to go to school. Mrs. Sunbury was anxious because she had never let him play with the children in the street.

'Evil communications corrupt good manners,' she said. 'I always keep myself to myself and I always shall keep myself to myself.'

Although they had lived in the same house ever since they were married she had taken care to keep her neighbours at a distance.

'You never know who people are in London,' she said. 'One thing leads to another, and before you know where you are you're mixed up with a lot of riff-raff and you can't get rid of them.'" W. Somerset Maugham, *Quartet*. New York: Avon Publishing Company, 1949, p. 100.

[30] In the 20th century, a trend in the direction of younger marriages has coincided with a trend toward home ownership, both of which are probably indications of early settling-down on definite status lines.

ture as such survives through temporary membership of individuals passing through on their road to ever-greater success.

From Class to Prestige. We have been told that the intermingling of many people in the cosmopolitan crowds of the large modern city tends to democratize social relations and to erase strict distinctions of class.[31] For the modern American city this assertion seems to hold true. Class lines in the modern American city have never been very distinct. It does not follow, however, that American urban structure lacks entirely in relations of social super- and sub-ordination. The individual city dweller is less likely to identify with a specific class position characterized by the role he plays in the process of production as either employer or employee. Still, he is acutely aware of the position he holds within a hierarchy of prestige that runs from the top to the bottom levels of urban society.

Status consciousness, in the city, replaces class consciousness. Symbols of status are strewn far and wide over the city environment. They cover the private as well as the occupational life of the city dweller. If the urban way of life appears, at times, as highly standardized at all status levels with little discrimination between rich and poor, the reason is often the outsider's lack of ability to read symbols of status which reveal themselves only to the initiated.

Status levels are clearly staked out from the second-hand car to the two-car garage. Club affiliations are not on the surface apparent as status symbols, yet for the initiated they are important indications of status. Whether a business executive has a private office at his command, whether he has his office carpeted or not, whether he has one or two secretaries at his command, and whether he has one or several telephone lines at his disposal; all these symbols of status are readily understood by those with whom official relationships are maintained.

Intense vertical mobility in the city has obliterated class distinction, which made a manual labor position, or home ownership or directorship in an economic enterprise, the inescapable social destiny of the offspring. On the other hand, status distinctions are all-pervasive in the modern city. They place the individual temporarily in a distinct position in a self-perpetuating status hierarchy. Relations

---

[31] "The social interaction among such a variety of personality types in the urban milieu tends to break down the rigidity of caste lines and to complicate the class structure, and thus induces a more ramified and differentiated frame work of social stratification than is found in more integrated societies." Louis Wirth, *op. cit.*, p. 16.

of sub- and super-ordination are just as prevalent in the city as they might be elsewhere. They are, however, not permanently attached to the individual in this environment. Status lines are more easily crossed in the succession of generations.

Social Change

Change and Urban Controls. The modern city is the climax area of social change. At a first glance, the prevalence of social change

SOCIAL CHANGE IN DIFFERENT IDEOLOGIES

Problem	Conservatism	Liberalism	Communism	Fascism
Historical Perspective	Emphasis on past, as reflected in present, and resisting change	Emphasis on future, and present means of attaining utopia	Present, and inherent conflict as basis for revolutionary advance	History irrelevant
Structure of thought	Morphological approach. Culture moves in life cycles	Causal explanation	Dialectic, eruptive development. Search for conflict productive of change	Anecdotal approach. Search for propaganda material
Implementation of action	Instinct of ruling class	Education, rationalization of the world	Analysis of conflict from class position	Leadership
Flexibility of change	Complete historical determination	Determination by various causal relationships	Theory integrated with action	Everything is possible
Political orientation	Experience rooted in tradition	Utopian goals and scientific means	Analysis of class struggle	Charisma and 'belief'
Action	Instinctual, freed from false rationalizations	Implementation of means for desirable ends	Revolution at the right moment	Follow the leader

in the city is easily explained through the absence of stable traditions. We want to know more in detail, however, how the agencies of social control in the city are handled in a sufficiently flexible manner not to obstruct, and perhaps even to promote, social change.

Resistance to social change is by no means unknown to the urban environment. There may be no resistance to change in principle; the status quo is not sanctioned as in the non-urban environment. Still, vested interests attached to the status quo put the majority of city dwellers on their guard whenever fundamental changes in their way of life or their economic institutions are considered.

New processes of production are watched with apprehension by all those who stand to lose their investments in earlier procedures. New scientific discoveries are watched with care and with suspicion lest their results might cause more harm than good in the long run. "Cultural" innovations may be sneered at even in the city by those connoisseurs who find themselves outdated in their tastes, in the cultivation of literary, artistic, and musical enjoyment.

The insecurities of urban life have a twofold effect upon the acceptance of change. On the one hand, the city dweller is more tolerant to change because he is not tied to absolute values. Previous experiences of change make him better able to readjust to new situations.

On the other hand, anxieties are produced by change in an environment in which the individual has been forced to readjust repeatedly.

A sound reaction to change is the attempt to assemble as fast as possible a new consistent pattern of routines to meet the new situation created through social change. Without such continuous reintegration of the urban way of life, society could not avoid complete disintegration. Naturally, the surplus energy required in this process of continuous reintegration may reach a point of exhaustion. The initiative may fail through which the city dweller makes himself at home in an environment of continuous social change.

Resistance. Resistance to change in the city may take a variety of forms. It may take the form of apathy, quasi-sanctions of the status quo, incrimination of the promoters of change, or violent resistance.

Apathy. Compared to the non-urban environment, the city appears as a breeding place of social change. Urban means of social control permit more freedom for the initiation of change than those of any other environment. The law consists of a broad framework only, much less specific in the determination of acceptable conduct than the stable tradition of pre-urban society. At that, the law can can be flexibly changed through the legislature if it fails to meet existing social demands. In detail, social conduct is prescribed only through status patterns, the adherence to which is enforced through the threat of economic failure and the loss of social prestige. In the long run, the initiation of innovations promises — if successful and accepted by the community at large — both economic and social rewards.

Still, it is safer even for the city dweller to submit to existing routines than to risk innovations that may either fail or succeed. In our culture, the desire for security has replaced, as a supreme value, the desire for riskful ventures with uncertain outcome.[32] The reason is undoubtedly tied to changes in economic conditions which have limited the chances for startling economic success. The city population follows eagerly in the wake of those economic trends which suggest the search for security as the wiser road for the individual breadwinner.[33]

In doing his own specialized job well, the city dweller makes his contribution to the community at large. The very complexity of urban social organization makes it impossible for him to look far beyond his immediate task. He loses interest in the organization of urban society as a whole. Urban society thus tends to travel like a ship with an efficient crew but without a captain. It is getting ahead fast, but there are no controls to keep its course in a definite direction. Nor is there anybody to decide what the direction should be. Social change in the city is implemented in many ways from day to day. There are no institutional guarantees that the trends of social development will further the welfare of the community.

The requirement for initiative in the urban environment is a requirement for partial initiative related to the specialized job for which the individual is best equipped. Unfortunately, this segmentary initiative is often accompanied by considerable apathy with regard

---

[32] About the shift of current values from "free enterprise" to "full employment," see Henry Pratt Fairchild, "Free Enterprise and Full Employment," *American Sociological Review*, Vol. 11, No. 3 (June, 1946), pp. 271-277.

[33] See also about economic institutions, pp. 342-348.

to the sum total of activities that perpetuate the entire city as a functioning social unit.

From the viewpoint of the individual city dweller, only a small fraction of the social mechanism which keeps the city going is understandable in its rational organization, its purpose and function. The rest is likely to appear as a chaotic blur of activities perceived only in their outside appearance. As an amateur in civics, thus, the city dweller tends to be conservative. Change is undesirable when the purpose of change cannot be comprehended. It calls for new adjustments where comfortable routines had already begun to establish themselves. The outcome of social change is never fully recognized until actual results are visible. Once results are visible, the city dweller may be willing to accept change. Unfortunately for the promoter of social change, however, it is difficult to demonstrate results without having the proposed change approved, accepted, and implemented.

Under the circumstances, urban change has always had to buck the countercurrents of a resistance not born of principle but carried by the fear of the unknown. We need only remind ourselves of the early resistance to vaccination, the present resistance to vivisection, or the forces which opposed the use of railroads, motorcars, sidewalks, and the construction of multistory buildings and of entire residential neighborhoods in uniform architectural styles.[34]

"Provincialism" is not lacking in the large modern city, if by provincialism we mean an attitude that resists change because of ignorance and fear of the unknown. One of the forms this resistance takes is that of apathy, of a lack of interest in the unlimited opportunities for the improvement of the urban environment.

Quasi-Sanctions. Another form of resistance lies in the establishment of sanctions of the status quo. Afraid of the uncertainties of

---

34 Resistance to social change is not just a whim of the urban population:

"A change in one part of the social structure will affect other parts connected with it. But the effects will not always follow immediately — an induced change may lag years behind the original precipitating change. These varying delays among correlated changes often mean maladjustment. They may arise from vested interests resisting change in self-defense, from the difficulty with which men readjust familiar ideas or ideals, or from various obstacles which obstruct the transmission of impulses from man to man." *Recent Social Trends in the United States.* New York: McGraw-Hill Book Company, Inc., 1933, p. 50.

social change, the city dweller gropes his way to something that will serve as a substitute for the stabilizing influence of tradition.[35]

In the modern city true sanctions are hard to establish. Nothing in the city is evaluated as being good or bad in itself. Social change is evaluated in relationship to the consequences it entails. Still, anxieties may cause resistance to change, and where religious sanction fails to operate, quasi-sanctions may take over.

By quasi-sanctions we mean irrational dedications to a way of life that is not questioned with regard to its consequences for the welfare of the community. When religion and tradition combine to enforce such irrational dedications, we are confronted with true sanctions. Substitutes for true sanctions will manifest themselves in a great variety of forms.

Quasi-sanction may be carried by sectarian fervor or political ideologies, by the vaguely consistent world views of the beer parlor politician or the paranoid anxieties of the individual plagued by prejudice turned defensively in all directions from which the established way of life may be challenged to change.[36]

As mass phenomena, such tendencies toward the establishment of quasi-sanctions of the status quo in the urban environment may lead to different types of more or less formal organizations. Under extreme circumstances of political unrest, when anxieties mount through the cumulative effects of poverty, unemployment, and fears for national survival, the entire citizenry combines in the support of stabilizing quasi-sanctions. The different outcome of fascist ventures all over the world can be explained by the extent to which such anxiety producing conditions did or did not prevail[37] We know that fascist tendencies are frequently limited to segments of the urban population. The assumption is justified that they remain limited to those sections of the urban population most exposed to conditions of the above-mentioned nature.

---

[35] "In contrast to the republican forms, the National Socialist Plebiscite Act of July 14th 1933 is a matter of propaganda rather than of constitutional law." Franz Neumann, *op. cit.*, p. 54.

[36] For the extent of intolerance in the United States, see "The Fortune Survey," *Fortune*, Vol. XXXVI, No. 4 (October, 1947), pp. 6-10.

A minority of 28 per cent of the American people is in favor of strong measures against intolerance.

[37] See Erich Fromm, *Escape from Freedom*. New York: Farrar & Rinehart, Inc., 1941, Chapter I, "Freedom — A Psychological Problem?" pp. 3-23.

In less blatant flare-ups of urban anxieties, quasi-sanctions may be carried by the type of social movement that has been known to precede totalitarian fascist upheavals.[38] Centered about a variety of deep emotional experiences, these social movements may emphasize the need for religious, moral, political, or economic security. They all have in common a disregard for the full understanding of the complexity of modern urban social organization. They make possible an escape from the responsibility of considering the detailed and manifold consequences attached to social change in the modern city. Instead of forcing the individual city dweller to accept such responsibility, they furnish him with an easy way out. They furnish him with short-cut interpretations of our highly complex urban social organization. They limit his responsibility for appropriate conduct to "good intentions" rather than full understanding of ensuing consequences.[39] They provide the shelter of a creed not questionable by rational argument.

Incrimination and Violence. The step to incrimination and violence is the natural consequence when fears and anxieties originating through social change rise to heights that call for an outlet in action. From race riots in housing projects to street fighting between opposing political parties, from bomb-throwing to enforce restrictive covenants to incriminating publicity devices, we are constantly surrounded in the modern city by some such release of tension.

This is the price we have to pay for social progress. Only if we fail to realize that the initiation of social change and the adjustment to it requires an unusual degree of initiative and emotional energy, can we hope to improve the urban standard of living without experiencing the counter-currents of anxious resistance.

Challenge to Progress. With further improvements of our material culture at heart, we may avail ourselves of different social techniques. We may attempt to promote social change by fashioning it as a social movement. We can try to move by gaining the support of those very tendencies which herd the city dweller into the confines of some creed, some sect or social movement. We can try to

---

[38] See Hadley Cantril, *The Psychology of Social Movements.* New York: John Wiley & Sons, Inc., 1941, Chapters 8 and 9, "The Nazi Party," pp. 210-270.

[39] For the ethical implications of science, see Max Weber, "Science as a Vocation," in H. H. Gerth and C. Wright Mills, *From Max Weber.* New York: Oxford University Press, 1946, pp. 150-156.

rally to the support of progress the very forces that tend to stem its tide. We can make a "social movement"of progress itself.

The danger of such paradoxical procedure lies in the circumstance that its ultimate purpose might be defeated once the irrational forces that have been gathered for support take over and become ends in themselves. Irrational enthusiasm, escapism, the shrinking from individual responsibility, and the search for refuge in a group attached to irrational loyalties is much more congenial to the resistance to change than to its promotion.

For the promotion of desirable social change, we had better look to the framework of democratic social institutions which are firmly anchored in the environment of the modern city.

SELECTED READINGS

1. Robert E. Park, Ernest W. Burgess, and Roderick D. McKenzie, *The City*. Chicago: The University of Chicago Press, 1925, pp. 1-46, 113-141, 156-160.
   Ernest W. Burgess, editor, *The Urban Community*. Chicago: The University of Chicago Press, 1926, pp. 3-64, 98-112.
2. Granville Hicks, *Small Town*. New York: The Macmillan Company, 1947, pp. 3-276.
3. Allison Davis, Burleigh B. Gardner, and Mary R. Gardner, *Deep South*. Chicago: The University of Chicago Press, 1941, pp. 3-539.
4. William Foote Whyte, *Street Corner Society*. Chicago: The University of Chicago Press, 1943, pp. 3-276.
5. Hadley Cantril, *The Psychology of Social Movements*. New York: John Wiley & Sons, Inc., 1941, pp. 3-270.

PROBLEMS

1. *Rural and Urban Social Control.* Read carefully the preceding chapter, and consult carefully the literature there referred to. Look up, particularly, Joseph S. Roucek and Associates, *Social Control.* New York: D. Van Nostrand Company, Inc., 1947, pp. 68-72.

   With the information gained, it will be your task to write an essay on the manner in which the individual city dweller is kept in line with environmental rules of behavior. This problem is entirely a matter of getting acquainted with all aspects of the problem, with different viewpoints related to it, and the development of well balanced judgment with regard to it.

   Your essay should contain indications of the manner in which urban social controls could be strengthened to avoid an excess of symptoms of social disorganization, and still kept flexible enough not to stand in the way of desirable social change, or progress.

2. *Economic Motivation and Land Values in the City*. Study carefully the main argument in Walter Firey's *Land Use in Central Boston*. Cambridge: Harvard University Press, 1947. In his first chapter, Firey claims that the determination of land values in the modern city cannot be fully understood without contributions on the part of the sociologist. In concrete examples, he demonstrates the impossibility of understanding urban values exclusively in terms of "economic motivation."

Consult, for information on the process of price formation, Joseph Schumpeter's *Business Cycles;* and Arthur M. Weimer and Homer Hoyt, *Principles of Urban Real Estate*. New York: The Ronald Press Company, 1948. Discuss the theoretical problem posed by Walter Firey in the first chapter of his book, and document your argument carefully from the above-mentioned and possibly further sources.

3. *Status Symbols*. Compile a list from 5 families, containing all items of expenditure that serve status functions as well as utilitarian functions. You will probably collect a considerable number of items.

Choose some families to be interviewed from different environments. Attempt a tentative estimate of the concentration of status-directed expenditures in different environments. Where are different social groups most likly to compete for status through their expenditure pattern? What research would be needed to confirm your findings?

CHAPTER 14

Social Institutions in the City

SOCIAL ORGANIZATION

The Secondary Group. Man in the city withdraws by emancipation from a network of social relations fixed by tradition. This does not leave him entirely free to do as he pleases. Various means of social control give direction to the conduct of urban populations. Most of these controls are not legally binding to all city dwellers. Some are not legally binding at all.

Yet, the urban environment is characterized by the great importance of "formal" means of social control. In the last chapter we concerned ourselves with informal means of social control active in the urban environment. The formal, or legally binding, means of social control are of a somewhat different nature. They establish group relations from which the individual can withdraw only at the penalty of legal prosecution or by relinquishing the privileges to which he is entitled as a member of such group structure.

The term "secondary group" is used to designate this type of group relationship.[1] In distinction to the primary group secondary

---

[1] "A distinction of importance is that between primary and secondary groups. In the first the relationship between persons is complete; in the second it is fractional. The result is that we feel we really know a person when we have a primary group relationship with him, but he remains for the most part a stranger to us if our only contact with him is in a group of the formal secondary type." William F. Ogburn and Meyer F. Nimkoff, *Sociology.* New York: Houghton Mifflin Company, 1940, p. 268.

group relationships are dedicated to specific, limited purposes. They consist of associations for some ulterior purpose. They are not entertained for their own sake.

Primary group relations tend to encompass the entire scope of activities in which the individual members of the group might be engaged. The interest of the members of the primary group in each other extends beyond specialized interests. Members of the secondary group, on the other hand, are tied to each other by the common pursuit of some specific purpose only. Beyond the segmental interests which the members of the secondary group share with each other, they stand in the same anonymous relationship to each other as do most city dwellers.

The concept of the secondary group covers a wide variety of social relationships. It covers the organization of government, business, and education. It covers the administration of different means of urban communication, church affiliation, and the network of voluntary associations which spreads over the entire urban area concerned with purposes of recreation and civic self-expression.[2]

A Social Technique. Secondary group formation is the social technique by which the urban community achieves most of its purposes. In contrast to the primary group, the secondary group must be considered a means to definite ends. The primary group — by contrast — is typically sufficient unto itself. It may exist for no other reason than its own self-perpetuation. The secondary group is called into being for the sole purpose of achieving some clearly defined task such as the education of children in our school system, the operation of an industrial plant or a trading center, or the cultivation of a particular religious creed.

Just as the stock company is composed of a membership tied by limited economic responsibilities, so does the secondary group consist of a membership held together for the sake of clearly delimited group activities. In the secondary group, the urban community has developed a form of social organization to be judged only from the viewpoint of whether it serves the purposes to which its membership has committed itself. This form of social organization is not com-

---

2 "There arise numerous associations on the basis of specialized interests differentiated out of the total community life. The city man substitutes a social life in associations for the community life which has lost its social effectiveness." Nicholas J. Spykman, "A Social Philosophy of the City," in Ernest W. Burgess, editor, *The Urban Community.* Chicago: The University of Chicago Press, 1926, pp. 56-57.

mitted to traditionally established routines.[3] The secondary group loses justification for its existence whenever the group loses interest in the purpose for which it has been established.

A ball club will not be continued for the sake of good fellowship, once the opportunity of playing ball has vanished in the city. However much fun the voluntary fire brigade in the small town might have had at fire practice, it will dissolve as soon as fire protection is placed on a professional basis.[4]

As purposes become obsolete and change, and as new purposes challenge the urban community, the organizational network sustained by the urban community in the form of secondary groups has to be changed, extended, and flexibly adjusted to new circumstances. As a "limited purpose organization," the secondary group is amenable to such change. It provides the flexible type of social organization of which our dynamic city culture stands in need.

Contract and Corporate Personality. The secondary group is founded chiefly on contract. Contracts establish legally-binding relationships between different individuals. The theory of contract is one of the major contributions of the city culture of Rome to later urban developments.[5] Contract consists of an exchange of commitments limited to specific content. Contracts are entered on a voluntary basis. Thus, a legal framework for the co-operation between individuals is provided in the city environment, where individuals are not otherwise tied to each other by bonds of loyalty.

In the corporate [6] personality, city dwellers unite for the common pursuit of common interests. This common interest may well be commercial or industrial organizations for the sake of economic profit. In this case, the stock company or the modern corporation — however defined by law — circumscribe the privileges and obligations of those individuals who decide to combine in concerted economic effort.

The corporate personality extends into other than economic activities. In the field of economic activities itself, it is not limited to the joint administration of pooled capital. It may cover with set

---

[3] Using Max Weber's conceptualization, the secondary group is "zweck-rational," not "wertrational."

[4] For the social function of the fire brigade in the small town, see Granville Hicks, *Small Town*. New York: The Macmillan Company, 1947, pp. 177-181.

[5] See pp. 15-16.

[6] "Corporate — formed into a body by legal enactment." *Webster's New Collegiate Dictionary*. Springfield, Mass.: G. & C. Merriam Co., 1949.

rules of conduct, with clear definitions of rights and duties, the relations of business partners toward each other. It may confine competition in a certain field of business according to voluntarily accepted rules; it may combine all participating individuals on either side of the bargaining counter in associations that commit their members to standardized conduct (trade associations).

As we understand the term here, it does not refer to legal incorporation under a charter. Some sort of contract, though, customarily solidifies the relationship between those individuals who join in a corporate personality. Such contract may be very specific, related to some unique effort or to some special situation. On the other hand, it may consist of no more than the payment of membership fees by which the individual becomes entitled to the privileges of some voluntary association.

The country club is a corporate personality in this sense. So is the service club of the Masons, the Lions, the Rotary, and so forth. The stamp collectors may unite in a local hobby club or in nationwide and international associations with clearly defined privileges and obligations to further the interests of a pastime fascinating to its members. Professional and occupational interests pull together in the promotion of internal cohesion, and in order to negotiate with related or conflicting interest groups. Collective bargaining, in our society, is predicated upon the existence of corporate personalities as bargaining partners representing either labor or capital.

Government agencies are corporate personalities in this sense. Negotiations between the government and broad interest groups in the community are thus turned into negotiations between corporate personalities with clearly staked-out rights and obligations. Political pressure is exerted by lobbyists in the service of interest groups organized as corporate personalities. Propaganda appeals to the community also originate in the well organized and adequately financed interest group.[7]

---

[7] "Since individuals have many diverse interests, they join various groups according to the purposes they have in view. Hence, an examination of group organizations shows that they are of many types: employers', workers', and farmers' groups, professional groups, religious and welfare groups, and many others. . . . Many groups of the "pressure type" require dues, build up large treasuries, employ expert lobbyists or political agents, and devote much time and effort to securing appropriate results through various governmental agencies." Joseph S. Roucek and Associates, *Social Control*. New York: D. Van Nostrand Company, Inc., 1947, pp. 94-95.

The corporate personality pervades all urban relations. As individuals, most city dwellers remain anonymous and ineffective in the promotion and guidance of social change. Through the vehicle of the secondary group and as members of several such secondary groups with clearly delimited purposes, the city dwellers join in the conduct of public affairs.

As voters, the city dwellers retain the last vestige of direct individual initiative. Even as such, however, they tend to be committed through secondary group pressures or party membership. Of course, the city dweller may remain entirely inactive through indifference.

Secondary Group and Corporate Personality. The origin of secondary groups is to be sought in the legislation passed by a community that enjoys rights of sovereignty.[8] A law grants the right to form compulsory associations for populations defined by the territory of their residence or other citizen attributes. Such legislation determines specific privileges and obligations. Participation in such secondary groups is not quite a matter of individual choice. Such participation is a necessary condition for making a living (for example, trade union membership and partnership in an economic corporation).

The origin of the secondary group may also be based entirely on voluntary contract. In this case, the secondary group constitutes itself and finds the legal basis best suited to its interests and purposes. This latter type of secondary group is frequently referred to as a "voluntary association," as contrasted with associations based on economic needs and prescribed in detail by commercial law or public statute.

The corporate personality — a fundamental legal concept in the formal organization of the secondary group — is not limited to group formation on the basis of individual choice. The corporate personality extends to comprehensive political organization where an entire citizenry — let us say a municipality — is organized to pursue as broad a task as that of promoting the welfare of the community in all its aspects. It also pertains to administrative bodies such as commissions, departments of city government, and public institutions based on statutory law or administrative action. The cor-

---

8 "Sovereignty — political authority independent of, and unlimited by, any other." *Webster's New Collegiate Dictionary*. Springfield, Mass.: G. & C. Merriam Co., 1949.

porate personality may lack the attribute of "membership by choice" which we consider an important characteristic of the secondary group in general.

Nor need secondary group relations necessarily find formal organization although they tend to do so. Common to all secondary groups is the circumstance that they are formed in relation to some objective, or group of objectives, in the pursuit of which the members of the group join their efforts. It is a purposive group. Formal organization on the basis of contract is the rule. An informally functioning secondary group, as a matter of fact, is hard to imagine, but must be considered as a possible borderline case. Such a secondary group is found when the purpose of the group is not as yet precisely defined, when commitment to membership is not as yet definitive; in short, in the initial stages of secondary group formation. Similarly, secondary groups without formal organization might be found operating in the debris left over after the abandonment of some formal organization. In the long run, the secondary group without formal organization has little chance of survival, due to the lack of cohesion of its membership in the anonymous urban environment.

Social Institutions. The social institutions in the city encompass secondary groups and corporate personalities of all types. We apply the term in a somewhat different manner than customary to many sociologists who talk about a limited number of some five social institutions, such as the institutions of government, the family, production, education, and recreation.[9] Our discussion will indeed be related to these basic functions of all social life. But social institutions will be sought for in all group relations that have found some kind of formal organization.

In summary: social control in the city tends to rise beyond the anonymous forces discussed in the preceding chapter, forces that impinge upon the individual city dweller and from the influence of which he is — as an economically successful city dweller — unable to withdraw. Social control, in the city, is to a large extent self-imposed control by means of purposeful social organization. In "limited purpose" organizations city dwellers unite for the achievement of specific ends that require concerted effort. Participation in this type of activity is largely based on free choice, although forms of possible

---

9 See William F. Ogburn and Meyer F. Nimkoff, *op. cit.*, Part Six, "Social Institutions," pp. 553-772.

organization may be prescribed by law. The city dweller moves in a flexible network of more or less well organized secondary group relations, a set of social institutions that he is able to bend to his needs. These institutions may terminate when their purpose vanishes, or when their work is taken over by some other institution. These urban social institutions are the vehicle for concerted effort, for premeditated social change of which we like to think in terms of "progress."

GOVERNMENT

Self-Government. For centuries, city government has meant self-government. In the city-states of antiquity, there was no higher authority than that of the urban community itself. In the Middle Ages, the chartered cities enjoyed privileges of self-government which gave them a special place in a world dominated by feudal powers.

From time immemorial, city populations have emancipated themselves from the influence of extraneous authority. At the beginning of urbanization in the Near East, the peasant populations that drifted into the rising urban centers had to make a break with the authority of local gods and traditions which they left behind.[10] All through antiquity, these emancipated peasants in the city needed the support of some substitute authority. Such authority was provided in the form of an urban deity assumed to wield supreme powers. At times, divinity was claimed for the house of ruling princes.

Urban self-government, in antiquity, never managed to free itself completely from the influence of caste and class structures. Political power was unevenly distributed. It was distributed according to criteria that had little to do with the urban way of life itself. Political power was based on either agricultural or military status, on land-holdings or military prowess. Under the circumstances, participation in urban self-government was not equally accessible to all city dwellers. It was not democratic in that sense.

During the Middle Ages, democratic urban self-government began to assert itself. At the period of medieval stagnation prior to the year 1000, feudal social organization withdrew from the city environment. When revived commercial activities later started to replenish the urban populations with roving adventurers and run-

[10] See pp. 6-7.

away serfs, individuals who came to the city not as feudal conquerors but after having severed their ties to the feudal system, these people had a chance to organize themselves in a manner congenial to the structure of urban pursuits. The merchants congregating in the suburbs outside the city walls were left to shift for themselves, to build protective stockades with their own means by levying taxes in their midst and by organizing for the pursuit of other common interests, such as fire protection, water supply, and so forth.[11]

Independent self-government of the city has remained an urban privilege since those early days.[12] It has not always remained entirely democratic (based upon equal rights of all individual citizens). Inequalities in property, home ownership, sex, or length of residence furnished criteria of selection for active citizenship. City government is still self-government today. The privilege is bestowed upon the urban community at its incorporation.

In modern times, the privileges of self-government have been extended beyond the urban environment. With the establishment of democratic rule on a nationwide basis in Western civilization, the city has had to relinquish some of its political independence. Rights of self-determination are now exercised on a more encompassing territorial basis. Urban democracy has ventured beyond the city limits. Some of the rights of self-determination are no longer exclusively a city privilege. The modern city in the United States competes with the state and the nation for the privilege of self-government. As participants in the democratic rule of state and nation, our urban populations join in the government of these large territorial units. They are to some extent made dependent upon social structures and interests extraneous to the urban environment.

The modern city charter grants rights of self-determination that do not approximate the complete sovereignty of the medieval city. Conflicts between the rights of self-government on the part of the nation, the state, and the city have led to clear legal definitions with regard to the issues the individual city is permitted to deal with by autonomous legislation.[13]

---

[11] See also p. 23 above.

[12] For the granting of "home rule" in the city charter, see Marguerite J. Fisher and Donald G. Bishop, *Municipal and Other Local Governments*. New York: Prentice-Hall, Inc., 1950, pp. 19-21 .

[13] *Ibid.*, Chapter 2, "The City in relation to other Units of Government," pp. 12-28.

Whatever these infringements upon the freedom of modern municipal government may be, they result from the circumstance that the urban principle of self-government has extended to the nation as a whole. In his triplicate role as a national, state, and urban citizen, the city dweller enjoys the highest degree of political freedom ever granted to man.

Informal Self-Rule. Spontaneous demands for self-rule on the part of select urban populations with special interests are as rampant today as during the early Middle Ages. The demand for self-government has its origin in the urban way of life. The law only crystallizes spontaneous processes of organization for self-government, processes which do not necessarily end where the law has been defined.

The constitutional framework of urban self-government is challenged at times, and circumvented and undermined by various social pressures. Where large and powerful sections of the urban population do not find their needs for political, economic, and social control adequately taken care of through existing political institutions, they are apt to venture into forms of organization suitable to their purposes. Such informal urban self-rule may well conflict with the constitutional municipal government. It develops to serve needs of social control arising on the side of, and sometimes in conflict with, the official democratic self-government of the total urban community. We are familiar with such developments in the form of boss rule, city machines, gang-rule, and organized graft and corruption.[14]

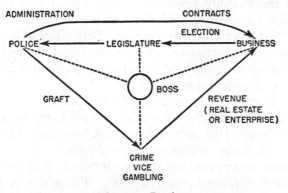

FIGURE 16. Bossism.

[14] See *The Autobiography of Lincoln Steffens.* New York: Harcourt, Brace and Company, 1931, Part III, "Muckraking," pp. 357-627.

"*Bossism.*" Various social needs coincide to promote such cancerous growth within the body politic of the modern city. Ambitious immigrant youngsters are excluded through prejudice from that advance in social and economic status they are taught to expect by our social philosophies. They may look for opportunities to get rich quickly where their ethnic origin presents an asset rather than a liability. Our city rackets are, indeed, staffed to a large extent by frustrated members of the first American-born generation and their associates in the urban slum.[15]

In spite of alleged desires for risk and concomitant opportunities, the business world tries to control as many variables as possible in the equation which spells either profit or economic loss. Thus attempts are made to corner contracts with the city administration for the delivery of goods or the execution of construction. Such guarantees, of course, fall under the heading of "graft and corruption"; they are obtained as payments for services rendered.

Racketeering, graft, and corruption play into the hands of boss-rule. Due to the illegal character of such activities, the placing of powers of supreme command in the hands of a boss is practically unavoidable. No participant in these activities has recourse to the law. If promises are broken, if sales territories are invaded by some aggressive racketeer on the liquor market, if delivery trucks are smashed while distributing goods for which there is no legitimate market, or if houses of prostitution are raided by the local police although the monthly bribe has already passed into the hands of some police representative, the law enforcement agencies cannot be approached for an equitable decision. Both litigants — equally involved in illegal operations — would soon find themselves behind bars without having their problem solved, a problem in which the community at large has no concern.

Illegal operations all stand equally in need of some extra-legal authority. Such authority must offer that minimum of security and control without which nobody would risk his money, his health, and his life in this daring pursuit of financial gain.

The entire underworld needs a boss for final decisions. If nobody assumed such dictatorial powers a boss would have to be forced into a position of control. The tremendous financial gain associated with

---

[15] See William Foote Whyte, *Street Corner Society.* Chicago: The University of Chicago Press, 1943, Part II, "Racketeers and Politicians," pp. 111-252.

the status of the "boss" is too tempting, however, to let the throne stand empty for long. Spontaneous self-government takes over where the official urban self-government is either unapproachable or unconcerned with the area of activities that needs to be regulated.

Control assumed under such circumstances depends for enforcement mainly on physical violence. Fines cannot be collected by legal means. They cannot be collected at all unless the threat of physical violence looms at least in the background. Thus are to be explained the gang wars that shock our urban communities at times of intensified illegal activities. Thus has to be explained the institution of Murder, Incorporated, which shocked the uninitiated, but which presents a recognized means of keeping order in the conflicting desires of underworld groups in competition and combat with each other.[16]

Control of Specialized Competition. Spontaneous self-government to control special interests in the city is not part of prevailing custom. Nor is it exclusively related to illegal activities. It may be related to matters of no concern to the community at large. The self-organization of the Chinese immigrant community in cities with large settlements of this ethnic group furnishes a good example for such a condition. At the height of racketeering and gang formation, the Chinese family tong often served as an extra-legal mediator in conflicts arising from illegal activities. For enforcement of authority some of these tongs, like other racketeering groups, had no recourse to the law and were dependent upon control by means of physical violence. In case of conflict between different racketeering groups or tongs full-fledged tong wars were resorted to for the settlement of the dispute.[17]

Today the function of the tong is by and large limited to that of an immigrant community center. The civic club encompassing the membership of all active tongs, is concerned with the mediation of peculiar problems of competition arising within this ethnic group.

---

[16] Lacking scientifically verified information about syndicated underworld activities and the enforcement of order in this environment through Murder, Incorporated, we have to rely on the plausability and the consensus reached in various popular sources. Among these, we quote two recent publications: Anonymous, *I, Mobster*. New York: Gold Medal Books, 1951; and Robert H. Prall and Norton Mockridge, *This is Costello*. New York: Gold Medal Books, 1951.

[17] See Herbert Asbury, "The War of the Tongs," in *Sins of New York*. New York: Bantam Books, 1950, pp. 147-162.

Outside the Chinese community, nobody is concerned with the manner in which the limited opportunities for business and employment open to this group are taken advantage of. Within the Chinese community itself, it may be considered a matter of unfair competition if a laundry business is established across the street from a similar establishment. Self-government, in the form of the board of the civic club or the civic council of the Chinese community, moves in to decide upon the situation with no other means of control at hand than that of possible expulsion from the ethnic group — a penalty with which the urban community at large has neither reasons nor power to interfere.

Government of Limited Control. Urban government, like most government, is a government of limited control. It protects the freedom of contract and the freedom of the city dweller to unite with others in the formation of corporate personalities that mobilize concerted effort in the pursuit of special interests. Spontaneous self-government is therefore not interfered with as long as it does not infringe upon the rights of other city dwellers.

The regulatory functions of modern municipal government itself, to be sure, surpass in scope and importance those connected with the self-organization of select groups of the citizenry for specific purposes. Municipal government is charged with the task of supporting law and order, of sustaining a smoothly operating system of communications, of caring for city services and public utilities, of sponsoring preventive medicine and preventive crime control, and possibly providing adequate welfare services and housing facilities in the community.

Extension of Government Controls. The borderline of what is considered the legitimate concern of municipal government is continuously being extended. Major political opinions divide on the question of whether urban self-government should, on its own initiative, assume more or less responsibility; whether it should limit itself to the minimum function of policing and protecting the ordinary routines of urban business life, or whether it should take positive action and improve living conditions in the city by contributing to the welfare of indigent citizen groups. It is open to dispute whether city government should assist its citizens with regard to those aspects of urban living — such as delinquency, crime, divorce, and housing — which can be improved only through concerted community effort.

Within the powers of municipal taxation, the city may want to
deal with the local housing situation, to provide for adequate services
by public utilities, to operate an efficient school system that does not
leave any educational needs unsatisfied, and to administer specialized
institutional facilities for the aged, the insane, neglected juveniles,
the diseased, and other needy and individually helpless citizen groups.
On the other hand, city authorities may refrain from taking such
action.

The never-ending controversy boils down to two questions:

1. By what social techniques are the desired objectives to be
achieved? Are they to be achieved by public or by private efforts?
Is it to be left to the free market to provide the desired services, or
are they to be furnished by municipal institutions? [18]

2. How is the financial burden of such institutional services to be
carried? Is it to be carried by fees or taxes, by those making use of
the institutional services (through fees levied by either private or
public institutions) or is the financial burden to be distributed among
all taxpayers of the community? [19]

Taxpayers and businessmen are interested in having these services
provided through private economic enterprise. This does not cost
the taxpayer anything, and private business is thus extended into a
field where it may yield reasonable profits. Both taxpayers and businessmen, on the other hand, are also recipients of public city services.
Particularly in individual emergency situations of illness or insanity,
there is an advantage in having the financial burden of such services
carried by the community as a whole. Moreover, we have learned
to recognize that not all city dwellers are able to afford the institutional services they need. To improve the general standard of urban
living, some institutional services — such as the care of tubercular
patients, the combat of venereal and other diseases, childcare activi-

---

[18] About the expanding field of community services, see Louis Wirth, Ernest
R. Hilgard, and I. James Quillan, editors, *Community Planning for Peacetime
Living.* Stanford: Stanford University Press, 1946, pp. 3-89.

[19] "We need to determine whether a certain facility is a private or public
responsibility. If it is regarded by a community or nation as so essential that
everyone should have it, irrespective of the individual's ability to pay for it,
the community maintains it."

"When the service can be measured, can be metered, it is likely that it will
be private, because then each individual can be charged for the amount he
uses. When it can't be metered, then generally it is made a public utility or a
public function." *Ibid.*, pp. 16-17.

ties, and, to a certain extent, even the provision of housing facilities [20] — are provided on a non-profit or even on a subsidy basis by municipal agencies financed by all the taxpayers of the city. The trend represents in many instances the only road to improvement. Those most in need of such services are the least able to pay for them individually.

The political struggle on these issues weaves eternally back and forth. Long term trends point toward an increase of publicly assumed responsibility. However reluctantly, the field for responsible urban self-government is being enlarged. Within the much maligned "welfare state," the citizenry takes over and provides through its governmental institutions those minimum facilities which otherwise remain outside the reach of substantial sections of the urban population.

Big Business in Municipal Government. In this process, the urban community has gone into big business. This development has not remained without influence upon the form of municipal government. The modern city operates vast enterprises. It has to buy supplies on a tremendous scale; it has become a large scale employer of all kinds of labor.[21] In the internal organization of its administration it is challenged to apply the same standards of efficiency practiced by the modern businessman.

That public administration can do the job as effectively as private industry and commerce has been denied often and by many. There

---

[20] "Housing is not merely a problem for the individual family; it is of vital concern to the community. . . . In the absence of a modern housing industry we face the problem of either subsidizing good housing or subsidizing slums (as we are now doing). Obvously it is in the public interest to aid the lowest income group to attain minimum standards of decent housing and to aid the next higher income groups up to a point where private industry can begin to serve them." *Ibid.*, pp. 45-46.

[21] "The urban governments of the United States perform those essential public services without which the inhabitants of the urban areas, containing the majority of our people and the bulk of the country's enterprise, could not continue to exist. Urban governments have been invested with the responsibility of providing for a range of services which affect virtually every aspect of the citizen's life. They provide water, dispose of sewage, prevent epidemics, guard the public health, protect life and property, control traffic, regulate and facilitate trade and industry, and furnish educational, recreational, and a host of cultural services. As urban centers have grown and civilization has become more complex, the services rendered by Government has expanded enormously." *Our Cities. Their Role in the National Economy.* National Resources Committee. Washington, D.C.: U.S. Government Printing Office, 1937, p. 48.

TABLE XIV

GROWTH OF GOVERNMENTAL FUNCTION

MUNICIPAL ACTIVITIES IN DETROIT

Year	Number of Activities
1824	23
1910	170
1920	251
1930	306

From: Lent D. Upson: The Growth of City Government. Detroit. Detroit Bureau of Governmental Research, 1931.

are those who feel that the sphere of private business activities has been dangerously limited in this manner. The lack of the profit incentive in public administration has been mentioned as a source of waste and inefficiency.

The proponents of public administration, on the other hand, proclaim that wasteful bureaucratic controls are by no means limited to public agencies. Bureaucratic waste is said to be part and parcel of large-scale modern enterprise, whether private or public. The costs to provide economic security for civil servants are matched today by similar expenses for employees of private enterprise. Public administration has possibly advanced further in granting tenure, seniority rights, sick leaves, paid vacations, old age pensions, and so forth. The difference, however, is only one of degree. Only a relatively small group of executives, at the bonus level, can be at all considered as operating under the profit incentive. Security, for better or worse, has come to be considered a more desirable goal than the profit incentive. While the profit incentive operates only at the top levels of industrial and commercial management, the desire for security pervades the rest of our economic life.

The City Manager System. The city-manager form of municipal government is presently spreading over this country.[22] Its purpose

22 "More than 900 cities have adopted the manager plan, and the current rate of adoptions is about 75 municipalities per year." Marguerite J. Fisher and Donald G. Bishop, *op. cit.*, p. 62.

is the concentration of administrative powers in the hands of an official well trained in methods of efficient public administration. The city manager is employed on the basis of merit and previous experience by an elected city council. He is subject to dismissal if his duties are not well performed. He is responsible to the council for all the work carried on in the different departments of the city government. He hires and fires department heads and controls their employment policies.[23]

At present, the city-manager system of municipal government prevails in about 20 per cent of all urban communities of 5,000 population or more in the United States. Although the trend of development is in the direction of the city-manager system, about 80 per cent of our urban communities with a population of 5,000 or more are governed by variations of the mayor plan.

The Mayor-Councilmen System. Individual cities differ in the powers granted the mayor. The so-called weak- and strong-mayor plans of municipal government differ primarily in the extent to which city officials, heads of commissions, and so forth are elected directly to their offices, or appointed by the mayor, who of course, is, himself directly elected to office as a political candidate.

In the mayor-councilmen system, the councilmen are (unless appointed by the mayor) individually responsible to the general electorate for the administration of the various city departments. These councilmen do the hiring and firing in their respective departments. Their personnel policies are checked only at election time by the general public. No wonder this system has often lent itself to appointments on the basis of faithful service in one of the political parties rather than on the basis of merit and experience.

In the mayor-councilmen system, control of the councilmen is indirect in nature. It is not based upon information about actual performance on the job. The same is true with regard to the councilmen in the city-manager system, but here the councilmen are not administrators; they appoint the city-manager and the city-manager appoints professional administrators. Nor does the mayor wield any great influence with the heads of the various parts of the city administration. Holding an elected office himself, he calls meetings of the city council, conducts these meetings, and has, therefore,

---

[23] For a full discussion of the city manager plan, see *Ibid.*, pp. 58-74.

some advisory influence on general administrative policies in addition
to his vote and veto powers.

Advantages and Disadvantages. Advantages and disadvantages of
either system are closely tied to advantages and disadvantages associated with centralized or decentralized control, to advantages of
either political office or professional competency. The present trend
of change toward the city-manager system is probably due to the
extension of the business end of municipal activities. As long as
the regulative functions of municipal government predominate, the
supervision of well-established restrictive routines can be handled by
a trustworthy non-specialist, elected to office. There is little need
for the co-ordination of different city offices concerned with bureaucratic routines rather than the promotion of community welfare.

Municipal government in the modern city is not so limited in its
tasks. It faces the challenge of social planning,[24] of proposing new
policies when old policies fail to meet the needs of the citizenry. It
faces the challenge of extending municipal services at the expense
of the tax-payer when benefits for the community as a whole justify such action. Such work demands the constant assessment of
available financial means to serve the various possible objectives.
Demands for administrative efficiency increase when municipal
government can extend its useful activities through wise husbandry,
when such efficiency can save the individual tax-payer a great deal
of money.

In addition, the complex operations of modern city government
increase the opportunities for the expert to do a better job than the
layman elected to office for his general intelligence, his political outlook, and his trustworthiness.[25]

The other advantage of the city-manager system is continuity in
the conduct of public affairs. Such continuity is best achieved with
a city manager at the head of the city administration. The city
manager is retained in his position as long as his services meet the
needs of the situation. He is retained or dismissed on the basis of
merit displayed on the job. He is less subject to uncertainties arising

---

24 See Chapter 15.
25 "The pure type of bureaucratic official is appointed by a superior authority. An official elected by the governed is not a purely bureaucratic figure."
H. H. Gerth and C. Wright Mills, *From Max Weber.* New York: Oxford
University Press, 1946, p. 200.

at election time inasmuch as he is hired and fired on a nonpartisan basis for his administrative abilities.

Objections have been raised against the unusual powers concentrated in the hands of the city manager, once appointed to his position.[26] These powers have sometimes been called "dictatorial," although they do not exceed the powers of the president of a large commercial or industrial corporation, powers which are controlled by the board of directors just as the city manager is controlled by the city council. Doubts about the efficiency of democratic controls in city-manager system are based upon the understanding that the expert knowledge vested in the good city manager can be exploited as a source of power in itself. As an expert in his field, the city manager may outmaneuver the members of the city council and the legislature.[27] This problem the modern city government shares with the large business enterprise of our days. Due to first-hand knowledge, management may control the directorate when conflicts of interest arise. Still, the advantages of the city-manager system lie in the facts that responsibility is clearly allocated and that the city manager is continuously subject to evaluation of his efficiency on the job.

Municipal Finances. Municipal finances provide the means with which to attain the objectives desired by the community.[28] In recent decades, urban communities have been concerned with the problem of tax avoidance. It takes the form of residential flight from the incorporated residential area. The resources of municipal taxation being largely limited to the taxation of real estate property, the

---

[26] For more specific disadvantages of the city-manager plan, see Marguerite J. Fisher and Donald G. Bishop, *op. cit.*, pp. 68-71.

[27] "Within the extension of administrative action . . . in the fields of welfare and rehabilitation, of city-planning and rural conservation, etc., the function of the 'expert' is by no means exhausted in the execution of routine jobs. He is charged to assume initiative. It is his task to propose new measures to the local or federal legislatures." Svend Riemer, "Social Planning and Social Organization," *The American Journal of Sociology*, Vol. LII, No. 6 (May, 1947), p. 514.

[28] "The sources of local revenue are five in number: (1) The general property tax, which provides around 90 per cent of the tax revenues of local governments; (2) miscellaneous taxes which vary from one local government to another, and include occupational taxes, business taxes, sales taxes, and so forth; (3) miscellaneous non-tax revenues . . . ; (4) the local share of state collected taxes; and (5) subsidies and grants from the federal and state governments." Marguerite J. Fisher and Donald G. Bishop, *op. cit.*, p. 215.

builders of expensive private homes are induced to withdraw from the city proper and to settle in some adjacent community that does not have the burden of expensive metropolitan services to carry, and, therefore, can keep the tax rate on residential properties low.[29]

The problem is particularly acute due to the present tendency toward decentralization. This trend leaves central areas sparsely populated, thus diminishing the tax basis of municipal government without leading to a proportionate reduction in the expense for city services.

To make matters worse, the indigent populations, the renters of run-down homes and apartments and others less well-to-do, stay in the city because they cannot afford to move. They lack private transportation or are unable to achieve home ownership in the urban periphery. These populations yield less in municipal tax returns, being at the same time most in need of institutional city services.[30]

Urban self-government has retained some of the challenge it presented to the city dweller in the early Middle Ages, although it operates today in a different institutional setting. It feeds upon the inclination of city dwellers to do things for themselves by way of concerted efforts; but it is hampered by the reluctance of the wealthier members of the community to rally to such concerted efforts. They are reluctant to co-operate because they are most likely to bear the costs and least likely to avail themselves of the public institutional services provided. Self-government is obstructed, furthermore, by the fact that the urban tendency toward spontaneous self-government makes many of our less privileged city dwellers rally to the support of city machines, gang-rule, and boss-rule. Defending themselves against the wealthy as well as the poor,

---

[29] "During the last 20 years numerous industries have moved from central to outlying urban areas and the employees of these industries are gradually moving out in order to live near the factories where they work. Moreover, it is well known that local business tends to follow population movements. As these movements take place, what is happening to the tax structure of the central city? The obvious answer is that sources of municipal revenue are drying up and disappearing." S. E. Sanders and A. J. Rabuck, *New City Patterns*. New York: Reinhold Publishing Corporation, 1946, p. 15.

[30] "Manifestly, this great deficit (in municipal finances) cannot be counterbalanced by extra taxes to be collected from those of the upper economic levels who have fled from the central city. It is also clear that a declining central business and industrial structure cannot continue to carry even the present tax burdens." *Ibid.*, p. 18.

only small, impartial citizen groups speak for the interests of the community as a whole, supported possibly by the professional enthusiasm of various experts.

BUSINESS

Economic Enterprise. Production in our urban society rests upon the foundation of modern economic enterprise. The economic enterprise, as we know it, is not a "natural" form into which economic endeavor must mold itself in the pursuit of ever-greater efficiencies. Modern economic enterprise is the outcome of unique historical conditions. These conditions have their root in the European cities of the Middle Ages.[31] Without the city of Western Civilization, modern economic enterprise would never have seen the light of day.

Modern economic enterprise is predicated upon the following institutional conditions: [32]

1. The existence of a *calculable law.* Law eliminates the possibility of arbitrary decisions in case of conflict arising in market negotiations. With the commitment of jurisdiction to either common or codified law, an element of insecurity is removed from the world of business. Thus business transactions are encouraged.

2. A *free labor market.* It must be possible for the entrepreneur to draw without restrictions upon readily available manpower for purposes of production. Serfdom had to be abandoned to allow the flow of labor in the direction where it would produce the greatest profit for the entrepreneur and the greatest productive benefit for the community.

3. The technique of *double-entry bookkeeping.* It permits the conduct of business to be constantly checked for profit. This technique places economic enterprise upon a strictly rational basis. It serves as a guide in the conduct of business, measuring its chances for economic survival, growth, or self-annihilation.

4. The *reduceability of all goods and services employed to their money value.* Landed property as well as raw materials, machines,

---

[31] See Henri Pirenne, *Economic and Social History of Medieval Europe.* London: Kegan Paul, Trench, Trubner & Co., Ltd., 1936, Chapters IV-VII, pp. 87-223.

[32] See Max Weber, *General Economic History.* London: George Allen & Unwin, Ltd., undated, Parts II-IV, pp. 115-369.

and manpower must submit to financial evaluation and must be made available on the market by way of commercial contract. Immovable property must be made available in the form of negotiable papers the transfer of which is regulated by law.

5. Peaceful market *competition*. The law and the machinery of law enforcement must appease the territory in which economic enterprise is to prevail as a form of production. It must impede the transfer of property by conquest or other forms of physical violence. Such law must be tacitly or explicitly approved by the general population.

Thus, the roots of modern economic enterprise are anchored in the folkways and mores of urban populations. All these institutional prerequisites of modern economic enterprise are inherent in any explicit definition of the "free market system" of production. We have only broken up this definition into its component parts to show in greater detail what this comprehensive term involves. Some have tried to explain the free market system through the psychology of the "economic man."[33] This approach fails to do justice to the capacity of modern economic enterprise to perpetuate itself regardless of individual attitudes toward the profit incentive. The market system prevails, even when individuals give their property away or squander it in inefficient business procedures. The background of modern economic enterprise is social rather than psychological in nature. It is fashioned as a social institution rather than a psychological attitude.

The urban origin of modern economic enterprise need not surprise us. The institutional setting in which it flourishes is congenial to our democratic way of life in the city. Within a framework of legal and institutional commitments to impersonal routines of business procedure, the individual city dweller is free to participate in a complex system of production directed toward the needs of the consuming populace. Our economic institutions are equally open to participation by all members of the heterogeneous urban community. Money is the impersonal measuring rod through which all city dwellers place themselves on a comparable basis. This abstract

---

[33] For a critical analysis of this approach, see Adolf Loewe, *Economics and Sociology*. London: George Allen & Unwin, Ltd., 1935, Chapter III, "Significance and Limits of Pure Economics," pp. 41-57.

measuring rod neglects qualitative differences such as ethnic backgrounds and individual attitudes. Without some such impartial coordination of the heterogeneous populations in the process of production, our democratic urban civilization would not have been able to survive economically.[34]

Monopoly. Still, some aspects of modern economic enterprise confront our urban civilization with a seemingly inescapable dilemma. Although fashioned for free competition, modern economic enterprise carries in itself the incentive to supercede free competition and to establish monopolistic or quasi-monopolistic market positions. Economic advantages, as a matter of fact, are enjoyed by large enterprise as such. Large enterprise has a tendency of increasing to the point of monopolistic market exploitation.

It takes a certain size of undertaking to carry the overhead of paying one man just for the task of cleaning up the plant and the office. It takes a certain size of undertaking to carry the overhead entailed in different types of capital investment, such as machines, office buildings, and plant construction. The conveyor belt offers its efficiencies only to those entrepreneurs concerned with mass fabrication. As the output shrinks in size, more and more efficiency devices, ranging from the employment of specialized labor to the installment of the conveyor belts, lose applicability: the overhead becomes too large to be economically distributed upon the individual unit of output. Economic efficiency increases continuously with the size of the enterprise.

Thus, modern economic enterprise is persistently challenged to enlarge its scope. The ideal of free market competition, on the other hand, requires an infinite number of relatively small-sized units of business enterprise. In this manner, modern economic institutions carry in themselves the seeds that tend to destroy their own foundation, the free market.

Attempts are made to arrest the growth of economic enterprise somewhere short of a full-fledged monopoly. Large combines are

---

[34] "Although the city, through the recruitment of variant types to perform its diverse tasks and the accentuation of their uniqueness through competition and the premium upon eccentricity, novelty, efficient performance, and inventiveness, produces a highly differentiated population, it also exercises a leveling influence. . . . A money economy goes hand in hand with such a (urban) system of production." Louis Wirth, *op. cit.,* p. 17.

assumed to compete with each other for available purchasing power by increasing their efficiencies and lowering their prices. Cancelled, however, is the opportunity for new enterprises to enter the field of competition. The capital investment required to enter the competition of large scale economic enterprise is enormous. Well established large scale enterprises today hold positions of relative security against new intruders on the market.

Bureaucracy. The economic endeavor of the individual city dweller, for these reasons, takes increasingly the form of a struggle for advancement not through independent enterprise but through promotion within existing economic institutions to positions of responsibility and high income. In large scale economic enterprise, the permissible overhead makes possible the employment of a sizable office staff exclusively devoted to the direction and the control of productive operations. The large enterprise furnishes the institu-

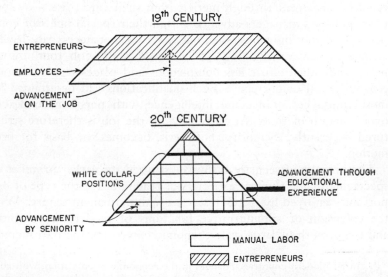

FIGURE 17. Structure of Economic Life. 19th and 20th Century. Schematic Presentation. White collar positions, in the bureacratic structure of modern economic enterprise, are both vertically and horizontally clearly set off against each other. Transition from one category to another tends not to be accessible on the job. Within each category, advancement occurs according to seniority. Transition into a higher category (status), or into a different occupational category (situs) is available only via educational experience.

tional background for the development of a business bureaucracy and a large population of white collar employees in the city.[35]

Such bureaucracy is relatively secure against dangers that threaten its survival. It may shrink or extend. A core of its staff will remain employed even in times of depression. It will be carried as a cost item to be written off against future profits. It will be retained to initiate extended operations once the tide of economic misfortune has passed. The more secure the market position of large scale enterprise, the larger the office staff that may feel relatively secure against temporary lay-offs.

Under the circumstances, new individual attitudes toward participation in the economic life of the city have developed in the last half-century. Hope for the amassing of spectacular fortunes has subsided and has been replaced by hope for relative economic security within the shelter of well established enterprise.

Specialization, moreover, has diminished the opportunities for rapid advancement through merit within such enterprise. Accountants and sales managers advance within their special fields of competency to top flight positions; but they will not necessarily have a chance to achieve eligibility for a directorship. Job routinization makes individual effort less conspicuous and places emphasis upon reliability and competency. Such qualifications can be attained by most employees of average intelligence with persistent endeavor over a length of time. Advancement on the job is therefore structured differently. Seniority, not merit, becomes the basis for promotion.

The promise of security is thus substituted for earlier promises of spectacular gain. Current expectations reach out for the type of opportunity enjoyed by the civil servant with permanent tenure. With the extension of administrative functions of modern government and the growth of large scale economic enterprise, the bureaucratic

---

[35] "In all modern countries, changes in the economic organization, with consequent alteration in social relations, have been accompanied by a movement of working population from agriculture to manufacture and from manufacture to commerce and services. This has been the mechanism of the increasing productivity of the European system throughout the whole modern period, and was the basic instrument of social transformation over the continental United States in relatively recent times." Eshref Shevsky and Marilyn Williams, *The Social Areas of Los Angeles*. Berkeley and Los Angeles: University of California Press, 1949, p. 3.

structure of job opportunities open to the modern city dweller displaces the flexible but less secure structures of economic success which dominated the occupational life of the city throughout the 19th century.

These fundamental changes in our economic institutions are not fully recognized by all city dwellers. Cultural lag and ideological resistances to change must account for the circumstance that the modern business executive and members of his clerical staff still think of themselves as participating in a world of flexible and independent economic enterprise, with spectacular opportunities for profit hovering over them.

Interest Associations. A systematic description of economic institutions in the modern city would remain incomplete without reference to that network of economic interest associations that is spread over our entire economic structure. The basic instrument of contract is used not only to protect the bargaining process on the market. It is used also for associational agreements by which various trades, types of participants in the productive process join their efforts to promote their respective interest positions.

Trade union membership provides a type of collective shelter against economic misfortune that would leave the individual laborer more vulnerable. It provides the means for collective bargaining through representatives elected by the group. Professional associations and business representations make it their task to further the interests shared by the affiliated membership. Politically, such interest groups function as pressure groups pleading with the community as a whole and its representatives in government for protection and privileges which — as the skillful lobbyist or the publicity agent tries to show — are in the best interests not only of those immediately involved, but of all citizens.[36]

In his occupational career, the individual city dweller does not move alone. Through his specialized occupational interests he enters into collaboration with others in a similar position. With these interest associations, he makes a stake for himself in the rationally organized group life of the urban community. As an individual, he can

---

[36] "Every ideology pretends that its primary loyalty is to universal value, thus sanctifying its partial and particular interests." Joseph S. Roucek and Associates, *Social Control.* New York: D. Van Nostrand Company, Inc., 1947, p. 193.

withdraw from such associations at any time — albeit at the cost of his occupational opportunities. These institutional devices, however, have a life of their own. Firmly rooted in the economic structure of our urban civilization, they pursue their course while an ever-changing individual membership jumps on or off the bandwagon.

WORSHIP

Religious Organization. In the modern city religious worship is also molded into the framework of social institutions. Innumerable denominations establish themselves through the right to contract and through the formation of associations. The membership combines to provide for the needs held in common. The means to accomodate these needs for worship and related social functions are furnished in the form of money levied through voluntary or assessed contributions.

Denominational differences in the modern city are closely related to ethnic background and social status.[37] This differentiation of membership occurs without compulsion. Yet prevailing ingroup ties are strong enough to guarantee a fairly consistent pattern of segregation. Differences of doctrine do not explain the manner in which the individual city dweller makes his choice between this denomination or that. Apart from convenience in close residential location to one church or another, the choice of affiliation is by and large a matter of family tradition that can be traced back through generations to some pre-urban residential location where denominational affiliation was not a matter of choice.

The institutional form which religious worship assumes in the city is therefore somewhat alien to its original intents and purposes. These purposes have become assimilated into the urban way of life.

Membership. The status of any given church membership is derived from that of the prevailing ethnic group.[38] Early immigrant arrivals, a majority of whom have acquired wealth and status in this country, crowd into one denomination; late arrivals with still

---

[37] See Liston Pope, "Religion and the Class Structure," in "Organized Religion in the United States," *The Annals* of the American Academy of Political and Social Science, Vol. 256 (March, 1948), pp. 84-91.

[38] For the relationship between class, status, ethnic origin, and religious denomination, see the source quoted in the preceding reference.

preponderantly low income and status will be found in another. With different degrees of wealth represented in their congregations, different denominations vie for the additional membership of individual city dwellers within the range of more or less delimited status groups.

Extent of church affiliation and the number of churches in relation to population are not lower in the city than in the country. The opposite is the case.[39] The reason may be found in the high degree of denominational specialization in this country, which calls for large population concentrations to provide sufficient membership for the different creeds. In the rural setting, distance may well be prohibitive for the building of churches and the holding of services to rouse all denominational preferences to active participation.

In the large modern city, there is room for the purposeful organization of even minor sects and creeds, but sectarian developments in the country are predicated upon the full participation of entire villages, towns, or farming neighborhoods. In the urban environment, membership can be drawn, on the basis of individual interest, from all over the city. Thus the urban environment provides more abundant facilities for worship; and they are made use of by a larger percentage of the urban than of the rural population — despite a more pronounced cultural secularization of the city population.

Urban Church Functions. With its congregation of either immigrant or in-migrant new arrivals to the city, the individual church finds its place first in the central residential districts of the city. In this environment, it serves more comprehensive functions than that of worship alone. It serves as a community center of the immigrant group. Its importance derives from the fact that it is the only pre-urban (non-specialized) institution carried from the village environment to the city.

The life of entire ethnic group, of recent arrivals to the city is centered upon the church. The attainment of adult status, weddings, and births are here consecrated. Death in the folds of the church is the desire of all members of the group. Associational and recreational activities are tied to the church organizationally. The clergy

---

[39] "Religion, it has been generally assumed, does not thrive in cities, which have been described by their critics as hotbeds of materialism, rationalism, and scepticism. But insofar as the facts about churches give us a clue to religious life, this view must be modified. *Our Cities, op. cit.*, p. 23.

stands by to assist and console the members of its congregation in times of social or personal crises.

Sooner or later, increasing numbers of the congregation begin to leave the central residential districts and move to better quarters more peripherally located. Temporarily, the individual church suffers from an awkward distribution of its membership. Due to difficulties of communication, the construction of a new church building in closer proximity to the bulk of the congregation comes up for consideration. The decision to build will come easier if the congregation has moved more or less in a group, establishing a secondary neighborhood of the ethnic group rather than scattering far and wide over the city territory. Early plans for a new church building, as a matter of fact, may have the effect of keeping the group together and retaining a consolidated community life within the ethnic group.[40]

After a further lapse of time, of course, the membership of the congregation will move again in a peripheral direction; sooner or later it will also spread thin. At this point, the church ceases to function as a general community center for the ethnic group. It specializes upon the more partial function of worship itself, and now stands more ready to accept into its folds other worshippers that share the creed, if not the ethnic background, of the majority of the congregation. In different residential neighborhoods of the city, a plurality of churches competes for membership from the more or less anonymous crowd of renters and home owners found in its vicinity.

In this manner, churches pursue their congregations into the urban periphery. In this process, they lose out in their community functions and start building their congregations through individual rather than group membership. The congregation of the peripheral church is selected more on the basis of residential location than social criteria.

In the meantime, the church structures left behind begin to be used for somewhat different purposes. They are retained to serve missionary purposes — particularly those left behind in the environment of urban slum and blight. Some of these churches may cater

---

[40] For a thorough discussion of the function of the Protestant Church, see H. Paul Douglass and Edmund S. deBrunner, *The Protestant Church as a Social Institution.* New York: Harper & Brothers, 1935.

to the recreational and associational needs of a population not held together through ethnic ties and unable to contribute to the organization of wholesome entertainment and adult educational activities. Missionary function is often combined with such community services provided within church buildings left behind by their congregations.

In the urban periphery, community facilities — for church suppers, adolescent sports, lectures, and so forth — are also increasingly provided for in the church although here for somewhat different reasons. Church facilities are used to proselyte among nearby urban residents, and to hold members of the congregation who are losing contact with the church to which they and their families were originally affiliated.[41]

In this manner, church functions undergo a complete cycle on the city gradient. From all-around community function they come to a point where they specialize in denominational worship. In the sparsely settled and undeveloped periphery of the city, they again devote themselves more to community functions. The similarity of beginning and end, however, is more apparent than real. A fundamental change takes place from the comprehensive functions of the ethnic church to the highly urbanized suburban church which provides a number of specialized community services for the convenience of its membership.

EDUCATION AND ASSOCIATIONS

Guidance For Conduct. In the city, education replaces the church to a certain extent in providing guidance for conduct. True, our educational institutions are committed to the unbiased communication of facts. They are not to teach what should be, but only what is. The very selection of factual material, the clarification of some techniques to achieve certain objectives and the omission of others, however, does influence the behavior of the city dwellers. They are, after all, particularly susceptible to educational influences because they feel the need for guidance in a complex environment after having emancipated themselves from tradition.

Government and private associations compete for the privilege

---

[41] See Paul Hanley Furfey, "The Churches and Social Problems," in "Organized Religion in the United States," *op. cit.*, pp. 101-109.

of offering educational services.[42] Religious organizations are particularly active in the field of private education. The trend, however, is in the direction of public instruction. This trend is retarded at the lower levels of instruction by religious interest groups.

The content of public instruction is held by the balance wheel of political pressures in some state of ideological equilibrium. Our educational system is suffused with those values and standards of behavior to which our urban culture has committed itself. These values emphasize advances in our material standard of living and democratic processes in the attainment of such material progress.

Construction. The government is committed to provide educational services for all city dwellers within reasonable distance from their residence. The acceptability of distances between home and school for different educational levels and purposes is determined by standards that are improved as more financial means become available in the community.

At elementary and high school levels, buildings are made to serve other than educational purposes in the most narrow sense. Similar to the church, the school at times assumes the function of a community center, providing space, particularly in the evening hours, for adult education, specialized leisure time activities, and some recreational needs of the surrounding residential areas.[43] Such broadening of function has been particularly conspicuous in the central areas of the city, where needs are probably most urgent, and in peripheral residential sections, where opportunities for communal leisure time activities have not been fully developed yet. In these 2 areas, community services are at a minimum, and therefore in greater demand.

Voluntary Associations. Voluntary associations on a neighborhood or on a city-wide basis spread over the entire urban environment. They represent concerted efforts by which citizen groups provide for their recreational needs, and their needs for club facilities to be used for meetings, conferences, and so forth.

---

[42] "In 1940, forty-nine per cent of American college students attended colleges not supported by public funds. Of the secondary school population, seven per cent attended private schools of one kind or another. On the elementary level, ten per cent attended non-public schools." Joseph S. Roucek and Associates, *op. cit.*, p. 132.

[43] For "Multiple Use of Facilities," see American Public Health Association, *Planning the Neighborhood.* Chicago: Committee on the Hygiene of Housing, Public Administration Service, 1948, pp. 44-47.

Such voluntary associations have importance beyond the alleged purposes for which they have been instituted. They provide opportunities for citizens to congregate outside working hours by status levels, and to assert and improve their status positions.[44]

Recreational Services. The spontaneous associational life of the urban citizenry competes with the associational life sponsored by both church and educational institutions. It is a social territory also invaded by commercial services. The impact of commercialized leisure time activities upon the "cultural" life of the city dweller was discussed in Chapters 11 and 12. In commercial entertainment urban culture attains some of its most unique features.[45]

SELECTED READINGS

1. Marguerite J. Fisher and Donald G. Bishop, *Municipal and Other Local Governments.* New York: Prentice-Hall, Inc., 1950, p. 1-603.

2. "Organized Religion in the United States," *The Annals* of the American Academy of Political and Social Science, Vol. 256 (March, 1948), pp. 1-164.

3. Joseph Schumpeter, *Business Cycles.* New York: McGraw-Hill Book Company, Inc., 1939, pp. 72-192.

4. James Burnham, *The Managerial Revolution.* New York: The John Day Company, 1941, pp. 71-77.

5. Joseph S. Roucek and Associates, *Social Control.* New York: D. Van Nostrand Company, Inc., 1947, pp. 79-182, 385-501.

PROBLEMS

1. *Participation in Social Institutions.* Compile a list from 5 families, containing all instances of participation of any member in some social institution. You will compile impressive lists of such participaton. Try to make these lists as complete as possible.

   Choose the families to be interviewed from different environments. Attempt a tentative estimate of the concentration of institutional participation in different environments. What patterns of social institutional participation prevail in different social groups?

---

[44] "It is largely through the activities of the voluntary groups, be their objectives economic, political, educational, religious, recreational, or cultural, that the urbanite expresses and develops his personality, acquires status, and is able to carry on the round of activities that constitute his life-career." Louis Wirth, *op. cit.,* p. 23.

[45] For recreational planning, see Chapter 18, pp. 446-447.

What research would be needed to support or refute your tentative hypotheses?

2. *Functional Analysis of Local Government.* To work out this problem, familiarize yourself with Marguerite J. Fisher and Donald G. Bishop, *Municipal and Other Local Governments.* New York: Prentice-Hall, Inc., 1950.

In addition, you will have to get information about the particular organization of municipal government in the urban community for which you intend to work out your problem.

Your problem is the determination of procedure required for the attainment of certain results in the local community. You will have to resort to interviews at city hall. You may select any urban community of 25,000 population or more.

What steps would have to be taken to get (1) a new high school constructed? (2) the fire engines in town painted blue? (3) the tax rate on an individual piece of property lowered. Your answers will have to be concrete and detailed. Where is the official decision made? What initiative has to be taken to achieve the desired result? Who has to be persuaded that your demands are reasonable? What would be the most expedient approach to such persuasion?

3. *Estimating Need for Church Building.* Ascertain the age and sex composition of active membership in the churches of your denomination in town. If more than three such church buildings in town are involved, limit your analysis to the three church buildings in your immediate environment.

Determine the function of these churches from their age and sex composition. Add to that, if available, a spot map of the residential location of active membership.

Consider the need for additional construction on the basis of your information. Discuss potential membership with the clergy. Take any further steps required to support your judgment, which ought to be checked with the clergy of your denomination.

CHAPTER 15

Social Planning

SOCIAL PLANNING AS A PRINCIPLE OF SOCIAL ORGANIZATION

Emergencies. At the beginning of the 20th century, human society stumbled into the cataclysm of worldwide war. Mankind recovered from destruction and disorganization, only to be blinded by the dazzling light of the prosperity of the 1920's, which seemed to carry us close to a millennium of comfort and wealth. The depression followed — a period of crushed illusion and courageous reorientation. Then, fascism forced the yoke of warfare and unprecedented destruction upon us again.[1]

After world war I, we commiserated with the "lost generation." Today, there are several lost generations. There is the generation that grew up during prohibition days, the generation that grew up during the depression years, the latchkey children of world war II and so forth.[2] Today, most of us look back upon a course of life which unfolded in the adjustment to a series of uprooting emergency situations. The first half of our century unwound itself while we were pushing along, unable to catch a breath, unable to look around, to find ourselves, or to get a bearing on our social, economic, and political destiny.

---

[1] For an unusual perspective, see Frederick Lewis Allen, *Only Yesterday.* New York: Bantam Books, 1946.

[2] See Joseph Schumpeter, *Business Cycles.* New York: McGraw-Hill Book Company, Inc., 1939, Vol. I, Chapter IV, "The Contours of Economic Evolution," pp. 130-192.

Regularities of the 19th Century. Glancing backward, the industrial fluctuations of the 19th century with their dynamic utilization and their unconcerned waste of human and natural resources appear to us orderly in comparison to the unheavals of recent decades. They appear as the rhythmical heartbeat of an era which, in steady progress, provided us with the steam engine, the railroad, electricity, chemical industries, and other blessings of our material culture.

Intellectually, we feel more at home in this era of gaslight and early industrial expansion than under present conditions. Its mechanism seems simple and translucent. It still shapes our social ideals because we have lost orientation in a world that changes under our feet while we are trying to understand it, that changes, as a matter of fact, because we are acting differently on the basis of our understanding in this era of inexpedient social planning.[3]

Change in Social Organization. In these later stages of industrialization and urbanization, our social institutions undergo changes so fundamental that they can be compared only to times like that of the very onset of the industralization process itself. It looks as if our market economy, our system of free enterprise, and the establishment of checks and balances in political institutions were very gradually being replaced by something else. We are not able, as yet, to form a clear picture of the general direction in which these various changes are headed.

When Adam Smith pondered the "Wealth of Nations," [4] when Saint Simon wrestled with the task of understanding the industrialization process that wrought havoc with the world of feudalism,[5] and when Karl Marx searched for fundamental principles in the social change of his times,[6] they did not receive their answers ready-made from empirical observations in their environment. They probed for essential traits in a maze of unorthodox and untraditional

---

[3] "A participant in a social exchange economy . . . faces data . . . (that) are the product of other participants' actions and volitions (like prices). His actions will be influenced by his expectation of these, and they in turn reflect the other participants' expectation of his actions." John von Neumann and Oskar Morgenstern, *Theory of Games and Economic Behavior.* Princeton: Princeton University Press, 1944.

[4] See Adam Smith, *Inquiry into the Nature and Causes of the Wealth of Nations.* 1776.

[5] See Claude Henri Saint-Simon, *Le Nouveau Christianisme.* 1825.

[6] See Karl Marx, *Zur Kritik der Politischen Oekonomie.* 1859; and *Das Kapital,* Volume I. 1867.

events which seemed beyond comprehension, which could not be understood with the help of traditional social science, nor accepted with the help of prevailing metaphysics.

We find ourselves in somewhat the same position. Things have changed, and while we have a fair conception of what they are changing from, we have difficulties in demonstrating what they might be changing to. Empirical observation and systematic speculation of more than a century have provided us with a fair conception of the principles of social organization which held the world of capitalism and early industrialization together.[7] Contemporary observations are often guided into these familiar channels. We cannot see but what we have been trained to see. We are somewhat blinded to the perception of new developments.

Broken Trends. During the 19th century, social change was determined by a number of one-directional trends. The standard of living improved constantly, and so did the national wealth as measured by various indices. In Western civilization, populations increased and cities grew. The scientific control and industrial exploitation of our natural resources progressed step by step.

The accumulated wealth seemed geared toward concentration in the hands of a few, and our industries expanded constantly through the drift of populations from the rural areas. Projected into the future, these trends promised ever-growing prosperity centered around an urban way of life, and the free market as the regulatory mechanism of population and consumption.

Today we are living in a time of broken trends. The population is still increasing, but it is increasing at an ever-decreasing rate. We foresee that day in the future (around 1980), when our population increase will come to a standstill, when it will start to shrink. The economic life of the country is burdened not only with cyclical fluctuations but with depressions of long duration.[8] These long-term depressions might be caused by the slowing down of population growth.[9] The consumers' markets are no longer subject to expansion through steady population increase, either natural or by way of immigration. Market expansion has become dependent upon the

---

[7] See pp. 342 ff.

[8] See Joseph Schumpeter, *op. cit.*, Vol. I, "Many Simultaneous Cycles," pp. 161-174.

[9] For the slowing up of urbanization, see pp. 56-58.

increase of individual purchasing power. The process of urbanization is slowing up noticeably. Our income distribution is subject to trends in favor of dissemination.

Although individual enterprises still enlarge their scope, ownership is dispersed to holders of stocks and bonds. The family-owned enterprise is vanishing from the picture. Economic power is concentrated in the hands of prominent executives with high incomes, yet incomes not commensurate to those yielded by full ownership. Individually, we strive for economic security instead of accepting the risks of oscillating opportunities. We marry earlier than ever before. We hope to settle down to a stable career in which we advance securely on the basis of seniority privileges.

A New Principle of Social Organization. We are drifting in a different direction than that indicated by a simple prolongation of the trends which manifested themselves in the course of the 19th century. In the maze of unexpected developments we have to discover some keynote that will explain to us the pattern of present social organization.

Social planning permeates the life of the country.[10] It is not a temporary phenomenon brought about by mobilization for World War II. The roots of social planning reach far back into the very beginnings of the industrialization process. Even the small entrepreneur plans, although his planning may be restricted to the organization of the work process inside his shop. Planning perspectives have gradually widened. As a principle of social organization in a democratic setting, social planning has escaped attention. It has been looked upon as a series of temporary adjustments to emergencies in the business life of the country.

Planning Concerns. Still, social planning has become the rule rather than the exception in ever-widening areas. We are far removed from the automaton of a self-organizing market society. Every large enterprise is guided by long-term policies which look far beyond present cost and price constellations. Administrative bodies have assumed responsibilities far beyond their original police functions. Organized labor is concerned with the standard of living

---

[10] "To plan or not to plan is no real issue. Planning even of economic affairs has existed at all levels of our national life, both public and private, since the beginning of our history." Charles E. Merriam, "The Possibilities of Planning," *The American Journal of Sociology*, Vol. XLIX, No. 5 (March, 1944), pp. 397-407.

of a large section of the population. Labor tries to consider wages as purchasing power as well as a cost factor. Employers and employees study the long-term effects of wage changes upon national production and consumption.

For decades the government has been concerned with the manipulation of the market by centralized monetary policies. In recent depressions, public works have been initiated to stimulate the producers' as well as the consumers' market. New agencies have been set up for the mastery of social and economic problems on a regional basis. The Tennessee Valley Administration is the most frequently quoted example of this nature.

A network of special purpose organizations for housing, farm security, family welfare, banking, and so forth is extended all over this country, concerned with planned action for the welfare of the community. Planning has become a civic responsibility in the school district meeting, in city planning associations, in the administration of neighborhood facilities, and in connection with citizens' action taken to combat juvenile delinquency.

The citizen does not limit his interest in public affairs today to casting his vote for an elected representative in the legislature. He investigates more closely than ever before the detailed issues at stake. He may take the initiative himself to propose, through pressure groups, new legislation needed in the community. We feel more responsible, today, for the details of governmental and administrative action. Citizenship does not stop at the election booth.

The emergencies of World War II did epitomize these trends in the direction of planning. With the mobilization for war and with planned reconversion, we have caught a glimpse of the tremendous potentialities inherent in a purposeful co-ordination of labor, capital, and natural resources.

Definition. We are confronted, thus, with a maze of "unorthodox" procedures in the economic and social field. What do these measures have in common? Is all of this planning? Is it social planning if various interest groups, following the fashion of the day, formulate their claims and objectives as planning programs? Is it planning if zoning laws are passed by the legislature of our large municipalities? Is it planning, if the TVA builds a dam, produces and distributes electric power, and combines these activities with related measures to benefit the welfare of a wide territory?

The answer is dependent upon our definition of social planning. A good definition will have to be problematical. It is not enough to gain a tool for purposes of crude classification. To cover a vast array of new situations, to provide a definition that will teach us to understand new problems and interrelationships, we shall have to choose a definition that will beg the answer to many questions that have never been asked. Our definition will have to contain the basic elements of a planning theory.

Social Planning and Science

Rational Action. To clear the field for our task, we must eliminate from our consideration 2 definitions of planning which tend to obstruct the view of the truly revolutionary changes brought about by social planning as a principle of social organization. In many discussions, social planning has been bound up closely with 2 misleading notions that have, nevertheless, something in common with it. Social planning has been used synonymously [11] with "rational" or "scientifically guided" behavior; [12] and it has been used synonymously with "bureaucratic organization." [13]

The scope of the planning field staked out by these definitions is either too wide or too narrow for our purpose. It either encompasses the entire field of science and technique, or it is limited to a very specific manner of co-ordinating human effort. Neither definition does justice to the planning function in our democratic society.

Social planning, as we see it is the late flower of a highly complicated urban civilization. We are interested in social planning as a new principle of social organization, as something unique to these times in which we are living. We are interested in *social* planning, not in planning as such.

Prediction. We cannot remain satisfied with a definition which considers planning as broadly identified with rational behavior. Plans are directed and consciously guided into the future. Therefore, they must indeed be based upon prediction. The instrumentali-

---

[11] "Synonymous — alike or nearly alike in meaning or significance." *Webster's New Collegiate Dictionary*. Springfield, Mass.: G. & C. Merriam Co., 1949.

[12] Such a definition underlies the entire discussion in Leonard Doob, *Plans of Men*. New Haven: Yale University Press, 1944.

[13] See Friedrich A. Hayek, *The Road to Serfdom*. Chicago: Chicago University Press, 1944.

ties for prediction are provided by modern science. As a matter of fact, modern empirical science finds its justification in its relationship to controlled action. The ambition of modern science and its very right of existence are linked closely with the hopes and purposes of our era of social planning.

Planning in this general sense, however, is not limited to any special type of social organization. It coincides with the development of modern scientific thought. This term does not help us analyze the crucial problems of our present social order. The concept assumes too wide a frame for our purpose. Prediction is needed for social planning; but social planning is more than that.

Science. Nor can the concept of social planning be limited to action guided by reliable scientific information. Many issues have to be worked out with little precise knowledge. Social action often cannot await final answers from social science research, answers that shall influence the planning decision. Social planning will often have to be undertaken without the assistance of conclusive research; it will be based on hunches, on the judgment of the expert with informal experience; it will be based upon persuasion when pressure groups succeed in convincing the citizenry of the general desirability of policies furthering their own interests.

Social planning strays beyond the narrow limits of applied science. Planning commitments are the outcome of compromise and arbitration. In science, we find out what is; in planning, we decide what should be.

Social Planning and Bureaucracy

Red Tape. Others have confused social planning and bureaucracy. They have had good reasons for doing this. There is scarcely any branch of administration or government that does not claim to be engaged in planning activities. If, then, planning is to be considered a standing feature of government bureaucracy, it is unfortunately made to share the antagonism directed against bureaucracy, red tape, and government interference. These terms are associated with the lack of efficiency that is said to sneak in wherever the stimulus of free competitive enterprise is missing.

Through the association of social planning and bureaucracy, it has become customary to mobilize highly value-burdened terms against any purposeful and far-sighted action of the community, against any action which requires concerted effort and against failure to rely upon the market alone for purposes of social control.[14]

Purpose of Bureaucracy. Government and administrative organizations have established a unique structure of working conditions, career, remuneration, and prestige for civil service employees. Government, however, has long since been joined in these developments by private enterprise in the management of working conditions for white collar labor as well as manual labor.

By itself, the concept of bureaucracy defies any attempt at being interpreted as a self-sufficient principle of social organization. Bureaucratic organization is a means to an end. It presents the most efficient way of organizing labor on a large scale for co-ordinated effort. It makes the entire enterprise greatly independent of the individual worker, who becomes an easily exchangeable part of the organization. Bureaucratic organization may be used to make profit in private business. It may be used also for some objective of public policy concerning welfare, war, or other matters of public interest.

Bureaucracy is a tool. It consists of an institutional arrangement which assumes that the initiative for the determination of purpose is vested somewhere else. Bureaucracy as such is entirely neutral to the political alternatives of democracy or dictatorship. The good bureaucrat can be made into anybody's servant. Bureaucracy, in itself, does not offer an alternative to the regulatory function of a free market system.

Robot? If, neverthless, the discussion of social planning is related to the consideration of pros and cons of either bureaucracy or free market economy, the cards are stacked in favor of the latter. Bureaucracy does not run itself. Bureaucracy is no possible choice as a principle of social organization. In itself, it does not contain a commitment on what purposes it is to serve. It could operate in a free market or in a totalitarian system of government.

Bureaucracy is bound to fail if it assumes the function of policy formation. Bureaucracy simply does not contain institutional instrumentalties for the process of decision-making. This being the case, bureaucractic autonomy is likely to mean arbitrary dictatorship.

We are familiar wtih the caricature of bureaucracy as an ungainly

---

[14] See Svend Riemer, "Social Planning and Social Organization," *The American Journal of Sociology*, Vol. LII, No. 6 (May, 1947), p. 508.

robot, a means without purpose, a civil service run wild in self-glorification and in the extension of self-assumed powers. So conceived, bureaucracy is bound to lead to dictatorship. The same holds true for social planning if closely identified with bureaucracy. The possible scope of social planning in a democratic society is obscured by confusing it with bureaucracy and by popular misunderstandings as to its function and purpose. This fallacy must be avoided in our definition of social planning.

PURPOSES AND CRITERIA OF SOCIAL PLANNING

Urban Social Organization. At the very beginning of urbanization, the turmoil of congregated living and a complex system of division of labor forced upon the city dweller new means of coordinating human effort. Slave labor and social stratification offered themselves as principles of social organization. Intitiative and command were allocated to certain groups of society. The toil of manual labor was allocated to others. An ideological superstructure served as justification for existing arrangements. Rulers and ruling classes claimed divine origin or divine sanction. Thus society stuck to traditional routines and resisted social change. The latter was brought about by conquest from the outside, by enslavement of the indigenous population, and by the infiltration by other cultures.

Hedonism. The great liberal revolution, which, from the Renaissance to the present day, advances on all fronts, political, economic, social, and cultural, imposes a different set of controls and sanctions upon modern urban society. Divine sanction is replaced by secular values concerned with contemporary community welfare. Over and above the remnants of a decaying feudal order the free market economy was established as a more democratic principle of social organization. The most fundamental contribution of this new social system was its orientation to secular values, its dedication to the achievement of the greatest happiness for the greatest number, happiness being conceived as the enjoyment of material things.

The liberal revolution failed us by accepting a highly individualized view on community welfare. Community welfare was conceived as the sum total of individual "happiness-es." Social organization was designed to promote highly individualized initiative within a broad framework of general social controls. The rules of the game were set, and it was left to the individual to adapt himself to them in a manner that provided for himself a maximum of wealth, comfort, happiness, and prestige. It was assumed — although never proved — that the sum total of collective happiness in the community would also be served best in this manner.

Economically, this conception led to the free enterprise system and to an economic theory which looked to the free market as a sufficient regulatory principle for the production and the distribution of goods, for a just arrangement of income levels and status groupings. The tremendous resources of individual initiative, freed from the fetters of feudal ties and unleashed for a rational exploitation of natural resources all over the world, led to a vastly improved standard of living.

Politically, a system of governmental checks and balances led to a framework of impersonal controls which allowed indirectly for individual participation in government. There was little interest in the development of political initiative. The social forces unleashed in the sphere of economic activities were supposed to take care of all that was needed of initiative and concern with community welfare. The state was to provide a framework only to protect a self-sufficient social body against destructive influences from the outside or from within.

Socially, the great liberal revolution led to a process of extreme individualization. Community responsibilities were cut down — in theory, if not always in fact — to a minimum. Community responsibilities were assumed to be best fulfilled by arduous work in the pursuit of individual interests. Family responsibilities were narrowed down to responsibility for the immediate offspring. Occupational responsibilities were left in the hands of entrepreneurs and business management. Neighborhood responsibilties deteriorated in the anonymous urban environment.

Community Welfare. Today social planning steps in to fill some of the gaps left by such a principle of social organization that was negatively conceived against the fetters of the feudal world.

We have run into many snares, due to the simple fact that community welfare is not always identical with the sum total of individual welfare. Untapped human resources have remained idle in the great potential of concerted action. Waste and confusion proved to be inherent in a principle of social organization that never was committed to definite goals of achievement, which left the advance of modern civilization to the guidance of arbitrary and atomized consumer preferences.

Concerted effort holds advantages over the co-ordination of individualized action. Co-operation is better than co-ordination because it involves a common goal. The assumption that the total result of innumerable activities in the service of self-interest will best benefit the community as a whole is not always borne out by actual conditions. We gain by the commitment to goals of achievement arrived at by discussions and negotiations among the citizens. Under the circumstances, we are looking around for a new principle of social organization that may benefit modern urban society by opening up new production and consumption potentials in addition to those disclosed by the liberal revolution. Social planning may be the answer to our prayer.

Criteria. Social planning is characterized, we plead, by three criteria. These criteria are related to each other, but it is difficult to subsume them under one general principle. They constitute three different aspects of one and the same thing. Here are the three criteria: [15]

1. Social planning is concerned with the concrete detail of its subject matter.

2. Social planning co-ordinates diversified technical skills and diversified professional training.

3. Social planning calls for the proclamation of values and the determination of specific objectives.[16]

Concreteness. At first glance, it may seem self-evident that social planning has to concern itself with the concrete detail of its objectives. All good science, as well as all good government, demands preoccupation with detail of observation, technique, or action. This is true enough. But in science and in government, past and future are visualized as linked with each other by causal relationships on a relatively abstract level. Economic, or social, or political, or technological, or historical connections are elucidated one by one. Predictions are made at any time with only one isolated factor in mind. The penetration of the future is limited to one partial aspect only.

[15] For an exhausting treatment of theoretical planning problems, see Karl Mannheim, *Freedom, Power and Democratic Planning.* New York: Oxford University Press, 1950.

[16] For city planning for limited objectives, see pp. 444 ff.

The entire approach is different in social planning. The emphasis is not on prediction of isolated factors but upon the projection of a concrete master plan into the future. The necessity, in science, of holding all but one of all revelant variables constant does not satisfy the planner who is well aware of the fact that he will have to deal, as best he can, with all facets of any given situation. He will have to concern himself with the indirect as well as the direct effects of any given planning measure. He will have to consider different planning measures and their diversified effects in order to weigh respective sacrifices and respective results against each other.

The social planner is moving along within a system of complicated interrelationships. His time perspective assumes a somewhat different quality than that of the social scientist. To him, time is more than a framework for the observation of isolated cause-and-effect relationships. He cannot apply the assumption of "others remaining equal." He bases his reasoning about future developments upon alternative assumptions of anticipated change and outright commitment to change which he himself, with the help of the community, will try to bring about. Time becomes a framework for action in a field of interdependent relationships which are not only studied by a passive observer, but manipulated from various leverage points simultaneously by means of co-ordinated social action.

To be sure, the penetration of the full detail of all causal cross-relations involved in the planning process suggests a task that can never be quite accomplished. We cannot investigate all facets of any given situation. In any planning report on housing or neighborhood development or on the exploitation of the natural and human resources of an area, it will never be possible to obtain complete photographic fidelity.

Yet, the challenge is always present to extend the investigation into further angles of the situation at hand. Because of the comprehensiveness of his task, the social planner will have to remain satisfied with information that will always be lacking in completeness. Where information fails, he may have to rely on improvised judgment. He will often have to yield to the pressure of impending action which cannot be delayed to allow all pertinent research findings to catch up with it.

Thus the conclusions of the social planner are never as final as those obtained in scientific investigations in which we enjoy the privilege of setting our own limitations, of isolating certain cause-and-effect relations by the very definition of our problems. The social planner cannot limit his task and plan a housing development with problems of family living in mind today, and with the problem of an efficient flow of intra-urban traffic in mind tomorrow. Whatever he does will affect the entire situation within reach of causal interconnection. His responsibility, if not his competence, is practically unlimited.

Where the social planner cannot do a perfect job, he will have to improvise. Nor is there, in social planning, a clear distinction — as in science — between relevant and irrelevant facts; there is a distinction only between conditions of first, second and third importance, and this distinction in itself is subject to changes of opinion.

Co-ordination of Skills. Our second criterion asserts that social planning is predicated upon the co-ordination of different technical skills and different backgrounds of professional training. The need for such co-operation follows logically from our first criterion, our discussion of the infinite planning task.

No isolated problem is abstracted, in social planning, to be dealt with competently by either architect, engineer, land economist, or sociologist. Ideally, all skills have to be invested, all viewpoints have to be brought to bear upon the master plan that is to be constructed into the future.

This need is not always recognized in present planning activities. City plans are being laid out with only the viewpoints of the highway engineer or the architect in mind. Resettlement programs have been carried through under the guidance of the agricultural economist only. As our definition would have it, this is not social planning proper. It represents applied science and falls short of the challenge contained in social planning as a principle of social organization. In practice, the architect, the engineer, or the land economist learns, as he goes along, something about the skills and the viewpoints of the borderline fields of scientific analysis. He has to acquire at least dilettant skills and interests in other professional fields. Fortunately, he often does quite well in this manner.

Values and Objectives. The task of social planning is different, also, from scientific investigation, in that it does not start out with a clearly defined goal. It is one of the tasks of the social planner to set his own objectives.

The social planner cannot eliminate or circumvent the value problem which the scientist pushes aside by proclaiming it "none-of-his-business." [17] The scientist may objectively investigate what the values of social groups or individuals are; he cannot objectively demand adherence to certain values which he thinks the community should strive for. Nor does the government executive bother about an objective justification of values or administrative objectives: these values or objectives are handed him by legislators, city councils, or similar bodies to whom the task of policy formation is assigned. The social planner does not share in any such clearcut division between initiative and policy formation, on the one hand, and expedient execution and administration, on the other.

In the abandonment of the traditional division of power lies the most radical break of social planning with the design of democratic institutions as we have known them. Under the impact of social planning, customary democratic form must be revised to retain democratic procedures in the face of new circumstances that have destroyed the efficiency of earlier democratic institutions and principles of government.

Problems of social planning are not posed in such a manner as to find their solution in the assignment of efficient means to the attainment of a set goal. Upon the planning expert rests the responsibility of proclaiming a system of values worth striving for. He is concerned with the determination of specific objectives and, simultaneously, with the best means of obtaining them. An integrated view is taken of both means and ends. Certain objectives are proposed because the means seem readily available and not too costly in relation to desired effects. Choices are made between different means for social improvement with their side effects upon a wide range of interlocking objectives in mind.

The necessity of deciding upon desirable goals in the process of social planning is often obscured by the delegation of powers to the social planner for the pursuit of broadly conceived objectives such

---

[17] "Have scientists, then, no special function or obligation in determining the ends for which scientific knowledge is to be used? As scientists, it is their business to determine reliably the immediate and remote costs and consequences of alternate possible courses of action, and to make these known to the public. Scientists may then in their capacity as citizens join with others in advocating one alternative rather than another, as they prefer." George A. Lunberg, *Can Science Save Us?* New York: Longmans, Green and Co., 1947, p. 29.

as the "welfare of the community." [18] While he is challenged to plan for the best interests of the community, it is left to him to decide what these best interests are. It is left to him to translate such general values into tangible objectives that can serve as a guide for concerted community action.

The value problem, as it confronts the social planner, has bewildered some of our social scientists trying to understand the function of social planning. In view of our scientific traditions, which exclude the concern with values from the task of scientific investigation, and in view of the practice of delegating the responsibility for social planning to the scientifically trained professional, this can scarcely surprise us. Concerned with the application of social science to the improvement of social conditions, Robert Lynd tried to settle the matter once and for all by proclaiming a set of social values sufficiently general to be acceptable to everybody.[19]

Unfortunately, Lynd had to raise himself to very lofty heights of abstraction to be able to reach out to something upon which all members of the community could *a priori* agree. The miracle of unquestioned consensus could not be performed without the introduction of a considerable amount of word magic. Contradictory values, such as the desire for the "realization of personal powers" and the "craving for physical and psychological security," stand side by side as goals to be obtained by a well guided process of social planning. There can be no doubt about the desirability of either objective; but the mentioning alone of these two highly conflicting objectives does not solve our problem. It does not tell us in practice what exactly we should do and strive for, nor does it tell us how to compromise between values that are bound to conflict in their implementation. It does not tell us how specifically to arrive at the relatively best solution of our problem under existing social conditions.

Social planning cannot deal with absolutes, nor can it be guided by absolute values alone. Political opinions will not clash at this level of abstraction. They will clash, however, when it comes to a

[18] It is the official purpose of the T.V.A. to "foster an orderly and proper physical, economic, and social development of the area." Although there are further specifications about the functions of this government corporation, the planning officials are operating within a wide framework of responsibilities, and are challenged to use their initiative. See David E. Lilienthal, *TVA. Democracy on the March.* New York: Pocket Books, Inc., 1945.

[19] See Robert Lynd, *Knowledge for What?* Princeton: Princeton University Press, 1939.

decision about the various means by which these general values are to be pursued.[20]

We disagree when we try to decide upon the specification of values, when we try to decide whether the rising tide of juvenile delinquency is to be curbed by the improvement of housing conditions, by the provision of recreational facilities, by changes in correctional treatment, or by religious education. The relative importance of specific implementation — as means for the obtainment of general values — will have to be weighed wherever different instrumentalities are recommended for the fulfillment of equally important basic desires.

Planning and Freedom. We run into a somewhat different confusion wherever the controversy of "planning versus freedom" raises its ugly head. The all-out opponents of social planning usually try to gain their point by a proper definition of the planning process, a definition which is bound to arouse animosity. They emphasize that restrictions involved in the commitments to concerted action are unavoidable in social planning. They stress the danger involved in the usurpation of dictatorial powers by an uncontrolled bureaucracy viewed as the only possible instrument for social planning.[21]

The promoters of social planning, are not without their own ideological trick-reasoning. Being well aware of the need for the determination of planning purposes, they gain their point by phrasing the general planning objectives in such a manner as to take the wind out of the sails of their opponents. They advocate "planning for freedom," [22] a scarcely objectionable but not very articulate undertaking. They tell us what they want to avoid, but they do not tell us how they want to avoid it. One of the major problems of social planning as a principle of social organization is thus brought into view.

We may do well to avoid the futile attempt of committing our-

---

[20] Values range from high levels of abstraction to relatively concrete means-ends relationships. This condition may appear obvious. Yet it is not generally recognized that the objectivity of social research may be affected by the level of abstraction on which it is conducted." Svend Riemer, "Values and Standards in Research," *The American Journal of Sociology*, Vol. LV, No. 2 (September, 1949), p. 133.

[21] See Friedrich A. Hayek, *op. cit.*

[22] "We shall have to make a distinction between planning for uniformity and planning for freedom and variety." Karl Mannheim, *Diagnosis of Our Time*. New York: Oxford University Press, 1944, p. 7.

selves, once and for all, to a series of planning objectives of general validity. It seems called for, rather, to make the proclamation of ends, and their specification in terms of tangible objectives, and the choice of adequate social and technological instrumentalities part and parcel of the planning process itself.

This view point does no injustice to the type of planning that is going on all around us in the urban and the urbanized rural environment. Social planning is well distinguished in this manner from many superficially similar processes of bureaucratic execution. If the determination of values is recognized as part of the planning process itself, it will be impossible for the promoter of social planning to impose his own values and preferences upon the situation with which he is concerned. The community is challenged to continuous criticism and to constructive participation.

Practical Problems of Social Planning

Citizen Participation. Democratic social planning is impossible without citizen participation. The planning expert has to promote his planning objectives successfully so that they will be accepted and approved of by the citizenry.

Social planning has been ridiculed by some as a selling job. There are those who regard with suspicion all expenditures for public relations in connection with particular planning ventures. It may indeed seem strange that the very public that is to be talked into the acceptance of a planning venture has to pay for being propagandized with the help of public relations funds made available to the social planner.

Yet intensive contacts between expert planner and citizenry are indispensable in good social planning. To plan for community recreational facilities on the school grounds, to plan for good neighborhood relations or a satisfactory commuting system in the metropolis is practically impossible without good public relations. Not even the best planner can derive a good plan for the people without knowing what the people want,[23] without having solicited some articulate expression of their preferences.[24]

[23] It has become customary to discriminate between wants, demands, and needs. Demands are considered as "effective" demands (backed up by purchasing power). Needs contain a normative element, the notion that by some objective standards people *should* have certain things, irrespective of purchasing power. Wants refer in the most general manner to people's interest in having certain things.

[24] For the self-organization of a community for purposes of recreational

Good public relations encompass more than a good selling job. To put a planning project across, the very people for whom the planning is being done have to identify with it. They have to feel that their own interests are being advanced, and they have to feel that they want to make the new facilities their own and use them, whether it is a matter of recreational facilities, a new school building for their children, or a new type of housing facility to be offered in the community. Some people can be talked into it. To that extent, social planning can be greatly aided by a good selling job. Planning experience shows that this is rarely enough.

The Planner and the People. To ensure full acceptance of a planning project, and to guarantee its survival in the long run, the plan must stem from the people themselves, and the people should feel that they are participants in the planning process. That requires more than a selling job.

To achieve citizen-participation, however, is easier said than done. There is astir among planners all over the country a growing interest in "methods," and thereby they mean methods to achieve full citizen participation in planning ventures. They are worried about gaining the co-operation of the right type of people in the community, not only a group of professional joiners and busybodies, but a group of citizens able to represent the true interests of the community and ready to assume leadership in the promotion and the acceptance of the planning project.

First, people have to gain an understanding of the fact that something can be done for them by way of social planning. They have to learn to think in broader terms than those of immediate self-interest. They have to realize that by concerted effort they can make the community a much more pleasant place in which to live, a better place to raise their children.

Citizens have to be alerted to latent potentialities in concerted action. Such concerted action does not necessarily consist of giving money for a good cause, although money is said to be quite helpful in almost any enterprise. It may consist of self-imposed commitments ("Let's not throw any more garbage on that corner lot to be

planning and the provision of recreational facilities, see Richard Waverly Poston, *Small Town Renaissance.* New York: Harper & Brothers, 1950, "Lewistown," pp. 102-113.

used as a baseball diamond for our teen-agers"), it may consist of
self-imposed restrictions and duties ("Let's have mothers take turns
in running a co-operative nursery school service"), and it may
consist in giving time to deliberations with the expert planner to find
out what the community can get within its budget, what are the
costs for further improvements and what are the projects that will
serve best the largest number of members in the community?

Initiative. How is the planner to instigate such general interest in
possible planning projects? He can talk his head off, and his efforts
may remain ineffective until somebody who is a member of the
group takes up the cue and carries his own initiative and enthusiasm
into this field of activity.

Entire communities have been made over from top to bottom by
a small core of active citizens. They have been provided with recreational facilities for all age groups; [25] they have been provided
with facilities for specialized leisure time activities; they have
worked for and obtained adequate nursery facilities.[26] Educational
facilities have been improved, and employment opportunities have
been planned to provide a better standard of living for all citizens.
Ghost towns have been converted into live communities, and dreary
dormitory suburbs have been pulled together into friendly and
sociable places in which to live. All this requires initiative, and it
should not be initiative by the professional planner alone.[27]

A quest for community leadership arises. Such leaders may be
people in different walks of life. Those who hold the purse-strings
are not the only important ones. Who are the true leaders? We do
not know for sure. We are trying to find out. It is one of the tasks
to which professional planners are devoting considerable attention.
When social planners enter a community, they often find themselves
surrounded by quaint people who do not carry much weight with
the rest of the group. Who are the people who can win others over
to their side, who can instill an interest in working together? Who

---

[25] For the quest for local initiative in community planning, see Richard
Waverly Poston, *op. cit.;* Jessie Bernard, *American Community Behavior.* New
York: The Dryden Press, 1949; and Arthur Hillman, *Community Organization
and Planning.* New York: The Macmillan Company, 1950.

[26] See Katherine Whiteside Taylor, "Parent Growth through Cooperative
Play Groups," *Marriage and Family Living,* Vol. VII, No. 3 (August, 1946),
pp. 61-63.

[27] See Arthur Hillman, *op. cit.,* pp. 35-205.

are the people who are looked upon as leaders, who are not under suspicion of working for their own individual interests? If we knew, we would have solved one of the most important problems involved in practical social planning.[28]

Arbitration. Once the community has been stirred up to do something for its own betterment, there remains the task of deciding upon priorities. What needs to be done most? Is it business and industry that needs a shot in the arm, or is it the social life of the community that is at a low ebb and requires special attention? Does the rate of juvenile delinquency make it apparent that the leisure time activities of the younger generation need more serious consideration?

No general answer can be given to this array of questions. In social planning, means and ends are so closely interrelated that a detailed description of conditions prevailing in the community is required to define the planning task.[29] Furthermore, the human factor is of overwhelming importance.

It depends upon the type of leadership available in the community how a planning program can best be turned into a self-perpetuating social process which, once underway, will shift its attention from the first problem to others. The community must learn to feel its own strength. It would be futile to impose standardized procedures from the outside, to achieve this end. The planner has to know the people themselves to know how to arouse them to work for a common goal. The outsider seldom does. He is dependent upon the people who have lived their lives in the community, have shared its tribulations and enjoyed its development. He is dependent upon people who know the people and can talk to the people in their own language. He is dependent upon people who are known to be in the same boat.

The training of the professional planner concerned with either construction or social relations enables him to make a valuable contribution in getting the planning process under way. His technical knowledge makes it possible for him to tell the people what they can get, and what it will take to get it.

---

[28] A simple compilation of census data will sometimes furnish an incentive to planning initiative within the community.

[29] In any community planning report, analysis of the economic base will always furnish a tie-up with nationwide or worldwide conditions. Economic conditions will be least amenable to treatment on a merely local basis.

The trained professional can propose planning alternatives that challenge the imagination of the citizens. He can visualize alternative solutions to one and the same problem. He may be able to recommend a constructive compromise between different interest groups who, for want of better understanding, have fought all social action to a standstill in the community. It will have to be the planner's task to translate blueprints and complicated technical, legal, and commercial schemes into a language which the average citizen, the non-specialist, can understand. He will have to stimulate and to encourage. He will have to give technical advice where such is needed.

Controlled Social Change. Once the community functions as a planning unit, the professional planner goes on to another difficult task. He will challenge the community to accept the responsibility of guiding social change, rather than letting it 'happen' to the community. Different planning projects will now have to be set into relationship with each other and pursued one by one in an orderly process. At this point, the community becomes the master of its own destiny, except for its economic dependence upon nationwide developments.[30]

The crux of the practical problem is the relationship between the professional planner and the people for whom he does the planning. The social planner cannot wait to have his task assigned to him by the community in need for his services. Still, he wants the initiative to come from the citizens themselves; there is no doubt that the citizens look to him for some leadership. It's a riddle that cannot be solved theoretically. Skills are being developed to arouse planning interests in the community without stifling spontaneous interest and initiative. Upon the success of such ventures hinges the future of social planning as a new principle of social organization.

SOCIAL PLANNING AND DEMOCRACY

For the People and by the People. Social planning should be thought of as a means of strengthening our democratic way of life. It is government for the people and by the people. That is nothing very new. But it is important to realize that democracy, as it has

---

[30] See Emil Lederer, *State of the Masses.* New York: W. W. Norton & Company, 1940.

come down to us with the principles and institutions of the 18th century, stands in need of an overhaul and new social inventions.

Social planning may be conceived as the adjustment of our social institutions to new social, economic, and political conditions by the application of democratic principles. Social planning does not aspire to anything more than government for the people and by the people. To conform to this principle, a system of government was originally conceived and put into practice by which legislative, executive, and judiciary functions were so interrelated, and yet separated from, each other as to guarantee equitable treatment of the individual citizen, and to guarantee his participation — by way of elected legislators — in initiative to promote the improvement of social and economic institutions. The concentration of government, however, and the assumption of greater responsibility for the well-being of citizens or citizen groups, have given unprecedented powers to executive government and administration.

Due to the size and complexity of modern urban society we do not identify with our governmental institutions to the extent that the member of the New England town meeting identified with its selectmen and their performance. Government is often considered as an anonymous power; the individual's participation in its conduct has become so indirect and relatively so insignificant that the feeling of responsibility is lowered and government decisions are not accepted any more as proclamations of the will of the people. The higher heads of government are, of course, more exposed to this estrangement; the Federal government more than the government of the state; and the state government more than the city government. Within the urban community, the city hall does not enjoy the same confidence as the ward boss or the district alderman.

Social planning may be looked upon as a substitue to fill this gap. Citizens' participation is much more easily stimulated in smaller governmental units, in the administration of common interests in the school district meeting, the country club, or the labor union, and in connection with special planning projects. Here, the results of concerted action are more tangible, and the efforts of the individual citizen will have more conspicious results.

Against Anonymous Government. Social planning can thus be understood as a counter measure or a spontaneous reaction against the growing anonymity of Federal, state, or municipal government.

It retains democratic thinking and scheming in a social setting where the earlier designed democratic institutions have lost their hold upon the imagination of the people.

There lurks, of course, the danger of parochialism and even separatism in the folds of a planning movement that glorifies the small homogeneous group as compared to the nationwide heterogeneous society of which we all are a part. The struggle for better integration of our highly urbanized society, carried by spontaneous planning activities, might suffer its defeat through the very instrument that it created for its purposes.

This would be the case if particularistic interests, instead of blending into national politics, were to establish themselves as stumbling blocks for a well-integrated system of national politics by ignoring the interests of the country as a whole. Social planning on the local or highly specialized level should, therefore, be conceived as a stepping stone only to an awakening and revival of a new consciousness of national citizenship, a revival that should lead to a more thorough interest in the control of larger economic and political issues which, at the present time, tend to drift along under the pressure of special interest groups, their lobbyists, their demagogues, and under the erratic influence of a disinterested urban and rural electorate.

Citizen Responsibility. This, however, is not the entire story of social planning. Inasmuch as neither legislation nor administration limits itself anymore to merely regulatory functions, inasmuch as the tasks to be performed by the government require increasingly more concern with detailed living and working conditions of the people, inasmuch as our techniques have improved to the point where the intelligent delegate of the people is far from able to understand without special training what could be obtained by economic, social, or physical planning; the task of arbitration must be handed back to the people, who must be enlightened by the expert and should express their preferences to the expert before they commit themselves to any given action program.

The importance of the planning expert, under the circumstances, moves somewhat into the background, while considerable attention will have to be focussed upon the relationship between the expert and the people. The growing use of opinion polls is only one instance that manifests the need for instrumentalities by which the expert is kept in contact with popular opinion between appointment or election times.[31]

Social planning as such is without either purpose or direction. In the hands of the demagogic promoter who has something to sell (if he has nothing to sell other than himself, we call him a dictator), it becomes a dangerous weapon that may lead us almost anywhere, to war or waste, to social turmoil or cultural stagnation. If, on the other hand, it is backed by a nationwide revival of citizen participation in the affairs of the nation, it might provide the leverage by which we shall be able to make ourselves masters of the complex urban environment in which we live.

SELECTED READINGS

1. Friedrich A. Hayek, *The Road to Serfdom*. Chicago: Chicago University Press, 1944, pp. 1-248.
2. Karl Mannheim, *Freedom, Power and Democratic Planning*. New York: Oxford University Press, 1950, pp. 3-313.
3. David E. Lilienthal, *TVA. Democracy on the March*. New York: Pocket Books, Inc., 1945, pp. 1-243.
4. Arthur Hillman, *Community Organization and Planning*. New York: The Macmillan Company, 1950, pp. 35-205.
5. Svend Riemer, "Social Planning and Social Organization," *The American Journal of Sociology*, Vol. LII, No. 6 (May, 1947), pp. 508-516.

PROBLEMS

Social Planning Processes. All 3 problems to be worked out in connection with the contents of this chapter are basically of the same kind. They are concerned with the application of our definition of social planning to practical planning projects.

With regard to each of the planning processes mentioned below (or whatever other processes there might be), collect as much empirical information as possible. Find out how the process or others like it got started, how it has been organized, how it has been staffed since being under way, and who determines what is to be done in connection with it and what is not to be done. Find out what the results have been so far.

With all this information at hand, consider whether all 3 of the

---

[31] For the use of an opinion poll in connection with the proposal of a city budget, see Don Cahalan, *Public Opinion on the City's Budget Planning*. Kansas City, Mo.: Civic Research Institute, March, 1943.

above-mentioned "criteria of social planning" apply to the process. Do different professional skills co-operate in the process? Are all or only a limited number of the aspects of the manipulated situation of importance to the people who carry out the process or for whom it is carried out? Is it a matter of using technical skills for the attainment of predetermined goals, or are the objectives of the process determined in the course of the planning process itself?

If the processes under your special consideration are not entirely covered by the three criteria of social planning as developed above, discuss their relationship to true social planning in the light of our definition. Discuss what other type of social process they might better be subordinated to, such as, for example, bureaucratic execution, social movement, or gang formation.

Below you will find an indication of the three groups of processes that you may select for analysis with regard to the absence or presence of planning criteria:

1. Apply the above to:

   a. Construction of a new high school building, considering the entire process from initiation to execution.

   b. The yearly handling of urban finances according to the city budget.

2. Apply the above to:

   a. The formation and functioning of a bridge club.

   b. An excursion to a nearby city in connection with your class in urban sociology.

3. Apply the above to:

   a. The activities of one of the local service clubs. (Rotary, Lions, Mason, and so forth.)

   b. The activities of that agency in the city government charged with the responsibility for city planning.

PART VI

Urban Planning

CHAPTER 16

Housing

URBAN RESIDENTIAL HOUSING

Separation of Work and Private Life. Residential housing separated from place of work is distinctly a phenomenon of the modern city.[1] On the farmstead, purposes of business and family living are so closely interlaced that the thrifty farmer is tempted to neglect his residential quarters in favor of business investment. In the modern city, occupational and private lives are separated from each other. There is no place for the pleasantries of family living in the barren and rationalized environment of factories and office buildings.

Private homes and residential districts must be designed with a variety of leisure time activities in mind. The backyard must serve as the children's playground; at other times it serves the purpose of adult relaxation in gardening, sunning, or just sitting in the fresh air. The backyard is a place to enjoy solitude as well as company. The living room of the family dwelling must accommodate a scope of leisure time activities no less varied.

Consequently, the private residence of the city dweller is not nearly as thoroughly rationalized as that part of urban shelter in which our occupational activities are carried out. It is based on tastes and preferences far more irrational than those determining

[1] For the combination of place of work and place of residence in the Middle Ages, see Svend Riemer, "Functional Housing in the Middle Ages," *Transactions of the Wisconsin Academy of Sciences, Arts, and Letters*, 1949, Vol. II; published Spring, 1951, Madison, Wis., pp. 77-91.

the layout of a modern factory or department store. The purposes of modern home construction are seldom clearly defined.[2] Individual preferences for the family home are as varied as those related to other items of consumption. Home planning purposes change continuously as time goes on.[3]

A Varied Panorama. Family housing in the modern city covers a wide range of conditions. The extremes are, on the one hand, the slums, where conditions are considered dangerous and detrimental to the health and safety of the inhabitants and, on the other hand, the fashionable suburbs.

Between these extremes, a varied panorama spreads before our eyes. Apartment hotels tower close to the center of the city. They contain provisions for meals, sleep, and recuperation; the downtown entertainment district is near enough to provide leisure time activities during the evening hours. These apartment hotels are intermingled with the slums as discussed previously.[4] Here, run-down and dilapidated buildings, built in a different era and for different purposes, hold a congested mass of humanity in overcrowded living quarters. Each structure clings to an adjacent one. They are not built to admit either sunshine or fresh air. Open spaces equipped for children's play are entirely missing. The vacant lot, muddy from the last rain or dusty from scorching sun and lack of vegetation, furnishes an outlet for the physical activities of the growing child.

Conditions in the area of "blight" are just one shade better.[5] Here, we find the slums of the future. Buildings may be in a better state of repair. They are not satisfactory, however, for the needs of family living. They are encumbered by industrial and other land

---

[2] Research to define the purpose of home construction is customarily related to the concept of "livability." Contributions are exceedingly limited. The most important empirical study to date is "The Livability Problems of 1,000 Families." Federal Public Housing Authority, National Housing Agency, Bulletin No. 28. Washington, D.C.: U.S. Government Printing Office, 1945.

The function of housing in studies like this is defined in terms of consumer preferences.

For the need for and the difficulties involved in livability studies, see Svend Riemer, "Architecture for Family Living," *Journal of Social Issues*, Vol. VII, Nos. 1 and 2, 1951, pp. 140-151.

[3] For the relationship between culture and home design, see Svend Riemer, "Designing the Family Home," in Howard Becker and Reuben Hill, editors, *Family, Marriage and Parenthood.* Boston: D. C. Heath and Company, 1948. pp. 493-504.

[4] See pp. 156 ff.

[5] For definitions of "slum" and "blight," see pp. 95-96.

uses detrimental to wholesome family living. Sanitary facilities may not be quite as objectionable as in the adjacent slum. Remodeling may have obtained a minimum degree of privacy for the individual family. Yet makeshift arrangements for family living are only too obvious. Most buildings in the blighted areas were designed for very different purposes from those which they now serve.

Beyond the inner belt of slum and blight, housing conditions pile up in a complicated mosaic. Vintages of different decades of construction follow upon each other. "Functional obsolescence" [6] is most pronounced in the center of the city. There are great discrepancies between the original and the present purposes of structure.

There are structures that came to life as mansions for the well-to-do, and others as one-family homes or duplexes built for the thrifty middle classes. There are tenements and single clapboard structures, brownstone houses in consecutive rows and single-family dwellings in the midst of spacious garden lots. At the periphery of the city, we come closer to an adequate fulfillment of contemporary housing needs. Even here, there is neither rhyme nor reason to the manner in which different housing conditions interpenetrate each other. There are attic rooms and basement apartments made available for family living. Families, in need of housing, find refuge in winterized summer cabins, in Quonset huts, and other temporary buildings. They may live within walking distance of their places of work, or they may have to commute for an hour or more to reach their private homes. They may have to pay from 10 per cent to 50 per cent or more of their family income for shelter. They may be able to rent their homes, or they may have to buy them. They may own them, or pay heavily on the mortgages. They may enjoy pleasant environs and companionable neighbors, or they may find themselves surrounded by scolding landlords and the riotous living of a motley and uncongenial crowd.

All this is urban family housing. Where the individual fits himself into the picture depends to a great extent, but not entirely, upon income. It depends upon the time when he settled down to family living, on whether he bought his home in times of depression or

---

[6] The term functional obsolescence designates a condition of deficiency (either in terms of utility, or in terms of sale value, or both) not due to physical deterioration but due to the fact that the needs have changed.

prosperity. It depends upon his tastes and preferences, on the compromise he is willing to make between his own needs and those of his children, between indoor comfort and amenities for outdoor living. It depends upon the amount he is willing to spend for housing as compared to all the other requirements for wholesome family living and child raising.[7] Housing conditions in the modern city are the result of unplanned growth, that is, of individual choices.

The Pioneering Stage. The western cities of this continent started as pioneering ventures. In the beginning they were cities without families, and they grew by immigration of single males. The problem of housing was to provide adequate shelter for the early arrivals of a single male population. They lived in hotel rooms, barracks, tents, and rented rooms; and later, in boarding houses.

Female companionship was of the less respectable type. Houses of prostitution provided not only for sexual needs; they furnished — jointly with bars, hotels, and taverns — centers for entertainment and leisure time activities as they develop in an environment without full family living.[8]

A residential pattern was established here which is still retained in the single men's districts of our large western cities, where cheap hotel facilities are made available as winter residences for tramps, bums, and hoboes, where inexpensive eating places cater to the simple needs of the bachelor with a minimum of financial resources, where red light districts and burlesque shows provide for different needs of contact with the opposite sex. In this environment, we also find the unattached old man who has to get along (or wants to get along) without family care up to the time of his death.[9]

---

[7] For the compromise nature of home planning, see Svend Riemer, "Sociological Theory of Home Adjustment," *American Sociological Review*, Vol. VII, No. 3 (June, 1943), p. 272.

[8] "There were not nearly enough dwellings in San Francisco to shelter even a small proportion of the new-comers, most of whom consequently were housed in leaky canvas tents or in hastily constructed board shanties with muslin or Osnaburg partitions. Many of the lodging houses, and some of the more pretentious hotels as well, consisted simply of one or more large rooms, with bunks fastened to the walls, and rows of uncomfortable cots on the floor." Herbert Asbury, *The Barbary Coast. An Informal History of the San Francisco Underworld.* New York: Pocket Books, Inc., 1947, p. 10.

[9] For Skid Road as a "natural area," see Calvin F. Schmid, *Social Trends in Seattle.* Seattle: The University of Washington Press, 1944, p. 295.

See also Walter Firey, *Land Use in Central Boston.* Cambridge: Harvard University Press, 1947, Chapter VIII, "The Role of Occupational and Kinship Patterns in Localized Anomie; the South End," pp. 290-322.

Early Family Dwellings. The earliest family dwellings confront us with facilities ranging from modest comfort to pompous ostentation, from makeshift shelters to elaborate mansions. The housing history of the Atlantic seacoast tells us about cellar dwellings as well as homes of prosperous merchants.[10]

In most of our large cities, the poor settled in the lowlands endangered by floods and high waters. The wealthier members of the community built their homes on more attractive and more sanitary sites. Segregation of homes by status is as old as the American city.

In one respect, early ecological patterns represent a contrast to contemporary conditions. Public buildings, store houses, docks, and shops were found in close proximity to the homes of the more well-to-do sections of the community. In view of the lack of industrial nuisances (odors or excessive noise), and in view of the advantages of living within short walking distance of the business and public centers, this arrangement was preferred by those who could make their demands effective by superior purchasing power.

The poorer people tended to live further away. When cities were first built the poorer people were forced to seek refuge in the periphery of the urban settlement.[11]

Congestion. Congestion fostered the development of slums. The residences of the lowlands were filled to overflowing. Immigrant families moved in and had to be accommodated regardless of home building activities. They moved into the basements of the homes

---

[10] The earliest mode of living for white settlers in America was of the congregate type. During the colonization period it was necessary that the colonists live in barracks during their first months in this country, either for protection from the Indians, or to give them the necessary time to work out plans for more permanent settlement.

The second stage for many settlers was the cellar dwelling. Quoting a contemporary source, "Those in New Netherland and especially in New England who have no means to build farm-houses at first according to their wishes, dig a square pit in the ground, cellar fashion, six or seven feet deep, as long and as broad as they think proper, case the earth inside all round the wall with timber, which they line with the bark of trees or something else to prevent the caving in of the earth . . . partitions are run through those cellars which are adapted to the size of the family." James Ford, *Slums and Housing.* Cambridge: Harvard University Press, 1936, p. 20.

Later, the term cellar dwelling was also used with regard to inhabited basements, endangered by floods.

[11] See footnote 2, p. 91.

of the well-to-do, frequently without having more than a single room at the command of the entire family.[12] Or they moved into more modest homes where they doubled up, sharing cooking and sanitary facilities with the host family. Or they spread out into the urban periphery where they housed themselves in most inadequate shelter: primitive log cabins, simple lean-tos, or other makeshift constructions.

To be sure, the early ditches dug by pioneers for their first hibernation cannot be considered part of the urban housing picture, but the cellar dwellings, the early log cabins, and the single rooms rented to the immigrant families are part and parcel of early American city life. There was not enough space to enjoy the luxury of privacy in the family home. A large kitchen-living-bedroom combination had to do for all needs of these early urban settlers.

In the early log cabin, sleeping quarters were frequently set off from the rest of the dwelling unit; they were relegated to the sleeping loft. The separation of kitchen and living room was part of the genteel European tradition, available in this country to the wealthier classes only. In the middle and lower income groups, the advantage of kitchen separation was long retarded, due to the need for doubling-up and the sharing of kitchen facilities.

Conversions. Doubling up on a temporary basis gradually led to conversions by which a residence planned and built for a single family was made suitable for two and more. For many immigrants temporary emergency arrangements had finally to be accepted as permanent housing.

Residential housing piled up in those sections of the city where land values had remained low. These less desirable neighborhoods were built up to the point of overflowing. Old homes were moved to the backs of their lots, and new structures erected at the street front. Every square foot of land available in the sections of poorer residences was utilized, until these sections consisted of jungles of

---

[12] "Many of the slums in the early history of the city were those on the edges of foul swamps and by the wharves where the poorer population lived. They are paralleled in every American city today." James Ford, *op. cit.*, p. 445.

"Several thousands of Italians are living in a manner to require constant watching; several families living huddled together in one large room, with mere boards and curtains for partitions between their scanty household goods." Edith Abbott, *The Tenements of Chicago, 1908-1933*. Chicago: The University of Chicago Press, 1936, p. 28.

wooden structures, dark alleys, stairs, fire escapes, and outhouses, in which only the initiated could find his way.[13]

As cities grew, the escape from the immigrant hovels became more difficult. Outlying lands had been pre-empted by the wealthier members of the community, eager to build on less congested land and able to do so because of better means of transportation available to them.[14]

Tenements. The first tenements built in the middle of the 19th century were hailed enthusiastically as an important step toward the improvement of urban living conditions. Philanthropy had to assume leadership and give financial assistance to the first efforts at tenement construction.[15]

Residential construction to be inhabited by more than one family was now built for this express purpose. The era of random doubling up promised to come to an end. Cooking and sanitary facilities were made available to each family.

These early tenements stand today as parts of our contemporary slums. That they have become symbols of slum living today is due to overcrowding and lack of maintenance and, last but not least, to their survival and continued use in an era that applies different standards to family housing.

Large scale tenement construction has always remained limited to a few of our metropolitan centers. It has flourished on Manhattan

---

[13] "In Chicago the frame tenement has lingered on and is still the predominant type. Many of these frame tenements were originally frame cottages of the prairie period and were expanded into tenements to provide cheaper housing facilities for the increasing population. The old cottage was raised up, new stories added above and below, and further additions built, not infrequently, both front and rear. In many cases the cottage has not only been raised but moved back to the rear of the lot, and a new house erected in the front. Sometimes the new front house is itself finally moved back to the middle of the lot, and a third house is built in front." *Ibid.*, p. 179.

[14] "The structure of American cities was also being shaped by purely internal means of transportation. At first movement by walking and horse-drawn vehicles on un-paved roads restricted the limits of city settlement to a narrow compass and forced families to live in tenements." Homer Hoyt, "The Influence of Highways and Transportation on the Structure and Growth of Cities and Urban Land Values," in *Highways in our National Life. A Symposium.* Princeton: Princeton University Press, 1950, p. 202.

[15] "Although many private dwellings had been occupied simultaneously by many families, or specifically converted for such use, the first tenement house originally designed for occupancy by several tenant families was constructed in 1833, according to Haswell, and was situated in Water Street." James Ford, *op. cit.*, p. 95.

Island because of the obvious lack of space for urban extension. In Chicago, tenements were never as prevalent because there were no natural obstructions to impede the horizontal growth of the city. In Philadelphia, the emphasis upon home ownership did not encourage the building of multiple dwellings.[16] In our smaller communities, the construction of tenements on a large scale would have been ludicrous and uneconomical.

During the second half of the 19th century, tenement housing became a means to supply economy shelter in the central areas of our large cities. With this objective in mind, the "dumbbell" tenements of 1879 were hailed as a prize design because they squeezed a maximum number of families into a densely built-up city block. Construction of tenements was often shoddy. Some brick walls collapsed before the buildings were completed. With construction geared to minimum standards of safety, and with high occupancy rates and reduced maintenance, these tenements were condemned from the beginning to become what they are today: the slums of the central city.

Standards. At the turn of the century, legislation was passed — under the leadership of New York, where conditions were worst — to guarantee minimum standards of health and safety to those parts of the urban population reduced by income to the use of economy shelter. Fire hazards and sanitary risks had been the concern of previous legislation dating far back to the early history of this country and to the Middle Ages in Europe.

Now the concern of the city fathers was extended to such items as light and air penetration, to the height of buildings in relation to their distance from each other, to the elimination of indirectly lighted rooms, to the provision of private sanitary facilities, and to other requirements with regard to the plumbing system provided for the individual family.

The public showed concern for the housing conditions provided for families living under conditions of economic stress. However, the public assumed responsibility only by way of restrictive legislation, leaving it to the forces of the housing market to provide the necessary dwelling units within a framework of carefully formulated housing standards.

---

[16] See Henry McCulley Muller, *Urban Home Ownership. A Socio-Economic Analysis with Emphasis on Philadelphia.* Philadelphia: 1947, pp. 73-79.

In the wake of such reform legislation, there followed late in the 19th and early in the 20th centuries, the era of reform tenements. For obvious reasons, restrictive housing legislation could not be made retroactive. The so-called "pre-law tenements" remained in operation. Some of them are still standing.

Secondhand Housing. With the growing population pressure in the late 19th century, the acceptance of secondhand or third-hand housing became standard practice.

Only a few members of the city population were able to build homes for themselves or to purchase new and "modern" homes at the periphery of the sprawling city. The majority of urban families had to take over where higher status groups had abandoned their homes for construction of a more recent vintage. Some remodeling took place in the process. Large mansions were refashioned for use as multiple-dwelling structures. Kitchen facilities and sanitary facilities were duplicated and multiplied. Awkward makeshift arrangements were forced upon the remodeling process, to impinge for ever after upon the usefulness of such quarters. Only a small number of homes in the American city are built for the people who live in them.[17]

Home Ownership. Since the turn of the century, home owner-

TABLE XV

INCREASE OF URBAN HOME OWNERSHIP

Percentage for Non-Farm Homes in the United States *

Year	Homes Owned	Homes Rented
1890	36.9	63.1
1900	36.5	63.5
1910	38.4	61.6
1920	40.9	59.1
1930	46.0	54.0
1940	41.1	58.9
1950	50.5	49.5 *

* 1950 Census of Housing, Preliminary Reports. U.S. Department of Commerce, Bur. of Census; Series HC-5. No. 1, Feb. 17, 1951.

[17] For the economics of "filtering-down," see Richard U. Ratcliff, *Urban Land Economics.* New York: McGraw-Hill Book Company, Inc., 1949, pp. 321-334.

ship has increased in our urban communities. This put new emphasis upon the construction of one-family housing. The rambling mansions of the 19th century were abandoned for smaller and more compact structures in all but the upper classes of society. The development of factory produced household equipment and increasing wages for domestic service also influenced conditions. The workshop of the housewife, the kitchen, moved closer to the living room. New equipment and new appliances made their appearance on the housing scene. Individual family housing thus became more readily "functionally" obsolescent.

In the busy barter for increasingly improved home conveniences and comfort, social segregation took place on a grandiose scale. The wealthier members of the community found themselves pushed toward the outer belt-line of urban residential construction, while a succession of lower status and income levels followed closely on their heels.

Only the innermost ring of urban residential housing, the slum, remained fairly static. Its development was retarded because its inhabitants were economically excluded from the rush for better housing facilities. This was not, to be sure, a stability of health and enduring equilibrium, it was a stability of hopeless deterioration, of slow death and social disorganization.[18]

Service Apartments. In the 1920's came the construction, on a sizable scale, of so-called service apartments. These multiple dwellings followed in the tradition of the tenements of the 19th century. They opened a new trend, however, in that they directed themselves to the needs and to the financial resources of an entirely different section of the urban population.[19]

These new apartment buildings provide shelter for relatively high-

---

[18] "Life . . . in blighted districts is becoming more and more squalid, wretched and intolerable. The health, safety and morals of some 25 millions of Americans are being seriously affected by the sub-standard housing, smoke, noise, vermin, dangers, confusion, and sordidness of slum and blighted areas, and the central business districts of cities are confronted with demands for rent reduction, tax delinquency, mortgage foreclosures, inability to maintain properties, flight of best customers to suburban areas, and numerous other problems." S. E. Sanders and A. J. Rabuck, *New City Patterns*. New York: Reinhold Publishing Corporation, 1946, pp. 4-6; see also Chapter 6.

[19] "The final form of multiple-family housing is, of course, the apartment. . . . Instead of ownership lodging with one of the residents of the building, the owner may be a corporation, with bond issues and stocks. Service has become centralized. Instead of separate heating plants for each home there is a central

salaried employees who want housing close to their places of work in the central business district. Now proximity to place of work is linked to the acceptance of rental housing and to the acceptance of multiple dwelling structures. It is linked to limited space in the individual apartment and the absence of outdoor spaces for adult recreation and children's play.

Some recompensation for these limitations is offered through rational design which guarantees the best possible usage of available space. Crowding is made bearable by the installment of efficient equipment and by the provision for centralized services (laundries, restaurants, nurseries, and so forth) to replace the household chores of a former day.[20]

A motley crowd of renters tends to assemble in these apartment buildings. They are used as bachelor's quarters (male or female); they lead to the formation of quasi-families on the part of two or

---

plant. The care of the building is entrusted to a paid janitor. The tendency is more and more to furnish *service* with the building as well as mere shelter, and in some cases this approaches hotel service, with maids, dining-rooms, garages, and so forth." George S. Wehrwein and Coleman Woodbury, "Tenancy versus Ownership as a Problem in Urban Land Utilization," *The Annals* of the American Academy of Political and Social Science, Vol. 143 (March, 1930), pp. 185-186.

"During the past few years a new type of multi-family housing unit, the apartment house, has been introduced into American cities. It is distinguishable from the older forms of multi-family dwelling known as the tenement house chiefly because of the better class of construction, the modern conveniences, and the high class character with which its promoter endowed it." Harland Bartholomew, *Urban Land Uses*. Cambridge: Harvard University Press, 1932, p. 43.

[20] "The movement into apartments is not solely because of greater economy. Many modern apartments cost more per family than good single family homes, but they have more rooms, are furnished more expensively, and the services rendered are more elaborate. Modern construction and invention have provided new comforts and conveniences, which are entirely absent or else very costly in the usual home. This is in line with the modern way of living. Women have more and more interests outside the home, and the workshop part of the house has shrunk in proportion. . . . Mechanical devices have taken the place of the vanishing servant, whose domain was once the single family home." George S. Wehrwein and Coleman Woodbury, *op. cit.*, p. 193.

"For many families . . . it will be well to provide more well-serviced apartment houses, or closely grouped single dwellings with various communal services. . . . Houses need to be planned with a view toward the cooperative employment of servants, the convenience of collective nursery rooms and nursery schools, and restaurants or other communal cooking and eating arrangements." Joseph Kirk Folsom, *The Family and Democratic Society*. New York: John Wiley and Sons, Inc., 1943, p. 573.

more single individuals inclined to set up joint housekeeping. The influx, after World War I, of female clerical workers to our large urban centers overflowed the previously customary boarding-house pattern of housing for the unattached, and had a great deal to do with the success of the modern service apartment in the 1920's.[21] Families are not entirely absent from this scene. At no point of the development, however, did the American public accept these downtown apartment structures as a suitable place for the raising of children. In the American scene, the renter never managed to escape the stigma attached either to the poverty of the early tenement dwellers, or the stigma attached to the service apartment, the inhabitants of which are thought of as shirking the duties of housekeeping chores, and the more important one of child raising.

Subsidized Housing. In recent decades, a variety of circumstances has called the attention of the public to the need for low-cost housing. "Housing" as a social movement starts with the assumption that housing facilities with certain minimum requirements must be made available to all members of the community, regardless of purchasing power, and in particular consideration of their willingness to raise children.[22]

This objective is very much in dispute. It originated in connection with other reform movements before and after the turn of the century. A full-fledged housing movement is nowhere experienced before the later stages of the industrialization period.[23] The housing movement is based upon the idea of joint community responsibility for the attainment of minimum living standards for all its citizens,

---

[21] "The over-all picture . . . is one of inadequate living-arrangements for the great bulk of the unattached population in American cities." Arnold M. Rose, "Living Arrangements of Unattached Persons," *American Sociological Review*, Vol. 12, No. 4 (August, 1947), p. 435.

[22] "We need to determine whether a certain facility is a private or public responsibility. If it is regarded by a community or nation as so essential, that everyone should have it, irrespective of the individual's ability to pay for it, the community maintains it." Louis Wirth, "The Strategy of Community Planning," in *Community Planning for Peace Time Living.* Stanford: Stanford University Press, 1946, p. 17.

The case for public housing is stated in Nathan Straus, *The Seven Myths of Housing.* New York: Alfred A. Knopf, 1944.

[23] A survey of housing measures in different European countries is offered in Catherine Bauer, *Modern Housing.* Boston: Houghton Mifflin Company, 1934, pp. 260-302.

particularly the responsibility of the community to give a "fair chance" for self-advancement to all its children.

Subsidized low-cost housing thus enters upon the contemporary housing scene. Initially carried by philanthropy, the provision of low-cost housing has now become the responsibility of our government. Under such auspices, it has become possible to consider, after a century of hand-me-downs and conversions, the building of homes directly for people with modest means. Such housing will have to remain economy housing, yet it will be geared to specific needs of the people who are going to inhabit these dwelling units.

This is the most striking achievement of modern housing. It eliminates the measuring rod of status as related to the age of housing facilities. It directs the attention of the architect to a highly differentiated system of contemporary family needs.[24] It restricts the sway of fad and fashion, it restricts abuses of conspicuous consumption in the contemporary housing scene.

THE IDEA OF FUNCTIONAL HOUSING

The Concept. Modern functional housing is concerned with the establishment of clear-cut means-ends relations in architecture and physical construction.[25] Modern functional architecture has been promoted by architects, craftsmen, engineers, and intellectuals who proclaimed the need for a new "morality" in physical construction.[26] They reacted against the spurious use of ornamentation, against the arbitrary application of different exotic styles in the private and public construction of the 19th century. They complained about the dishonesty inherent in building practices which allowed willful ornamentation to dominate construction and the purposes it was to serve. They deplored the loss of a meaningful relationship between the appearance and the function of any given structure.

---

[24] See Svend Riemer, "Architecture for Family Living," *op. cit.*

[25] "It (modern functional architecture) aims at once more relating methods of building as closely as possible to real needs. In fact it is nothing more nor less than the exact modern equivalent of the architecture that flourished in previous ages, but fell into decay during the last century through architects having got out of touch with life and having forgotten what architecture was really for." J. M. Richards, *An Introduction to Modern Architecture.* Hammondsworth, Middlesex, England: Penguin Books Limited, 1940, p. 10.

[26] "We are returning to honesty of thought and feeling." Walter Gropius, *The New Architecture and the Bauhaus.* London: Faber and Faber Limited, 1935, p. 17.

Private residences had been decorated in Gothic, Oriental, Classic, Renaissance, or Romanesque style without any apparent relationship between these style elements and the way of life assumed by the occupant. Not even individual tastes and preferences or esthetic considerations were, necessarily, the determinant factor in the selection of the individual family residence.

Fashions and fads ruled the taste of the hour. At times these fashions coincided with similar preoccupations in other leisure time activities. The Gothic revival coincided with the superficial romantic indulgence in the novels by Sir Walter Scott in the early decades of the 19th century.[27] Both private and public buildings were affected. European and American arctitecture both participated in a wild spree of medieval embellishment. The absurd discrepancy between style and function was only too obvious where an efficient municipal administration housed itself in construction topped with the defensive ramparts of a medieval burgh.

Modern architects rebelled against the obvious incongruity between the structure and its function. The architect of the 19th century was called to task for his interest in the ornamentation of a building while simultantously neglecting the design of the basic structure. The important functions of a building were distorted to provide more surface for ornamental stucco façades. Waste space was a standard feature of residential construction, which abounded in picturesque nooks, corners, and turrets, flattering the fancy while forgetting the real needs of the occupant.

Obsolete Function. In a manner of speaking, we may even consider the ostentatious mansions, the fake castles and palaces, the Greek-temple banks, and the Gothic college dormitories as functional; to do so we have to use the term in its widest connotations. The ornamental use of historical style-elements in structures devoted to functions incompatible with the images of Greece, Rome, Carcassonne, or Venice reveals an attitude interesting in itself.

---

[27] "Sir Walter Scott is probably responsible for the Capitol building (in Baton Rouge); for it is not conceivable that this little sham castle would ever have been built if he had not run the people mad, a couple of generations ago, with his medieval romances . . . it is pathetic to see this architectural falsehood undergoing restoration and perpetuation in our day, when it would have been so easy to let dynamite finish what a charitable fire began, and then devote this restoration money to the building of something genuine." Mark Twain, *Life on the Mississippi*. New York: Bantam Books, 1946, p. 281.

Two conceptions of functional architecture:

I

Relation to Needs and Techniques of
Cultural Environment

| Greek Temple | Medieval Castle | Railroad Flat |

II

Relation to Specific Modern Needs and the
Use of Modern Industrial Techniques

| Devices for Mass Production (one-level plant) (conveyor belt) (access to transportation) | Devices for Informal Family Living (kitchen close to livingroom) (elimination of parlor) (second livingroom for younger generation) | Use of Modern Techniques (flat roof — rainproofed material) (steel construction of tall buildings) (skeleton of ferro-concrete, glass encased) |

It reveals the attitude of the newly rich, who find themselves in the process of conquering a world of natural resources and new techniques in a competitive rush which does not leave time for contemplation and self-expression. Ornamentation is borrowed from the open book of history. The function and purpose of such architecture is pomp, ostentation, conspicuous consumption.

The economy housing of the same era does not fare worse if seen in proper perspective. The design and construction of tenements, with their neglect of sun and air penetration, filled the function of providing economy shelter for the immigrant family arriving in this country. Such housing could be made available at low rentals. A maximum of sheltered space was provided in the metropolitan center, on valuable land where even today no better housing can be provided without government subsidy. Privacy, low occupancy standards, the provisions of halls for interior communication, southern exposure, and segregated sanitary facilities were luxuries not available for unskilled immigrant labor.[28]

---

[28] "The New York Tenement Law, which had been passed in 1901, accepted the fact that tenements were commonly built for investment, and on small plots of land; that the investor (or speculator) was not as a rule concerned with the quality of the living conditions, but sought to produce as much rentable space as possible on each lot." George Herbert Gray, *Housing and Citizenship*. New York: Reinhold Publishing Corporation, 1946, p. 11.

If, then, the patrician mansion and the economy shelter of the 19th century can both raise the claim of being "functional" adjustments to existing circumstances and contemporary needs, if both make use of available means of construction and ornamentation for prevailing purposes, if both can be considered "functional" in a special sense of the term, we have to look for more than an emphasis on clear-cut means-ends relations in the message propounded by modern functional architecture.

New Purpose. Modern functional architecture does not gain its foothold in the contemporary scene by stressing function, any function, and teaching us to consider, in any structure, first the utilitarian factors, and second, the esthetic aspects. The message of modern architecture extends to the proclamation of a specific set of ends. It calls our attention to the importance of new and changing functions, of which traditional architecture had remained oblivious.

Modern urban society is not dedicated to any unifying purpose. Temples and cathedrals do not hold the center of the stage. Our churches are hidden in the shadows of Wall Street, or mold themselves, beside bank, courthouse, and postoffice, into the street-front of the small town's public square. Our factories are pushed aside as nuisances. Our railroad stations are submerged in the turmoil of our central Zones of Transition. Our tall office buildings in the center of town perhaps give symbolic expression to administrative powers concentrated in our metropolitan settlements. Specialization is the key-word in modern urban civilization. This leaves us without a common denominator for physical construction. Each building stands on its own merits. It must be evaluated with one criterion in mind only: its usefulness for its own particular purpose.

Residential housing, under the circumstances, gains merit through its fitness for private family living. Private family living, for the first time in history, is considered an end in itself. It is not made subservient to any ulterior purpose, such as worship, occupational work, wage slavery, or conspicuous consumption. It is freed to be true to itself.

In view of the predominantly negative orientation of the movement of modern "functional" architecture, this problem has never been faced consciously. Modern residential housing has been freed from subservience to ulterior purposes, but it has not been given a purpose of its own. Under the guise of rebellion and refutation, however, new forces have been stirring. Some sort of tacit agreement seems to stand out with regard to the purposes of modern residential construction:

1. The recuperative functions of private family living have become the primary concern of the residential architect.

2. Comfort is stressed rather than efficiency of production; convenience rather than high standards of performance.

3. The recuperative functions of indoor and outdoor living are moved into juxtaposition to each other; they are planned to supplement and interpenetrate each other.

4. Gregarious patterns of home life are given preference over requirements for privacy, specialization of activities, and individual isolation inside the family home.

These 4 emphases of functional residential architecture have something in common. They all are reactions against the specialized, efficient, closed-in, and enervating performances demanded of the modern city-dweller during the workday.

The main purpose of modern residential housing is informal relaxation and recuperation. Remaining housekeeping chores are not rationalized with increased efficiencies of home production and food preparation in mind, but geared to the reduction of labor and the avoidance of discomfort. In reaction to the strain of our occupational lives, ours is a home culture that relaxes from strain and sends us back — with some of our energies restored — to factories and office buildings.

HISTORICAL BACKGROUNDS OF FUNCTIONAL ARCHITECTURE

Functionalism in modern architecture is the hybrid child of both rational and romantic tendencies. John Ruskin and William Morris, in England, made themselves spokesmen for a revival of the "organic" qualities inherent in good architecture. They rejected, early in the 19th century, the jumble of style elements that characterized building activities.[29]

John Ruskin. Ruskin glorified medieval architecture as a true expression of the spiritual qualities of an era. He observed the close interrelationship in medieval architecture between available tech-

---

[29] For historical backgrounds, see J. M. Richards, *op. cit.*, Chapter V, "The Growth of the Idea," pp. 54-68.

niques and modes of expression. He admired the naturalness and spiritual honesty of medieval construction. He saw how, in the Middle Ages, esthetic values had been the natural outcome of available construction methods.

Ruskin glorified medieval architecture in contrast to "dishonest" ornamentation, in contrast to arbitrary, meaningless, and artificial use of style elements unrelated to the inherent purposes of a building. But he was unable to achieve more in this manner than to create a new fashion of design and ornamentation, a preference for pseudo-medieval style and construction.[30]

William Morris. William Morris went further in exploiting the object lesson of medieval architecture. His name is associated with the English Arts and Crafts Movement. He pointed his finger at the modern machine as the basic cause for cheap imitations of style and and deterioration of good taste. The machine, he thought, had stepped between the product and the producer, and guided the latter according to its own artificial laws.[31]

To regain a feeling for materials and what they can do if shaped by the human hand and simple tools, William Morris pointed the way back to crafts production. He concerned himself with hand weaving and the construction of simple handmade furniture. In home construction, he favored the use of native materials that easily blended into the site upon which the building was constructed.

William Morris turned his attention to the humble task of providing residential housing instead of trying to gain fame by working on spectacular public buildings. The homes he built were characterized by rustic simplicity; they were built for a pleasant informal life in the country. If they borrowed from any style, it was from that of the native farmer.[32]

The Out-of-Doors. One of the tenets of modern functional archi-

---

[30] "(John Ruskin's) writings are full of serious disquisitions on the philosophy of architecture; but his influence, too, did little more than set a fashion for particular medieval styles." *Ibid.*, p. 55.

[31] "William Morris's struggle to restore the spirit of hand-craftsmanship in the face of the advancing power of machinery has already been spoken of. But in spite of this struggle being doomed to failure he has a very important place in the early history of modern architecture. This place is symbolized by the house at Bexley Heath in Kent, which he had built for himself in 1859." *Ibid.*, p. 56.

[32] The publication that linked English experimentation with domestic architecture to the development of functional architecture on the continent was Hermann von Muthesius, *Das Englische Landhaus. Berlin:* Wasmuth, 1904.

tecture is the demand for a close relationship between indoor and outdoor living, the demand for a home life close to the heart of nature. The tendency to place indoor design in direct relationship with the garden outdoors, the park, or the uncultivated countryside goes back far beyond William Morris. It goes back to the days when the city fortifications were eliminated as useless because of the invention of gunpowder.

In the France of the 17th and 18th centuries, the rational design of interior space projected out into the landscape. Garden and park continued a motif first presented in the pattern of an interior floor plan. A park-like landscape surrounds the famous Palace of Versailles, with every path and opening in the woods, every highway leading as far as Paris seen in relationship to the rational layout of rooms in this late Renaissance castle.

Later, the procedure was reversed. In English park planning, the landscape was left close to the original state of nature with pleasing views and scenic surprises. Romantically, all traces of man-made rational design were eliminated. Natural growth was encouraged, and irrational changes and shifts of scenery were accentuated.[33]

In the long run, this cultivation of nature had its repercussions upon the interior design of residential architecture. The floor plan lost its domination by a symmetrical interior design. It rambled loosely and informally, according to the needs of the occupants.

Rational Construction. The other source of modern functional architecture emphasizes rational design and the use of modern construction methods. It reached residential housing much later. This trend was progressive rather than romantic and reactionary. It did not reject the modern machine, but tried to bend it to use for human purpose.

Modern functional architecture learned to borrow from the engineering feats of the 19th century. For a long time, new construction methods had not been permitted to exert their influence upon domestic architecture. The use of cast iron as a support for construction, of ferro-concrete, and, later, of steel girders was long limited to other purposes than residential construction. As these techniques advanced, the engineer crowded into fields previously

---

[33] See Puckler-Muskau, Fuerst von, Hermann Ludwig Heinrich: *Hints on Landscape Gardening.* Boston: Houghton Mifflin and Company, 1917. The belated translation of an early German publication.

reserved to the architect. He built bridges and tried his hand at the construction of large public buildings.

Public Buildings. The Crystal Palace of London's first International Exhibition in 1851 was not only the first building to apply cast iron construction; it was also the first prefabricated building with factory-produced parts, a building easily assembled on the site and later removed to a different location.

The large vaults of the growing national libraries in France, England, and Switzerland posed problems of construction that demanded the co-operation of the modern engineer. Warehouses, railroad stations, factory buildings, and department stores had to avail themselves of construction methods which made it possible to enclose large interior spaces and yet keep them open to the penetration of sunlight. Where stronger supports could be used more sparingly, glass could be used as a wall surface to an increasing extent.

The Skyscraper. From the use of such construction methods in the warehouse and the department store, it was only a step to their use in the modern office building. In the 1880's, the Chicago School of Architecture built up the "loop" of that city in an unprecedented manner. Here the modern skyscraper was born.[34]

This development came to an abrupt conclusion with Chicago's International Exhibition of 1893 which turned the attention from modern construction methods to the neo-classicist architecture cultivated at the Beaux Arts school of architecture in Paris.[35] The new continent forsook the potentialities inherent in the lack of stultifying traditions. For years to come, delight in unnecessary ornamentation was to crowd out concern with the purposeful application of new materials and new construction methods.

L'Art Nouveau. Shortly before the end of the 19th century, the 2 trends that fed the development of a modern functional architecture met. They met in Belgium, both of them contributing to the *l'art nouveau* movement.[36]

---

[34] J. M. Richards calls the skyscraper "the disappointing child of four grandparents: steel frame building construction, the electric lift, high city land-values, and the American belief in competitive advertising." *Op. cit.*, p. 63.

[35] "In Sullivan's own words spoken at the time: 'thus architecture died in the land of the free and the home of the brave — in a land declaring its democracy, inventiveness, unique daring, enterprise and progress. . . . The damage wrought by the World's Fair will last for half a century from its date, if not longer.'" *Ibid.*, p. 64.

[36] For *l'art nouveau*, see *Ibid.*, pp. 59-61.

Like the teachings of Ruskin and Morris, *l'art nouveau* asserted that structure, rather than ornamentation, was to be the true basis of architecture. Not all the artists and architects of this circle shared with Ruskin and Morris the contempt for the modern machine. They did not limit themselves to the re-creation of simple medieval crafts production. They looked and searched for new forms adapted to the age of industrialization.

They were concerned with more than architecture. They were concerned with the beauty of utensils and tools to serve the needs of everyday living. This beauty was not necessarily to be hand-shaped. To do justice to the way of life of the 19th century, the possibilities of machine production were conscientiously exploited. Yet the machine was no longer used to mass-produce cheap imitations of the hand-carved and hand-knit household goods of a former era. The machine was encouraged to be true to itself. The perfection of simple and utilitarian forms was no longer distorted to give the false appearance of hand-produced irregularities. Appreciation of the type of beauty was developed which today we like to call streamlined.

The *l'art nouveau* movement had many cobwebs to brush away. During the 19th century, the adherence to different "styles" of construction had been frozen into so many dogmatic codes. The creative urge of young architects and artists yearned for freedom from formula. They abandoned accredited patterns of design and learned to see things in a different way. Flowery, informal lines of decoration wound their way through interior hallways and staircases. A new style of ornamentation was added to the existing ones: the style of *l'art nouveau*, with winding, meandering, circling lines, which refuted definition in terms of any historical style.

New Techniques. A more enduring contribution of *l'art nouveau* was its affirmative attitude toward the unlimited possibilities inherent in modern techniques. Once the spell of dogmatic historical imitations had been broken, the scene had been cleared for the self-expression of the machine age.

The beauty of simplicity and economic purpose inherent in American patent furniture was rediscovered only lately.[37] But supporting walls were freed from distracting stucco ornamentation. Iron con-

---

[37] Siegfried Giedion, *Mechanization Takes Command*. New York: Oxford University Press, 1948, "Patent Furniture and Ruling Taste," pp. 389-396.

struction was allowed to remain visible, thus adding new esthetic values to contemporary buildings. Structural elements were not hidden away shamefacedly as something ugly and vulgar. If there was to be beauty in modern construction, it was to flow from purpose and structure rather than from ornamentation plastered on top of it.

The Bauhaus. In the German *Bauhaus*, a school of architecture and industrial design, the creed of functional architecture achieved concise formulation.[38] Principles of fitness-to-purpose were now applied to industrial buildings, as well as to residences, machines, motor cars, school buildings, household articles, and industrial tools. Engineer, architect, and designer now worked together as a team to give fit expression to the modern urban environment.[39]

Frank Lloyd Wright. Two gigantic masters of modern architecture carry the zest of "functionalism" into the contemporary scene: Frank Lloyd Wright [40] and Le Corbusier.[41] The former, with his farm background in the Middle West of this country, retains many of the romantic elements of the movement. Like Morris, he searches for simple, regional materials that will easily blend into the building site. The family homes from his drafting board appear as refuges from modern civilization.

As the genius he is, however, he branches out beyond personal idiosyncracies and aids in the development of the modern office building, the hotel, the museum, and other public buildings. He ingeniously tests the possibilities of modern construction methods, and

---

38 The new architecture was to be "simply the inevitable logical product of the intellectual, social and technical conditions of our age." Walter Gropius, *The New Architecture and the Bauhaus.* London: Faber and Faber Limited, 1935, p. 18.

For designs from the Bauhaus and its philosophy, see also Herbert Bayer, Walter Gropius, and Ilse Gropius, editors, *Bauhaus, 1919-1928.* New York: The Museum of Modern Art, 1938.

39 "Peter Behrens, the most important of the new Continental architects, was appointed, as a result of the Werkbund movement, by one of the leading electrical firms in Germany, the A.E.G., both as architect *and as designer of their products, and even their advertisements.* His appointment is a landmark: once more the architect was in his rightful position as the expert on design and master of the machine." J. M. Richards, *op. cit.,* p. 62.

40 For an introduction to the work of Frank Lloyd Wright, see his book, *An Autobiography.* New York: Longman's Green and Company, 1932.

41 Two recent publications will furnish excellent introductions to the ideas of this eminent author and architect: Le Corbusier, *Concerning Town Planning.* London: The Architectural Press, 1947; and *When the Cathedrals Were White.* New York: Reynal & Hitchcock, 1947.

applies them to contemporary demand. He tries to envision and proclaim the needs of the future.

Le Corbusier. Le Corbusier's work is more closely allied to modern engineering feats. He does not flee from modern civilization; he worships it. Almost playfully, yet to definite purpose, he experiments with the possibilities of modern construction methods.

He delights in having his buildings start on the second floor, because modern steel construction can do just that. He wants fewer, but higher skyscrapers to allow for the influx of air and sunlight into the dwellings of the city center.[42] He does not want his buildings to blend into nature; he wants them to master nature. He wants to create a man-made environment to fit the purposes of modern existence. He wants to master modern civilization, or perish in the process. For him, there is no escape.

There are none, in the younger generation of architects, to equal the grandeur of these two. The most important task of modern residential architecture seems to be a tenacious fight against the appalling lag of contemporary tastes which survive despite the inconveniences they impose upon the modern way of life.

SOME ECONOMIC ASPECTS OF HOUSING

Basic Needs. To many, the problem of getting any housing at all is more important than the problem of architecture and purposeful design. The housing supply in Western civilization is far from adequate.[43]

American housing is more ample than that of Russia, France, or Germany, and most other countries. But whether the housing supply of a nation is adequate or not must be considered a matter of consumer opinion, dependent upon the ambition of its citizenry. The play of forces on a free market does not necessarily alleviate the pressure of urgent needs.[44]

Consumer purchasing power is not necessarily spent wisely. Whether it is or not, to be sure, is a matter of value judgment. Without hesitation, however, we can state that a large section of the popu-

---

[42] "The skyscrapers of New York are too small and there are too many of them." Le Corbusier, *When the Cathedrals Were White, op. cit.,* p. 55.

[43] For an estimate of housing needs in the United States, see Charles Abrams, *The Future of Housing.* New York: Harper & Brothers, 1946, pp. 62-71.

[44] The interplay of market forces to be considered in the estimation of housing needs is best discussed in Alexander Block, *Estimating Housing Needs.* London: The Architectural Press, 1946.

lation of the United States is not provided with housing that answers family needs according to prevailing opinion.[45] Different goods compete on the market for the purchasing power of the consumer. The individual dollar held by our urban consumers is not attracted in the direction of housing to an extent at which desirable housing standards could be obtained.[46]

Housing involves a commitment to a fixed level of expenditures

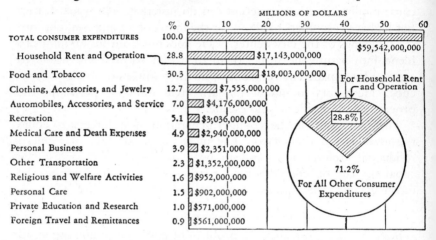

MILLIONS OF DOLLARS

	%						
		0	10	20	30	40	50	60
TOTAL CONSUMER EXPENDITURES	100.0						$59,542,000,000
Household Rent and Operation	28.8			$17,143,000,000			
Food and Tobacco	30.3			$18,003,000,000			
Clothing, Accessories, and Jewelry	12.7		$7,555,000,000				
Automobiles, Accessories, and Service	7.0	$4,176,000,000					
Recreation	5.1	$3,036,000,000					
Medical Care and Death Expenses	4.9	$2,940,000,000					
Personal Business	3.9	$2,351,000,000					
Other Transportation	2.3	$1,352,000,000					
Religious and Welfare Activities	1.6	$952,000,000					
Personal Care	1.5	$902,000,000					
Private Education and Research	1.0	$571,000,000					
Foreign Travel and Remittances	0.9	$561,000,000					

For Household Rent and Operation

28.8%

71.2%
For All Other Consumer Expenditures

FIGURE 18. Housing in the Consumer's Budget. Average for 1930-1939. From: Svend Riemer, Designing the Family Home, in *Marriage, Family and Parenthood*, edited by Howard Becker and Reuben Hill. Boston: D. C. Heath and Company, 1948, p. 505.

reaching far into the future. Economic insecurities, labor turnover, and industrial fluctuations cause the avoidance of such commitments on the part of the economically less firmly established members of of the urban community.

This is true even with regard to rental housing, where the cost of moving and the loss of local credit act as impediments to frequent

[45] "What sort of homes do the American people live in? One-third good. One-third fair. One-third bad." Edith Elmer Wood, *Introduction to Housing. Facts and Principles*. Federal Works Agency, United States Housing Authority. Washington, D.C.: U.S. Government Printing Office, reprinted May 1940, p. 9.
[46] "Housing came second in order of outlay (1935-36)), taking $9.5 billion, of 16 percent of income. . . . Household operation formed the third largest group of items, with a total expenditure of $5.3 billion — nine percent of total income." *Consumer Expenditures in the United States. Estimates for 1935-36*. National Resources Committee. Washington, D.C.: U.S. Government Printing Office, 1939, p. 5.

change. To pay for adequate family housing requires a degree of economic security not within the reach of large sections of our population.

Industrial Organization. Another point to be considered is the somewhat parochial organization of our housing industry.[47] It is small business, local business, which rarely avails itself of the advantages of mass-prefabrication of either parts or total units. Production methods lag behind the general trend toward cost-reducing efficiency.

The consumer's dollar finds its way easily into channels where more spectacular advances in the level of living are promised in exchange for expenditures. Radios and cars — both factory produced — are bought instead of housing space. The level of nutrition may be improved instead of the level of home living. The trend toward the small compact modern house must be understood in connection with differential advancement in industrial organization. Space is relatively expensive because it is produced on a crafts basis. Our dwelling units are reduced in size and made tolerable by the installment of mass-produced efficiency equipment.

Community Responsibility. To meet prevailing needs in the housing field, and to turn them into effective demands, is no easy matter. A variety of crutches are provided to enable the consumer to get what he wants. They range all the way from loan insurance to outright subsidy. For decades the government has assumed the responsibility to fill the gap between needs and effective demand. Loans on second and first mortgages are insured to pump more money into the housing market (Federal Housing Administration). Our financial institutions have developed loan instruments that make it possible for the consumer to buy a house by committing his earning power for many years to come.

IMPLEMENTATION OF SUBSIDIZED HOUSING

Public assistance to urban housing has in principle been offered in two ways:

(1) The former *United States Housing Authority* gave loans and offered outright subsidies to local housing authorities for slum clear-

---

[47] For the economic and social structure of the American housing industry, see *American Housing. Problems and Prospects.* New York: The Twentieth Century Fund, 1947, Chapter 2, The House as an Industrial Product, pp. 38-58.

ance. Small, well planned neighborhoods were created to replace demolished slum housing. Eligibility to occupy the new houses was limited according to need (i.e. number of children, income, previous location of residence, etc.) and to a certain extent also according to ability to take advantage of offered conveniences in the improvement of morale. Rents were adjusted on a sliding scale according to family income. The excess of costs over income was in part covered by funds of the Federal Agency.

(2) The *Federal Housing Authority* limited itself to the insurance of loans made by various credit institutions for the purchase of family residences. This indirect means of assistance was aimed to help wide ranges of the middle classes, who were able to squeeze the purchase of a home into the family budget only on a long-term credit basis. The security of Federal insurance made it possible to offer loans at reasonable cost. Since loans were granted only when certain normative standards were met and on the basis of an official evaluation of the property, they contributed to the stabilizing of the housing market.

In the changing contemporary scene, these two basic principles of subsidy are still used, although carried by new agencies and supported by sometimes ample, sometimes scanty means, according to political expediency.*

Low-cost rental units are put at the disposal of needy families in the lower income groups. This is done by subsidy and loans for building activities initiated by local housing authorities to meet local needs (U.S. Housing Authority). Insurance companies have invested large amounts of money — tax-free but at low interest rates — in large scale rental housing projects in our metropolitan centers.

Underlying all these activities is the idea that the effect of housing conditions upon our children is so important that their needs should be considered even where purchasing power fails. Housing at adequate standards should be available to all, regardless of their ability to pay. Housing may be considered somewhat like a public utility; it may be considered a matter of public as well as private responsibility.

---

* From: Svend Riemer: "Designing the Family Home," in *Family Marriage and Parenthood*, edited by Howard Becker and Reuben Hill. New York: D. C. Heath and Company, 1948, p. 508.

Home Ownership. During the last half-century, home ownership has been increased in the United States. It is tied to the ideal of the permanent family home with ample play space for children easily supervised from the kitchen window, and to prestige in the community because the ownership of real estate is associated with civic responsibility and interest in community affairs.[48]

There is nothing wrong with the dream of home ownership, as long as certain pitfalls are avoided. In the purchase of a family home, the hidden costs of assessments, taxation, and maintenance are easily ignored. No future home owner should tell himself that he will "pay like rent," and in the end will "have something saved up." That is not necessarily so. Our homes are being used up while they are being paid for. They deteriorate physically, and they become obsolescent "functionally," due to new inventions, equipment that was not foreseen at the time of home construction, and to new fads and fashions as well as undesirable changes in the neighborhood. At resale, there may be something left over. It all depends upon the purchase of the home as a business venture.

SELECTED READINGS

1. J. M. Richards, *An Introduction to Modern Architecture.* Harmondsworth, Middlesex, England: Penguin Books Limited, 1940, pp. 9-80.

2. James Ford, *Slums and Housing.* Cambridge: Harvard University Press, 1936, Vol. I, pp. 1-509.

3. *The Livability Problems of 1,000 Families.* Federal Public Housing Authority, National Housing Agency, Bulletin No. 28. Washington, D.C.: U.S. Government Printing Office, 1945, pp. 1-67.

4. Nathan Straus, *The Seven Myths of Housing.* New York: Alfred A. Knopf, 1944, pp. 3-227.

5. *American Housing. Problems and Prospects.* New York: The Twentieth Century Fund, 1947, pp. 3-171.

PROBLEMS

1. *Status and Change of Local Housing Conditions, 1940-50.* This problem is based entirely upon the use of materials derived from the U.S. Census of Housing for the years 1940 and 1950.

   Select one or several urban communities from your state, a neighboring state, or the state in which your university or college is lo-

---

[48] Problems of home ownership are excellently discussed in John P. Dean, *Home Ownership: Is It Sound?* New York: Harper & Brothers, 1945.

cated. Compare housing conditions in these communities with regard to the information offered in the U.S. Census.

You will find interesting data about facilities available, about home ownership and other types of tenure, about crowding and size of homes, and about the relative numerical importance of one-family and multiple dwellings. Record the change of these conditions between 1940 and 1950 in simple tables and graphs.

The value of your contribution will be increased (1) by the amount of comparative materials drawn into the picture, and (2) by the explanations you may be able to offer for differences, similarities, and patterns of change.

Comparative data should certainly be furnished for the state and the nation as a whole, for neighboring states, and for other urban communities.

2. *Social Values in Functional Architecture.* Acquaint yourself with the work of one of the leading modern architects. This will require some library work. You will want to know what these architects have written; more important, study their designs. Books and articles, moreover, have been written about these prominent architects. They are also mentioned in texts and other books about modern architecture. You will have to canvass periodicals as well as magazines for helpful information.

Frank Lloyd Wright, Le Corbusier, and Gropius are strongly recommended as objects of your study because they have expressed themselves freely about the objectives of their work, and they have been freely discussed by others.

Study in detail architectural design as well as the written word of the man you have selected, and take notes as you go along. Record functional features of the design promoted and invented. Account for the social objectives to which your architect has dedicated his work. Although the architect tries to design functionally and usefully, you have to answer the question, "Useful for what?" What social values has he tried to serve? Can you interpret his work as a consistent effort to serve definite social values?

3. *Factors Determining Local Housing Needs.* Consult Alexander Block, *Estimating Housing Needs.* London: The Architectural Press, 1946; and Edith Elmer Wood, *An Introduction to Housing.* Federal Works Agency, U.S. Housing Authority. Washington, D.C.: U.S. Government Printing Office, reprinted May, 1940.

From these sources, compile systematically a list of the type of information needed to estimate the future housing needs in some urban community in this country. Go as far as you can in compiling this information. The closer you get to an actual estimate, the better your contribution will be.

You may add a critical analysis of other estimates made for urban communities, states, or the nation as a whole.

CHAPTER 17

Neighborhood Planning

A New Perspective. The beauty of modern residential architecture is not apparent from a fixed point of observation. We do not recognize the charm of a modern housing project by staring at the standardized dwelling units which repeat themselves monotonously in shape and form. The well-planned neighborhood spreads out like a fan as we drive by.

In movement, the logic and design of the street system is translated into visual experience. The neighborhood alternately opens up with hospitable welcome or turns its back to protect itself against intrusion. It beckons and withdraws. It gives a glimpse of interior parks and playgrounds to stir our envy. Some monumental buildings, a market place or community center may try to impress us with the dignity of a well-organized environment for friendly, neighborly living.

The modern real estate development requires that we retrain our powers of observation. From the contemplation of static perspectives, we are called to an appreciation of moving patterns. Such fundamental change in attitude occurs slowly. Much resistence will have to be overcome before we can call ourselves free to delight in the residential architecture of the 20th century.

The residential architecture of the 19th century was built for the pedestrian observer. He stood transfixed in front of the individual family mansion. Behind the foil of trees and shrubberies, well

411

framed by a decorative garden lot, the structure rose to express grandeur and pride, shelter and coziness.

If this type of architecture is seen from a passing automobile, the eye is unable to rest peacefully upon the ornamental detail. The variety of design produces confusion. The inability to absorb changing and irrelevant details causes irritation and esthetic dissatisfaction. The speed of the car demands an architecture cast into a different mold.

Backgrounds of Neighborhood Planning

Origins. Esthetic considerations, however, do not explain the contemporary demand for neighborhood planning and large scale real estate developments. Different historical sources contribute to this unique feature of contemporary housing in the city. Some of the most important backgrounds of modern neighborhood planning are: (1) the Garden City Movement; (2) large scale real estate developments; (3) the settlement movement; (4) concern with natural areas in the modern city; (5) problems of social control; and (6) economies of design, construction, and operation.

Garden City Movement. The Garden City Movement is closely associated with the name of Ebenezer Howard, who, at the turn of the century, published a book in which he proposed a systematic reform of modern city planning. The book appeared first in 1898 under the title *Tomorrow: A Peaceful Path to Real Reform;* in 1902 it was republished under the more revealing title: *Garden Cities of Tomorrow.*[1]

The first title reveals clearly that more than a technical innovation in the field of city planning was intended. Interest in the Garden City grew as part of the social reform movement that flourished at the turn of the century. At that time, the industrialization process showed the first signs of slowing down. The exuberance of early industrial expansion had worn out, and social reformers found time to look around and assess some of the effects of the machine age.[2]

---

[1] In recent years, this book has been reprinted with an instructive contribution by Lewis Mumford on "The Garden City Idea and Modern Planning." See Ebenezer Howard, *Garden Citites of To-Morrow.* London: Faber and Faber Ltd., 1945.

[2] For the onset of reform movements in the industrialized cities of England, see J. L. Hammond and Barbara Hammond, *The Bleak Age.* New York: Penguin Books, 1947.

What they saw, in our large cities, was not good. The urban pioneers of machine production had encapsuled themselves in a desert of stone from which there was no escape. London, the capital of an empire, sprawled far into its hinterland in a confusion of unplanned growth. The smoke of factories enveloped large residential sections. Crowded quarters in the central city lacked open parks and playgrounds.[3]

In this situation, Ebenezer Howard conceived the idea of stopping the growth of the modern metropolis. He suggested that the suburban sprawl be replaced by the construction of self-contained communities removed from the orbit of the built-up metropolis. These garden cities were to fulfill 2 requirements. They were to contain sufficient occupational opportunities within their own confines to make commuting to the central city the exception rather than the rule; and they were to be separated from the central city by a green belt of open land never to be used for purposes of urban construction.

Ebenezer Howard combined with his vision the businessman's interest in practical detail. He coped with the legal, economic, and architectural problems of the Garden City movement which he had initiated. Letchworth and Welwyn, in the outskirts of London, stand as examples of what he was striving for.

Residential planning was considered, in the Garden City movement, a tool for the fundamental refashioning of our urban civilization.[4] The Garden City did not limit itself to concern with physical shelter. It was to reshape the urban way of life. It failed in its main objective, but it sowed the seed for many ideas and useful improvements still to be implemented in modern neighborhood planning.

Real Estate Developments. It is frequently overlooked that neighborhood planning has been practiced by realtors and contractors concerned with just plain business. They stumbled into neighborhood planning without welfare considerations. In the growing modern city, they were faced with the problem of how to protect real estate values against depreciation brought about by the intrusion of undesirable land uses.

---

[3] For the squalor of towns during the earlier phases of the industrialization period, see *Ibid.*, Chapter VI, "The Loss of Playgrounds," pp. 52-90.

[4] "The Garden City, as Howard defined it, is not a suburb but the antithesis of a suburb: not a more rural retreat, but a more integrated foundation for an effective urban life." Lewis Mumford, "The Garden City Idea and Modern Planning," in Ebenezer Howard, *op. cit.*, p. 35.

Some contractors went so far as to throw walls around small surburban settlements. Individual homes were attractively arranged around a central park or playfield remindful of the old village green. A building to hold the social functions of the community was provided as a focus of interest. At times, there was even a swimming pool. Residents of the neighborhood thus had access to services otherwise provided in the country club.

Residents of such "guaranteed" neighborhoods were carefully screened before being admitted to ownership of private homes and membership in the community. Protection of this nature is expensive, and therefore, the "guaranteed" neighborhood remained a phenomenon closely linked to advanced economic status.

Some features of neighborhood planning result naturally from the scope of modern real estate developments. We know about the speculative building boom in Florida during the 1920's. Entire villages and small towns were sprouting at that period, catering to highly standardized demands on the part of a homogeneous clientele. It was both natural and economical to give an appearance of pleasing unity to such real estate development by the use of a uniform style of architecture. Small town centers were planned in their entirety, including banks and restaurants, drug stores and grocery stores.[5] Large scale real estate developments drift automatically in the direction of unified planning.

There are few cities in the United States without real estate developments in the suburbs containing at least some tentative features of neighborhood planning. Prominent among such features is a layout of winding streets, which serves well the purpose of protecting the residential area against unnecessary through traffic. There may be joint lakefront development such as swimming piers and bathing beaches. There may be a community center or a country club in central position. At times, a grade school on ample playgrounds in the center of the village may pull children and parents together into some kind of community living. Consumer preferences lead to various experiments of this kind.

The Settlement Movement. Neighborhood planning has its roots also in concern with social problems. We must remember the settlement movement of the late 19th century. Educational settlements

---

[5] Frederick Lewis Allen, *Only Yesterday. An Informal History of the Nineteen-Twenties.* New York: Bantam Books, 1926, Chapter XI, "Home, Sweet Florida," pp. 301-321.

were established in the central areas of our large metropolitan cities. It was their purpose to make the educator and the social worker, the minister and the doctor, the sociologist and social reformer residents and participants in the neighborhood to which they were carrying their services.[6]

Such professionals sought their way into areas that suffered from poverty and depravation, where juvenile delinquency was rampant, where drunkenness flourished as a relief from sordid environments, where families were torn into fragments of individuals with conflicting interests. They approached the problem through education and enlightenment, by provision of playgrounds and facilities for indoor athletics, by way of extension work that carried the challenge of modern hygiene and nutrition and modern child raising practices into the individual family home.

The pioneers of settlement work must be considered the forerunners of later attempts to give focus to community activities, to provide facilities, and to stimulate constructive citizen participation in community affairs.

Study of "Natural Areas." It was left to the sociologist to discover the constructive forces inherent in close neighborhood living. He discovered these forces at work even in the most disorganized areas of urban residential slum and blight.[7] The sociologist discovered the natural areas as a social fact in all parts of the modern city.[8] The observation of patterns of unplanned association in the large city revealed tendencies toward segregation of unlike people and tendencies toward clustering between people with similar background.

Our mind turns to the clustering of immigrant groups with different nationality backgrounds. Chinatown and Little Sicily are no inventions of the New York tourist trade. They are spontaneous

---

6 "The social settlements had set for themselves the task of reconstruction of city neighborhoods as the best means of approach to social problems. At first, however, their emphasis was not primarily upon the neighborhood as a geographical or social unit but rather upon the people who lived near enough to participate in their activities. The settlement was to be the center of a radiating culture rather than the center of a natural community." Jesse F. Steiner, *Community Organization*. New York: The Century Co., 1930, p. 14-15.

7 See Ernest W. Burgess, "Can Neighborhood Work Have a Scientific Basis?" in Robert E. Park, Ernest W. Burgess, and Roderick D. McKenzie, *The City*. Chicago: The University of Chicago Press, 1925, pp. 142-155.

8 See Harvey W. Zorbaugh, "The Natural Areas of the City," in Ernest W. Burgess, editor, *The Urban Community*. Chicago: The University of Chicago Press, 1926, pp. 219-229.

formations which repeat themselves in other American cities. They indicate lack of assimilation on the part of the ethnic group. With the help of Americanizing influences in school and playgroups, the first and second generations of American born citizens learn to withdraw from the ethnic village within the city and to disperse into less homogeneous residential sections.

While clustering and neighboring of like and like-minded people is most intense in the immigrant communities, it is not limited to these. Less stringent patterns of residential segregation follow lines of income and professional status, are based on race prejudice and different phases of the family cycle. In his private life the urbanite tries to escape the association with heterogeneous crowds.

Natural areas are not limited to homogeneous groupings either. Groups of people *dependent* upon each other for a livelihood are drawn into proximity of each other. Catering services — as furnished by druggist, grocer, shoe-repair shop, and laundryman — find their way into the commercial districts of all but the most exclusive residential neighborhoods, which rely entirely on delivery service and car trips to the nearest shopping district. Our urban natural areas are based upon interdependence relations as well as on homogeneity of the resident population.

This tradition of urban living could not help but influence our thinking about urban residential settlement. Neighborhood planning follows existing patterns of segregation.[9]

At that, neighborhood planning is encouraged at a time when influences of the wider American community are gradually dissolving the need for neighboring on the part of immigrant groups. Neighborhood planning may well revive and re-inforce an otherwise vanishing tendency toward segregation.

Means of Social Control. Sociologists encourage neighborhood planning because it is expected to strengthen informal means of social control.[10] City-ways are far removed from folkways.[11] The

---

[9] Neighborhood planning has been condemned because it is said to re-inforce existing patterns of segregation. See Reginald R. Isaacs, "The 'Neighborhood Unit' is an Instrument for Segregation," *Journal of Housing*, Vol. 5, No. 8 (August, 1948), pp. 215-218.

[10] For rural-urban differences in social control, see Joseph S. Roucek, *Social Control*. New York: D. Van Nostrand Company, Inc., 1947, pp. 68-73.

[11] "Folk societies have certain features in common which enable us to think of them as a type — a type which contrasts with the society of the modern city." Robert Redfield, "The Folk Society," *The American Journal of Sociology*, Vol. LII, No. 4 (January, 1947), pp. 293.

law and the police keep the city dweller in line. If he is told to do something or to stop doing something else, he wants to know the reason why he should. Walking down Broadway with his arms swinging wide, he may be surprised to learn that "his own freedom ends where the next man's nose begins." He obeys the written law, as manifest in legal codes, city ordinances, or statutes. His behavior is not governed by concern for other people and their well-being.

Conditions are very different outside the city. Individual behavior, in the small town or the rural neighborhood, finds itself under much closer scrutiny by friends and neighbors. "What they don't know," a small town person writes, "they do not hesitate to ask about." Nor are they inclined to hold back their opinions about a person. Outside the big city, the line of least resistance for individual behavior lies in doing exactly what people think you ought to do. Conformity of social behavior and permanence of social structure is enforced by informal mutual supervision.

Such means of social control, ranging all the way from a sneer in public to gossip behind one's back, are lost in the anonymous city environment. Symptoms of social disorganization in the large city have been attributed to the lack of informal means of control.

The control value of neighboring has been one of the cornerstones in the argument for neighborhood planning. Clarence Perry referred to Cooley's and W. I. Thomas's discussion of the primary group and the constructive forces inherent in knowing your neighbors intimately.[12]

Neighborhood planning tries to recapture for big city living those values of informal social control otherwise associated with the small town.[13] How effective such transplantation can be, remains yet to be seen.[14]

---

[12] Clarence A. Perry, *Housing for the Machine Age.* New York: Russell Sage Foundation, 1939, "Function of the Face-to-Face Community," pp. 215-221.

[13] For an early statement about the constructive aspects of neighboring, see Robert A. Woods, "The Neighborhood in Social Reconstruction," Papers and Proceedings, Eighth Annual Meeting, American Sociological Society, Vol. VIII, 1913, pp. 14-28.

For a recent statement on the same topic, see Judith Tannenbaum, "The Neighborhood. A Socio-Psychological Analysis," *Journal of Land Economics,* Vol. XXIV, No. 4 (November, 1948), pp. 358-369.

[14] See Svend Riemer, "Villagers in Metropolis," *The British Journal of Sociology,* Vol. II, No. 1 (March, 1951), pp. 31-43.

Economy of Design and Construction. Not the least important challenge in favor of residential neighborhood planning comes from the professional architect and engineer, the landscape architect, and the city planner. Henry Wright was the first in this country to point out concisely and sytematically the economies to be gained by large scale planning of residential housing. His emphasis was not only on mass production but upon the joint consideration of all the needs of a sizable residential population.[15]

Henry Wright showed that the needs for private living in a residential neighborhood can better and more economically be provided for if they are considered jointly. Among the features he proposed and which now have come to be accepted as standard practice in neighborhood planning are the following: (a) differentiation of the street system; (b) combination of garden lots and other out-door spaces for common usage; (c) consideration of economies accruing from attached housing; (d) centralization in the provision of services (technical and social); (e) large scale operation and maintenance.

Most of these proposals are retained in Perry's classical statement on modern neighborhood planning.

THE CLASSICAL DOCTRINE OF NEIGHBORHOOD PLANNING

Clarence Perry. To Clarence Perry we owe the formulation of the neighborhood unit formula.[16] He set down in terms of definite principles the elements of design and construction that ought to go into neighborhood planning. This undertaking was of great merit

---

[15] See Henry Wright, *Rehousing Urban America.* New York: Columbia University Press, 1935, Chapter V, "The Case for Group Housing," pp. 29-50.

[16] "The neighborhood unit — 'a scheme of arrangement for the family-life community' — was first described in one of the three monographs that made up volume 7, Neighborhood and Community Planning, of the Regional Survey of New York and Its Environs." (1929)

"In 1933, a supplemental study of the neighborhood unit idea as applied to a particular field of housing was undertaken by Perry. It was presented in a volume entitled The Rebuilding of Blighted Areas, and was issued by the Regional Plan Association, a body formed to carry out the purpose of the New York Region Plan." Clarence A. Perry, *op. cit.,* "Prefatory Note," pp. 11, 12.

The final and most comprehensive formulation of the idea is to be found in Clarence A. Perry, *op. cit.,* Chapter III, "The Neighborhood Unit Formula," pp. 50-82.

because it focused the planner's attention upon fixed specifications.
Not every suburban settlement with a meandering street layout
can be considered a planned neighborhood. A community center,
as such, does not make a neighborhood. Nor are the full opportunities of neighborhood planning automatically taken advantage of
wherever a large number of family homes are built simultaneously

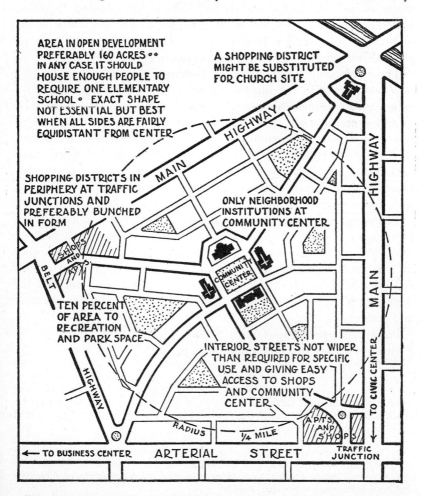

AREA IN OPEN DEVELOPMENT
PREFERABLY 160 ACRES °°
IN ANY CASE IT SHOULD
HOUSE ENOUGH PEOPLE TO
REQUIRE ONE ELEMENTARY
SCHOOL ° EXACT SHAPE
NOT ESSENTIAL BUT BEST
WHEN ALL SIDES ARE FAIRLY
EQUIDISTANT FROM CENTER

A SHOPPING DISTRICT
MIGHT BE SUBSTITUTED
FOR CHURCH SITE

HIGHWAY

MAIN

HIGHWAY

SHOPPING DISTRICTS IN
PERIPHERY AT TRAFFIC
JUNCTIONS AND
PREFERABLY BUNCHED
IN FORM

ONLY NEIGHBORHOOD
INSTITUTIONS AT
COMMUNITY CENTER

SHOPS
AND
APTS

BELT

COMMUNITY
CENTER

MAIN

TEN PERCENT
OF AREA TO
RECREATION
AND PARK SPACE

INTERIOR STREETS NOT WIDER
THAN REQUIRED FOR SPECIFIC
USE AND GIVING EASY
ACCESS TO SHOPS
AND COMMUNITY
CENTER

TO CIVIC CENTER

HIGHWAY

RADIUS   ¼ MILE

APTS
AND
SHOPS

← TO BUSINESS CENTER   ARTERIAL   STREET   TRAFFIC
JUNCTION

FIGURE 19. The Neighborhood Unit Formula According to Clarence Perry.
From: Clarence A. Perry, *Housing for the Machine Age*. New York: Russell
Sage Foundation, 1939, p. 75.

on contiguous sites. The requirements of modern neighborhood planning are far more specific.[17]

The Scope of Private Living. For planning purposes, the neighborhood is defined as "that area which embraces all the public facilities and conditions required by the average family for its comfort and proper development within the vicinity of its dwelling."[18] All facets of private living are to be covered by planned facilities. Whether these facilities are to be provided in the individual home or through joint service facilities has to be decided on the basis of available techniques and consumer preferences.

The practice of neighborhood planning has opened our eyes to new possibilities in the improvement of home environment. On a community basis, necessary services (such as heat) can frequently be provided at less cost. Recreational and social facilities have been provided for modest income groups who previously considered such services a rich man's privilege. Standards of residential living have been noticeably raised by a process which, for better or worse, has transferred important functions from the individual family home to joint facilities available for the entire neighborhood.

The neighborhood is to be established as a relatively self-sufficient unit, the borderlines of which are to be crossed for highly specialized purposes only. There ought to be many days on which no member of the family leaves it for other purposes than occupation or advanced education. It will have to include, therefore, facilities for daily shopping, for leisure time activities, for social life, and for play and recreation.

Perry has provided us with 6 principles to be checked in the evaluation of any given neighborhood plan: [19]

Size.

"A residential unit development should provide housing for that population for which one elementary school is ordinarily required, its actual area depending upon population density." [20]

---

[17] For the most recent and the most systematic presentation of standards of neighborhood planning, see The Committee on the Hygiene of Housing in the American Public Health Association, *Planning the Neighborhood.* Chicago: Public Administration Service, 1948.

[18] Clarence A. Perry, *op. cit.,* p. 50.

[19] *Ibid.,* p. 51.

[20] *Ibid.,* pp. 52-56.

According to this principle, Perry estimated that the size of planned neighborhoods might well vary from residential housing provided for 3,000 to 10,000 people. Present estimates allow for a margin from 2,000 to 8,000 persons, with an optimum size of about 5,000 persons.[21]

TABLE XVI

ACCESS STANDARDS FOR COMMUNITY FACILITIES

WITHIN THE NEIGHBORHOOD

Recommended Maximum Limit

Neighborhood Facility	Walking Distance (one way) from Farthest Dwelling
Nursery School	¼ mile [a]
Kindergarten	¼ to ½ mile
Elementary School	¼ to ½ mile [b]
Playground	¼ to ½ mile [c]
Park	¼ to ½ mile
Shopping Center	¼ to ½ mile
Indoor Social, Cultural and Recreation Center	½ mile [d]
Health Center	½ mile [d]

[a] Where nursery school cannot be provided within ¼ mile it should at least be within 15 minutes elapsed time by public or special transit.

[b] In exceptional circumstances, the limit may be ¾-mile walk or 20 minutes elapsed time by school bus, if children may obtain hot lunches at school at nominal cost.

[c] One-half mile permissible only in planned neighborhoods meeting all requirements for safe access, and where playground is adjacent to elementary school.

[d] Where facility cannot be provided within neighborhood or walking distance it should at least be within 20 minutes elapsed time by public transit.

From: Planning the Neighborhood. Public Administration Service. Chicago, 1948. p. 44.

The experience of recent building activities has shown this principle to stand up as a fairly valuable rule of thumb. It provides a scope large enough to include most facilities required for daily needs. At the same time, it leaves the neighborhood small enough to permit

[21] See *Planning the Neighborhood, op. cit.*, p. 2.

the formation of a tight network of personal acquaintances within its boundaries.[22]

The elementary school located within the neighborhood covers an essential need for small school children. "Children of the elementary school grade," we learn, "should not be required to travel more than one-half mile to school." [23] This requirement is most easily met if the grade school is located in the very center of the real estate development. A school building at this location can provide space for many social activities of parents and older children. It can be used in the evening hours as well as during the day. Playgrounds and recreation areas surrounding the school building should attract all age ranges of the resident population.

Other requirements for daily living include the grocery store and the drug store to be sustained by a population of the above-mentioned size. These shopping facilities are customarily placed somewhere at the periphery of the neighborhood site. This location eliminates heavy truck delivery service in the residential area. It also makes it possible for the local store to cater to a wider consumer population attracted from adjacent residential districts. At the periphery, these stores will be close to similar stores geared to the needs of adjacent residential areas, thus forming a small shopping center that makes for competition and better service.

Boundaries.

"The unit should be bounded on all sides by arterial streets, sufficiently wide to facilitate its by-passing, instead of penetration, by through-traffic."[24]

This principle contains implicitly another specification with regard to neighborhood size: The size of the neighborhood area must not be so large as to make it impossible to have it by-passed by through traffic.

All traffic that does not terminate in the neighborhood itself passes around it without disturbing its internal peace. In between major

---

[22] The problem of neighborhood planning is judiciously appraised by Richard Dewey, "The Neighborhood, Urban Ecology, and City Planning," *American Sociological Review*, Vol. 15, No. 4 (August, 1950), pp. 502-507. Consult the works referred to in the article.

[23] Quoted from the New York Regional Plan in Clarence A. Perry, *op. cit.*, p. 55.

[24] *Ibid.*, pp. 56-57.

traffic arteries leading to and from the central city, the neighborhood lies protected against intrusion, an oasis of stability in a wider environment full of movement.

To emphasize the visual unity of the neighborhood area, the planner is likely to take advantage of man-made and natural boundaries. Freight-yards or canals may serve as examples for the former, rivers and steep hillsides for the latter. It is intended, in this manner, not only to eliminate undesirable intrusion but also to stimulate a feeling of belonging by creating a visual image for identification.

Park belts may run along the boundary of the residential neighborhood. For the protection of residential peace inside the planned unit, this device is not always successful. If parks and playgrounds are lacking in adjacent residential areas, a defensive park belt will not serve its function. It will attract the outdoor leisure time activities of other than neighborhood residents. It will cause, rather than impede undesirable intrusion.

Open Spaces.

"A system of small parks and recreation spaces, planned to meet the needs of the particular neighborhood, should be provided." [25]

If centrally located, such recreation spaces will turn the eyes of the neighborhood inward. The most pleasant associations of neighborhood living, it is assumed, will be evenings of outdoor play and informal recreation. The important task of furnishing a functionally adequate as well as esthetically pleasing layout of the recreation area is demanded of the landscape architect.[26]

Perry estimated that something like 10 per cent of the total area would have to be devoted to open green spaces.[27] This prerequisite, however, is flexible and subject to revision depending upon the outdoor recreational facilities of the wider environment. To guarantee

---

[25] *Ibid.*, pp. 57-62.

[26] The social objectives of park and recreational planning have been well stated in S. R. Sanders and A. J. Rabuck, *New City Patterns*. New York: Reinhold Publishing Corporation, 1946, "Recreation Areas and Facilities," pp. 131-146.

[27] A study of recreation areas suggests "a flat ten percent as a good figure to aim at in open or suburban unit subdivisions." Clarence A. Perry, *op. cit.*, p. 59.

an open development, it is furthermore required that "each structure
be separated from its neighbor by a distance equal to its height." [28]

These requirements for open spaces in the planned neighborhood
will not necessarily cause an undue increase in cost for the individual
dwelling unit. To a large extent, open spaces will be gained by
economies inherent in a well planned layout. A differentiated street
system, with narrow streets inside the planned area, saves land to be
used for the benefit of the residents.

Institutional Sites.

"Sites for the school and other institutions having service spheres coinciding with the limits of the unit should be suitably grouped about a
central point, or common." [29]

The emphasis is upon a central focus of attention to give visual
expression to neighborhood unity. The image of the village common
is to be reproduced in the city environment to create the mood for
a more stable and self-contained way of life. The "other institutions
having service spheres coinciding with the limits of the unit" present
a problem. Institutions in the city are of so specialized a nature that
their service can rarely be limited to a population of no more than
about 5,000 persons.

It would take a very homogeneous population with great interest
in religion to make it reasonable to provide even 1 church for the
individual neighborhood. There is little opportunity to provide for
various denominational needs within the boundaries of the planned
neighborhood unit. Nor is there enough patronage for a single
movie theater.

A community center, serving simultaneously a great variety of
purposes, is the only other institutional building to be considered
within the confines of the neighborhood. The limited scope of the
individual neighborhood might even suggest a combination of
school and community center within the same structure. There are
disadvantages connected with such a combination. As Perry says,
"A community clubhouse, in these modern days, must permit
smoking, keep open until late hours, and altogether encourage an

---

[28] *Ibid.*, p. 62.
[29] *Ibid.*, pp. 62-65.

atmosphere of gaiety and freedom that is quite foreign to the traditional school." [30]

Stores.

"One or more shopping districts, adequate for the population to be served, should be laid out in the circumference of the unit, preferably at traffic junctions and adjacent to similar districts of adjoining neighborhoods." [31]

The internal peace of the self-contained urban neighborhood and the interests of business suggest peripheral location. When talking about a business district for a population of 5,000 persons, Perry seems unduly optimistic. It is necessary to transcend the limits of the individual neighborhood in the planning of urban commercial districts. Perry hints in this direction when he refers to the patronage of adjacent areas. [32]

Our city environment is said to be over-zoned for commercial districts already. Rezoning will never allow for the revival of the village grocery store and the village druggist. Even daily shopping needs of the resident urban population stretch out their feelers in the direction of larger districts with more specialized services than can be provided on a neighborhood basis.

Street System.

"The unit should be provided with a special street-system, each highway being proportioned to its probable traffic load, and the street-net as a whole being designed to facilitate circulation within the unit and to discourage its use by through traffic." [33]

---

[30] *Ibid.*, p. 63.

[31] *Ibid.*, pp. 65-72.

[32] "Each neighborhood, being a concentration of families, whose workers pass daily through one, two, or possibly three main portals, the canalization of traffic is automatic . . . residents frequently find it convenient to stop at a local store on their way to or back from 'town.' It is that convenience and the courses of the traffic streams which determine the neighborhood portals as the proper locations for local shopping districts.

Another advantage in having business in the periphery of a unit is that frequently it is only across the street from a retail district in an adjacent neighborhood. Sometimes four such districts, in the corners of their units, will be found in a cluster. Thus residents of those four neighborhoods will all enjoy a wider range of shopping opportunity." *Ibid.*, p. 69.

[33] *Ibid.*, pp. 72-75.

Sudden bends and steep slopes will not discourage the child from walking to the playground, to school, or to the grocery store. It will discourage, however, the motorist whose destination lies diagonally across the planned neighborhood.

There have been neighborhoods planned in locations where through traffic could not be entirely avoided. In such cases, the planner is challenged to devise means (underpass or overpass) whereby the two streams of communication can be held separate from each other.

Trends Toward Neighborhood Planning

Neighborhood planning is more than a passing fashion. We have mentioned a number of social conditions in the past that encourage the modern movement in favor of neighborhood planning. Some of them, like the early settlement movement and the interest in natural areas, are apt to lose importance as time goes on. Yet there are two fairly consistent trends in the contemporary social scene that are apt to encourage the further development of neighborhood planning. This is not to say that neighborhood planning will retain forever those features laid down dogmatically in the neighborhood unit plan by Clarence Perry.

Of these two trends, one is primarily economic, the other primarily social in nature. Economically, the savings involved in large scale residential planning are so compelling as to promise the perseverance of current developments. Socially, the transfer of functions from the individual family home to community facilities is so thoroughly based upon current needs of the urban family that a reversal of this trend is practically unimaginable. Neighborhood planning, in some shape or form, is here to stay.

Large scale production of housing leads to a consideration of advantages inherent in mass production. Factory production is economically superior to the production of the individual family home by successive teams of craftsmen. We know about the difficulties of co-ordinating crafts labor in an efficient work process. Advantages of division of labor, such as the employment of unskilled or semiskilled labor and the reduction of transportation in the work process, cannot be utilized in piece-construction on the individual lot.

Large scale home construction, furthermore, makes accessible the economic advantages inherent in the provision of specialized rather than individualized services. These possibilities offer themselves where the needs for shelter on the part of relatively sizable populations are envisioned jointly.

Imagine the development of a residential area for a population in which the need for desk work at home, for purposes of study, bookkeeping, and so forth, can be considered an exception rather than the rule. In this case, nearby library facilities with a few study-desks can eliminate the burden of an extra-room or study-corner from the individual dwelling unit.

There are many similar examples. Consider the need for formal entertaining. One housing project in New York City provided for this need by making a specially furnished apartment, with kitchen equipment installed and presentable furniture in the living room, available successively to all residents in a large apartment house. By eliminating the function of formal entertaining from the individual dwelling unit, from all individual dwelling units, these could be planned much more economically for purposes of everyday living.

Facilities for active recreation, for social gatherings and study groups and business meetings can be considered in a smiliar light. In order to reduce the cost of housing, unnecessary duplication of services can be readily avoided, if not every dwelling unit is fully equipped for all such needs.

Transfer of Family Functions. To most of us, the use of some joint facilities will be perfectly acceptable; the use of others will be refused. We may stall at the idea of dining facilities through which all members of the neighborhood have their dinners prepared in a community kitchen, from which it is transported to the individual dwelling unit for consumption.[34] Others will shrink from holding their bridge games in the community center, while permitting their children to enjoy themselves in public parks and playgrounds.

In earlier days, the individual home shared in the fulfillment of community functions. Parlor or living room provided occasional shelter for social meetings and get-togethers. The life of the com-

---

[34] Such facilities are available in two experimental apartment structures in Stockholm, Sweden, aimed at the needs of gainfully employed married women.

munity extended into the individual home. Today we observe the reverse tendency. The family branches out into space designed and constructed for community functions.

But whether community facilities are made use of or not, there can be no doubt about the elimination of an increasing number of functions from the individual family home. To attend nursery school, the child leaves the orbit of parental protection earlier than ever before. Teen-agers congregate in the ice-cream parlor, the tavern or the poolroom, at the street corner or in the movie theater, if no better outlet is provided for them.

More frequently today, we invite our friends to share a meal with us in a restaurant rather than our own dining room. Our games are in demand of equipment which only the wealthiest can afford in their own recreation rooms or backyards. The billiard room of the fashionable mansion is on its way out; the poolroom is here to stay as a recreational establishment.

The reason for the specialization of individual leisure time interests is discussed elsewhere.[35] For neighborhood planning remains the task of providing for such interests in close proximity to the individual family home. In the future, the livability of residential housing will not be measured alone by space and equipment provided for the individual dwelling unit; it will be judged by the extent to which all family members can find their recreational needs fulfilled within walking distance.

The Challenge of the Mixed Neighborhood

Neighborhood planning perpetuates the trend toward residential segregation in the city.[36] The city dweller is inclined to seek refuge in his private quarters from the bewildering contact with all sorts of people with whom he is compelled to deal, barter, haggle and struggle, and whom he must flatter in the downtown environment, in factory and office building or wherever he makes his living, gets his education, or joins a citywide association for recreational or civic purposes.

In his home environment, the city dweller wants to replace complexity with simplicity. In his neighborhood, the city dweller wants

[35]See beginning of Chapter 11.
[36] See Reginald R. Isaacs, "The 'Neighborhood Unit' is an Instrument for Segregation," *Journal of Housing*, Vol. 5, No. 8 (August, 1948), pp. 215-218.

to relax and be himself, and he does not want to be confronted with different opinions. In and around his home, the city dweller wants to have his own attitudes and manners taken for granted.

Neighborhood planning enforces such patterns of segregation. Not all aspects of segregation are necessarily desirable. Segregation stifles the city dweller's quest for a full experience of the social scene of which he is participant.

Neighborhood living may well accentuate the curse of over-specialization. The occupational life of the city dweller is limited to some very partial aspect of the entire productive process. If he is also limited in his private life to one-sided views, to partial slants on public events, to a limited set of manners and customs, he will become unnecessarily limited in his views of life and living.

The "Full Experience." These dangers of neighborhood planning have been well recognized. To avoid them and yet to retain the advantages of neighborhood planning, the planning of "mixed" neighborhoods has been promoted.[37] The idea is to plan neighborhoods catering to the needs of a somewhat differentiated population. In this manner, it is hoped to circumvent the stagnating influences of provincialism and ethnic isolation.

Secondary objectives joined in making the mixed neighborhood attractive to the city planner. By inducing different income groups to live in close proximity to each other, it was hoped to encourage better maintenance and upkeep than is to be expected where a settlement exclusively of lower income groups is left to deteriorate for lack of financial resources. Similarly, a more equal distribution of fiscal income and expenditure over the entire city area was to be implemented through unsegregated urban settlement.

By providing for differentiated housing needs in one and the same neighborhood, by providing rental as well as owned housing, single

---

[37] "In the past . . . the majority of planners have contended that the 'neighborhood' unit should be 'unmixed,' that is, the 'neighborhood' should be characterized by a high degree of homogeneity with respect to type of housing and especially its residents. . . . Another group of planners . . . insists that the neighborhood should be both 'mixed' and 'unmixed' — mixed as to structural type of dwellings, but unmixed or homogeneous in regard to race, religion, and economic level of the occupants. . . . There is also a small, but growing, group of planners who, in their adherence to democratic principles, maintain that the neighborhood unit must be mixed as to housing types and racial occupancy." Reginald R. Isaacs, "Are Urban Neighborhoods Possible?" *Journal of Housing*, Vol. 5, No. 7 (July, 1948), p. 177.

family structures as well as multiple dwellings, the planner envisioned a neighborhood to which the individual city family could adhere through all phases of its development.

At first arrival in the city or during the first years of family formation, the city dweller may well be satisfied with rental accomodations; later he may want to buy a home of his own. Apartment living may suit his needs while he is single or recently married, or later when he is old and his children have left the parental home.[38]

Ordinarily, each step in this process demands a shift from one residential neighborhood to another. If neighborhood ties are considered worth preserving, different types of housing needs should be served in close proximity to each other. As the family unfolds and shrinks, neighborhood ties will not necessarily have to be severed.

Prejudice. Planning for mixed neighborhoods has also been geared to the elimination of status and race consciousness. Mixed neighborhoods have been suggested to break down prejudice by teaching different people to live together, by letting them get to know each other and by forcing them to develop an understanding of their differences.

This noble intent may fail because it runs counter to popular demands and existing prejudice. In low cost subsidized housing, some successful ventures of interracial neighborhood construction can be recorded. Yet, the danger of interracial conflict has never been absent.

Housing encompasses more issues than mere shelter; so does neighborhood planning; and so does the planning of mixed neighborhoods. Some of the above-mentioned issues may be better attacked with means other than those of physical construction.

SELECTED READINGS

1. Ebenezer Howard, *Garden Cities of ToMorrow.* London: Faber and Faber Ltd., 1946, pp. 9-159.

---

[38] "Typically, the cycle of life of a couple begins with a kitchenette apartment; a larger apartment with the birth of a baby; a single home in the suburbs as the first child is ready for school; return to the city apartment with marriage and departure from home of the children; and finally, refuge in an apartment hotel in old age." Ernest W. Burgess and Harvey J. Locke, *The Family.* New York: American Book Company, 1945, p. 520.

2. Clarence Arthur Perry, *Housing for the Machine Age*. New York: Russell Sage Foundation, 1939, pp. 11-221.

3. The Committee on the Hygiene of Housing in the American Public Health Association, *Planning the Neighborhood*. Chicago: Public Administration Service, 1948, pp. 1-72.

4. Granville Hicks, *Small Town*. New York: The Macmillan Company, 1947, pp. 3-276.

5. James Dahir, *The Neighborhood Unit Plan. A Selected Bibliography with Interpretative Comments*. New York: Russell Sage Foundation, 1947, pp. 5-83.

PROBLEMS

1. *Neighboring and Neighborhood Construction.* The question is whether neighborhood construction as such is conducive to the practice of neighboring. To find out, select in some urban area 2 residential districts: 1 planned, designed, and constructed for purposes of neighborhood living, and the other not. Design for neighborhood living is recognizable by a number of different criteria. A planned neighborhood will be separated from its surroundings by traffic thoroughfares, the homes may be of uniform style, commercial and public community facilities may be provided for in central location. State precisely which of these, or which other criteria you are using to distinguish between residential housing planned for neighborhood living and that not so planned.

Within the scope of a semester's work, your project cannot lead to definite conclusions. Under the circumstances, select 5 families inside the neighborhood, and another 5 in a comparative residential area not designed for neighborhood living.

Subject these 10 families to intensive interviewing. Find out whether the families in the planned neighborhood are spending a greater share of their leisure time within walking distance of their family homes, whether they have more speaking acquaintances within walking distance from their family home, and whether they have been in more of the homes situated within walking distance than those not living in homes constructed for neighborhood living.

You will be given credit for clear statement of procedures, for the information gained in your interviews and their interpretation.

2. *Recent Changes in Neighborhood Planning Practice.* This project consists of a careful comparison between the "classical doctrine of neighborhood planning" and a more recent formulation of standards of neighborhood planning.

The 2 sources to consult are Clarence A. Perry, *Housing for the Machine Age*. New York: Russell Sage Foundation, 1939; and the

Committee on the Hygiene of Housing in the American Public Health Association. Chicago: Public Administration Service, 1948. Compare in detail the standards of neighborhood planning set forth in these 2 publications. Record any change that might have occurred and consider the reasoning that has led to such change.

What type of research or experience has led to change and improvement? What further research would be needed for further improvements in the practice of neighborhood planning?

3. *The Future of Neighborhood Planning.* Read carefully Chapter 17 and consult the literature quoted in it. State factors in favor of urban neighborhood planning, and other factors that tend to obstruct the tendency toward neighborhood living in the urban environment.

Weigh the positive and the negative factors against each other and try to arrive at a judgment about the future of neighborhood planning in the modern city.

CHAPTER 18

City Planning

CITY GROWTH AND CITY PLANNING

The Individual Lot. The challenge to modern city planning derives
from the many undesirable features of unplanned city growth in the
19th century.

The slums in the center of the city do not serve their purpose well.
They have happened planlessly. We have not bothered to eliminate
or to replace them. Nor is there rhyme or reason to the insecurity
imposed upon the urban home owner even outside the slum environment. His residence is endangered by the inroads of undesirable land
uses. Apartments and commercial land uses penetrate into areas of
single-family housing, thus reducing both convenience and sale
value. Garages and filling stations, unless restricted by zoning ordinances, may turn the peace of the quiet residential neighborhood
into areas of buzzing motor traffic.

Our cities have been built up by a gradual disposal of individual
lots. No other purposes than those concerning the individual home
on the individual lot were taken into consideration while the urban
mosaic was being filled in. Yet residential needs transcend the confines of the individually owned lot. There are needs for parks and
playgrounds, for well-organized shopping districts and commercial
entertainment. These services have been provided by happenstance.

At the periphery of the modern city, the situation was always temporarily undefined. Nobody knew whether an area would finally stabilize into a fashionable suburb, a workingman's district, a factory zone, or apartment blocks close to rapid transit lines. We know that land uses in the periphery of the city gravitate in the direction of the least desirable land uses, others being pushed out by evasion.[1] Without city planning, competition for space never came to a rest. There was no opportunity for the provision of well balanced services within reasonable distance of the individual family home.

Organic Disorder? Modern city planning, however, is not only opposed to unplanned and disorderly growth. Modern city planning is opposed, also, to the unimaginative gridiron pattern of the urban street layout and the tendency to obscure rather than to take advantage of irregular topographical features of the urban site. Modern city planning is carried by rational as well as anti-rational sentiments.

Some city planners make their goal the establishment of "organic order" in the urban community.[2] The term "organic" serves to confuse rather than to clarify the issue. Our eyes are guided to the well-proportioned beauty of the medieval city which seems to have been built by individuals eagerly trying to fit each part of physical construction into a pleasing whole. Architects are wont to compare colonial cities, built at the stroke of a pen, with those that have

---

[1] "We find in the rurban fringe three land use characteristics which are common to all marginal areas, and two additional characteristics unique to the rurban fringe but nonetheless resulting from its marginality. They are, respectively, as follows: (1) a capriciousness and diseconomy in private developmental plans; (2) variability and instability in the spatial patterns of land use; (3) a tendency for residences to gravitate to the lowest use in terms of class status; (4) an irrelevance of settlement patterns to soil capability; (5) the removal of the land from agricultural productivity." Walter Firey, "Ecological Considerations in Planning for Rurban Fringes," *American Sociological Review*, Vol. 11, No. 4 (August, 1946), p. 413.

[2] "The principles of expression and correlation are not independently functioning principles, but rather daughter-principles of that all-governing mother-principle of 'organic order' — which in fact is the very principle of architecture in the universe."

"This can be achieved only when the town designers . . . have absorbed the meaning of these principles into the very blood of their veins." Eliel Saarinen, *The City*. New York: Reinhold Publishing Corporation, 1943.

For contrast, see Le Corbusier's attitude toward the gridiron system of street-layout:

"This grille of streets, this 'American lay-out,' is precisely the excuse for the attacks of academicians and romantics. It is our particular vanity to be plunged in disorder down to the very base. We make a virtue of it; we affirm that it is life, rich, subtle, agreeable, and what not." Le Corbusier, *When the Cathedrals Were White*. New York: Reynal & Hitchcock, 1947, p. 48.

grown.[3] They are inclined to prefer the latter for their "organic fitness."

Such views are not free from romantic misinterpretation. It is true that the purposeful foundation and construction of entire cities has always favored a somewhat monotonous rectangular layout. They encourage straight lines of construction. The first planned urban development in the cities of Western civilization, the Piraeus at Athens, offered also the first example of the gridiron pattern.[4]

The organic variety of the medieval city reveals itself at closer inspection as the outcome of planless growth. Many disadvantages were inherent in the layout and construction of the city of the Middle Ages. Only our ignorance of the hardships of medieval urban living sustain our admiration. The people of the Middle Ages judged their cities by standards different from those of the modern tourist. At the beginning of their existence, these cities were laid out simply and rationally, following simple geometrical patterns. The organic variety which we admire in their present remnants is the outcome of later growth and congestion within the confines of the defensive walls.[5]

Growth of Planning. Neither planning nor unplanned city growth, to be sure, is an intrinsically modern urban phenomenon. Neither process guarantees better results than the other. Unplanned growth involves risks, cumulative congestion, and functional disorders. But city planning also can be either good or bad. To be good, city planning must encompass both the spatial and the social dimension. It cannot be limited to vague esthetic criteria. The test of the goodness of cities, as a matter of fact, will have to be found in the social dimension.[6] We have to ask ourselves what a certain city environment — whether planned or grown — will do for the people who live in it.

---

[3] "Colonial cities . . . were always founded and built according to a simple geometrical plan." L. Hilberseimer, *The New City. Principles of Planning.* Chicago: Paul Theobold, 1944, p. 28.

[4] "Under Pericles, Hippodamus (ca. 450-400 B.C.) laid out the Piraeus on the checker-board plan in the first effort at city planning in the Western world." Ralph Turner, *The Great Cultural Traditions.* New York: McGraw-Hill Book Company, Inc., 1941, Vol. I, "The Ancient Cities," p. 479.

[5] See pp. 22-24.

[6] Consider the interesting attempt by E. L. Thorndike to measure the "goodness" of cities, *Your City.* New York: Harcourt, Brace and Company, 1939. Such measurements, needless to say, are dependent upon arbitrary indices of readily available data. The problem is to find some objective criterion for the index of "goodness." Even then, there remains the question of "goodness for whom?"

The City as a Way of Life

Social Objectives. What do we expect from the layout of physical construction in our urban environment? We expect:

1. that the layout of construction follow some easily recognizable geometrical pattern,

2. that buildings be so related in space to each other as to minimize the total amount of movement required in the course of daily activities, and to provide proximity or distance between different construction as functionally demanded,

3. that buildings be so related in space to each other as to give symbolic expression to existing relationships in the social dimension.

Geometrical Simplicity. Our esthetic perception has been so trained by the view of cities built in a circle, a square, a rectangle, or a semicircle that any less decisive layout of construction would leave us esthetically dissatisfied. Still, the layout of urban construction in easily recognizable geometrical patterns is desirable for other than esthetic reasons.

At arrival in New York City, Le Corbusier expressed his spontaneous delight in the much-maligned gridiron pattern.[7] It gave him a feeling of freedom. Simple arithmetic made it possible for him to find his way from any part of the city to any other. On Manhattan Island, any address gives an absolute indication of location, once the simple principle of numerical sequences has been grasped.

This offers freedom for the mind, Le Corbusier asserted; freedom to concern itself with other matters of greater interest than pathfinding. An easily perspicuous city plan turns orientation, for the city dweller, into a matter of simple routine and makes it possible for him to focus his attention on social relationships.

Movement Between Construction. More specific is the demand to have physical construction functionally related in space. It forces

---

[7] "The streets are at right angles to each other and the mind is liberated." Le Corbusier, *When the Cathedrals Were White.* New York: Reynal & Hitchcock, 1947, pp. 47-51. (The above sentence is used as a caption for the discussion of the gridiron pattern.)

The poet Heinrich Heine saw an expression of the idea of infinity in the straight-line construction of Berlin's Friedrichstrasse.

upon us a consideration of prevailing social relationships. We have to know what buildings are used for, how frequently and at what times of the day, whether there are combined uses which invite the placement of different constructions in close proximity to each other, or whether there are buildings — such as church and brothel — which serve such different social dimensions that they are better segregated in space.

A functional city plan is dependent upon the usage made of urban construction. It is dependent upon prevailing social relations and, therefore, time-bound. A city can well outgrow the purposes of its original design.

The centrally located castle of the medieval city became meaningless when the aristocratic family learned to prefer a suburban residential location. Resplendent churches may be left behind in the environment of central urban deterioration long after their congregations have moved to the urban periphery. A rapid intra-urban transportation system makes unnecessary the location of interurban railroad stations close to the downtown business district.

Symbolic Expression. In city planning, we often neglect the demand that urban construction should express visibly prevailing social relationships. To some extent, this demand is fulfilled by the functional location of buildings in space. The temple, the palace, or the large office building in the center of the city calls attention to the focus of urban values at the time of construction. On the other hand, the escape of the residences of the more successful members of the urban community into the parkland of the suburbs or the countryside of the hinterland fails to give visible expression to the social structure of the large modern city.

Because factories and workingmen's districts have also moved into the rurban fringe, the panorama of the modern city has lost the faculty of giving symbolic expression to the system of social organization which it shelters. The modern city does not confront us any longer with a universe of construction that easily reveals its social meaning to the observer.

Early City Functions. Most cities of the historical past can be interpreted as expressions of a way of life. They are built for specific functions and they are limited to the construction techniques available to their era. Planned cities as the outcome of colonization enterprises are more apt to express originally intended city functions, while cities that have grown naturally carry the signs of successive phases of changing functions to which construction activities have currently been readjusted.

Early urban culture knew the city as a center for religious worship. This placed the temple in the very center of the urban construct, with direct routes leading from its entrance to the city gate. Residences of the priesthood were located in the temple itself or in other public structures in prominent position. The residences of urban labor were moved into the background to fill the space between the ecclesiastical buildings and the defensive walls.

Before the invention of gunpowder, the defensive wall was rarely lacking from the urban environment. Then, walls disappeared because they no longer served their purpose.

In addition to serving the needs of defensive warfare, the walls of early cities gave a more unified appearance to the urban settlement, before it went aimlessly sprawling into the urban hinterland, with individual structures shooting far out in advance of the built-up city. The urban in-group was visibly held together in the protective arms of urban fortifications.

As the priesthood lost power and prestige to the king and his feudal consorts, the central location of the palace replaced that of the temple. The nobility, retained its urban domiciles in a close huddle around palace and temple. Here they remained, as a matter of fact, until the close of the Middle Ages, basing their prestige alternately upon military or political leadership, upon commercial wealth or absentee ownership of rural states, upon republican, or monarchial, or dictatorial governmental office.

The cities of the Middle Ages have come down to us in the overgrown state of late developments. At the beginning of their existence, they were planned spaciously and in simple geometrical outlines. So generously were these cities laid out at the time of their foundation that their walls enclosed both farm land and vineyards.[8]

As the cities of the Middle Ages passed from the 12th and 13th to the 15th and 16th centuries, they vastly increased in population. The open spaces adjacent to the city walls were built up. Urban residences crowded into every nook and corner of the former farm-

---

[8] See Svend Riemer, *Functional Housing in the Middle Ages.* Wisconsin Academy of Sciences, Arts and Letters, Transactions, 1949, Vol. II, Spring, 1951, pp. 77-91.

stead or vineyard. Because the city could not extend horizontally beyond the city walls, residential housing grew to the height of several stories. Floor space within the dwelling unit was precious, and buildings were made to protrude slightly in the upper stories; they often met at the height of the gable.[9] Finally, these cities overflowed. Non-citizens without residential leases inside the city walls nestled together just outside the city gates in small suburban clusters.[10]

The Sprawling Modern City. After the invention of gunpowder the cities of Western civilization lost the confining belt-line of their walls and sprawled into the hinterland. Gradually, the spatial order of status was reversed. The residences of nobility and wealthier citizens withdrew from the unsanitary conditions of the inner city into the open country. While palaces, parks, and mansions lost themselves in the urban periphery, the residences of the less affluent citizens remained in stifling congestion within easy walking distance of the central market place. Beyond an inner ring of public buildings and ornate, official residences of nobility and powerful merchants, the status of urban residents gradually increased from the center to the far periphery of the city.[11]

For purposes of public display, attention was still focused upon the city center. After the French revolution, the aristocracy and officialdom of a decaying monarchical order reasserted themselves through corrections of unplanned urban growth which had got forcefully under way on the wings of the industrialization period.

---

[9] Informative foreign-language sources on housing in the Middle Ages are Rudolf Eberstadt, *Handbuch des Wohnungswesens und der Wohnungsfrage.* Jena: Gustav Fischer, 1910, "Zweiter Abschnitt: Das Mittelalter," pp. 23-43; and Alwin Schultz, *Deutsches Leben im XIV und XV. Jahrhundert.* Wien: Grosse Ausgabe, 1892, "Die Burgen," pp. 7-16, "Staedte," pp. 16-145.

[10] "Soon the space that cities and burgs had to offer these new-comers (the merchants), who became more and more numerous and embarassing in proportion as trade increased, was no longer sufficient. They were driven to settle outside the walls and to build beside the old burg a new burg, or, to use the term which exactly describes it, a faubourg (forisburgus), i.e. an outside burg." Henri Pirenne, *Economic and Social History of Medieval Europe.* London: Kegan Paul, Trench, Trubner & Co., Ltd., 1936, pp. 42-43.

[11] "The strengthening of the power of the central state brought greater security for trade and to the individual. The town house grew into a mansion with gardens, and the shop moved out of the house to specialized structures. . . . The country estate came into being." Henry S. Churchill, *The City is the People.* New York: Reynal & Hitchcock, 1945, p. 18.

These corrections are associated with the work of the well-known city planner Haussmann in Paris.[12]

By means of straight avenues radiating from the public squares at the city center, he conducted the eyes of the spectator toward the pomp and splendor of the Second Empire. Simultaneously, Haussmann razed the girdle of remaining fortifications and opened the newly gained space for the construction of wide boulevards and fashionable apartment housing. City planning, in this era, represented the interests of the upper and upper middle classes at the beginning of the industrialization period. Remnants of the feudal system and the successful pioneers of the modern business world walked hand in hand for many decades.

Industrialization. Unplanned order characterizes the modern city under the impact of the industrialization period. The simple logic of effective competition for space segregated different land uses from each other. In the center of the city, business and light industry had no difficulty in displacing other land uses. With regard to the status arrangement of residential housing the sequence customary in the Middle Ages had become reversed throughout. The wealthier members of the commercial community crowded toward the very periphery of the built-up city. Here was escape from a city environment that had become ugly in appearance and insanitary as a human residence.[13]

The city of the industrialization period, of course, expresses its own way of life and a unique set of values and purposes. It is best represented by the rapidly growing cities of the late 19th century. The gridiron pattern of Oklahoma City, systematically imprinted

---

[12] "Perhaps the most spectacular of all the large-scale projects for correcting city-wide mistakes was the construction of the great boulevard system of Paris under the direction of Baron Haussmann." Harold MacLean Lewis, *Planning the Modern City.* New York: John Wiley & Sons, Inc., 1949, Vol. I, p. 24. For similar corrections, see pp. 24-26.

[13] See footnote 11.

In the industrialized landscape, escape from the city was not always easy. "Healthful exercise in the open air is seldom or never taken by the artisans of this town, and their health certainly suffers considerable depression from this deprivation. One reason of this state of the people is, that all scenes of interest are remote from the town, and that the walks which can be enjoyed by the poor are chiefly the turnpike roads, alternately dusty or muddy." J. L. Hammond and Barbara Hammond, *The Bleak Age.* New York: Penguin Books, 1947, p. 82.

upon the plains of the Southwest 10 years after the foundation of the city, furnishes an early example.

With purposeful economy, land had been divided into equal units. The rectangular street system was forced upon the topography. The traditions of this era went back to the colonization of the Atlantic seacoast, when equal and generous allotments of land were made available to each freeman in the community. From such early hold-ings — built-up and subdivided — originated the city block of more or less standardized size in the modern American city.[14] The real estate ventures of a later date accepted the principle of equalitarian subdivision which came to serve the purpose of easy commercial handling rather than that of just distribution.

In both cases, the intent was the rational exploitation of land. Variations in topography presented a nuisance, an economic liability to be leveled by unskilled labor or the steam shovel. Man not only made himself a master of his physical environment, he shaped it to suit his purposes of rational economic exploitation for industrial, commercial, or residential land uses.

Toward the end of the 19th century, the relation of different land uses superimposed a distinct pattern of growth upon the original gridiron layout. Commerce and light industries clustered in the center. Residential competition scrambled into the open country-side at the periphery of the city. Successive status groups followed each other to inhabit second-, third-, and fourth-hand residences. The slum still girds the city center as a reminder of impending growth of the downtown busines section. Within this general scheme, members of nationality and status groups find their way to each other and segregate themselves from other groups.

The Structure of Modern City Planning

Corrective Measures. City planning today seldom involves the task of building an entire urban settlement from scratch. The in-vestment in existing structures and services is too colossal to be re-

---

[14] "New Haven, a coastal town, was also planned. It was laid out as a square, diagonally to the harbor. The square was divided into nine blocks, the central one served for public use. Each of the nine squares was 858 feet on a side, so that . . . the "home lot" was ample for subsistence at least. As the town grew these lots were subdivided, and the squares themselves were split by new streets into four more squares." Henry Churchill, *op. cit.*, p. 26.

peated in replacement of an already standing city. Most measures of modern city planning are corrective and ameliorative.

The rapid growth of the modern city encourages a type of planning that looks ahead but bides its time for gradual changes in the city pattern. The master plan of the modern city is based on the assumption of fairly rapid replacement needs. Wholesale tearing down and rebuilding is the exception rather than the rule. More practical are procedures which determine future land uses in various parts of the city. Building permits are made conditional to coincidence with a master plan that is projected into the future. Thus, a new city layout will emerge on the site of existing construction.[15]

Zoning. An invisible network of building intentions, related to future function, is overlaid upon the map of existing land uses. As buildings are torn down, the mosaic of a consistent new city plan is gradually being fillled in. The new "city beautiful" is thus expected to rise from contemporary obsolescence and deterioration.

There are difficulties involved in this aspect of modern city planning. Barring destructive warfare, there is rarely an opportunity for the modern city planner or the resident of the modern city to experience in his lifetime the realization of future possibilities. The city rejuvenates itself piecemeal in parks and playgrounds, in shopping centers and housing developments, which may temporarily stick out like a sore thumb in the present picture and which may thus discourage the completion of plans as originally intended.

Time Perspective. Under the circumstances, modern city planning frequently gives way to short-term corrective measures appreciated as such. Modern city planning practice concerns itself with improvements of street layout and highway systems, with the opening up of parks and playgrounds, with restrictions of commercial land uses, and with spotty slum clearance projects, all of which are intended to meet pressing needs and, at the same time, to add up to something like a well organized whole in the long run. The difficulties of combining immediate correctives with long-term planning objectives are often insurmountable.[16]

Different time perspectives of planning are apt to interfere with

---

15 About the function of the master plan and about techniques of Land Use Survey upon which the master plan is to be based, see Harold MacLean Lewis, *op. cit.,* Vol. I, pp. 45-58.

16 *Ibid.,* Chapter III, "The Correction of Mistakes," pp. 24-38.

each other. To provide transportation facilities to outlying residential districts may meet urgent needs as they are felt at present. On a basis of long-term planning and replacement, we may well find that the outlying residential districts we are trying to serve should not have been located there in the first place. We may place parks and playgrounds where a few decades hence there will be no residents to enjoy them. We may provide parking space in the central business district while the planner is at work to diminish the need for parking in this area of high land values.

Flexible Planning. Ideally, city planning consists of mutually interdependent commitments projected toward some future date of full realization. While a given plan is on its way toward realization, the assumptions on which it was based change under the hands of the city planner. In addition to conflicts between immediately pressing needs and long-term planning perspectives, the planner is confronted with harsh and unpredictable facts of changing technology, changing social conditions, and changing city functions.

For such reasons, the need for flexible planning policies has been emphasized. As the planner gains new information, he is required to reconsider his previous thinking and to plan all over again. Such reconsiderations force themselves upon the planner incessantly. In this manner, modern city planning loses its utopian character. There are no fixed ideas about the city beautiful which are gradually but surely approximated as urban construction rejuvenates itself. The immense complexity of long-term city planning derives from the fact that the specifications for the plan are continuously changing.

Fifty years from now, urban needs are bound to have changed in a completely unpredictable manner. As we advance through the decades of the immediate future, our recognition of urban needs in the year 2000 will gradually clarify. As this happens, city plans will have to be revised repeatedly by either patchwork or complete reorganization.

Planning Levels. Modern city planning stands as a combination of many different processes. It consists of (1) complete layouts of city patterns to be built at one sweep; (2) corrective measures to improve conditions of life and work in our built-up cities; (3) master plans, to guide future building activities into desirable channels; (4) processes of replanning on the basis of new information; and (5) reconciliation of short-term and long-term planning measures.

CITY PLANNING PRACTICES

Multiple Purpose. Through city planning, we are trying to achieve a great many things. Through city planning, we try to reduce the commuting distance between place of work and residence. We attempt to provide adequate recreational facilities close to the private residence of the city dweller. We see to it that the flow of traffic proceeds unimpeded between homes and offices, between shopping districts and factories, between the dormitory suburb and the city church.

City planning is the means by which we permit light and air to penetrate into the tightly-knit urban fabric. City planning helps either to segregate or to fuse different types of residential neighborhoods in the urban environment. City planning places parks where parks are needed; it may have to provide for an ostentatious civic center to promote civic pride. City planning directs the flow of communication to its own hinterland, to adjacent cities, and to other lands.

Physical Planning. City planning is concerned with physical planning only. Were it not so, the city planner would have to carry the entire burden of social and economic policies. For this he is as little equipped as anyone in any other single profession. The city planner works in the spatial dimension; he molds in wood, brick, concrete, asphalt, and landscaping a stage for the entire field of urban activities.

The streets, buildings, parks, and highways, however, which develop under the city planner's direction take their function from the social dimension. They are to serve social purposes. The city planner understands his task badly who does not keep himself accurately informed about the social life of the community he is trying to shelter.

Teamwork. His vast task could make of the city planner a jack-of-all-trades with supreme skill in none. There is no single social scientist, who would dare to undertake the analysis of all those social conditions that have bearing on measures of city planning. Under the circumstances, the city planner finds himself in danger of setting himself up as a prophet or dictator who develops a utopian scheme for city life as he wants it.

We are not unfamiliar with the visionary approach to city planning. It has furnished many constructive ideas; but it has not always kept in step with the times, nor has it always correctly anticipated future social needs. If we are to avoid arbitrary planning schemes, we have to establish city planning as a co-operative venture between different scientific skills and fields of study. The economist is needed for the task as well as the sociologist, the engineer as well as the architect, the physician as well as the geographer. The task of city planning points toward the need for teamwork.

While the administrative setting for such teamwork is being developed, city planning proceeds on the basis of highly conventionalized routines. It does the things which the modern city planner, trained in engineering and architecture, knows how to do. City planning does things about the usefulness of which there can be little doubt.

Streets. City planning is sometimes understood as predominantly a matter of highway planning and street layout. It is treated as if intra-urban and interurban communications were the most important issue of city construction.

Communication conquers space, but it is not related to the possibilities of reorganizing existing spatial relationships. To permit easy access to the downtown theater district, radiating cross-traffic routes may be sent out into suburban areas. Another solution to the problem would be the decentralization of facilities for passive commercial entertainment. The highway engineer is professionally tempted to leave existing construction as it is, but to connect it by efficient means of transportation.

The congestion of intra-urban traffic in our growing cities impresses us with the need for ameliorative measures to bring quick relief. A limited number of streets radiating from the city center are widened to provide for rapid transportation. How many such through streets will be needed depends upon the actual flow of traffic between the central business district and the urban periphery. The city planner gains such information from now highly standardized investigation procedures.[17]

To alleviate congested downtown traffic, the highway planner considers the possibility of cross-routing all traffic that does not terminate in the downtown area. Even smaller cities try to keep

---

[17] For traffic planning, see *Ibid.*, Part II, "Communications Master Plan," pp. 59-194.

transcontinental transportation by bus, truck, and automobile away from their central business and shopping districts by letting the main highways bypass the inner parts of the city.

The winding street system of residential areas presents [18] a counterpart to the widening of cross traffic routes. It is to discourage traffic for the benefit of residential quiet and playing children; it is to squeeze through-traffic into arteries for rapid transit. The winding suburban street layout and the barring of streets to traffic in the central zones is useless unless accompanied by street widening where such is needed.

Parking. In our large metropolitan areas, motor traffic in the central city has swollen to unmanageable proportions. The downtown parking problem has become notorious. The provision of parking space in central locations is not the only answer to the problem. It is, as a matter of fact, a very expensive solution to our difficulties. Both underground and elevator garages are costly.

Street and highway planners have tried to force motor traffic to terminate somewhere at the fringe of the business district. Generous allowance for parking space is to be made on present slum properties where incoming motor traffic is to be brought to a stop. The inner city, then, is to be provided with a clearly arranged system of public transportation, with bus lines or subways.

Green Spaces. The landscape architect is primarily concerned with the opening up of green spaces within the built-up city.

Plans for improvement start with an inventory of existing parks and playgrounds and their location in relation to the distribution of urban residence. The land use map of the city is carefully perused and circles drawn around all open-air recreational facilities, the diameter of the circle being proportionate to the size of individual park or playground. In this manner, gaps in the park planning structure become easily apparent.

In addition to the question of whether enough outdoor recreational space is available, it will be a matter of concern whether such facilities are available at reasonable walking distance from all urban residences. An inventory of the above-mentioned kind will suggest where further space for parks and playgrounds will do the most good, where the need is greatest and adequate facilities most badly lacking.

---

18 See also Chapter 17.

Some park planners go so far as to include the layout of highways and boulevards in their activities. They are concerned with easy access to recreational facilities in the outskirts of the city.

Well known is the manner in which problems of communication have been solved in conjunction with the provision for outdoor recreational areas between Riverside Drive and the Hudson River on Manhattan Island. Underground railroads were overlaid with a belt of park and playgrounds, while the highway at the river bank carries an unobstructed flow of motor traffic back and forth between the outskirts and the central business district.

Park planning may extend into residential neighborhood planning. In the residential neighborhood, parks may be provided to segregate the individual neighborhood from adjacent areas. Interior parks and playgrounds may be devised to make the residents of the neighborhood independent of facilities catering to a wider range of urban residents. School playgrounds frequently serve others than pupils and, thus, contribute to the recreational facilities of the community as a whole.[19]

Park planning penetrates into many issues of general city planning. The focus of interest, of course, is bound to remain somewhat one-sided.

Slum Clearance. The same may be said about the city planner who organizes his thinking around the important issue of slum clearance. Esthetic as well as humanitarian purposes may guide his activities.

An efficient advance of slum clearance activities is predicated, like any other type of city planning, upon a detailed inventory of existing conditions. Detailed investigation procedures have been worked out to permit precise measurement of the degree of obsolescence reached in the individual city block and on the individual lot.[20] With such information available, the city planner can determine the sequence in which undesirable housing conditions are to be considered for rehabilitation.

The clearance of existing slums in the center of the urban settle-

[19] For park planning techniques and principles, see *Ibid.*, Vol. I., Chapter 10, "Parks and Recreation Facilities," pp. 195-214.

For the study of design, see George D. Butler, *Recreation Areas.* New York: A. S. Barnes and Company, 1947.

[20] American Public Health Association, Committee on the Hygiene of Housing, 1790 Broadway. *An Appraisal Method for Measuring the Quality of Housing: A Yardstick for Health Officers, Housing Officials and Planners.* New York: 1945, Part I, "Nature and Use of Method."

ment is beset by one major difficulty. As deteriorated and insanitary dwelling units are torn down, new housing must be made available for the inhabitants of the demolished area. If not accompanied by a plan for resettlement, slum clearance may impose an intolerable burden upon that part of our city population it is supposed to benefit most. At times of a citywide housing shortage, to be sure, no responsible city planner is willing to consider the demolition of slum structures unless there is a guarantee for rebuilding, on the same location or elsewhere.

New construction must be of such a nature as to accommodate the previous slum dwellers. It must be low-cost housing. To build such housing on previous slum location is almost prohibitive due to extremely high land values close to the center of the city. That low income groups were able, originally, to settle here at all was due to a crowding of individuals and families in itself sufficient to create a slum environment. Resettlement will, ordinarily, have to occur at lower densities. This makes rebuilding on the site practically impossible.[21]

Deteriorated dwelling units will have to be torn down. Low-cost housing will have to be provided wherever feasible. New land uses will have to be attracted to the site of previous slums. At times, tax exemption and public subsidy have been granted to facilitate the building of low-cost housing on previous slum location. Economically, such ventures are operating at a loss, even where the construction of high apartment buildings tries to accommodate relatively high population densities.

If, on the other hand, resettlement is to occur farther out in the periphery of the city where land values are still relatively low, hardships and resistance are encountered in the resettlement of a population that is very neighborhood-conscious and dependent upon associations with friends living in close proximity. There is no easy solution to this problem.

THE ZEST FOR DECENTRALIZATION

In modern city planning, decentralization is said to be desirable (1) for purposes of defense;[22] (2) as a measure against urban con-

---

[21] See Harold MacLean Lewis, op. cit., Vol. II, "Problems of Redevelopment," pp. 38-40.

[22] William F. Ogburn, "Sociology and the Atom," American Journal of Sociology, Vol. LI, No. 4 (January, 1946), pp. 270-275.

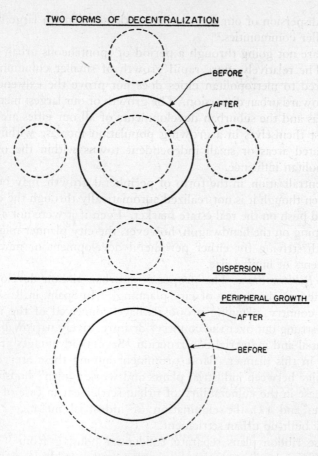

TWO FORMS OF DECENTRALIZATION

BEFORE

AFTER

DISPERSION

PERIPHERAL GROWTH

AFTER

BEFORE

FIGURE 20. Dispersion and Peripheral Growth.

gestion;[23] (3) for industrial location;[24] and (4) for the purposes of large scale residential neighborhood planning.[25]

Dispersion. Decentralization, of course, can mean two different things. The term can be applied to peripheral urban growth or

---

[23] "When too many people try to get to the same place at the same time, especially over an outmoded transportation system, congestion and strangulation are inevitable. Severe congestion tends to force decentralization." S. E. Sanders and A. J. Rabuck, *New City Patterns.* New York: Reinhold Publishing Corporation, 1946, p. 63.

See also Gerald Breese: *The Daytime Population of the Central Business District of Chicago.* Chicago: University of Chicago Press, 1949.

[24] "The main new industrial belt . . . will probably be located on the outer rim of the present city along major water courses and railroad belt lines."

to the dispersion of our large urban settlements into a large number of smaller communities.[26]

We are not going through a period of spontaneous urban dispersion. The relatively more rapid growth of smaller communities as compared to metropolitan cities does not prove the existence of a trend toward urban dispersion. The growth of our largest metropolitan areas and the suburban developments of all our cities are apt to manifest themselves in a growing population increase within unincorporated areas or small independent towns within the orbit of metropolitan influence.

Decentralization, in the form of peripheral growth, may be desirable even though it is not realized automatically through the existing pull and push on the real estate market. Even if it were not a matter of jumping on the bandwagon, however, the city planner might find it worth striving for either peripheral development or new urban settlements of limited size.

The Ribbon Plan. The proposal of urban ribbon developments is not new to the theory of city planning. [27] In Spain, in Russia, and in this country, planning proposals have conceived of the modern city as strung out over the countryside in relatively narrow bands of residential and industrial construction. Several advantages are to be gained in this manner. Most prominent among these are: (1) the proximity between industrial plants and workingmen's housing; (2) a decrease in the vulnerability of urban settlement in case of atomic warfare; and (3) the elimination of industrial nuisances from a densely built-up urban settlement.

These ribbon plans separate residential housing from industrial construction by lines of communication, and possibly by park belts, running through the midst of the settlement. The transportation system retains contact with other residential, commercial, or industrial facilities in the far distance, up and down the "line." The dis-

Homer Hoyt, "The Structure of American Cities in the Post-War Era," *The American Journal of Sociology,* Vol. XLVIII, No. 4 (January, 1943), p. 481.

[25] "There have been vast vacant areas at the peripheries, but within the boundaries, of the larger cities in the United States. These peripherical vacant areas have been developing while the central districts lost population." Harold MacLean Lewis, *op. cit.,* Vol. II, p. 94. Consult Chapter 18, "Decentralization of Industry and Residence," pp. 91-116.

[26] See pp. 58 ff.

[27] For the "ribbon system of town development," see L. Hilberseimer, *op. cit.,* p. 68.

tance to be covered between place of employment and place of residence is reduced to walking distance running at a rectangle through the narrow band of construction. Careful consideration of prevailing winds and topographical variations, furthermore, will make it possible to let industrial nuisances drift off and drain off into the surrounding countryside without annoyance to the urban dweller. Moreover, an urban ribbon development does not offer a very eco- nomical target for the atomic or any other bomb.

Residence close to his place of work is not an unadulterated advan- tage to the workingman.[28] Although this may not make him quite as dependent upon his employers as housing in the old company town, the workingman may be tied to an environment that permits advan- tageous employment in only one industrial plant. The mobility of modern labor is not taken into account in the proposal of urban construction that locates only one place of work in proximity to the worker's residence.

Moreover, while people are gainfully employed as individuals, they live as families. The entire workingman's family, not only the main breadwinner, would be tied down to a location favorable to the labor supply of one single industrial plant only. The rest of the family may be riding up and down the communication lines of the ribbon development to gain jobs elsewhere or to attend educational institutions. The advantage of an easy walking distance to place of work, the elimination of commuting, will be achieved for one family member only. For the rest, such urban development is more likely to prolong than to shorten commuting distances.

Industrial Dispersion. Dispersion from the large city into a large number of relatively small industrial settlements can attach itself to already existing communities. It can proceed gradually in the re- location of industrial activities. It does not require a complete re- building of our urban structure. It can experiment with limited in- vestments and reap the harvest of improvements as they are achieved.

The following alternatives offer themselves for industrial de- centralization:

1. A single factory and the houses of its workers may be built in the countryside away from an existing village or town.

---

[28] See Kate K. Liepmann, *The Journey to Work.* New York: Oxford Uni- versity Press, 1944, Chapter III, "The Price of the Daily Journey," pp. 26-66.

2. A single factory or a group of factories may be set up in a rural area, workpeople being transported daily from one or more towns in the surrounding district.

3. A group of factories and the houses of the workers in them may be established in a new place.

4. A group of factories and associated houses of this kind may be attached to an existing village.

5. A single factory, or perhaps two, may be attached to an existing village.[29]

The one-industry settlement will have to be avoided to eliminate the danger of a local monopoly on the labor market. Single factories that move away from the large city will, therefore, do well to establish themselves in already existing communities which provide the factory worker with alternatives of employment in the diversified occupational structure of the small town. If the labor supply is to be imported, new housing facilities will have to be provided. If these residences are attached to an already existing community, there will be an opportunity for the industrial worker to assimilate himself to the social life of the settlement; institutional services may be needed to facilitate the assimilation of the newcomers.

If the labor supply is to be drawn from the resident population, the planner's interest will shift from the provision of housing to the provision of transportation facilities to accumulate sufficient labor from the wider regional territory. The location of the industrial plant will then gravitate to the center of population, not necessarily coincident with the location of any of the already existing communities.

Industrial Fringe Location. The major efforts at metropolitan decentralization will find their outlet at the very fringe of these same settlements by way of peripheral growth. At this location, industries will not have to draw their labor supply by new transportation facilities from other areas. They will have the opportunity of drawing from the entire labor potential of the metropolitan area. At this location, industries gain the advantage of relatively low land values.

Industrial fringe location benefits business by accommodating the increasing space needed for the modern industrial plant. Space is

---

[29] See Thomas Sharp, *The Anatomy of the Village*. Harmondsworth, Middlesex, England: Penguin Books, 1946, pp. 41-42.

needed for private freight yards and spurs connected with the commercial transportation system. Space is needed, also, for the layout
of the plant itself which, in the age of mass fabrication and the
assembly line, consists preferably of a vast one-story construction.
The modern factory has outlived the era of multiple-story construction in the downtown Zone of Transition.

Residential Decentralization. Decentralization is not exclusively
an industrial problem. It must be considered a residential problem in
its own right. For the childbearing phases of the family cycle, it is
considered desirable to obtain residence in the outlying districts of
the city, where children's play is not interfered with by traffic, where
lots of relatively generous size leave space for recreational activities,
where the air remains free from impurities, and where sunlight is
not obstructed by tall and densely crowded buildings.

Residential decentralization is closely tied up with neighborhood
planning. Residential decentralization has been viewed as a means
to provide for the spontaneous neighborliness that is absent from the
inner city zones.

Residential dispersion is recommended to counteract the narrow
specialization of human contacts prevailing in the purposeful atmosphere of city living. If the urbanite longs for the small town, he
longs for something that will provide him with the full experience
of life in all its facets. In reaction to metropolitan conditions, he
yearns for an environment where people get to know each other in
more than one segmentalized way.[30] He hopes to get to know the
grocer as a member of his service club, and to establish acquaintance
with his children's teacher over the garden fence.

Still, we have to ask ourselves whether the city planner should
go all out for decentralization within the metropolitan region. The
advantage of cheaper land values in the urban fringe cannot be
gainsaid. The suburbanite, moreover, gets more for his money by
escaping the nuisances that are today associated with residential
location in the central city. He escapes the roar of traffic, the
gasoline fumes, and the shadow of the skyscraper or the apartment
building. But there is a price to pay. The suburbanite is burdened
with the cost of ever increasing commuting distances. He has to

---

[30] For an excellent descriptive account of overlapping social roles in the
small town, see Granville Hicks, *Small Town*. New York: The Macmillan
Company, 1947, Chapter VIII, "Institutions and People," pp. 164-194.

work for the privilege of his residential location by spending hours in either bus or train, by depriving himself of valuable hours of home life. If this is what the city dweller wants, the city planner has his task set for himself.

Central Rehabilitation. We want to know whether the urban public moves to the periphery because it wants to locate there, or because that alone is where livable homes can at present be either bought or rented.[31] We want to know the opportunities for central urban rehabilitation, what the costs would have to be for the individual involved, what the costs would have to be for the community as a whole, by either tax exemption or subsidy. We want these costs checked against the costs that will have to be carried sooner or later if we permit our urban settlements to sprawl far into the hinterland, forcing us all to live in a doughnut-shaped suburban belt-line that stretches far and wide into the landscape while leaving a desert of urban deterioration in its wake.

The people of the city should be enabled to make an intelligent decision. For that purpose they need the help of the expert city planner.[32] What to do with the city is not for the planner to decide. The city is of the people, they must see that it is built well, to serve their needs and those of their offspring.

Selected Readings

1. Le Corbusier, *Concerning Town Planning.* London: The Architectural Press, 1947, pp. 9-127

2. L. Hilberseimer, *The New City.* Chicago: Paul Theobald, 1944, pp. 17-192.

3. Henry S. Churchill, *The City Is The People.* New York: Reynal & Hitchcock, 1945, pp. 1-186.

---

[31] See Richard Dewey, "Peripheral Expansion in Milwaukee County," *The American Journal of Sociology,* Vol. LIV, No. 2 (September, 1948), pp. 118-125.

[32] "(The social planner) is called upon to plan for the 'welfare of the community,' but it is left to him to specify such general statements in terms of tangible objectives that can serve as a guide for concerted community action." Svend Riemer, "Social Planning and Social Organization," *The American Journal of Sociology,* Vol. LII, No. 6 (May, 1947), p. 514.

4. Harold MacLean Lewis, *Planning the Modern City.* New York: John Wiley & Sons, Inc., 1949, Volume I, pp. 1-273, Volume II, pp. 1-204.

5. S. E. Sanders and A. J. Rabuck, *New City Patterns.* New York: Reinhold Publishing Corporation, 1946, pp. 1-181.

PROBLEMS

1. *Zoning Practice.* You will have to inform yourself about and report upon current zoning practices in a city of 50,000 or more.

Find out what branch of the local government is responsible for the proposal and administration of local zoning ordinances. There may be a city planning office, a land commissioner's office, or the entire responsibility may be vested in the office of the city engineer. Find out where building permits are granted: that will lead you to the appropriate authority.

Compare a good land use map with the zoning ordinances under operation. What changes in the structure of the urban community are intended through existing zoning ordinances? Are commercial areas to be concentrated or widened? What is the land use future of outlying areas going to be?

Through informal interviewing, find out as much as you can about pressures to change the zoning ordinances. Interview realtors and home owners to find out how they view the building needs of the future. Have you any constructive suggestions?

2. *Decentralization.* Consult the literature quoted in Chapter 18 that is related to the problem of decentralization. Quote the arguments brought forth in favor of and against decentralization. Weigh them against each other, that is, try to assess which of them are based upon more certain trends of social and economic development.

Try to arrive at a balanced judgment that will give decentralization its proper place in the future of the modern American city.

3. *The City of the Year 2000.* This is a project in tentative city planning. Without previous training, nothing like perfect design can be expected of you. You are challenged, however, to explore different possibilities of designing the arrangement of different types of urban construction in relation to each other.

Consult the literature on city planning quoted in Chapter 18. That will give you ideas about various possibilities.

Consider only the following types of construction:

    1. Places of work.

    2. Places of residence.

3. Places of entertainment and association.

4. Schools.

5. Public administration buildings.

6. Commercial services.

7. Routes of transportation.

Sketch these types of construction in different spatial relations to each other. Discuss the advantages and disadvantages of different arrangements.

You will not design the city of the future, but you will gain some understanding of the difficulties involved in basic city planning proposals.

Index

457